CAPTAIN AUSTRALIA

ALSO BY ROLAND PERRY

The Don

Bold Warnie

Waugh's Way

The Fifth Man

Hidden Power: The Programming of the President

Mel Gibson, Actor, Director, Producer

The Exile: Wilfred Burchett, Reporter of Conflict

Lethal Hero

Elections Sur Ordinateur

Shane Warne, Master Spinner

Programme for a Puppet

Blood is a Stranger

Faces in the Rain

CAPTAIN AUSTRALIA

A History of the Celebrated Captains of Australian Test Cricket

ROLAND PERRY

RANDOM HOUSE AUSTRALIA

Random House Australia Pty Ltd
20 Alfred Street, Milsons Point, NSW 2061
http://www.randomhouse.com.au

Sydney New York Toronto
London Auckland Johannesburg

First published 2000 by Random House Australia

National Library of Australia

Cataloguing-in-Publication Entry

Perry, Roland, 1946– .
Captain Australia
Includes index.
ISBN 1 74051 001 1.

1. Cricket captains – Australia – Biography.
2. Cricket players – Australia – Biography.
3. Cricket – Australia. 4. Test matches (Cricket).
I. Title.

796.358650994

Typeset by Midland Typesetters, Maryborough, Victoria
Printed and bound by Griffin Press, Netley, South Australia

10 9 8 7 6 5 4 3 2 1

To Sir Donald Bradman
Captain of Australia's team of the twentieth century

CONTENTS

PREFACE

My thanks and appreciation go to the captains who granted interviews and supplied information that helped in the writing of *Captain Australia*. It would not have been possible without additional assistance from historians, academics, administrators, umpires, journalists and players past and present. As ever, the MCC library aided my research. A special mention also to historian/librarian Rex Harcourt, Thos Hodgson, Tony Maylam, Jack Grossman, Tim Burstall and Alan Young for supplying photos and information from unpublished player memoirs that helped give a broader picture of events that occurred before living memory. A special thank you to Ken Kelly, curator of the cricket museum at Edgbaston and a vice president of the Warwickshire C.C.C.—for kindly granting permission to reproduce photos of the earlier cricket captains.

Roland Perry
2000

INTRODUCTION

ALWAYS NUMBER ONE

Ever since Test cricket began, the position of Australian cricket captain was the top sporting job in the country. It has had enormous prestige, and has been held by men more popular than any governor, state leader or prime minister. In the early years, educated and moneyed men often took the position. To tour the country and England a cricketer needed funding. That didn't mean that a privileged background was the only criterion for leadership, but it helped. Billy Murdoch, a hedonist lawyer with wit and personality, was Australia's best nineteenth-century bat and a popular skipper in the 1880s. His successors were less impressive. Henry Scott, a doctor and the son of a pioneering captain in the Royal Marines, was a determined bat but a less successful skipper. Percy McDonnell, a Greek scholar and son of a barrister, was a bat with style and courage. But he presided over a losing streak of five Tests.

It took all-rounder Harry Trott, a postman from Collingwood in Victoria, to create the first real sense of superiority over England in the field. Harry didn't achieve it by exhortation. Nor was he driven by some chip-on-the-shoulder 'we'll show you' inferiority. Harry was an amiable character who was simply smarter in the field and better able to manage his team than any rivals. He acquitted himself well in England in 1896 against Dr W G Grace and then in 1897–98 led Australia at home to its most resounding win to that point, beating an England led by Andrew Stoddart and Archie MacLaren four–one.

Federation's forgers

In the 1890s, the colonial leaders were trying to forge Federation and a sense of nationhood. Trott's great leadership delivered wins against the 'mother country' and the first sustained sense that the 'best of us' could be better than 'the best of them'. The cricket team was called 'Australia' a generation before the new nation was to emerge from a group of dispirited, often squabbling, colonies. Yet somehow they set aside differences to unify for cricket matches against England. There was an expected measure of parochialism in selections, but by and large the best squads were chosen to represent a nation that was yet to exist. The press responded with jingoistic fervour because it had something to be jingoistic about. Brilliant, close-fought Tests, including thrillers, galvanised interest in Australia and England.

Joe Darling, the son of a rich South Australian grain king, followed Trott and maintained the pattern of consistent competitiveness against England, taking the next series in England one–nil in the 1899 five-Test series. This was the first time Australia had taken a series of three Tests or more away from home. It fuelled a sense of pride and achievement and was significant in creating an atmosphere conducive to the founding of nationhood.

When Australia became a federation in 1901, Darling put his imprint on the unity by issuing his team in the First Test of the 1901–02 Ashes with velvet skullcaps. He ordered each player to wear the cap throughout the game. The no-nonsense skipper wished to present the England opposition with the perception of a unified squad. Australia won the 1901–2 series four–one, and celebrated the birth of a nation. The next outstanding leader was New South Wales's Monty Noble. He maintained Australia's raised standard into the 1900s and was a strong captain. Noble superseded George Giffen as the best all-rounder the nation or any colony had produced. It would be another half-century before another cricketer—Keith Miller— would rank with him as an all-rounder.

The spirit engendered by Trott, Darling and Noble carried through until the First World War, when tens of thousands of Australians travelled overseas to fight, and often die, for the British Empire.

Warriors for Warwick and Woodfull

After that conflict, the big, autocratic Warwick Armstrong, the son of a wine and spirits merchant, restored a sense of dominance in Australia's cricket prowess over England in 1920–21 and the 1921 series after a pre-war period of internal dissent that led to on-field capitulation. He captained Australia to eight successive wins, a record that lasted eighty years. Gambling addict Herb Collins succeeded him. He did well until a controversial last Test in the 1926 series. Either his ineptitude or the temptation to throw a game led to a one–nil series loss in England in 1926.

The pendulum swung hard back to England under the talented Percy Chapman, who had a batting colossus in Wally Hammond and the world's fastest bowler in Harold Larwood. In 1930 the selectors turned to Bill Woodfull, the non-drinking headmaster son of a preacher, to restore Australia's fortunes in England after a four–one thrashing in 1928–29.

Woodfull's team was not as strong as Chapman's, except for one batting phenomenon, Don Bradman. Bradman emerged at twenty-one to make scores of 132, 254, 334 and 232 in an aggregate of 974 at an average of 139.14, to effectively make the contest unwinnable for England. The popular Woodfull returned with the Ashes after a two–one win in 1930. He continued on with runaway series wins against the West Indies in 1930–31 and South Africa in 1931–32. Woodfull's main weapon, Bradman, dominated.

England's establishment could accept the odd series loss, but Bradman represented the possibility of long-term Australian dominance that would mean a decade or more of humiliation for the seat of the Empire. This was unacceptable. So England enlisted a high-born Scottish lawyer, Douglas Jardine, to destroy Bradman. Jardine devised bodyline, a method of bowling and field placement designed to either bruise or dismiss batsmen. Many considered the tactics clever. Like any good lawyer, Jardine stayed within the rules and did not bend them. He cut Bradman down to almost half his average of 100 runs an innings and won the 1932–33 series four–one.

The Australian public thought Jardine's methods reprehensible. The 24-year-old Bradman was the country's hero. He represented something special. He was better at what he did with a willow than anyone else in history. During the Depression Bradman was the best Saturday afternoon entertainment going. Only the great horse Phar Lap was a surer bet. Punters, working class or wealthy, could put their money on that amazing animal and be sure of a return. When it was rumoured that Phar Lap had been poisoned in the United States, the 'Yanks' were loathed. Give Don Bradman two innings in a match and he was bound to deliver a fine performance at least once. No other sportsperson in history performed so brilliantly and consistently at the highest level of any game for so long. So when the Empire tried to do him down, there was hostility towards the English. There were rumblings that Australia should withdraw from the British Common-wealth. Some even mumbled the shock word *republic*.

The main problem was that the brilliant Jardine—with a 60 per cent Test-win ratio, statistically England's most successful skipper—had gone too far. He had strayed outside the bounds of fair play that had been a hallmark of cricket since its inception. Jardine was not playing in 'the spirit of the game'. When bruised after batting against bodyline bowling, Bill Woodfull told England's management that its team was not playing fairly. If anyone but the courageous, high-principled captain had uttered such a denunciation they would not have made the same impact. The cantankerous, dictatorial Warwick Armstrong would have received a negative reaction in England. Herbie Collins would have been ignored, and investigations made into his betting. But Woodfull was a man of impeccable character. His protest struck home. Within eighteen months he had his way and bodyline was effectively outlawed. The disgraced Jardine would never play for England again.

In 1934, Woodfull led Australia to a two–one win in a titanic series struggle decided in the last Test at the Oval. Victory came thanks to the biggest of big-occasion performances in the history of series deciders by Bradman (244) and Bill Ponsford (266), who put on a record 451 for the second wicket. From Australia's point of view, justice had been done. The Ashes were taken back and Bradman was restored to his former unassailable position.

Woodfull returned home a conquering hero and retired at the peak of his leadership powers, a luxury attained by few.

Bradman unbeatable

Don Bradman, neutralised for that one series in 1932–33, succeeded Woodfull for the long-term. Ultimately he fulfilled England's worst fears by denying it an Ashes victory for another twenty years. But Australia lost its first two Tests under Bradman in 1936–37. His own form and the weather conspired to defeat the relatively weak home team. Then his form returned. He lifted for the grand performance three times, scoring 270, 212 and 169. Australia came back from the dead to win three–two.

Bradman, the game's foremost batting dominator, was not a natural leader. Yet he learned on the job better than anyone. Once confident in tactics and strategies, Australia was as close as could be to unbeatable. After the first two losses at the helm—which could be put down to the weather more than Bradman's aptitude—he lost just one of the next twenty-one Tests, at the Oval in 1938. Bradman injured his ankle and could not bat. Had he been fit, Australia might well have forced a draw.

So was Bradman Australia's best ever captain? It's difficult to judge. He was his own greatest asset. Put any other player in his place in every series he was in and Australia would have lost or struggled. He won the big games—the ones that decided a series' fortunes—literally off his own bat, or he saved them. The record is unambiguous.

Bradman was popular with most under him, but he had his detractors and enemies. His direct style ruffled feathers. He said what he meant and meant what he said. He never wasted a syllable in comments or analysis. In the 1930s, Jack Fingleton, Bill O'Reilly and Clarrie Grimmett had their moments with him. They caballed against him when his captaincy looked shaky.

Yet not being loved by every player paled in importance compared to winning. His antagonists within the 1930s team buried their differences and saluted him when it came to beating other nations.

This humble son of a country carpenter proved to be the most intelligent, shrewd and tactically brilliant leader since Harry Trott. And no one in the history of cricket ran a better strategic campaign and tour than Bradman in 1948. Australia played thirty-four games and didn't lose one. It was only challenged in two matches against the counties. Bradman, who turned forty during the season, as ever led from the front, scoring eleven tour centuries in an aggregate of 2428 first-class runs at an average of 89.92.

Bradman elevated the status of Australian captain to new heights. Both the country's main political parties approached him. Labor looked at his background and universal popularity with the public and thought he was one of them. The conservative Liberals under Menzies observed his establishment profession—stockbroking—and considered him one of them. But he had no interest in going into politics.

Like all skippers before him, Bradman had always played virtually as an amateur. Despite his universal popularity, skill and the unparalleled prestige he brought Australia, he was paid a pittance. It worried Bradman that he didn't have a profession or a regular source of income. At one point early in his career he was briefly unemployed. While a vast audience smothered him in adulation, Bradman in 1930 wondered in private if he would earn enough to marry and have a family. He began in a profession—stockbroking—in Adelaide, aged twenty-six in 1935. It was late to find a work direction for that era.

Don Bradman's experience determined his later attitude. He thought that cricketers should treat the game as a sport, not a profession. He believed that all players should develop lives and work outside the game. After they finished playing, what would they do? This was a half-century before some professional cricketers could set themselves up for life with ACB contracts and commercial endorsements after a decade at the top.

Miller's misfortune

Don Bradman's successor was his impish deputy, Lindsay Hassett, the private school-educated son of a real estate agent. Hassett's wit, diplomatic style, cricketing skills and background were a throwback to Billy Murdoch. He maintained Australia's post-war dominance until 1953, when England regained the Ashes. There followed a period of contention regarding the Australian captaincy. The leadership baton passed to a good player, off-spinner Ian Johnson, rather than Australia's finest all-rounder, Keith Miller. Johnson, according to most experienced observers, was a fair, battling skipper. The spirited and attacking Miller was regarded as gifted. In 1954–55 he led New South Wales to a draw with and win over England, and he captained his state to two Sheffield Shield wins. Richie Benaud regarded him as the best leader he played under.

In the 1950s, individuals with flair like Keith Miller were not in favour. It was an era when independent minds were discouraged. Cricketers, it was felt, were very much amateurs who should stick to playing and let administrators dominate proceedings and do the thinking. Johnson, a well-liked, capable individual was a diplomat, an ideal establishment man, who wouldn't cause trouble. Richie Benaud, like Miller, incurred the wrath of the cricket establishment at one point after the 1956 tour of England. They were both marked out of contention for national leadership.

Rumours abounded that Miller fell out with Bradman and that was why he missed out. Some have even made the inane suggestion Miller never made it because he bowled bumpers at Bradman during his testimonial in the 1948–49 season. In 1954–55, Bradman was one of thirteen members of the Board of Control for International Cricket, who determined the captaincy on a vote, with the then chairman, Roy Middleton, having the casting vote should the vote be split. There were three representatives each from Victoria, New South Wales and South Australia, two from Queensland, and one each from Tasmania and Western Australia. Bradman always remained mute on the subject of selection and for whom he voted as leader. But even if Bradman wanted Johnson or someone else and not Miller, he could not deliver more than one vote. Because Bradman had been a towering figure in the game, some assumed that he always achieved what he wanted. Yet it simply wasn't the case. Even when he was chairman (1960–63, 1968–72) Bradman wasn't the autocratic type. On occasions Bradman had been out-voted as a selector for South Australia and Australia. Others did manage their way against Bradman's will. But their arguments had to be cogent and free of sentiment. All of those who ever worked with him regarded him as the best selector ever.

Whatever the reason, Miller missed out on the chance to display his natural leadership talents at the international level. Had be been at the helm, would Australia have done better in Ashes contests in the mid-1950s? As it turned out, probably not. No one could have countered the shooting star of English fast bowler Frank Tyson, who dominated in the 1954–55 Ashes in Australia. Miller had a poor season with the bat, scoring just 167 at 23.86, and a lean time for him with the ball, taking just ten wickets (yet at a good rate of 24.3 runs a wicket). In 1956, again, no one could have made a major difference with tactics or strategy in facing the inspired off-spin of Jim Laker, who took a freakish forty-six wickets at 9.61 on English wickets. He was unplayable on awful strips doctored to his advantage. (Miller, like all the Australians, failed with the bat. He was near his peak with the ball, taking twenty-one wickets at 22.24.)

After that 1956 disaster, critics called for the wholesale dumping of the veterans in the team, including Johnson, Miller, Ray Lindwall, and keeper Gil Langley. Miller saw the writing on the wall. He had back problems, but was fit enough to go on to South Africa in 1957–58. Yet without the incentive of the coveted leadership there was nothing left to achieve. He had done it all except captain his country. It was the most outstanding non-appointment in Australia's history.

Benaud's ball game

Keith Miller's misfortune was followed by perhaps the most disappointing elevation ever. Not because the appointee to the captaincy— pharmacist Ian Craig—wasn't equipped. He was a teenage prodigy with a blade. But it was an elevation too early. Ian Craig became captain at twenty-two. He couldn't make runs and win Tests at the same time. Craig did exceptionally well in South Africa, leading his team to a three–nil win, no mean feat during the period following the Second World War. But he failed with the bat, and kept failing. In the end he was swamped by the form of a preponderance of top-class bats all competing for too few places. Craig fell ill just before the 1958–59 Ashes series in Australia. He decided not to play.

Richie Benaud, the star of the 1957–58 South African tour with both bat and ball, was in the right place and ready to lead. Whatever thwarted an earlier ascension had evaporated. This time the selectors got it dead right. Benaud was twenty-eight. He was experienced and successful at the Test level. He even had his off-field achievement calibrated professionally. He had been a daily journalist—a crime, court and general news reporter—in Sydney. This gave him abundant contacts in the media. Benaud knew how to put the correct spin on events as well as a cricket ball. He could talk journalists' language and craft a succinct press release. On top of that, he had courage to spare and had modelled himself on the attacking style of his hero, Keith Miller. Now Australia received some idea of what cricket leadership under Miller might have been like. Benaud led Australia to the top of world cricket again after a half decade in the backblocks. His leadership collided with the best English and West Indian line-ups in history. In monumental series contests he moulded a strong Australian side and guided them through to victories. Like Bradman and Armstrong before him, he never lost a Test series. Like Bradman and Trott, he was a superb tactician.

An injured shoulder forced Benaud out, not quite with the timing of Woodfull and Bradman, but with much kudos. He stepped down with Australia the clear, dominant cricket nation in a world of ever-increasing competition. The West Indies had developed through the 1950s and into the 1960s as a brilliant, attacking combination. South Africa was a threat at home or away for the first time in seventy years. India and Pakistan were now very tough to beat in their own territories. Every cricket tour was anything but a holiday, putting demands on the leadership. Yet the meagre remuneration for the captain and the players meant their time was limited in the game. Poor match payments had been a concern for all except a few since the mid-1800s. It was an added stress factor on families already deprived of their breadwinners for most of each year.

Another problem was the addiction players developed to international cricket and the leadership. Each man who took on the captaincy enjoyed it so much he didn't wish to give it up. The thrill of winning was a drug. The fun of touring from locker room to locker room was not to be missed for most. The camaraderie of a national representative team often on top of the world was the strongest bonder of 'mates' known to man outside war. Most leaders did not leave the game of their own accord. More often than not, injuries, lack of form and series losses put paid to careers. Most wished to go on. Many loved the limelight, an aphrodisiac in itself. Others feared the afterlife. Some had forsaken marriages and family to be in the game at the top.

Not just for openers

Bob Simpson, the son of a Scottish printer, succeeded Benaud in 1964. Simpson had essentially been without a line of work he could rely on for income during his emerging years. So he became a quasi-professional, playing league cricket in England during the northern summers. He supplemented his income with journalistic work, but dedicated himself to being a Test cricketer above all else. Simpson's sides won or drew all home series in his first period as skipper but lost to the West Indies under Gary Sobers in 1965 and South Africa under Peter van der Merwe in 1966–67. Opening bat Bob Simpson was talented, reliable and driven, but was less inclined to lead with the flair of his predecessor. His opening partner, Bill Lawry, a plumber by trade and a pigeon fancier, was also a leader who tended to suppress enterprise with both the bat and leadership. Like Simpson, he was courageous at the wicket but he wasn't aggressive in batting tactics or field placements. Too often when leading he refused to let free his inspired side, which had been seen, for instance, during his 1961 tour of England. In 1968, Lawry preferred to hang onto the Ashes in a drawn series rather than win them.

Lawry took over in a series already won against India in 1967–68, and had big wins against the West Indies at home and versus India away. He was unfortunate to run into a powerful South Africa away in 1969–70, when Australia received a rare and humiliating hiding. Its top ranking among world Test teams was lost. Yet Lawry was kept on as leader. If he could win or control the Ashes at home in 1970–71, all would be forgiven. This time he met an equally obdurate and cannier captain in Ray Illingworth. Australia lost two–nil, with four draws. Lawry was dumped for the last Test, treated without due respect for enormous service rendered.

The Chappells' challenges

The man who took over from Bill Lawry was Ian Chappell, and he was determined not to be given such short shrift. Chappell was driven even more than his predecessors by the aim to make Australia the top cricketing nation again after the seven up-and-down years under Simpson and Lawry. He was a 'player's man', who engendered team spirit. Chappell—in the line of Trott, Bradman and Benaud—was an outstanding tactician. He wasn't afraid to follow his instincts, an important characteristic when a captain needs to take risks in order to win.

Chappell was also a maverick who dared to suggest that cricketers should think for themselves and move towards semi-professionalism. His success as a leader—he went through seven successive series without a loss—gave him a tenuous power, which he used to push for cricketers' rights and better pay and conditions. He retired as skipper in 1975—on his volition as he vowed he would—but kept playing until the advent of Kerry Packer's World Series Cricket (WSC). Chappell's militant drive—he was like a union official representing the cricketing workers—dovetailed with Packer's desire to make money from tele-vising the game. The media tycoon was prepared to pay cricketers what they wanted to achieve his aims. When his goals were reached and he had the rights from the ACB to televise Tests and one-day games, cricketers were offered better contracts. It still wasn't huge money, but it was a beginning. The players had made headway against a board caught in an amateur time warp, when the growing demands of the sport were forcing it towards professionalism.

Ian's brother Greg Chappell was handed the captain's chalice for the 1975–76 season, and he led a strong team to a crushing win against the West Indies. But 1977 proved a nightmare year for the new man. The secretly brewing WSC venture became public. Greg Chappell, a participant in it, was snubbed by officialdom. That would have been bearable if his side was winning. But it lost three–nil to Mike Brearley's Ashes team in England. Greg Chappell, like his brother Ian, went two seasons with WSC before returning to the official Test team as captain. Greg was one of the country's finest ever bats, but his capacities as a leader were sorely tested in the post-WSC amalgam. The Test team was not as unified or as dedicated as it had been when he first led. It lost to the West Indies, beat England, lost to Pakistan and beat New Zealand. It was back to the yoyo years of the 1960s.

Bob Simpson at forty-one answered the call of a desperate ACB and came back for a second life as captain in 1977–78, a decade after he had first retired. But the WSC defections meant he was running a second XI. Simpson won against India, then ran into reality against the West Indies away. Australia was thrashed. The reins were handed to Graham Yallop, an underestimated, good bat. Yallop failed as a skipper by default during this period of upheaval, as did the dashing stroke maker Kim Hughes, who was a makeshift leader filling in for Greg Chappell when he didn't tour. Hughes, particularly, would have done better had he had a more supportive, stronger squad under him. But he encountered dissent from the WSC veterans. Dennis Lillee and Rod Marsh, both battle-scarred heroes from Packer's alternative competition, thought that they could do a better job as captain. Hughes was left with disgruntled elements in his squad.

Greg Chappell's later years as leader were more fruitful. He did not lose in the last six series in which he captained.

Border battles

When Greg Chappell, Rod Marsh and Dennis Lillee retired, Kim

Hughes was left with more unity but less skill, and the Australians were no match for the rampant West Indies at home in the 1984–85 series. Sections of the media screamed for Kim Hughes's removal. Hughes fell on his sword mid-series and was replaced by the reluctant Allan Border. By this time, Test players were more or less professional.

Allan Border was a fighter who never gave up. Like Ian Chappell he made it his career's work to put Australia on top again. But it was a much harder chore than ever before. The final blast of WSC—a price paid for better player conditions and professionalism—was felt in the late 1980s, when Australia was left with a lack of fully developed, skilled players. Border refused to believe that Australia didn't have another ten players with 'ticker' like he had. Gradually, painstakingly, the team improved amid setbacks and crushing defeats from the West Indies.

Border's leadership was a mirror image of his batting. He was at his best when fighting to save a game, which he was so often forced to do. During this era there was no other way he could captain. Border tended to be defensive, for there was less opportunity to go for dashing wins. When he emerged in the early 1990s in control of a strong unit, he tended to go in for overkill to make a game safe before winning it, rather than, say, declaring early to give the opposition the semblance of a chance. It was a hangover from all the beatings and humiliations during the decade between 1978 and 1988. Border enjoyed revenge against all teams (except the West Indies), particularly England.

By 1993, after eight years, Border had shaped a tough and talented squad. It fell one run short of toppling the West Indies, which had not been beaten in a series for thirteen years. After a record ninety-three Tests as skipper and completing a magnificent job of restoration, Border handed over to his deputy Mark Taylor, in a smooth transition. It was a departure from the chaos of the years 1977 to 1984, when Greg Chappell threw the baton to Simpson before it went to Yallop, then Hughes then Chappell, and back to Hughes again before finally going to Border.

Taylor's triumph and Waugh's winning ways

The WSC experience was now a matter of history, but it had brought in a new era of professionalism. Most players in the mid-1990s were on contract to the ACB for between $250,000 to $480,000 a year. It was serious money to go with endorsements, promotions and other deals that cashed in on the team's high-profile success. The team was unified under Mark Taylor as it had been under the Chappells from 1972 to 1976. Mark Taylor directed his side to a record nine series wins in a row before Sachin Tendulkar and India beat Australia two–one early in 1998. Undeterred, Taylor added another two series wins in his final year against Pakistan, which made up for his first-up loss in 1994, and a final victory against England.

Mark Taylor was a harmonising skipper, who kept his squad happy, alert and motivated. He was skipper in fifty Tests and won twenty-six, twice as many as he lost. Taylor, an opener of quality, maintained Australia as the number-one Test nation for five years from 1994 to 1999. But he didn't go easily. Mindful of a horror stretch with the bat lasting eighteen months until mid-1997, he decided to get out not long after he gained everlasting fame with a score of 334 not out against Pakistan away. If he had lingered, lost form again and left the game in ignominy, he might well have been glad of his university degree in quantity surveying. Instead, his timely retirement meant he was swamped with promotional and advertising offers that would prolong the income to which he had become accustomed while skipper.

The last captain of the twentieth century was Steve Waugh. Aged thirty-three when he took over, Waugh had never been employed outside cricket. He was in the Chappell mould of militant leader, if with a more subtle approach. Waugh had lobbied and threatened to strike in 1997 for better conditions and a wider spread of pay for all first-class cricketers. This was achieved. He was less of a diplomat than Taylor, but after fourteen months in 'office' had a fair and workable alliance with his employer, the ACB. Waugh was much maligned as a skipper early, but the sheer weight of Test and one-day wins (record streaks in both forms of the game) during 1999 and 2000 shut up his critics. Steve Waugh proved to be an outstanding captain, who had the faith of all his charges. Many Test players put their development as top professional Test performers down to his personal touch.

Waugh may not have been the great natural tactician or strategist to begin with, but he learned. His acquired as opposed to innate leadership skills, combined with his fighting qualities with the bat in the Border mould, made him a formidable figure in cricket into the new millennium. After seventeen Tests and twelve wins, ten of those wins in succession until November 2000, he had taken Australia into a new dimension of winning and professionalism, with coach John Buchanan assisting. Waugh had set new and different standards for his successors. He could look forward to a lucrative cricket afterlife following sensible investments with the 'hay' he made while the sun shone on a long Test career.

After more than 120 years of Test cricket, the position of captain of Australia had maintained its high-profile image, prestige and popularity beyond any public office. And income for the position from the 1990s on was commensurate with that status.

This book begins, not with the first official Test captain, Dave Gregory, but the man who had the unique double distinction of being in the first England team to tour Australia in 1861, and in the first Australian team to tour England in 1868. His name was Charles Lawrence. And he could lay claim to being a, if not *the*, founding father of international cricket.

Prologue

CHARLES LAWRENCE

....

16 December 1828 – 20 December 1916

A FOUNDING FATHER OF ASHES CRICKET

Charles Lawrence, a forty-year-old Sydney publican and professional cricketer, arrived at Lake Wallace in Victoria's Western District in mid-July 1867, intent on gathering a squad of Aborigines for a tour of his home country, England. It would be the first ever tour by an Australian team. Lawrence was a mild John Bull type, with handsome aquiline features and a goatee beard. He was intent on returning to his homeland if not a new-world conquering hero then a successful entrepreneur, by creating a cricketing circus from down under. Lawrence had a quasi-missionary zeal. Like many pioneers of the nineteenth century, he wanted to make his fortune in an acceptably Christian way. Rather than 'using' the Aborigines, he wanted to be seen as 'bettering' them, along the road to his own goals. He regarded and dealt with the Aborigines as equals.

Charles Lawrence could be both shrewd and single-minded. He knew from contact with the Aboriginal players on their first trip, earlier in 1867, through Victoria and New South Wales that they loved alcohol. In order to get their attention, he had drunk with them. In

the first week this had had unfortunate consequences. Three ended
up in the Edenhope town gaol. Lawrence had not set out to get them
drunk, but their excitement over his plans had led to over-exuberance.

Lawrence met with the local policeman, Mounted Constable
Thomas Kennedy, at the lock-up to bail out his prospective charges.
Kennedy was unhappy with Lawrence's approach, complaining that 'a
glass of grog was a potent reasoner with a blackfellow'. Lawrence
explained that he would be imposing a moderation-with-booze rule.
Kennedy remained unconvinced. He wrote to his superior at Portland
on the south-west Victorian coast and requested that the Central
Board for the Protection of the Aborigines stop Lawrence's proposed
tour. Kennedy complained about the earlier tour of Australia in 1867
(that Lawrence did not organise, although he did once captain the
team at Wollongong). The Aboriginal team had been allowed to drink
too much and it had led to the deaths of three players: Watty (Bila-
yarrimin was his real name), who died on the team cart just short of
Edenhope, Jellicoe (Unamurramin) and Paddy (Pappinjurumun). The
causes for their demise had been said to be 'stress, city life, alcohol
and lung disease'. Their 'captain' or manager was Tom Wills, an alco-
holic, who didn't discourage his men from consuming too much liquor.
He was blamed for the problems. Kennedy also noted the fact that
several of the new team had 'chest ailments'.

The police complaint, together with a supporting letter from local
medico, Dr Molloy, who said that a change of climate would be fatal
to many of the team, was posted to the Protection Board.

Lawrence continued with his quest. He knew that his main hope
of avoiding the team's roistering would be to give them a full program
of games and to keep them away from bars. Lawrence set about
explaining the tour and providing incentives to each player. Some
prize money for events such as running was promised. All expenses for
the entire trip to England and back, lasting eighteen months, would
be paid. Lodgings and food would be 'good'.

This was enticing enough for every member of the prospective
fourteen-strong group. It was portrayed and seen as better than
another year of hard labour on pastoral properties. None was forced
into the tour. All were prepared to go willingly. They were going to be
exploited but in a way acceptable to them.

Charles Lawrence didn't boss his charges. He told them he would organise the tour and lead in most of the games. His open, genial, polite manner endeared him to the Aboriginal players. Lawrence gained their trust. He coached them in cricket, which was not always easy. They were not enthusiastic about training. But when he organised them to practise their traditional skills with spear and boomerang he received a better response. Lawrence encouraged one of the players to perfect his ball-dodging ability, where three others threw cricket balls at him from ten paces. He explained that in Australia and England they would be required to exhibit all their abilities during and after cricket matches.

Confident that he had a team that would stand up against all comers, Lawrence began to beat up publicity by issuing a challenge in the *Hamilton Advertiser* to any team in the Western District that could field sides of sixteen or eighteen players. They played three games, the last on 28 August, winning two and drawing one. It gave Lawrence a chance to select the best Aboriginal players for his team.

At the end of the training period, he presented each one chosen with a distinctive, warm uniform. It consisted of white flannel trousers, a red Garibaldi shirt, diagonal blue sashes, hatbands, belts and neckties. Then in a ceremony at Edenhope cricket ground, he handed each man a peak cap of a different colour, which would be theirs for the entire tour and would distinguish them. It was an important moment for the Aborigines. One by one the well-whiskered players stepped forward to receive their equivalent of the later 'baggy green': the brilliant all-rounder Johnny Mullagh (Unaarrimin); classy stroke player Bullocky (Bullchanach); hard-hitting, 'amusing' Dick-a-Dick (Jumgumjenanuke); fast-running, steady bowling Twopenny (Jarrawuk) from Bathurst in New South Wales; fragile King Cole (Bripumyarrimin); multi-talented all-rounder Johnny Cuzens (Yellanach); Charley Dumas (Pripumuarraman), from Wollongong, the only other player from New South Wales; accurate bowler Tommy Red Cap (Brimbunyah), who was handed a black cap; Harry Tiger (Bonnibarngeet); Peter (Arrahmunyarrimun); Mosquito (Grongarrong); Jim Crow (Lytejerbillijun), Sundown (Ballrinjarrimin), Billy Officer (Cungewarrimin), Harry Rose (Hingingairah) and Tarpot (Murrumgunarrimin). (Later, Harry Rose, Tarpot and Billy Officer would drop out.) This event made them all feel part of a special mission.

After a solid two months' preparation, Lawrence and a local

pastoralist, William Hayman, twenty-six, who had begun the Edenhope Cricket Club, had moulded the squad into a well-knit group. On
16 September 1867, they and the Aborigines piled into an American-
style covered wagon and a cart and set off from Edenhope on their
adventure. Lawrence planned to escort his cricket team most of the
way from Victoria's Western District to Melbourne and other major
towns before a boat trip to Sydney. After touring New South Wales and
playing several matches over two months, they were scheduled to be
on a boat to England where they would play nearly fifty matches. The
England tour, set to begin early in February 1868, Lawrence hoped,
would be the first ever by an Australian team. Every cricketer except
Lawrence was Aboriginal.

Bush and board trouble

The squad endured a tough wagon trip and were once bogged in the
wet. Later a wagon overturned and the four horses bolted. Johnny
Cuzens, one of the Aboriginal drivers, fell on his head but recovered
after mild concussion. Despite these minor mishaps, camping out as
an ensemble brought them closer together over the eight-day journey
to Warrnambool. Along the way they took time off for hunting and
traditional dancing.

Lawrence used the nights around the campfire to begin his prose-
lytising, beginning with the concept of Our Saviour as represented by
the child in the manger. Dick-a-Dick became confused and distressed,
thinking that 'the baby Jesus' had been killed. He wanted Lawrence
to explain it. Lawrence didn't want them to be distracted. He wished
'to have them inclined to a belief in the afterlife'.

It was not easy. The Aborigines had powerful spiritual beliefs based
on big concepts, including mountains, the earth and the sky. The idea
of worshipping a baby in a stable didn't grip them.

'When one of your tribe beats the other in a fight,' Lawrence asked
them, 'who do you believe in?'

'Our king,' they replied.

'Well, that's right. Now suppose we beat Warrnambool [in cricket].
Who will you believe in?'

'You, of course.'

'Why?'

'Because you are our captain.'

Lawrence went on to tell them how the baby wasn't killed but that he grew into the son of God, and went to heaven. If they were good and kind to each other they would end up there too. Lawrence was not too sure if they accepted these ideas. But he often worked these themes and promised to take them to church in Warrnambool.

One evening an Aborigine wandered into their camp and said he wanted to join them and play cricket. The team were suspicious of him and suggested that he might have mates ready to ambush them. Lawrence said he could stay the night and he would test his playing ability in the morning. If he was good, he told the new man, he might stay with them. Lawrence then ordered all of his men to load their guns. Should anyone come near the camp, he would give the order 'to fire up in the air'. The Aborigines made a bed for him in a huge gum tree, so that he could be the look-out. Lawrence didn't think he could sleep.

Not long after he had bedded down, he heard 'a terrible noise, like the galloping of cattle'. In fact, it was six horsemen. Lawrence called for his men. 'Be ready!'

The invaders yelled they would smash the camp and kill everyone.

'Fire!' Lawrence ordered.

He and the Aborigines aimed their weapons above the heads of the would-be attackers and let go a volley of shots. It sent 'the brave men away quicker than they came', Lawrence noted in his memoirs. The new Aborigine in the camp claimed that the intruders were Aborigines from his station. They had come after him to stop him leaving the station and joining the team. The Aboriginal cricketers were still unsure about the stranger. Lawrence bowled to him the next day, and gave him a bowl. The interloper wasn't good enough.

'I gave him some money,' Lawrence recorded, 'and told him to go back to his station.'

The incident caused Lawrence to ride shot-gun on the wagon for half the day. He could not be sure if they had been set up or the outsider had been telling the truth.

Lawrence was relieved when the eight-day trek was over.

The team rested for a week in the Warrnambool hotel and relaxed by playing billiards and dancing waltzes and polkas at night. A big crowd filled the bar and dance area each night. Lawrence and Hayman mingled with the Aboriginal team members, making sure they didn't drink too much. They wanted the lads to make an impression in their first game. And they did, thrashing Warrnambool in front of a crowd of more than a thousand. It was a fine start to a tour. The Aborigines certainly believed in their captain.

On the Sunday after the game, he took them to church, as promised.

'They seemed to like it,' Lawrence noted.

They were attentive and put money in the collection plate.

Lawrence asked them about the experience. They replied:

'Music very nice and him (the minister) talk a lot and get a lot of money.'

'And what do you think he does with it?' Lawrence asked.

'Keep it, don't he?'

'No. He gives it to the poor people.'

They were 'astounded' and commented:

'Does he then? Well when we go to church again I will always put my money in the plate.'

Lawrence was pleased to report that they did.

Morale was high. But disaster was never far away from the squad. One member of the team arrived home late and wanted to light his pipe using a chandelier in a dormitory where the rest were asleep. He had to jump for it, but in attempting to pull it down he brought it crashing to the floor. Kerosene spilt and fire engulfed the room. It was extinguished. No one was hurt, despite the damage, which was paid for out of Lawrence's contingency funds.

The team was set to play exhibition games around Victoria, but a major problem developed that threatened the trip. The letters of complaint about the tour from Constable Kennedy and Dr Molloy arrived at the Protection Board early in October 1867. While no law prevented Lawrence from taking his men to other colonies and England, public pressure could see the government prevent it. The board was then drafting the notorious Aborigine Protection Act (which became law in 1868), that would force Aborigines to relocate to missions and reserves. It was, in part, in response to the disaster of the early 1867 tour and an attempt to 'protect' Aborigines from exploitation. But the proposed Act would have its own sinister ramifications. No Aborigine would be able to travel without the board's permission, creating a police state for Aborigines and a form of 'apartheid'. Had the Act been law then, Lawrence would have had no hope of getting his men out of Victoria, let alone Australia. (This law was still on state statute books in the 1930s. Then, the great Aboriginal fast bowler, Eddie Gilbert, had to get written permission from the Queensland board in order to travel interstate to play in Shield matches.)

The Victorian board, frustrated in the knowledge that it would be a toothless tiger until mid-1868 when the Act was expected to become law, began a press campaign against Lawrence. It was to the point. Appeals were made to put an end to the 'heartless proceedings of the speculators who unscrupulously endanger the lives of the blacks for the sake of sordid gain...'

Lawrence received support from *The Age*, the most influential paper in the state. It reported a game at Corio and complimented the team for their behaviour on the field. They were not being 'used up' as Dr Molloy had told the board. On the contrary, in *The Age*'s view, the players seemed as 'temperate as anchorites, as jolly as sandboys and as supple as deer'. In other words, they were mentally and physically alert.

In a game at Corio there was a good deal of feeling between Tom Wills and Lawrence. They had been friends since meeting in Ireland in 1854 during a cricket match between the Phoenix Club, where Lawrence had a coaching appointment, and a Liverpool team. Wills, a hero in Victoria for founding and playing Australian Rules Football, was bitterly disappointed about not being involved in the planned 1868 England tour. He was aware of his former companion's concern about the Aborigines' drinking. Wills assumed that this was the reason he had not been invited to join the squad. He was right.

He bowled with anger that day at Corio and took four Aboriginal wickets in his first eight overs. But he couldn't remove Lawrence. When Corio batted, Lawrence brought himself on to bowl immediately Wills came to the wicket. When Wills was 6, Lawrence trapped him lbw. It didn't bring them any closer. Rain killed the game, which was drawn.

Backers of Lawrence's squad lobbied for a fixture at the Melbourne Cricket Ground in November to coincide with a visit by the Duke of Edinburgh, but the Melbourne Cricket Club (MCC) rejected them. The impact of the Protection Board's press push to stop the tour was having an effect. Wills, a 'ground staff' coach at the MCC, influenced the decision not to stage a game.

Lawrence was aware of the building pressure to stop the Aborigines leaving Melbourne. There were strong rumours that the Victorian government would order the police to intervene at the Melbourne port from which they were due to leave. He planned a return match at Corio and was reported in the press as scheduling further games. Lawrence instructed all the players to talk about upcoming matches. Secretly, he made arrangements for the team to leave by boat for Sydney not from Melbourne but from Queenscliff, close to Corio. Players were told they were going on a 'fishing trip' from Queenscliff. They boarded the *Rangatira* off Port Phillip Bay heads late in October and it sailed to Sydney with its happy extra cargo.

The press supported the 'fugitives'. It was more attractive to readers than backing the Protection Board. *The Age* suggested the board had been 'checkmated by the speculators' and sent a reporter to cover the team's exploits in New South Wales. These began with a win at Wollongong against Illawarra, followed by an athletics exhibition. At Wollongong the crowd was unruly. It surged near the track when Dick-a-Dick and Cuzens raced over 100 yards and the two runners careered into spectators. Cuzens was concussed. Dick-a-Dick knocked over a horse and its rider. This kind of incident brought more headlines than the cricket, but the team continued to perform well, with wins over West Maitland, Singleton and Newcastle.

It went on to Sydney and was based at Lawrence's Pier Hotel on the Esplanade at Manly Beach. Lawrence had sold the hotel and planned to be out of it by the time he caught the boat to England.

He continued to monitor the team's drinking. Lawrence was protecting his players and doing everything to ensure a successful mission. His management methods helped their performances, although a strong combined Sydney team beat them at the Albert Ground in Redfern. They also lost to Bathurst on Boxing Day 1867.

On a return game at the Albert Ground in early February 1868, this time against a combined army and navy team, the Aborigines played brilliantly in front of big crowds—4000 and 9000—on two days. Each day the Duke of Edinburgh was among the spectators. On the first, he was introduced to and mingled with them, much to their delight. On the second, enchanted by their cheerful, polite manner, he mixed with them again. The Aborigines were inspired. They rolled the army and navy team for 64, thanks to Johnny Cuzens, who took eight for 23. The Aborigines replied with 237, with Cuzens smashing a top score of 86, Mullagh 64 and Bullocky 39. Mullagh had a correct defence, and a fine, wristy style that allowed him to play all round the wicket. Bullocky was aptly named. He liked to hit hard and often. The army and navy combine was two for 51 in its second innings when the game ended in a draw.

It was followed by an athletics show. The strong, 180-centimetre, 80-kilogram Mullugh jumped 172 centimetres in the high jump. Then there was a mock battle of six men a side. Each man had a spear and some hurled their weapons 85 metres, causing the human target to dodge or be struck. The Aborigines appeared in a new costume of colourful dress and headgear featuring lyrebird plumage. The bigger second-day crowd loved it. Lawrence was satisfied. His troupe, he felt, would more than pay its way and maybe even return a profit for the main investor, George W Graham, a Sydney solicitor, who was making the trip. William Hayman left two weeks earlier to smooth the squad's entry into England.

England ho

The first Australian cricket team to tour England sailed from Sydney on 8 February 1868 on the *Parramatta*, a wool ship, almost to the day when the last convict ship was leaving England for Australia after eighty-one years of transportation. The Aborigines were given a big cabin just below the first-class area and were treated well. Lawrence continued his simple religious instruction and it helped calm them on the voyage. The man in charge of the ship, Captain Williams, they were told, had prayed to Jesus in heaven for their safe journey. Lawrence made an effort to teach them to read and write, but gave up when the team members lost concentration and began drawing animals and birds. During the day they carved wooden needles, hair clips, bracelets and other items, making them a hit with the ladies and children on board. At night after dinner the team played draughts and various card games. They joined in dancing, again to the pleasure of the women passengers. Their agility and graceful movements made them naturals on the dance floor. Captain Williams occasionally joined them for the evening meal and even tried his hand at cards.

Return to green fields

Charles Lawrence was thrilled to be travelling to his former homeland after seven years in Australia. He had come out with H H Stephenson's first All-England XI in 1861 for a tour of Victoria. Born in Surrey, Lawrence told his team how as an eleven-year-old he hitched a ride on a cart from his home that took him fifty miles to London, where he walked a few kilometres to Lord's to see his hero, batsman Fuller Pilch. Lawrence remembered settling in at a place near the boundary only to see Pilch caught first ball. At eighteen, after he had played for Surrey a few times, he hitched his way to Scotland to stay with a relative in Edinburgh. He found a job as an assistant stationmaster at a railway station. Lawrence played as much cricket as possible and established himself as a capable all-rounder.

At nineteen, in 1849 he was selected to play for Scotland against William Clarke's All-England XI. Lawrence made a name for himself by taking ten for 53 in one innings. He bowled four batsmen.

In 1850, he met and married Ann Elizabeth Watts. (They were to have four children—Elizabeth in 1856, Anne in 1858, Charles in 1860 and Maude, who died at birth in 1866.) William Clarke was impressed by Lawrence and obtained a professional appointment for him in Ireland in 1851 as a coach at Dublin's Phoenix Club. He also became a tennis coach, but that business did not develop and Lawrence lost money for investors. He had returned to England to play for Surrey again when he was invited to join the All-England team to tour Australia in 1861. The new land was enticing and he brought out his family. Sydney, rough and rustic as it was, offered opportunities, especially for a professional sportsperson who knew much about outdoor games. Cricket was the boom sport in Australia, with clubs springing   up like mushrooms. Lawrence opened a cricket goods shop and cafe at 353 George Street, played five games for New South Wales versus Victoria and coached the cream of Sydney between 1862 and 1864. A fellow Surrey man, William Caffyn, also coaching in Sydney, said of Lawrence in 1864, 'By his perseverance, energy and ability, he did a great deal toward the raising of the game to its present high standard.'

In that year, George Parr brought out his All-England team. Lawrence played in the New South Wales twenty-two and scored 25 out of the first innings of 135. In another game against England, bowling fast-round-arm, and experimenting with the new, legal overarm (the 'Windmill'), he took six for 29 in one innings.

In 1866, Lawrence bought the Pier Hotel at Manly. Now he had sold that to pursue the biggest adventure and gamble of his opportunistic career so far.

Happy landing

Even before the team landed, there was a mini-crisis when those on board learned that the Duke of Edinburgh had been shot and wounded in Sydney. The Aborigines were distraught. They vowed to perform games of welcome in front of him.

They were also upset when the ship's captain bade them farewell before the boat docked at Gravesend. They had felt safe in his company and with him at the helm over the three-month voyage until mid-May.

Hayman was waiting for them dockside and led them in two coaches to their base at West Malling in Kent. Lawrence continued on with the boat to London. He was due at the Surrey Cricket Club's annual dinner the night he arrived. Lawrence used the night to 'network' with the one hundred guests. He drank with jolly Surrey secretary, William Burrup, who had been a keen instigator of the All-England team's 1861 tour. In correspondence begun in mid-1867, Burrup had been interested in staging the first game of the current tour against Surrey at his new, beloved Oval at London's Kennington. Lawrence, aware that every such match meant money in the bank, was delighted when they firmed up on the fixture that evening. They agreed on the dates: 25 and 26 May.

The following day Lawrence rejoined his squad and told them the good news about the Surrey match. Lawrence found them raring to play cricket. And play they would. The schedule was not well structured, and would grow as the tour progressed and the novelty of the 'troupe' was publicised. As it turned out, there was to be a 126-day itinerary from the first match at the Oval. The team was to perform on ninety-nine of them. Take out eighteen Sundays, when sports were banned, and it was left with just nine days' break. Even by mid-nineteenth century standards, this was demanding, given the time to travel from town to town. On top of this, every day was long. The gruelling schedule allowed little else beyond playing, travelling and sleeping. In a way, it suited Lawrence. He knew he had to avoid, as much as possible, his players having idle time, where they would be tempted to hit the grog. His main challenge would be keeping harmony. It said much for the Aborigines' toughness, team spirit and self-discipline that Lawrence was confident they would get through the five months without a drop off in form.

West Malling was Hayman's family home and the Aborigines had an immediate impact. Few people in Britain had seen a black. Their dual demeanour of dignified grace and ready laughter and fun-loving behaviour were a novelty. Ignorance abounded. Later in the tour a hotel proprietor at Brighton insisted that they 'scrub off the dye' before they had baths. He thought that they were white men, who had 'dyed for the occasion', a bunch of early-day Al Jolsons. But in general they were well received. On one occasion Lawrence walked into the local draper's shop at West Malling. The owner invited him behind the shop into his drawing room. Lawrence noted in his memoirs that the man's 'daughters were entertaining my gentlemen with a little music ... Three of the blacks were reclining upon sofas whilst the ladies were playing and singing. They all seemed delighted with the evening's amusement and [the Aborigines] promised to call again.'

The Aborigines' colourful reputation preceded them to the Oval, where 7000 spectators turned up, many of them women, who walked from all over London or arrived 'on horseback and in carriages'.

Before the first ball was bowled, the Aborigines gathered in a group, gave three cheers to the opposition and ended with a shriek that sent a laugh and a buzz through the crowd. Spectators were amused that the Aborigines fielded barefoot, but soon became appreciative of their fielding and throwing skills. They moved swiftly across the uneven outfield. Instead of the high lobs to the keeper that featured in local cricket, they would 'spear' the ball in, low, fast and accurately.

A full-strength, first-class Surrey made 222. Mullagh, bowling overarm, took three for 100 off fifty-two overs. Lawrence, in fine form, with his accurate mix of over and round-armers and the odd over of slow underarm, took seven for 91 off forty-nine overs. In reply, the Australians collapsed for 83, with Mullagh making 33 and King Cole

14. The crowd was further amused by the excited chatter of the Aborigines at the crease. They yelled to each other in their own language, and made many false starts up the wicket.

The tourists were forced to follow on and did better, making 132, Mullagh this time stroking 73, Lawrence 22 and Bullocky 19. Surrey won by an innings and 5 runs. It was a result that reflected the standard the tourists would put up—below first-class level but with the skill to upset quality teams. The upright Mullagh was the star with bat and ball. Lawrence, a neat, light figure, standing about 174 centimetres, would give him good support with his technically correct if a tad defensive style. Then there was Cuzens, who was the third all-rounder. After that it was hit or miss, with Red Cap, and later Twopenny, capable of a top performance here and there.

The press was generally supportive and optimistic. *Reynolds News* took the long view and called the match a 'new epoch in the history of cricket'. Given the touring teams that would follow from Australia over the next 130 years, this was a more prophetic observation than the reporter could have imagined. *The Sheffield Telegraph*, not to be outdone, saw it as 'the Event of the Century'. But *The Times*, 112 years short of Australian ownership, was less kind. Its reporter saw 'second-rate bowling', and batting 'sadly wanting in power'. Running between the wickets was 'slow and uncertain'.

It didn't put the crowds off. Twenty thousand attended over three days. A third day, 27 May, was set aside for sports. There were races, boomerang and spear throwing, high jump, running backwards, hurdles, pole vaulting, and cricket-ball throwing. A boomerang just missed decapitating a small dog that strayed onto the Oval. Spectators who underestimated the weapon's sweeping curve were forced to duck.

Lean, bearded W G Grace, twenty and making his name as a champion all-rounder, competed in the ball throwing. He won the event with hurls of 116, 117 and 118 yards, beating Mullagh (104 yards—below his best of 120 yards achieved at Harrow) and Dick-a-Dick (107 yards). It wasn't the last time Grace would see them on the tour. He wrote in his book *W.G.*, 'The team went up and down the country, playing matches against clubs, including several of the counties, and acquitted themselves very well.'

Lawrence tried other events such as his own feats with bat and ball.

A ball would be thrown from a distance and he would stop it with the bat without the ball hitting the ground. The feat didn't capture the crowd's imagination. He reduced his act and it wasn't always in the show. Lawrence took note of the spectator reaction to the more popular ball-dodging act by Dick-a-Dick, who defended himself with a shield and leangle, a curved wooden blade similar to an old-style cricket bat. This performance would later be given third billing behind the spear and boomerang throwing.

After expenses paid to Surrey, the police and the umpires, there was a 300 pounds profit. It was a strong start, but Lawrence knew it would rarely peak like this. Weather, less suitable grounds, the novelty wearing off and defeats would lower the gate here and there.

Three days later, the Australians played an upper-class team led by Lord Paget at Maidstone. The visitors, thanks to Lawrence (four for 68 in Maidstone's 151, and 57 not out from four for 119), were on the way to victory when Lord Paget decided the game should be called a 'draw' in order that the Aborigines could perform their acts and sports.

Lawrence took the team to the Derby, and was able to keep up public interest. They were intrigued by the Aborigines at a time when Darwinism was fashionable and many unscientific theories about human origins were flying around in England's journals. Most of the comment about the tourists was polite, even glowing, while often at times patronising. Yet it was always more respectful than press remarks at home.

England observations such as 'adroit hunters...skilled trackers ...natural sportsmen...agile athlete...fair cricketers...' abounded.

Lord's, ladies and lubrication

The tourists toured on to Gravesend and were beaten by an innings by the Gentlemen of Kent, while the genteel women of Kent admired the Aborigines and their fashion. At Deer Park in a game against Richmond early in June, the former Governor of New South Wales, Sir William Denison, presented each Aborigine with ten shillings. With such interest from England's ruling classes, the ultra-conservative Marylebone Cricket Club at Lord's, cricket headquarters, relented. It agreed to a game but at a price—fifty per cent of the gate, which was twice as much as paid to Surrey at the Oval.

Before the big Lord's match, the Aborigines challenged Sussex at

Hove, leading on the first innings but losing the game. Then they beat Lewisham at Ladywell by six wickets. Mullagh and Lawrence starred both times.

The Lord's game of 12 and 13 June brought further big London crowds, eager to see the black tourists. (When the next white team played at Lord's, members were heard to express their shock and disappointment that the players were not black.) The Marylebone Cricket Club did not field all its 'ground' staff—the professional players retained by Lord's—a sign that it saw the foreigners as easybeats. Instead, the lofty club selected half the side from its social and military elite: two earls, a viscount, a lieutenant colonel and an army captain, all of whom regarded the game as more than social fun. They fancied themselves with bat and ball and took their performances seriously.

The home side batted first. Early on, the Marylebone Cricket Club's attitude at the selection table looked like causing serious embarrassment. Mullagh bowled the Earl of Coventry with a terrific leg cutter that slid alarmingly off the infamous Lord's ridge (known then as the 'lip') and sent his off stump cartwheeling. The crowd roared. Soon afterwards, Cuzens, who had been practising overarm after watching opposition English bowlers, sent down a very quick delivery from a four pace run-up. It uprooted the Earl of Bathurst's middle stump. The Australians, sometimes referred to in the common parlance of the day as 'savages' by fascinated onlooking anthropologists, were colourful and cheerful. And they could play. The aristocrats, who may have thought themselves superior in every respect, had a sudden dose of inferiority. In the space of five minutes, the tourists earned solid respect. Now Australia was seen to produce more than just gold. It had cricketers not to be taken lightly.

Mullagh delivered forty-five overs in that Marylebone Cricket Club first innings and removed four others, including Richard Fitzgerald (50), the Marylebone Cricket Club's best bat on the day. The home team succumbed for 164. Mullugh took five for 32; Cuzens four for 52.

Lawrence thought the total was gettable and asked the tired Mullagh for a special effort. The brilliant Aborigine, who displayed all-round skills to match any player alive, responded with a well-crafted 75, including a strong partnership with Lawrence (31) of 60. It was enough for the tourists to reach 185 and a slender lead of 21.

At the close of play on day one, Dick-a-Dick stood in front of the members and cheekily invited any of them to throw cricket balls at him for a shilling. He offered five shillings to anyone who could hit him. In an early forerunner to the movie *The Matrix*, where the hero dodged bullets, the sprightly, lean figure again used a shield and a leangle to parry everything hurled at him. A line of members formed and dropped their money into a hat. Some cribbed closer than the ten paces allowed, but the Aborigine brushed off the head-high missiles with the shield and the ones directed at his legs with the leangle.

No one could hit him. Dick-a-Dick walked away with a tidy sum, which according to custom would be distributed among the players once he had bought an item or two for himself. This act brought Dick-a-Dick extra money through the tour. Sprinting did the same for Cuzens. He was never beaten in any race on the long tour.

The next day at Lord's, England could only manage 120, Cuzens taking six for 65, giving him ten for 117 for the match. It would be a long time before an Australian in any fixture would do as well with the ball at Lord's. Cuzens was well supported by Mullagh, who took three for 19, giving him eight for 51 in the two England innings.

Charles Lawrence was nervous. His team had an even hundred to get for victory. He was savouring the meaning of a big win at Lord's against the much-vaunted Marylebone Cricket Club when his team collapsed for 45. Cuzens, 21, and Mullagh, 12, resisted. The 55 run win to the MCC was a big disappointment. Yet the competitive performance assured the tourists of a well-attended, full itinerary of games. Clubs that had been a little sniffy or indifferent about playing them now lined up across the country to play them.

At the end of the game, there was a reception under a marquee where the Aborigines mingled with the English players and their families, Lord's members and other invited guests. The handsome, dignified Johnny Mullagh was the centre of attention, especially with the women. He was photographed and one of the attractive young women promised to send him a portrait of herself.

The ever-lurking drink problem also emerged at Lord's. Some of the hosts insisted on drinking to the Aborigines' health. The sad irony was that alcohol threatened their wellbeing. These 'cricket lovers ... chatted with them,' according to Lawrence, 'until the poor fellows got quite helpless to refuse.'

Lawrence objected to this pressure, only too aware after the experience at Edenhope how easily too much conviviality could set them off. The hosts responded that the Aborigines 'were not slaves'. They kept plying them with drinks, saying that 'they should have what they liked'. When Lawrence further remonstrated with them, he was told that 'they [the Aborigines] were in a free country'.

It would be a constant worry for Lawrence on tour. Related to the drinking was homesickness, which had emerged by mid-June. Being away from home so long was alarming for some of the Aborigines, who needed to relate to their home territory. They had left home in September of the previous year. It had concerned them to be months away travelling Victoria and New South Wales. Now, several months on and in a strange land 20,000 kilometres from Victoria's Western District, some were depressed. They missed family and traditions. Lawrence counselled them as best he could. But it was a problem that would not leave the squad. It increased the likelihood of some of them getting drunk, and others becoming sick.

Death and glory

Illness unrelated to alcohol or depression was the fate of thirty-year-old King Cole after the Lord's match, in which he batted well and made 14. Lawrence checked King Cole into Guy's Hospital, London. Hayman remained in London to look after him as the 'caravan' moved on to Southsea versus East Hampshire. The tourists were thrashed by an innings, despite Cuzens taking six for 71, and Mullagh (40), Bullocky (30), and Red Cap (23 in the second innings) all getting runs.

King Cole was diagnosed with tuberculosis as the team went down to Bishop's Stortford by eight wickets on 20 June. Hayman sent a message to Lawrence that King Cole was deteriorating. Now he also had pneumonia. Lawrence dropped out of the next (drawn) game at Hastings on 22 and 23 June and travelled back to London to see the ailing Aborigine. But King Cole died on 24 June. With a heavy heart, Lawrence organised a burial in Victoria Park cemetery. He read the eulogy.

Lawrence couldn't be held responsible for such a tragedy. He had treated all his men well. Yet the warnings about the Aborigines' 'chest ailments' by Constable Kennedy and Dr Molloy would haunt him.

The tour had to go on, but Lawrence was now more acutely aware of each player's condition. He noted that two team members—Jim Crow and Sundown—were suffering from homesickness. Lawrence needed them, but acknowledged that their health came first. The next possible ship that he could trust to take them home safely was the *Parramatta*, again under the control of Captain Williams, in mid-August, still two months away. Lawrence made arrangements for Crow and Sundown's return to Australia. He was taking no risks, even if he would be left with only eleven men for a further two months and nearly half the games.

Despite the anguish over King Cole's death, the team began to perform better. They lost just one game, drew two and won two, versus Halifax and South Wales. The latter, at Swansea, was one of the big victories for the tour. South Wales was reduced to 68 by Mullagh (five for 17) and Lawrence (four for 38). The Australians replied with 193 (Cuzens 50, Red Cap 37, Mullagh 25) and then dismissed the home team for 92 (Mullagh four for 23, Lawrence four for 40), giving the tourists a win by an innings and 33 runs.

The team visited the Swansea Fun Fair in high spirits, where Dick-a-Dick spent five pounds on the 'wheel of fortune'. He won several prizes. Generous as ever, he handed them out to Mosquito, Red Cap and some of the others. He kept a Swiss imitation clock for himself and became attached to it.

Lawrence's absence against a full-strength Yorkshire County team on 13 and 14 July at York had much to do with the thrashing by an innings and 51 runs. Only Cuzens, with 32 and 42, presented opposition with the bat, while Red Cap took a career best of seven for 34. The Aborigines were not allowed into the lunch marquee on the first day. It appeared to be the first act of racism, as opposed to ignorance, they had experienced. They had encountered such positive, sometimes overwhelming sentiment so far that it was a shock. Once over it, they were angry. Mullugh vowed not to take the field on day two.

The lunch snub made the papers. Editorials attacked the Yorkshire Club. The club president denied that any discrimination had occurred. He said that the lunch had been prepared, but that the Aborigines had not turned up. He claimed they had gone to the local hotel for their meal. A supportive crowd on day two gave the Aborigines prolonged applause. But Mullagh was not among them.

Lawrence regretted not being present to support his men. Later he let the Yorkshire Club know of his feelings, although its president stood by his claim. The fact that he did showed that most people were sensitive to the race issue.

Tiger trouble

Charles Lawrence returned to the squad and lifted their rating at Manchester against Longsight, top scoring with 37 and taking five for 49. A few bad umpiring decisions went against the tourists and they lost by four wickets. They then thrashed the Carrow Club at Norwich and prepared for a game against Keighley in Yorkshire. Keighley batted first and Lawrence opened the bowling with Red Cap, who took five for 54 in Keighley's first innings of 118. The tourists made 101 and then Lawrence took seven for 54 in Keighley's second innings of 146. The Australians had a 154-run target for victory. Lawrence made 28, while Cuzens, in striking form, smashed 70 and nearly stole the game. The Australians were on eight for 142 with just 12 to make at the close of play.

On a mid-tour roll, they beat the Bootle Club by nine wickets at Liverpool. It was a windy day and the Aborigines decided not to throw their boomerangs. The crowd booed and catcalled for some time. Johnny Mullagh, the best thrower, reluctantly bowed to spectator pressure. His first throw curved close to, but above the crowd, who first responded with an 'oooooh', then applauded and yelled for more. Mullagh obliged. The weapon was caught in a sudden wind drop and slid into a small section of the crowd near the edge of the ground. It struck a boy wearing a straw hat. He went down, stunned and with a bleeding face. A doctor ran across the oval and treated the unintended victim for a superficial wound. His hat had saved him from something more serious.

In a return match against Longsight at Manchester, the Australians avenged an earlier loss by winning by 107 runs. Lawrence took eight for 48 and three for 25. Mullagh batted and bowled superbly once more. He was emerging as the stand-out tourist, returning better figures with bat and ball than almost all top players in England in 1868. Lawrence and Cuzens backed him all the way with consistent performances, while Twopenny's bowling efforts were the surprise in the latter weeks.

Rain intervened at Bramall Lane versus Sheffield, with the Australians on track to win. Hours of idle time led to more chances to booze than normal in a summer so far mainly uninterrupted by the weather. Bullocky drank heavily and could not leave the team lodgings. In the early hours of day two, 11 August, Harry Tiger assaulted two policemen, who found him wandering Sheffield's King Street. He thumped one of them and tried to strangle the other. Tiger was over-powered. One of the policemen used a baton to quell him. He was dragged to the police lockup. A doctor was called to dress his head wound. Lawrence asked the Sheffield Club secretary to intervene. He paid the one-pound fine and Tiger was released.

Lawrence was furious. Tiger, like Bullocky and some of the others, blamed the 'gentlemen'—the members and spectators—for giving them too much drink. Over breakfast the next morning, he and Bullocky were warned that they would be sent home if they didn't improve their behaviour. They were so contrite that, as ever, Lawrence forgave them by the time breakfast was over. It was a constant theme, especially during down time in hotels and boarding houses on their long trek up and down England. Drink would lead to fights between team members. Lawrence would intervene. There would be sulking. Later, during card games or other leisure activities, the Aborigines would 'profess their love' for Lawrence and do anything 'to please' him.

Lawrence always ended up showing compassion. 'Whatever else could I do than forgive and hope for improvement,' he wrote in his memoirs.

There was only one near-altercation between Lawrence and one of the team. It happened in the next game at Dewsbury versus the Savile Club. The team was in low spirits after being soundly beaten by an innings, despite a top score of 20 from a sober Tiger in the first innings, and 48 from Mullagh in the second. The team members straggled up to the station and were waiting for a train. Dick-a-Dick became agitated. He had left his beloved Swiss clock at the hotel. He wanted to retrieve it. Lawrence, aware that the train was already overdue, blocked his path. Dick-a-Dick remonstrated with his captain, baulked around him and sprinted off. Lawrence gave chase but couldn't catch him. The Aborigine returned with the clock under his arm just as the train pulled in.

The match schedule ended as it had begun—at the Oval against

Surrey, where the tourists were beaten again, this time by nine wickets. The bowling was as steady and penetrative as ever. The batsmen handled speed and medium pace well. But spin and slow bowling was the team's undoing. It was the biggest single weakness of the squad for the tour.

A near-disaster was again averted during the boomerang throwing when a man was struck. Also again, a hat saved him. The 'very frightened' victim approached Lawrence and threatened him with legal action. Lawrence apologised, pulled five pounds from his pocket and handed it to the man, telling him to buy a new hat. 'He went away quite satisfied,' Lawrence noted, 'as the injured one was very old.'

A team of character

In all, the team played forty-seven matches from May to November, mainly in the rapidly growing industrial centres, and in front of fair to excellent crowds, who paid sixpence to half a crown at every venue. They won fourteen, lost fourteen and drew nineteen of their fixtures. Their form held through the arduous season. These 'Stalwart Men' as the press acclaimed them, never wavered as a unit in five months. They were performing as well (if not better) in the last month as in the first. It was a remarkable feat of character, endurance and stamina, especially as Lawrence had just eleven men to select for half the season. The problem with alcohol was ever-present, but no more so than would be experienced by many Test squads to tour England in the next 130 years. Jack Blackham's squad in 1893, for example, made the Aboriginal cricketers seem like choirboys by comparison.

Lawrence and Mullagh were the 1868 team's stars. Lawrence played in forty matches and scored 1156 at 20.16, with a top score of 63 versus Sussex at Hove. To appreciate his average, it must be doubled (at around 40) to judge it against performances in the twentieth century, due to the awful state of pitches, which gave bowlers a decided advantage. Lawrence's bowling statistics were impressive: 250 wickets at 12.1 runs a wicket. Again the wicket-taking rate figure should be doubled (to around 24) to make a comparative analysis with today's players. Mullagh also did well. He made 1698 runs at 23.65, with a highest score of 94 versus Reading. He played in forty-five matches, taking 245 wickets at 10. These were both outstanding all-round figures. Mullagh at least had to be rated as first-class standard. He might have acquitted himself well at Test level, but he preferred to return to the Western District and play local cricket.

The third strong performer was Johnny Cuzens, who in eighty innings made 1358 runs at 19.97 (with a top score of 87 against the Carrow Club) and took 114 wickets at 11.3. Bullocky, when sober, also had moments with the bat, scoring 579 at 9.33, as did Red Cap with bat (630 at 8.4) and ball (fifty-four wickets at 10.7). Twopenny, especially late in the long, demanding season, lifted his rating with the ball and took thirty-five wickets at 6.91. He had learned to bowl overarm during the long season, and at speed, which accounted for his improved figures. Improved overarm styles were coming into vogue during 1868. The Aborigines would take home with them advanced variations of the new technique that had only been used proficiently by Mullagh in the Western District. (Until 1864 any delivery above the shoulder line had been deemed a throw, and therefore a no-ball. For many years after 1864, any one match would see overarm, round-arm and underarm.)

While a profit analysis of the trip has produced rubbery figures, depending on the analyst, the tour seemed to have made about 1000 pounds for the investor, George Graham. Lawrence and his Aborigines received nothing beyond what they picked up as prizes, usually for non-cricket performances. Yet the tour's overall 'success' encouraged others to consider future trips.

Now forty-one, Lawrence returned to Australia feeling that he had to find greater security for his wife and three children. His touring, risk-taking days were over. Recalling his experience in Scotland as a railway stationmaster's assistant, he joined the New South Wales railways and worked for them for the next twenty-two years until he retired in 1890. His cricket continued, this time with the Newcastle Club, where he became known as 'the Old Master'. Lawrence it seemed, no matter who the company, performed near the top. Well into his forties, he led the Newcastle batting average in 1870, 1871 and 1872. His stamina was remarkable. At an age when others would like plenty of spells from the bowling crease, he delivered unchanged in three games against Maitland in 1871, taking thirty-one wickets for 117. Lawrence played on until he was fifty-six in 1884, when he made his last appearance in New South Wales. It was a benefit match at the

Sydney Cricket Ground. He scored thirty-one. But the Lawrence name lived on in Newcastle. His son Charles was one of the club's leading bats in the 1880s.

Full circle

In 1891, Charles Lawrence, now sixty-three, with greying facial hair beyond the mutton-chops and goatee beard of his youth, was appointed coach to the Colts, the junior members of the Melbourne Cricket Club.

William Hayman had kept Lawrence informed about the lives of his team. Johnny Mullagh, the team's champion, became a professional at the Melbourne Cricket Club during the 1869–70 season. He was paid a pound a week and half his travelling expenses, and given free lodging. He played for the Melbourne Cricket Club for just six weeks (scoring 209 at 34.83, and taking eight for 300) and was selected to play for Victoria. But no amount of cajoling could keep him in Melbourne or persuade him to travel to Sydney. The pull of his homeland was greater. He had been away too long and became ill, probably from the worry of being dislocated from his roots. He was back in the bush at Harrow by Christmas 1869. This meant he missed playing for Victoria against New South Wales and was never chosen again. The MCC made sure he was in the Victorian squad for the following season 1870–71, but he refused to return to city life.

Mullagh had had enough. He restricted his cricket to bush matches for Harrow, which he enjoyed in his own quiet way, except for some racial incidents that brought back memories of the incident at York. He was batting well against the Apsley Club when its captain remarked to one of the bowlers, 'Let's get this nigger off the field.' Mullagh pulled away when the bowler was running in. When he faced up again he deliberately hit a catch. He let it be known to his teammates that he didn't wish to play against a team with such attitudes. It was a quiet, dignified yet poignant protest.

On another occasion when Harrow was playing away, according to John Mulvaney and Rex Harcourt in their book, *Cricket Walkabout*, all except Mullagh were shown to bedrooms in an inn. The innkeeper ushered Mullagh to a room across the yard by the stables. The Aborigine, in another civil protest, left the premises and slept the night in the open.

Although a colonial hero, Mullagh worked as a farmhand and rabbiter, and struggled during the 1870s. His affection for the English lured him back to Melbourne in 1878–79 to play for Victoria against Lord Harris's All-England XI. Although then in his mid-thirties and past his brilliant best, he managed a majestic 36, top score in Victoria's second innings.

The hat was passed around for him at the MCG. Fifty pounds were collected. A local jeweller donated a gold watch, which Mullagh treasured nearly as much as the portrait of the 'Lady from London' he met at Lord's. When asked later in life why he had not married he replied with all the pathos of opportunities lost: 'A white woman won't have me, and I will never marry a black one.' His prejudice against black women was puzzling, given his own stand against racism.

Mullagh kept playing for Harrow in the Murray Cup competition until nearly sixty in 1890. A year later, local Harrow boy Jack Minogue came across sheepskins hidden in a tree at James Edgar's Pine Hills Station, where Mullagh lived and worked. He told the police. They investigated and found Mullagh with more hides. He had been killing sheep to help feed himself and his dogs. Instead of being charged, he was thrown off the station. A few weeks later, Minogue found Mullagh under a tree. He was weak and complaining of a sore side. Minogue went to the station, found James Edgar and they returned, but too late. Mullagh was dead.

One of Lawrence's first acts when he arrived in Melbourne with his MCC job was to attend Mullagh's funeral at the Harrow cemetery. He joined the Harrow team, who threw sprigs of wattle and blackberry on the casket. (Each year now an Aboriginal team plays the Glenelg XI at Harrow for the Johnny Mullagh Memorial Trophy.)

Charles Lawrence was interested to know what had happened to his favourite team member, Dick-a-Dick. Hayman told him that he had 'gone bush' in the Little Desert area of Western Victoria soon after the England tour. It was where he had once tracked and found three lost children, an act that had brought him fame throughout Australia and England. He was later seen working as a drover and fencer along the Murray River near Mildura. Johnny Cuzens, another of Lawrence's favourites, had also been an MCC professional. But like Mullagh he became homesick and ill. Destitute, he returned to the Western District and died, it was said, of a cold in 1871.

Tiger continued to live up to his name and reputation after the tour, being in and out of gaol for drunken behaviour. He died in 1884. Red Cap married and had a family. He was granted forty acres on the Glenelg River and was a successful shearer until his death in 1893.

Lawrence, as an MCC professional, had come full circle since his professional days in Ireland from 1851 to 1861. He was a fine, popular coach, with an eye for technique and courage. He had seen plenty in his decades in and around the game. In 1898 at age seventy, he played his last game, a charity match at the MCG, making 7 runs in a stay at the crease of just under an hour. Lawrence's strokes no longer had the brash force of his youth, but his eye and technique, especially in defence, were a model for any of his charges.

As the years rolled on, that mighty venture of 1868 slipped into perspective for him. In his eighties, Lawrence began writing his memoirs. Perhaps exhausted by recalling the high dramas of that history-making venture, he gave up after sixty pages of notes, just at the point where he recalled the team docking in England. (A few other extra notes were later discovered by relatives and associates.) He died soon afterwards.

Charles Lawrence's endeavour in touring England and his handling of a mercurial, talented Aboriginal team created a significant break-through in 1868. It led to Tests between Australia and England less than a decade later, and soon afterwards, the Ashes, the longest-running international competition in sporting history.

Charles Lawrence has the unique distinction of playing in the first England team to tour Australia, and the first Australian team to tour England. It qualifies him as a founding father of Ashes and inter-national cricket.

1

DAVID GREGORY

....

15 April 1845 – 4 August 1919

Tests: 3; Captain: 3; Wins: 2; Losses: 1;
Win ratio: 66.67 per cent

A TRIM BEGINNING

Every few weeks, David William Gregory, one of Australia's best cricketers of the 1860s and 1870s, would have his mighty beard and
whiskers trimmed in dusty George Street, Sydney. His barber was
William Caffyn, a refugee from Surrey, England, who just happened
to be the finest cricket coach in the New South Wales colony.

The two always talked cricket, from the merits of W G Grace, the
most outstanding all-round English cricketer of the nineteenth
century, to the impact of the overarm delivery; from the influence of
gambling on the game in England to the tricks of the underarm
grubber. The friendly, brown-eyed 'Handsome Dave', as women of
Sydney dubbed him, would listen, learn and ask questions. He was
keen to absorb everything he could but not slavishly follow the English
way. In his quiet, analytical way, Gregory wanted to apply verve and
energy to Australian cricket, which was the dominant sport in the
country. Football codes of the times were only just emerging, and
were seen as winter pastimes for keeping cricketers fit. Cricket was the
thinking man's sport that was developing and evolving. People such as

Gregory and Caffyn were stamping a style and approach that would have ramifications right through to the end of the twentieth century.

Gregory was the most imposing skipper Australia has had, the 133 kilogram Warwick Armstrong notwithstanding. He stood 187 centimetres high and weighed 90.7 kilograms. His genial good looks were hidden or accentuated, depending on the beholder, by his grand beard and whiskers, which were the most impressive and well-known in Sydney in the 1860s, when he built his reputation as an efficient operator in the New South Wales Government Audit Office. On the cricket field he was an accomplished batsman and expert slipper. He kept himself in shape by walking, particularly in the Blue Mountains, and building boats that were solid enough to venture beyond Sydney Harbour's heads. His hobbies were fishing and gardening, which also kept him healthy.

Gregory's reputation for enterprise was established at fifteen when in December 1860 he was awarded a 'meritorious medal' for conduct at St James' Church of England School. He visited the Governor, Sir William Denison, and asked for a job, reminding the Governor that His Excellency had told the school a few years earlier that if they obtained 'good passes' they would get jobs. His reputation for cricketing ability reached a zenith a decade later in April 1871. Around his twenty-sixth birthday, he and his brothers Ned and Charlie beat a brilliant Victorian trio—Tom Wills, John Conway and Sam Cosstick—in a single-wicket championship that drew a 7000 crowd at the Albert Ground, Redfern.

Conway was impressed with Gregory's leadership skills. 'He not only looked the part,' Conway wrote to a relative in Melbourne, 'he *was* the part. Dave Gregory would be ideal to lead a combined colonies team against England.'

Conway, another instigator of Test cricket, had longed for the day when one of England's touring sides—there had been three before 1876—would play a side representing Australia, which was still a quarter-century away from Federation. Until now the tourists, who in the 1873 tour numbered among them W G Grace himself, had taken on the colonies separately, often playing teams of eighteen and more. Conway, a Melbourne Grammar School–educated journalist, suggested to James Lillywhite, who led the tourists in 1876, that they play a truly international match of eleven players a side. The Englishman was confident his squad would cope with anything mustered by the colonies. But he had not quite calculated on the spectacular growth of cricket in New South Wales and Victoria. Lillywhite was therefore happy to tack on an international fixture at the Melbourne Cricket Ground when his team returned from a New Zealand tour in mid-March 1877.

Conway was elated. He set about the unenviable task of selecting the Australian eleven. His first coup was to select Gregory as captain. There was a strong, sometimes bitter, rivalry between the two biggest colonies of Victoria and New South Wales, which stemmed from more than the distance that separated their capitals and climate. Victoria had been free settled while New South Wales had begun as a penal colony. There had been a lack of trust between the two colonies based on ignorance and parochialism, which has continued on into the twenty-first century. Yet in the choice of Gregory as leader, no mumble of disagreement was heard in Victoria. Gregory's reputation had preceded him over a decade. Never had the selection of a standout skipper in the long history of Australian cricket been so universally accepted.

However the rest of the team was not so easy to secure without dissent or protest. Conway bravely contracted players and ignored protests from the New South Wales Cricket Association. But then the problems began. Conway and Gregory badly wanted to choose the overarm paceman, Fred Spofforth. But 'the Demon', whose hirsute, rugged appearance was reminiscent of another devil of a bowler, D K Lillee, one hundred years later, would not join other New South Wales players unless his mate Billy Murdoch was chosen as wicketkeeper. Spofforth had been bowling at Murdoch since they were kids in Balmain's Gladstone Park. Fred Spofforth knew he would be Gregory's first pick, and thought he could use his power to get his way. But he was not as resolute as Gregory, who could be as authoritative as he was easygoing. 'No Billy Murdoch, no Fred Spofforth,' Spofforth had told Gregory over a conciliatory drink at Gregory's home.

'No Spofforth,' Gregory said, then paused, sucked on his ever-present pipe and added, 'would be a shame.'

Spofforth thought his reputation would see that he and Murdoch played, but sole selector Conway and skipper Gregory wanted the dashing South Melbourne Club's Jack Blackham to keep. The speedster, who loved to frighten and hurt batsmen, had no choice but to honour his stand. Spofforth, then, was left out of the first-ever Test match, and the beginning of Test cricket's rich history.

The team's players from New South Wales were Gregory, brother Ned Gregory, Nat Thomson, Tom Garrett and Charles Bannerman. The Victorians were Blackham, Tom Horan, Bransby Cooper, Billy Midwinter, Tom Kendall and John Hodges.

England stumbled off the boat from New Zealand after a rough trip that had caused much seasickness. The team was without its only wicketkeeper, Edward Pooley. He was languishing in a Christchurch gaol after a betting incident. Pooley had bet a man in a bar that he could predict every individual score of the eighteen Christchurch players in the game against England. He wrote a zero beside each batsman's name, and said he would take a pound for every right guess and pay a shilling for every wrong guess. Nine batsmen made ducks, which meant that Pooley made a tidy profit of more than nine pounds, a considerable sum at the time. There were reports of a near riot and fights in the pub when Pooley came to collect. The man with whom he had made the bet told the police he had been duped. They charged Pooley with 'malicious damage'. Pooley was later acquitted of the charge but was fined for having 'created a disturbance'. His only real crime, it seemed, was knowing from experience that England dismissed most local sides in their tours for low scores and that ducks were made by many of its opponents.

England then had to play the day after arriving and without its keeper, but observers reckoned that this made the teams even. Australian didn't have the lethal Spofforth–Murdoch combination.

The England team in batting order read: H Jupp, J Selby, H R J Charlwood, G Ulyett, A Greenwood, T Armitage, A Shaw, T Emmett, A Hill the captain, James Lillywhite, and J Southerton.

The game began at the Melbourne Cricket Ground, among the gum trees not far from the Yarra River. Only about 900 spectators were there for the first ball. Several English teams had toured before. There was not much novelty in that. But no side representing Australia had ever played them. This was a first. No one running the beer tents, or the Melbourne Cricket Club (MCC), expected a bonanza, just perhaps a curiosity to see if the two fledgling colonies could stand up against the might of England.

Test beginning

David Gregory was smoking his pipe as he came out to toss the first coin ever in a Test. He won and decided to bat.

At 1.05 pm on sunny 15 March 1877, overweight, bearded Alfred Shaw from Nottingham, wearing a tie and black sash to keep his trousers up over his considerable pot, became the first bowler ever to sense the hushing of the crowd for the initial delivery in a Test. He bowled line and length to Charles Bannerman, the Kent-born Sydney batsman. Bannerman, with a great sense of the anticlimactic, blocked it. He maintained his scorn for theatrics by nudging the second ball forward of the wicket on the leg side for a single—the first Test run ever. A cheer of relief and derision went up from the small crowd, who didn't rate the Australians' chances high.

Bannerman's opening partner, Nat Thomson, made a single before the Yorkshire beanpole Allen Hill bowled him. The score was one for 2, and most observers thought events were unfolding as predicted. Bannerman, on 8, drove hard to mid-off and hit Armitage in the stomach. The fielder clutched at the ball but didn't get a hand to it. It was a chance of sorts. Bannerman took his life and ploughed on, with drives in the arc between cover and mid-wicket. He eschewed any glances or cuts, and thus reduced the chance for a mis-hit as his score mounted. He was still there at 2 pm for the forty-minute lunch break.

Bannerman resumed after the interval in front of a crowd that had more than quadrupled. Tom Horan, an Irish free settler, went after lunch for 12 at 40. David Gregory marched out to the biggest cheer of the game so far, took a single and then responded hesitantly to another. He was run out. He trudged off, more than a trifle disappointed that he had not made his mark on the game as a batsman.

Charles Bannerman continued to dominate as wickets fell. He shocked the purists by dancing down the wicket to several of the bowlers, including the pacey Hill and George Ulyett, to reach the pitch of the ball. He could do no wrong as he drove on. His success frustrated the English. Lillywhite spoke to Yorkshire bowler Thomas Armitage, who switched from innocuous line and length to the dreaded lob. The ball was tossed high with the hope of it lobbing on the stumps. Bannerman played back and swiped the ball forward of the stumps. The English skipper and bowler consulted again. Armitage switched to underarm grubbers, a common ball that flattered bowlers' figures more than took wickets. It was a hard ball to drive effectively. Bannerman, in only his tenth first-class innings, blocked and shovelled his way out of trouble.

The first day of Test cricket belonged to Bannerman as he reached his century in 160 minutes before a demonstrative, convivial crowd, which filled beer tents to applaud and toss hats in the air. Bannerman walked off at stumps at 5 pm with his score on 126 not out in 195 minutes. Australia was six for 166, about a hundred more than the betting predicted.

The next day, the crowd had tripled to 12,000, with Bannerman an instant colonial hero. He continued his plunder and reached 165 in 285 minutes with 15 fours, before a rising ball from Ulyett split his finger and forced him to retire hurt. The jolly Yorkshireman, known as 'Happy Jack' for his endless wit, remarked, 'Always wanted six fingers on bowling hand. Arranged it for opposition instead!'

Australia reached 245. (Bannerman's effort represented 67.3 per cent of his team's records, still a Test record 123 years later in 2000. It is also still the highest score by an Australian on debut.) Captain Gregory was pleased and admitted his team had collected more than he had hoped. His simple philosophy was to score as many runs as possible. Now he relished the chance to drive home a win for the underdog colonials.

Gregory's hours in the barber Caffyn's chair had paid off. They were both early proponents of unorthodox fields and reacting to each new batsman with bowling and field changes. Gregory urged keenness in the field and his players responded, sensing a chance to create history. England reached 196, mainly thanks to the opener Jupp (63) and Charlwood (36). Midwinter took five for 78.

The Australian second innings followed more or less the plan of the first, except that Charles Bannerman, with his bandaged finger, made just 4 instead of a century. This reduced the Australians to just 104, with Shaw taking five for 38, including the wicket of Gregory, bowled for 3.

England needed to make 154 to win.

Now the skipper's skill in a tense finish would play a major part in winning or losing. Gregory threw the ball to Bedford-born Victorian Tom Kendall, a left-armer, who bowled medium pace with flight and variety. Kendall had been steady without being penetrating in the first innings, taking one for 54. But Gregory, who had only sighted him during this game, had faith in his ability.

James Lillywhite sent in Hill (35 in the first innings coming in at number nine) and Greenwood to open. Kendall removed them both by the time the score was 7. At four for 22, Ulyett and Selby lifted English hopes with a stand of 40. Gregory rang the changes and shifted his field, trying everything to break this dangerous partnership, including bringing himself on for five overs, which conceded just 9 runs. Finally he brought back Kendall, who broke through again, bowling Ulyett (24). Hodges had Selby caught for 38, effectively ending England's chances, the tourists crumbling to be all out for 108 and beaten by 45 runs. Kendall took a match winning seven for 55. A key to the win was Gregory's favouring of Victorian bowlers, who sent down nearly four times as many overs as their New South Wales teammates. They took seventeen of the twenty wickets. Had he been sentimental or parochial, Australia would have lost.

After the game the excited crowd gave more than eighty-three pounds to a collection for Bannerman, who was the unofficial man-of-the-match. Another forty-six pounds was raised for Kendall and Blackham. The latter's tremendous keeping, especially up at the stumps to the pacemen, was appreciated.

Gregory paid tribute to the 'sound good sense and fighting temperament of his team' and to 'Willie Caffyn, who taught me all I really know about cricket'.

The *Argus* newspaper said David Gregory's leadership proved the difference between the two evenly matched sides.

Spark of centuries

The interest in this initial international match ignited a fire throughout the colonies that was never to expire. Suddenly there was a feeling among Australians for *the best of us* against *the best of them*. There was tremendous demand for a second encounter. This time Fred Spofforth was selected and there was no argument about who should keep. The Demon realised that to be left out of such a contest would mean he would miss out on the best competition the game could provide, and history in the making. Gregory also brought in Billy Murdoch, at the expense of his elder brother, Ned, but retained Blackham. Just to show who was boss, Blackham was told to keep. James Kelly was also selected. Horan and Bransby Cooper were omitted. England, still without Pooley, made no change for the Second Test, also at the MCG. It began on 31 March.

Gregory won the toss and batted again. Australia could reach just 122, and perhaps the skipper's only major error in the two games was to drop himself down the order to number ten. He made just 1 not out. Only Midwinter (31) got going. Hill took four for 27.

England built a steady team score (Greenwood 49, Ulyett 52, Emmett 48, Hill run out 49) of 261, with Kendall (four for 82) the pick of the bowlers. Spofforth (three for 67) bowled fast but was not the force expected. His grumbling about who should keep to him was silenced forever in his third over, when he bowled a quick lifter outside off stump. The batsman, Shaw, slid out of the crease in his attempt to strike it. Blackham took the ball one-handed and in almost the same action whipped off the bails.

Gregory decided that the Australians needed a good start. Instead of exhorting his openers to do better, he decided to lead from the front. He opened with Thomson and asked Bannerman to bat at three. The skipper's instinct proved correct again. The opening stand was 88. Gregory made 43 (top score) before Ulyett had him caught. Thomson made 41 and Bannerman 30 (in just eighteen minutes). New man Kelly, who made a competent 19 in the first innings, crashed eight successive fours in a quickfire 35. Australian managed 259 and Gregory was confident his bowlers could again contain England. This time the target was 121 for victory. Kendall again burst through early and at one point England was three for 9. A steadying partnership between Greenwood (22) and Ulyett allowed the tourists to reach four for 54. Spofforth then bowled Selby (2), swinging the game Australia's way again. The score was five for 76. Ulyett (63) took charge and England ran out the winner by four wickets.

A sense of unresolution and hunger for more of this kind of high-level competition pervaded the colonies.

Ungracious games

John Conway organised a tour of England the following year, 1878, with David Gregory as skipper again. But the English would not put up a national Test side, fearing the Australian tourists would take gate receipts from county games. They lost the first game against Notts in the freezing cold, but found their form by the time of an important match against the Marylebone Cricket Club, beginning on a wet day on 27 May at Lord's. About 1000 turned up to watch the game, many surprised that the Australians weren't black, a misconception caused by the talented Aborigine team that had toured a decade earlier.

Spectators thought they would be in for a batting exhibition when W G Grace cracked the first ball of the game for 4. They were shocked when Allan had him caught next ball. Allan struck again with the following delivery, bowling Clem Booth. At two for 25, Gregory put Spofforth on. It took him 23 balls to take six wickets, including the hat trick as the Marylebone Cricket Club collapsed for 33. Australia's reply wasn't much better—it was bundled out for 41. Shaw and Morley took five wickets each and only Midwinter reached double figures. The crowd grew to 10,000 as the Marylebone Cricket Club began its second innings. It made just 19, with Boyle taking six for 3 and Spofforth four for 16. Australia went on to win by nine wickets.

This crushing defeat forced the Marylebone Cricket Club to rethink international cricket, such was the interest now generated by this highly skilled, fit group, which had been drilled into a tight unit by the tough-minded Gregory. They were so outstanding by the eleventh match of the tour, against Middlesex at Lord's, that Grace 'kidnapped' one of its number, William Midwinter, for a Gloucestershire game just before he was due to bat for the Australians. Midwinter had spent just sixteen days in Gloucester in his life but they happened to have been his *first* days. It was enough for Grace to claim the all-rounder, who became a truly international cricketer. Midwinter ended up spending half the year in England playing for Gloucester and the other half playing for Victoria.

Grace and a Gloucester player, James Bush, arrived at Lord's. Grace lost his temper and abused Conway. He pushed the dithering Midwinter into a carriage, which took them back to the Oval. Conway reported the conflict to Gregory, who was incensed. He, Conway and

Harry Boyle, a friend of Midwinter's, then jumped in another carriage that gave chase across London. They caught Grace and Bush outside the ground just after they had shoved Midwinter through the gate. Another bitter altercation ensued.

Grace's parting shot to the Australians was, 'You haven't got a ghost of a chance against Middlesex.'

Ironically, Midwinter's replacement, Allan, put that ghost to rest by bowling the Australians to victory, taking seven for 38 and six for 76. Meanwhile, at the Oval, Grace's team went down to Surrey. The news brought a big cheer from the Australians at Lord's.

Grace's graceless intervention angered Gregory and his team enough for the skipper to declare that the tourists wouldn't play against Gloucester, unless he, Conway and Boyle received an apology from Grace. Aware of the terrific attendances at all the Australian games, Grace put pen to paper in a suitably abject manner.

Midwinter's defection left a hole in the middle-order. He was the only tourist with sound experience of wet pitches. It also reduced the Australians to just eleven men for the rest of the tour. Spofforth vowed to upset Grace in their game against Gloucester, the reigning county champions, which he did. He bowled his quickest for the tour and took seven for 49 and five for 41. The Australians went on to an easy ten-wicket victory early on the second morning.

Gregory kept his team united throughout and there was not one reported spat between the rival New South Wales and Victorian representatives. It developed into a strong fielding unit. Bannerman and Murdoch batted as well as anyone in England, while the bowling line-up of Spofforth, Allan, Boyle and Garrett was devastating. Blackham proved brilliant behind the stumps, standing up to the pacemen.

The English critics appreciated the value of outstanding leadership. *The Sporting Times* wrote, 'Mr Gregory was the difference. He has no peer in England today...'

The pressure of four months touring in England and Scotland got to the normally urbane captain on the return trip via the United States. He lost his temper at a bad, perhaps biased umpire in Philadelphia.

However, the world tour was a success and each player earned more than 1000 pounds—equivalent in purchasing power today to several million dollars—which promised to set them up for life.

Harassing Harris

Cricket surged on as the colonies' most popular sport. Intercolonial competition stepped up. The MCC brought out an England team led by Lord Harris for an Australian tour during 1878–79. Gregory again captained the Australians in the Third Test between the two countries, which began on 2 January 1879, again at the Melbourne Cricket Ground.

Lord Harris's squad had an aristocratic, if not educated, ring to it, most players being graduates from Cambridge and Oxford universities. Over the recent world tour, Spofforth had become Gregory's favourite bowler, living up to his formidable reputation by taking 764 wickets in all matches at just 6.08. Very few bowlers ever took five for 30 or six for 36, but this was the Demon's amazing performance rate. In the history of the game it could only ever be compared with Bradman's batting feats over two decades at all levels of cricket.

At Melbourne in the only Test of 1878–79, Gregory opened the bowling with Spofforth and Allan. Spofforth bowled Ulyett in his first over. Soon he and Allan had two wickets each and the score was four for 14. England recovered thanks to Lord Harris (33) and Charles Absolom (52), but Spofforth, with the first hat trick ever in Tests— Royle, McKinnon and Emmett—put paid to any chance of a reasonable score. England made 113, Spofforth snaring six for 48.

Gregory juggled the Australian batting according to current form, putting Alick Bannerman at four, Spofforth at five and himself in last, which raised many eyebrows. After a shaky start, in which Australia was at one point three for 37, Alick Bannerman (73), also a star over the recent long tour, took charge in a 64-run partnership with Spofforth (39). Australia rattled on in an even performance to nine for 234. The skipper came in, scored 12 not out in a 22-run last-wicket stand with Kelly. Australia made 256.

Spofforth, who had bowled almost unchanged in the first innings, was asked by Gregory for a special effort to reduce England to the smallest score possible. He had clean-bowled four batsmen in the first innings and repeated the feat in England's second dig, taking seven for

62. Only Lord Harris (36), Emmett (24 not out) and a late flurry from last man Schultz (20) gave England's effort of 160 some respectability.

Australia knocked off the 18 runs without loss, giving it a ten-wicket win. This spurred on the New South Wales Cricket Association to stage its first Test in Sydney, scheduled to follow a tour game against New South Wales.

Lord Harris was so impressed by an umpire in the Melbourne Test—George Coulthard, a champion Aussie Rules player for the Carlton Club—that he hired him for the tour north. Coulthard stood with a Sydney lawyer–politician Edmund Barton (who, in 1901, became Australia's first prime minister) in the New South Wales match.

Heavy betting was a feature of the lead-up to the contest, and New South Wales was well favoured after the Test win. The ground was festooned with warnings of heavy fines and imprisonment for betting, but it began in earnest as soon as the game started. Every umpiring decision was scrutinised and cheered or booed, according to how it might sway fortunes. England led by 90 runs at the end of the first innings on Saturday, the second day of the game. New South Wales was forced to follow on. Billy Murdoch, Australia's greatest batsman, opened and was crucial to the big money hanging on a New South Wales recovery. He had scored 82 not out, top score, in the first innings of 177. Many a punter would be in debt after this match if New South Wales did not win. Never until this point had a game of cricket been so well watched by a packed crowd.

With the score at 19, Murdoch on 10 went for a dangerous run and was run out. Umpire Coulthard would not have called for the video replay if it had been available. His finger went up with the vigour he applied to leaping for a high mark in football. At the other end, Barton saw it the same way, as did the players in positions to give a reasonable opinion.

The many gamblers, who thought the run-out meant they would lose their money, howled at the umpire. Suddenly this respected referee was the embodiment of all that was wrong with the world for average spectators—a Victorian in the pocket of the Poms, their former masters.

Murdoch trudged off. Instead of the next batsman in, Gregory appeared at the players' gate. Barrackers became more vocal.

'Go back, Murdoch...Get another umpire...Don't play them, Gregory...'

Harris strode over to the gate.

'What's the matter?' he asked. 'Where's your next man?'

'In the name of the New South Wales team I object to George Coulthard,' Gregory replied.

'On what grounds?'

'He's incompetent.'

'I don't agree, sir. I suggest he is a fine umpire.'

Angry crowd members, fuelled by prospective losses or alcohol or both, jumped the fence and rushed the players. Coulthard moved close to Harris, as if to protect him. A spectator belted Coulthard across the back with a stick. English player Albert Hornby took on some of the mob and in a wrestle that followed had his shirt torn off. Amid the mêlée, the players shoved and jostled their way to the safety of the pavilion, where Hornby had managed to drag and push an offender. The mob wanted to free him.

Attendants took half an hour to clear the ground. But the spectators stayed, expecting a resumption. The umpires asked both captains to resume.

'Not until you are replaced,' an angry Dave Gregory said to Coulthard. Harris had the power to agree to a change, but to his credit refused. Gregory's request highlighted a weakness that had surfaced in England and the US. He was not one to abide always by the umpire's decision, especially if he sniffed bias, real or imagined. In the game so far, there was no evidence that Coulthard had favoured the tourists. The source of Gregory's grievance came from two refused appeals in England's first innings—one for a run out and the other for a catch at the wicket.

The umpires, attendants and members of the New South Wales Cricket Association tried twice to get the game resumed. Gregory refused. Harris led his team back onto the pitch to stop New South Wales claiming the match on a forfeit. The crowd booed and catcalled. They hoped that all bets would be off if the game were abandoned. Harris and his men occupied the pitch until 6 pm, thus forcing a resumption on Monday after the Sunday rest day. New South Wales collapsed for 49, Ulyett taking four wickets in four balls. England ran out easy winners by an innings and 41.

Harris, affronted by what he viewed as a lack of sportsmanship, refused to play the scheduled Test in Sydney, thus depriving Gregory of a suitable end to his fine career. A cricket furore followed that set a tone for future Test encounters. In essence Harris—accurately—claimed that the betting had led to the problem. The New South Wales Cricket Association could not attract the numbers of spectators to the Sydney Cricket Ground that the MCC could entice to the MCG. Gambling for the Sydneysiders was a necessary inducement.

The affair became a black mark on Gregory's fine career. He was thirty-three at the time and battled on, playing inter-colonial cricket until he was thirty-seven in 1882–83.

He made 60 runs in his three Tests at an average of 20, and did not take a wicket. He played 41 first-class matches, making 889 runs at 14.57 and taking 29 wickets at 19.06.

In 1883, the year he retired, Dave Gregory was promoted to Inspector of Accounts in the New South Wales Audit Office. He became Paymaster of the Treasury in 1897. Gregory had sixteen children from his first two wives, who both widowed him. He married a third time at sixty-seven, and died of a heart attack seven years later.

Despite his lapses in accepting umpires' decisions, Dave Gregory was a fitting figure as Australia's first Test captain. Few that followed him had his bearing, leadership skills or determination to win. He set trends in approach, planning and strategy that would last well beyond his lifetime.

2

WILL MURDOCH

18 October 1854 – 18 February 1911

Tests: 19; Captain: 16; Wins: 5; Losses: 7; Draws: 4
Win ratio: 31.25 per cent

THE SOVEREIGN WINNER

In the first Test ever in England, just after the home team was dismissed for 420, William Lloyd Murdoch, the well-built, tanned Australian captain with the neat black moustache, congratulated the legendary W G Grace. He had hit a sensational 152 in his typically intelligent, elegant style.

'I can top your score,' the cheery yet determined 25-year-old Billy (or Will as he was also known) Murdoch told Grace.

His confidence and cheek stunned the English champion. 'A sovereign says you won't,' Grace replied.

They shook hands. It rained at the Oval on day two, 7 September 1880, and held up play for more than an hour. Batting on the uncovered wicket would be tough. Murdoch opened and had one of those horror starts where his timing was out. He also kept missing the strike. Bannerman, his partner, was in better touch. By the time the score was 28, Bannerman had all the runs; Murdoch had none. Steel put him out of his misery by having him caught for a duck.

During a tea break, Grace came over to Murdoch.

'About that sovereign,' he said.

'Ah, yes,' Murdoch replied with a wide grin. 'You don't have to pay me until after the game.'

Grace smiled, shook his head and walked off.

Australia reached just 149, Boyle top-scoring with 36 not out. The tourists were 271 in arrears. England's captain, Lord Harris, enforced the follow on. Murdoch sensibly let the warmed up, in-form Boyle open with Bannerman and dropped himself to number three.

The move didn't work. Boyle was run out for 2. Then Shaw dismissed Bannerman (8) and Morley had Groube (3), leaving Australia three for 14. England relaxed a fraction, and the crowd prepared for an early finish.

Murdoch belied his cheery exterior and dug in with Percy McDonnell. Grace seemed to be irritated by the link. He spoke with Harris several times and suggested field placings. He advised Harris that he (Grace) should come on to break the partnership. The England captain relented. Murdoch struck Grace to the boundary through cover with the shot of the match. Two balls later he struck another four through mid-on. The batsman smiled, but not with malice. It was his way at the crease. Grace was not to know this. He scowled.

'About that sovereign,' the Australian chided in an early form of sledging. Grace ran in with more zest and in two overs removed McDonnell (43) and Jim Slight for a duck. Australia was five for 101, still 170 short of making England bat again. Murdoch reached his fifty, doffed his cap to the crowd but received no congratulations from Grace.

Murdoch went into his shell with Blackham (19) and they added a stodgy 42. With the score at six for 143, Murdoch poked his head out and attempted to calm down the aggressive George Bonnor (16), the 198-centimetre heavy hitter, who had one batting gear—forward at pace. Steel bowled the big man and soon afterwards caught and bowled Palmer (4). Australia was eight for 187—now 84 behind and with two tailenders to come. Murdoch was 90. The game seemed over.

The Australian captain was about to step up a notch when his number ten, George Alexander, pulled out some powerful drives and outscored him. Murdoch reached a century, the second by an Australian in Tests. First Harris shook his hand, then Grace, but with less enthusiasm. Murdoch made no reference to that sovereign this time. It was now not a joke but, with luck, a prize to be had.

'Murdoch was always graceful,' observer Sir Home Gordon noted in a London paper. 'He cuts beautifully . . . He is a jolly genial man with much appreciation of other players . . .'

This great knock included many powerful off and cover drives. Murdoch's footwork was quick. No bowler bogged him down. Yet it was asking a lot for the tailenders to perform miracles. Finally Morley had Alexander caught for 33. Australia was nine for 239—32 behind—and still facing an innings defeat. Murdoch moved to take charge and was again pleasantly surprised as the number eleven, Moule, had a successful dip. The score mounted. Australia reached 271, and ruined England's plans for an early finish. The crowd grew. Murdoch sliced and drove his way through the 120s, then the 130s. Now spectators and players alike were interested in how much the lead would be, and whether or not Murdoch would overtake Dr Grace's 152.

Moule was determined to be there so his skipper would at least have the honour of the highest score for the first Test ever in England. Murdoch reached 150 and then passed Grace. Soon after William Barnes bowled Moule for 34. Murdoch was left on 153 not out, and Australia was all out for 327, just 56 ahead.

Murdoch walked off to a standing ovation for his batting and the fight the Australians had put up. He was full of thoughts about what a lead of 100 would have meant, or what a difference the injured Spofforth would have made.

His *what-might-have-beens* were accentuated by England's struggle. Edward Grace (W G Grace's elder brother) was bowled by Boyle for a duck and the home side was soon five for 31. Only a defiant 27 not out by Frank Penn saw England home by five wickets.

Murdoch was proud of the guts his side had shown. At the end of the game he had a secondary glow from knowing he had topped that 152.

The sovereign was paid up with good grace. It hung on Will Murdoch's watchchain until the day he died.

Cricketer, lawyer...

Lawyer William Lloyd Murdoch was the perfect choice to captain Australia in 1880 on a peace-making tour. After the gambling mob incident of the previous year in Sydney, fences needed mending and egos soothing. Lord Harris was still smarting when the Australians arrived. Something more than an unctuous public relations man was needed. Will Murdoch had everyone's respect as a batsman. He was a fluent, brilliant bladesman, comparable with England's finest and judged by some to be even better than Grace, or at least as accomplished. More importantly, he was free of vanity and positive, and was never seen in a foul mood, an achievement given the ups and downs of big cricket.

When the Australians had arrived in England, there was a snooty attitude towards them, in part due to the furore in the press after the violent ground invasion at Sydney. The visiting troupe was snubbed. They were hoping to play mainly first-class matches—at least one Test and up to three if possible. But the updated schedule they received when they disembarked, mainly influenced by Harris and the Marylebone Cricket Club, listed just five first-class games and no Test. However, Will's goodwill to all rubbed off on many of the squad's hosts. The diplomacy that he led with, and engendered in the tourists, meant that teams began queuing up to play them. Five extra first-class fixtures were added for the final month in September, making it ten in all out of thirty-seven matches played. And there was that one memorable Test at the Oval.

Another factor that endeared Murdoch to the English, as it did to everyone in Australia, was his use of language. Murdoch was creative, cliché-free and humorous. He wouldn't say, 'You look ready for action today, Fred,' to Spofforth, but instead, 'You have a demonic demeanour today, Fred.'

Umpires were referred to as 'whitecoats'. Spectators were 'paymasters' and journalists 'honoured scribblers'. Murdoch refused to refer to the swallow-like six birds embroidered on blue Sussex caps as martlets. 'Nonsense. They are crows,' he would say.

Murdoch returned home late in 1880 with the broken relations between England and Australia repaired and his own reputation magnified to heroic proportions. Yet he still had to earn a living. He turned to his qualification and began practising law in Cootamundra. He would often write to his more experienced brother, Gilbert, in Sydney's legal centre of Phillip Street, for advice. Gilbert was referred to as 'the oracle'. To a sheep stealer, who sought Murdoch's services when caught, he advised, 'Migrate to New Zealand. I think the silly beasts are free there. At the very least they are more numerous, and perhaps less coveted.' To a man accused of being a bushranger and horse thief, he remarked, 'You would have more chance [of acquittal] in Kelly country, but that is in Victoria, outside my jurisdiction.'

He became impatient with incompetent magistrates and referred to them as 'a lot of fossils, and when I'm here a bit I'll warm their tails for them'.

Murdoch enjoyed his work, indeed everything he did. He was keen to play big cricket again, and not just to while away Saturday afternoons playing for Cootamundra in games on matting against Grenfell, Temora, Junee and Yass. So at 27, he made himself available for the New South Wales and Australian sides for the 1881–82 season. England was touring again, led by three professionals—James Lillywhite, Alfred Shaw and Arthur Shrewsbury. Murdoch was again appointed Australian captain by John Conway, who set up the summer schedule.

Melbourne was once more the venue for the First Test. It was drawn, with Tom Horan hitting 124 (run out) in four hours in Australia's first innings of 320, following England's 294 (Ulyett 87). In the second innings, John Selby completed a fine double of 70 after a first innings of 55 (run out). Australia's William Cooper took six for 120 in a marathon sixty-six (four-ball) overs. Australia was three for 127 at the end of the final day, with Murdoch on 22 not out (after 39 in the first knock). The game was evenly poised when drawn.

Murdoch carried his fair form into the next game against the real enemy—Victoria—and wrote himself into the record books with 321 at Sydney—the first triple century ever in Australia. He batted most of two days and hit 38 fours, giving just one chance at 120. New South Wales reached 775 on day three, and Murdoch, demonstrating impressive stamina, kept wicket as Victoria reached six for 206. Showing flexibility, the two teams tacked on two more days' play. Murdoch had to rush back to the Cootamundra court, where he was involved in a breach of contract case between a builder and a farmer. He missed day four.

Both parties and the magistrate congratulated him on his batting feat. 'If the court permits,' he said to the magistrate, 'I wish to return for day five to help New South Wales win it.'

He caught an early train before dark and made it back by noon to oversee victory from behind the stumps. New South Wales, not surprisingly, won by an innings.

Will Murdoch's 321 was to stand as a Sydney Cricket Ground record for another forty-seven years. It took Don Bradman, peaking as the great accumulator at age twenty, to beat this score with 340 not out, again against Victoria. (A year later, the Don ran up 452 not out against Queensland, to put the record out of anyone's reach in Australia for at least the rest of the twentieth century.) Murdoch's grand effort was the best ever by a wicketkeeper. Only Rod Marsh challenged it ninety years later. But his clubbing 236 for Western Australia against Pakistan was still 85 short.

For the first time Sydney hosted a Test at the SCG in mid-February 1882. Murdoch took over as keeper from Blackham, who could bat but was not fit enough to stand behind the stumps. He showed no mercy for either England or his own bowlers when the tourists batted first. Medium-pacers George Palmer (fifty-eight four-ball overs) and Ted Evans (fifty-seven overs) bowled unchanged right through England's mediocre innings of 133. Was this a sign of the captain's inflexibility or flexibility? The two bowlers in question did not complain. They took wickets (Palmer seven for 68, Evans three for 64) and were most economical. The 'ploy' set Australia up for a win, although the home side's equally stodgy batting left it at just 197 after a good start from Blackham (40) and Hugh Massie (49).

Murdoch was forced to field bowlers other than Palmer and Evans when Ulyett (67) and Barlow (62) pushed England's second innings off to a start that threatened to steal the game. But Palmer's off-cutters swung the contest back to Australia. He took four for 97, giving him his first ten-wicket haul in Tests (eleven for 165). England scored 232. Murdoch (after 10 in the first innings) lifted for a top score of 49, helping Australia to a five-wicket win.

Two weeks later, again in Sydney, the two countries clashed once more. A similar pattern to that of the previous Test emerged. England made 188 and 134 (Shrewsbury justifying his big investment in the tour with 82 and 47, top score in both innings), and Australia answered with 260 (McDonnell 147, Bannerman 70) and four for 66, giving it a win by six wickets. Palmer was once more the match winner, taking nine for 90 for the game.

For the first time ever, the teams travelled by train (with a change at the Murray River border) all the way from Sydney to Melbourne for the Fourth Test, which began on 10 March. England scored 309 (Ulyett 149, Garrett five for 80) and two for 234 (Ulyett 64) against Australia's 300, in which Murdoch maintained his fine season with a top score of 85.

Leader, diplomat

The English were still reticent about playing Tests when Murdoch and his squad landed there in May 1882. The schedule listed the only international beginning on 28 August. Nevertheless, the Australians went about the task of beating the lesser opposition with the same spirit with which it would tackle England. Massie began the tour (in much the same way that Bradman would nearly a half century later) against Oxford with 206 in three hours of savagery. Then, in the second game, versus Sussex at Hove, Murdoch launched into the zone he had reached in Sydney five months earlier and crafted a brilliant 286 as Australia amassed 643. The visitors won by an innings and 355 runs (Palmer taking a hat trick).

Sussex county officials were so impressed by Murdoch's batting and his mien, which projected such a positive image and bonhomie, that they approached him about playing for the county.

Murdoch liked Brighton. 'It's not Sydney,' he remarked, 'but it has a vibrant sea air, the theatre is excellent and the cricket first-rate. I shall think about it, but cannot guarantee an answer within years.'

'The offer stands as long as you do,' an official responded flatteringly.

Buoyed by fine form and perhaps those overtures for his services and his exceptional companionship, Murdoch slammed a distinctive 107 not out in the next contest against the Orleans Club, which included his great combatant, Grace, whom he dealt with severely.

The thirteen-man group trooped up, down and across England, experiencing a couple of defeats, a few draws and mostly victories, until encountering the national side at the Oval on 28 August in their thirtieth match.

The Australians disgraced themselves with a pitiful first innings of 63 (Barlow five for 19), but England did little better, struggling to withstand the ferocity of Fred Spofforth. He began by scattering

Grace's stumps for 4 and didn't stop, thanks to Murdoch's instinct for the bowler with stamina and desire. He let the Demon rattle off thirty-six consecutive overs for a return of seven for 46, which included a spell of three wickets in four balls to go with his hat trick in a previous Test. England scored 101.

Massie (55) and Murdoch (29 run out) were the only two batsmen to resist the accuracy and swing of Peate (four wickets in each innings), as Australia crumbled to six for 99 in the second innings. Sam Jones, just twenty-one, came to the wicket and started well, collecting 6 in a few deliveries. Murdoch was batting with him and took a single to Grace at point. Young Jones touched his crease and walked away from it to do some farming. He patted a few spots on the pitch. Grace ran in, removed the bails and appealed. Jones looked up and wandered back to his crease, only to see the umpire's finger go up. The batsman stood his ground and looked up the wicket to see his skipper's reaction. Murdoch shrugged. Jones trudged off, head down.

The astonished crowd reacted. The Australian dressing room was agitated.

Spofforth was furious at what he saw as poor sportsmanship. When his skipper was run out—legitimately—soon afterwards, the speedster came up to him. 'What do you think of what happened to young Jones?' Spofforth asked Murdoch as he removed his pads.

'It wasn't the most courteous piece of sportsmanship I've seen, Fred.'

Murdoch's words were just enough to incite his main weapon. 'I swear to you England will not win this,' he said angrily.

Murdoch nodded in agreement. He knew his charge. The lean, 187-centimetre Spofforth was a man of his word, a no-nonsense bloke and a true sportsman, who, at times, had a short fuse. If ignited strategically by his leader, the effects were devastating. Spofforth had blasted through England with alacrity in the first innings. Grace's unsporting indiscretion had made him determined to be just as explosive the second time around. And it was needed. Australia only scored 122 in its second innings, leaving England just 85 for victory.

Grace let his opening partner Barlow take the brunt of Spofforth's early overs, grabbing quick runs off Boyle at the other end. He watched as Spofforth uprooted the stumps of English skipper Albert 'Monkey' Hornby, with a ball described by a journalist 'as the quickest on English soil in a decade'. More hyperbole would follow as the Demon then bowled Barlow for a duck. England was two for 15.

Ulyett—the best player against Australia in Test cricket's short history—joined Grace, who sensed the ill-feeling from the Australians over the controversial run-out. This made him just as determined as Spofforth to win. He dug in and played shots to the few balls that allowed them.

These two put on 36, taking the score to 51, which the 20,000 spectators thought would see the home side sail home. Murdoch noted that the sky was darkening. He cajoled Spofforth into bowling up the slope from the pavilion end. This way his long right arm would be less easy to pick up in the poorer light. The Demon responded and lifted his rating even further. Surrey Secretary Charles Alcock, founder of *Cricket* magazine, noted how rattled the English dressing room became as the home team watched the world's fastest bowler tear away from them and in at the wavering batsmen. 'Our finest lost their nerve,' he said. 'The collective cool dissipated.'

Spofforth bowled his famous 'break-back' ball—which cut into the right-hander from outside off stump—ten times in succession then zipped through a straight one. It confused Ulyett (11). He was good enough to get an edge to Blackham, who was literally breathing down the batsman's neck.

England was three for 51. There was still no need for panic, with only 34 runs to make and seven wickets in hand. With the score at 53, Grace (32) drove at Boyle but failed to get to the pitch of the ball. A catch was struck to Bannerman at mid-off. He snaffled it. It was four for 53.

Lyttelton off-drove Boyle for 4, and he and 'Bunny' (his nickname, not his batting status) Lucas, coming in at number five, lifted the score slowly. There were six wickets in hand. Murdoch urged his team to concentrate and his bowlers to deliver accurately. His hope was that this would force errors. Twelve successive maidens were bowled. Lyttelton had managed to avoid Spofforth. The speedster had a quiet word to Murdoch. The skipper then spoke to three players forward of the wicket, including Bannerman. Boyle delivered a slower ball. Lyttelton drove to Bannerman, who misfielded deliberately, letting the batsman take a single. Lyttelton had to face Spofforth. Four maidens followed. Lyttelton was stranded at one end facing the

Demon, who finally delivered an unplayable break-back that crashed into the batsman's stumps. England was five for 66, 19 short with half the side still to bat and no time restraint.

Maurice Read, batting at number seven, had made an impressive 19 not out in the first innings. He ran hard as Lucas took twos. But after an over he had to face Spofforth. The first ball shaved Read's off stump. The next one bowled him, sending the middle stump metres back. England was six for 70, still 15 short of victory. Next ball, Spofforth caught and bowled Steel for a duck. It was seven for 70.

'With such bowling,' Alcock wrote, 'it could have been 150.'

However, England was still in the box seat. Lucas was still in. He had been joined by number nine, William Barnes, a top-class professional. The number ten, Charles Studd, had made two centuries against Australia and in theory would be able to polish off the few runs needed. But his nerve had gone. He was walking around the pavilion with a blanket over his head, trying to keep warm while blocking out the view of Spofforth charging in and the cries from the stunned crowd. Studd was praying he would not have to bat.

Lucas and Barnes scrambled 5 runs off Boyle's over, taking the score to 75. Spofforth, showing no signs of fatigue, charged in and forced Lucas (5) to play on to the last ball of his over. England was eight for 75, 10 away from a win. At this moment a spectator had a heart attack and died. Another finally chewed through his umbrella handle.

Studd walked to the players' gate, the blanket still round his body. He dropped it on a seat and walked out, his legs jelly and his brain spinning.

'I'm facing, Mr Studd,' Barnes informed the newcomer.

'Oh, thank God,' Studd said.

Barnes made a decision to keep the strike. Studd, normally a fine stroke maker, was not up to it this day.

Barnes took the beginning of Boyle's twentieth over. The first ball jumped awkwardly. Barnes fended it off. The ball flew off his glove to a gleeful Murdoch at point. England was nine for 75. Peate came to the wicket. He had a wild swing and collected 2 to leg. The score was 77. England had 8 to win, 7 to draw. He played and missed the next ball and then swung mightily at a third. It bowled him.

The crowd was hushed for a moment. Then they jumped the

fence, yelling and screaming. Spofforth was lifted shoulder-high and carried to the pavilion. Once inside, he danced a jig of victory, thrilled with his magnificent fourteen for 90. He was the best player of the game. He was appeased for what he saw as Grace's unsporting transgression in the Jones run-out. He had vowed vengeance and achieved it.

Spofforth and Boyle had taken six wickets with their last twenty balls, while just two scoring shots were made for 4 and 2, thus ensuring an amazing Australian victory by just 7 runs.

The electricity generated by the close encounter boosted cricket to an unprecedented level of interest in England and Australia. This infuriating, taxing game that could bore to tears demonstrated to a wide audience that it could also excite like no other sporting contest.

The game invoked songs, scenes in the New South Wales parliament and even poetry by poet laureate John Masefield, who penned '85 to Win', a dramatic reconstruction that included a line for the poor fellow who died in the excitement.

After the amazing contest, death was a continuing theme. A writer at *Sporting Times* published a mock obituary notice:

In Affectionate Remembrance
Of
ENGLISH CRICKET
Which died at the Oval, 28th August, 1882

Deeply lamented by a large circle of
Sorrowing friends and acquaintances

R.I.P.

N.B. The body will be cremated and the
Ashes taken to Australia.

Thus Will Murdoch's pressure and leadership skills in the tense final hour led to the introduction of 'the Ashes', the longest-running international competition for any sport. During the tour he made 1711 runs and topped the averages with 30.55, which many English observers felt even Grace could not match.

Murdoch and his squad played another eight matches and then returned home via the United States. The trip had lasted eight months. The players were heroes after the narrow Oval success and fêted in every capital city on their return. In Melbourne they were given a torchlight procession and awarded medals.

Bountiful Captain Bligh

The Oval Test sparked so much passion that Ivo Bligh's England team was set to play four Tests during the 1882–83 southern summer.

In the first, 'Mr Murdoch's Eleven', as the home team was officially called, was successful by nine wickets against 'The Hon. Ivo F W Bligh's Team'. Murdoch batted well, making 48 and 33 not out in front of a total crowd of 54,000 at the Melbourne Cricket Ground over the New Year.

Australia lost the Second Test beginning 19 January 1883, when England notched 294 and then bundled out the Australian team for 114 and 153. The teams barely had time to get off the train before they were at it again in Sydney in the Third Test. England kept the pressure on, scoring 247. The world's best bowler, Spofforth, finding the SCG wicket much more to his liking, took four for 73.

The home team, with opener Bannerman (94) in form, struggled to 218. Fred Spofforth (seven for 44) then reduced England to 123 in its second innings, which set Australia 153 to win. It was the time for Australia's collective nerve to fail, and it did. Australia only reached 83, with Barlow (seven for 40) the destroyer. England won by 69 runs and took the series two–one.

In keeping with the spirit created at the Oval and the notice in the *Sporting Times*, a group of young Melbourne women led by Florence Rose Morphy presented an urn containing burnt bails to England's Bligh. Bligh and Morphy married a year later. Now the Ashes had 'substance'. The urn was eventually given to the Marylebone Cricket Club at Lord's. England and Australia fought for it from then on.

In another trend that would last as long as the game was played, the captain of the losing team was criticised. Journalists noted Murdoch's penchant for shooting, parties, 'picnics and champagne', which were 'not conducive to good cricket'.

Will Murdoch kept up his socialising despite the criticism and led Australia to a win in the Fourth Test, which had been added as an afterthought. The game was played at Sydney, beginning 17 February, and England once more began well with 263. Australia replied with 262, putting the contest on an even keel and promising the possibility of an Oval-like finish. England made 197 in its second innings. Murdoch decided to lead from the front in the chase for 199 to win. He opened and took seventy minutes to score his first run. Either he was very keen to make sure the Australians won, or all that champagne and good living had caught up with him. He scored 17 while his fellow opener Bannerman (63) and keeper Blackham (58 not out) ensured a four-wicket victory for Australia.

England, 1884

The two–all series finish meant Murdoch retained his captaincy for the 1884 tour of England. Fewer grumbles were heard about his hedonist lifestyle. He went on enjoying champagne, picnics, parties and shooting in England, where such activity was encouraged.

In the First Test, according to *Wisden*, 'Old Trafford immediately established its unenviable reputation as the rain centre of Britain when the first day (10 July) was washed out.'

On day two, England was all out for 95, thanks to Boyle (6 for 42) and Spofforth (4 for 42). Australia replied with 182. England managed 180 in its second effort, leaving Australia 94 to win, but no time for its second innings.

After this uneven draw, Australia was favoured to win in the initial Test at Lord's beginning on 21 July. The tourists' first innings score of 229 did nothing to dispel that prediction. It might have been a bigger score had not Murdoch been so sporting. When Grace injured his hand in the field, the Australian skipper acted himself as substitute fieldsman for England, as was the custom of the time. He then took a good catch to dismiss Henry Scott for 75. According to observers, he could easily have faked a miss, but it would not have crossed Murdoch's mind. He held up the catch, and his own team's progress.

Allan Steel's 148 helped England to 379, a nice lead of 150. Australia was then put back for just 145, a defeat by an innings and 5 runs. Australia was one down with one Test to play.

At the double

Murdoch put on a special performance in the Third Test beginning at the Oval on 11 August, making the first double century in Test cricket. He and McDonnell (103) accumulated 143 for the second wicket. This was followed by a record partnership with Scott (102) of 207. Murdoch fell to W Barnes for 211, and Australia made 551, a lot more than required. The skipper would have declared at 400 if it were possible (declarations could not be made until 1889).

England made 346 and two for 85, thus forcing a draw and winning the series one–nil.

Murdoch's squad entertained England on its own terms, insisting on pay that upset local 'professionals'. The Australians didn't wish to be branded in the class-riddled way predominant in England, with its amateurs and pros. They just wanted to play cricket and take a share of the gate for their efforts. The tours were costly and the Australians were justified in claiming returns for their crowd-pulling style. They won eighteen of thirty-two matches, lost seven and drew seven. Murdoch again topped the batting averages with 1378 at 30.62, followed by McDonnell (1225 at 23.55) and G Giffen (1052 at 21.04). Spofforth topped the bowling averages with 216 wickets at 12.23, followed by Palmer with 132 dismissals at 16.14.

Murdoch's lifestyle took a new turn on the way home on the boat after the 1884 tour, when he met heiress Jemima Watson. Their 'whirlwind romance' ended in marriage in November.

The thirty-year-old Murdoch was still reeling when he turned up at Adelaide for the First Test of the 1884–85 season against the England side jointly sponsored by professionals James Lillywhite, Alfred Shaw and Arthur Shrewsbury. Not surprisingly, Murdoch failed twice. The English team led by Shrewsbury won by eight wickets, despite good performances by McDonnell (124 and 83 run out) and Blackham (66). England's William Barnes (134), William Scotton (82) and Ulyett (68) helped set up an eight-wicket win for the tourists in their first innings of 369.

Murdoch and his team wanted half the profits from all matches between Australia and the tourists after the Adelaide Test. Terms couldn't be agreed upon for the Second Test in Melbourne beginning early in January 1885. The Victorian Cricket Association was staging the game and didn't like Murdoch's demands. It sacked Murdoch and his entire team and announced a new Australian side lead by Tom Horan.

Will Murdoch could afford to hold out for more. He had his law practice and he had married well. He returned to his practice at Cootamundra. He had played in sixteen consecutive Tests, thirteen as captain. It seemed that his career had been cut short, but six years after his forced exclusion, he was asked to captain Australia on a tour to England in 1890 that included two Tests played and one—at Old Trafford—that was washed out without a ball being bowled.

Australia lost the first at Lord's in July by seven wickets, and just lost a thriller at the Oval, when Australia's J E Barrett returned wildly from the covers. The two runs that resulted won the game for England by two wickets.

The Australian team was accused of drunken brawling on the tour. *The Bulletin* remarked tartly, 'The Australians always bat on a wet wicket after a banquet.'

Murdoch's four innings of 9, 19, 2 and 6 did not reflect his true form for the 1890 northern summer. He topped the averages for the fourth time in five tours.

Will Murdoch's complete Test batting figures were eighteen matches, thirty-three innings, five not outs, and 896 runs at an average of 32. He captained seven Test teams, for five wins, seven losses and four draws.

At thirty-six, Murdoch decided he'd had enough of Australian Test cricket. After the 1890 tour he left to take up Sussex's longstanding offer to join the county. His form was so impressive during 1891 that early in 1892 he and Australia's J J Ferris were chosen to play for an England team under Walter Read against South Africa at Newlands in Cape Town. Murdoch batted at number three and made just 12. England won by an innings and 189 runs, mainly due to Ferris's bowling (six for 54 and seven for 37). These two defections were not taken well back in Australia, where the moves were regarded as 'calamitous'. Murdoch took over as captain of Sussex from 1893 to 1899. Between 1901 and 1904 he played in the London Counties XI, with his old friend W G Grace, now in his mid-fifties. In 1904, Murdoch, just short of his fiftieth birthday, cracked 140 for the Gentlemen against the Players at Lord's. It was his twentieth century from 17,070 runs in 684 first-class innings spread over twenty-nine years. The eloquent gent could still deliver.

England and Sussex's C B Fry, in his book *Giants of the Game*, viewed Murdoch in his later playing years thus:

> His gait and gestures are full of the direct, hard-bitten energy that distinguishes Colonials . . . Not only in batting but in all else our Bill carries a style all his own . . . He walks, talks, eats, drinks, smokes and wears a hat distinctively; he does nothing by formula . . . a great cricketer and the best possible pal, before, during and after a match wet or fine . . .

Will Murdoch returned to Australia in 1911 for the disposal of his father's estate in Victoria, and attended a Test between South Africa and Australia at the MCG on 18 February, the first day of the game. Murdoch predicted that the South Africans would lose five wickets in the pre-lunch session. Right on lunch the fifth wicket fell.

The 66-year-old Murdoch felt he had cursed the tourists. He was upset. 'I shall never make a prophecy about cricket again,' he said. 'I've brought bad luck to those boys.'

Just after lunch he suffered a stroke, slipped into a coma and died in hospital an hour later. He was buried on 18 May at Kensal Green, England. Play on all county grounds was suspended.

This and the fact that Will Murdoch led his country in a record seven series against England is testimony to his popularity as a person and leader. Will Murdoch was Australia's best bat of the nineteenth century.

3

TOM HORAN

....

8 March 1854 – 16 April 1916

Tests: 15; Captain: 2; Losses: 2

THE LUCK OF THE IRISH

Thomas Patrick Horan always thought he had the luck of the Irish. Born in County Cork, his building contractor father, James, and mother, Ellen, took him and his siblings from their troubled homeland to free-settle in Melbourne, Australia. The freedom in a tough, challenging new land, where survival and mateship took precedence over colonial domination, famine, religious bigotry and war, was, he claimed often, the making of him. He counted himself fortunate to have attended the Bell Street School in the Melbourne suburb of Fitzroy, where he befriended a young Jack Blackham. The latter's enthusiasm for cricket enthused Horan. He fell in love with the game at ten and the two boys and other schoolmates played endless scratch games during long summers.

The courage of his family to migrate to a new land began his fortunate life. An accident of timing and background saw him selected to play in the first Test ever between England and Australia at the Melbourne Cricket Ground in March 1877. He was just twenty-two years old when he heard a roar from the small crowd on the first day in front of a sceptical Melbourne crowd. The first wicket ever had fallen in a Test match. The time was 1.10 pm, just five minutes into the match. New South Wales's Nat Thomson had been bowled by England's seamer Allen Hill. The round-faced, high-browed and balding Tom Horan strode out with his mutton-chop whiskers bristling to join Charles Bannerman. Horan was the third batsman in the history of Tests, which was a bit like being the third man on the moon: he wouldn't be remembered for it, but it was a quaint claim to fame. He lasted only forty minutes for his 12, yet he had at least steadied the ship with Bannerman, who was already signalling something special, and left with the score at two for 40. Horan did even better in Australia's second innings, top-scoring with 20 from 104. He also took a difficult catch off John Hodges to get rid of the dangerous John Selby (38), who until then looked likely to lead England home to a win. Australia won by just 45 runs. Again, Horan counted his blessings.

Twelve days later he lost his place for the second historic game, but as chance would have it, Australia lost. 'If only they had chosen me,' he joked forever afterwards.

Horan, a chief clerk in the Victorian Audit Office, toured England with Dave Gregory's team in 1878, and in the following year, at twenty-four, married Kate Pennefather, the daughter of a local police sergeant. (Before he was forty, he would have nine children with her.)

Horan played in the third-ever Test in January 1879 then in December 1881 was at the MCG again, four and a half years after his first Test, when Alfred Shaw's team toured Australia. The game began on 31 December 1881. Horan, in another achievement, became the fourth batsman—behind Bannerman 165, W G Grace 152 and Will Murdoch 153 not out—to hit a century in Test cricket. He wrote himself into the record books again, this time with a first: the initial Australian century partnership—107—for the fifth wicket with George Giffen (30). Horan was run out for 124. Onlookers considered he was set for a double hundred, so dominant was his batting. He hit 26 in the second innings.

A month later, he played in the first ever Test in Sydney. His luck ran out when he was run out for just 4 in the first innings, and received the 'best delivery of the match' from George Ulyett, who bowled him for 21 in the second. Nevertheless, Horan was once more part of a winning team. Australia was victorious by five wickets. He was in the right place and the right time again ten days later, in Sydney for the Third Test of the series. Australia won by six wickets. Horan hit 1 and 16 not out and then another 20 in the drawn Fourth Test back in Melbourne.

Five months later, in August 1882, Tom Horan played in the first great Test thriller, at the Oval, London, which Australia won by seven runs. The articulate Horan had more than just kissed the Blarney stone of his homeland. He had been in six Tests without experiencing a loss. 'Tommy's our lucky green charm,' captain Will Murdoch declared during the tour. 'We must select him every time.'

This extraordinary run continued at the end of the year in Melbourne. Despite scoring a duck, he still found himself in another victory celebration. Australia won by nine wickets.

Horan's serendipity deserted him temporarily at the MCG in January 1883, when Ivo Bligh's team routed the Australians. Horan managed 3 and 15. After eight Tests, he knew of international defeat, and just so he would not forget its cruel bite, he was part of Murdoch's team that went down to Bligh's side in Sydney in late January. Yet despite his mediocre batting efforts—19 and 8 run out—he showed that he was no mug with the ball. Murdoch turned to his innocuous-looking round-arm medium-pacers 'just for luck', when he was having trouble shifting England's openers. Dick Barlow, seeing the chance for easy pickings, was caught trying to belt Horan in his first over. The bowler implored his skipper for more chances. He felt he was worthy of more than a quick trundle to allow Fred Spofforth to change ends. Murdoch acceded. Horan then bowled Walter Read (66 and top score in England's first innings) for 21, when no one else could penetrate his solid defence. He ended with three for 22 off seventeen overs with ten maidens, and a promise from his skipper not to ignore him in the future.

Tom Horan helped Australia back to its winning ways at Sydney in the attempt to save face against Bligh's team in the Fourth Test. He scored only 4 and 0, but took the bowling figures in England's second knock, with two for 15 off nine overs, including two maidens. Murdoch swung him into the attack early, and Horan bowled the stylish Charles

Leslie (19). Later in the innings Horan forced captain Bligh himself to spray a catch to Murdoch. Australia won by four wickets.

Horan's family was growing, which stopped him from any more long tours of England or the world, but he returned to the Test team two years later, in early January 1885, as captain. When Murdoch's team was replaced in a pay dispute, the Victorian Cricket Association chose Horan to lead the Australian team of tyros. He led from the front with a gritty 63 in the first innings (and 16 in the second), but England was too powerful. It overwhelmed what, in effect, was the country's Second XI by ten wickets.

Horan was critical of Will Murdoch's stance for a better share of gate receipts. Despite his good fortune at leading the Australians, he would not remain silent. He condemned Murdoch and his men and said they conspired to prevent the English visitors from making money. The 'conspirators' had damaged the goodwill between the two countries' cricketers and they had been discourteous to the tourists.

This was tough rhetoric, considering his good mate Jack Blackham was one of the players holding out for more. Horan and Blackham argued in private, but didn't let the disagreement develop into a feud after a twenty-year friendship. Horan was replaced as skipper by Hugh Massie for the next Test in Sydney beginning 20 February 1885, and had an ally among the old guard in Fred Spofforth, who expressed his disgust at the push for more pay. Spofforth was picked for a comeback at Sydney. Only four of the makeshift team in Melbourne were retained—Horan, Sam Jones, Arthur Jarvis and John Trumble.

Australia batted first and play was interrupted by a storm for two hours. The difficult, sodden wicket reduced it to just 181, with last men in, Tom Garrett and Edwin Evans, saving embarrassment with a stand of 80. Fred Spofforth returned to Test cricket with a fury, taking England's first three wickets in four balls. However, the tortoise, Horan, with his accurate round-arm trundling, seemed quicker than normal as he slid balls off scuffmarks from Spofforth's follow-through. Horan took the figures (six for 40). Spofforth took the other four for 54. England made 133. Australia struggled in its second knock, yet Horan top-scored with 36 from 165. He was having a good match and was confident with Spofforth in the line-up that Australia could hold the tourists under the winning target of 214.

The Demon came through, cutting England down to six for 92 in a long first spell. While Massie rested him, England's number seven, Wilfred Flowers, and number eight, Maurice Read, got their eyes in, and put on a seventh-wicket stand of 102. With the score at six for 194, England had just 20 to make with four wickets in hand.

The crowd had sat out the long fightback and was resigned to seeing the home side beaten. Then Massie asked Spofforth for one last spell. The bowler produced a Spofforth special 'break-back'—or fast in-swinger—to scatter Read's stumps. A terrible mix-up followed and saw number nine William Attewell run out for a duck. England had not budged from 194. Suddenly the Australians sniffed a win. Flowers (56) couldn't shield number ten Bobby Peel, who was caught behind by Jarvis off Trumble for 3.

The score was nine for 199.

Fifteen to win and the last men in. It was the stuff of drama and poetry, and what better performer than Spofforth to bowl at the death. He had done it at the Oval in the legendary 1882 Test. The score edged up to 207, one lusty hit away from a tie. The Demon then produced a sharp lifter at Flowers's throat. He edged the ball to point where Evans took a 'blinder'. Australia won by 6 runs.

Spofforth came through, taking six for 90 from 48.1 overs (which still consisted of four balls each) with 22 maidens, and probably would have taken the man of the match award. Yet he would have been pushed by Horan, with his fine double with bat and ball.

In the Fourth Test the following month, Australia, now captained by Jack Blackham, won again, this time by eight wickets. Horan had a quiet game with bat and ball, while George Giffen took seven for 117, and 198-centimetre 'giant' George Bonnor played the innings of his career, with 128. The difference again was Spofforth, who took five for 30 in England's second innings of 77.

Horan became Australia's fourth change of captain in the series when he took charge again, but his 0 and 20 didn't help his team, which went under by a whopping innings and 98 runs. England won the series three–two.

It was Horan's last Test. In all he had played in fifteen—two as captain—and had batted in 27 innings, scoring 471 runs at an average of 18.84. He also took eleven wickets at a flattering 13.

Horan played on until 1892 for Victoria and East Melbourne. He had 182 first-class innings and scored 4269 runs at 23.27. His highest score was 141 not out against Gloucestershire. He took 35 wickets at 23.68.

He may have retired from the game, but he could not leave it after the good fortune he'd experienced for most of his career. He kept on as 'Felix', the cricket critic, covering the big Tests, tours and inter-colonial games. 'Critic', it transpired, was a misnomer. Horan, who died of heart failure at sixty-one, never wrote a specious or spiteful word about any player in thirty-seven years working for *The Australasian*. He often remarked on his good luck to be born at the beginning of an era and a great sporting tradition. Those who played with and knew Tom Horan considered themselves richer for the experience.

4

HUGH MASSIE

....

11 April 1854 – 12 October 1938

Tests: 9; Captain: 1; Wins: 1;
Win ratio: 100 per cent

CLANSMAN IN A HURRY

Lean, moustachioed Hugh Hamon Massie strode out to bat with Alick Bannerman at the Oval on 28 August 1882, day two of the second Test ever played in England. It had rained hard that morning and the wicket would be an impossible 'sticky' when it dried out in an hour. In that time, Australia would either lose or give itself a chance in this game. In the first innings it had been rolled for 63. Fred Spofforth (seven for 46) had just held England (101) enough to give Australia a slim chance, if it could wipe out the deficit before the wicket took spin.

The field was muddy in places. Buckets of sawdust were on hand to fill bowlers' footmarks. Bannerman was under instruction from skipper Will Murdoch to hold up one end while Massie, the team's hitter, had been told to chase quick runs.

Sometimes this directive led to a win. On other occasions, when it failed it caused chaos to the batting order. But Murdoch felt there was no option. England had a lead of 38, which on this wicket was a lot. He had to get runs before the bad wicket caused his team's demise. Massie took strike and gave notice in the first over of his intentions.

He swung at everything and collected a boundary. Bannerman went onto the front foot to combat the low-skidding balls, with defence only in mind. Within a few overs, Massie's big wind-up shots had caused confusion for the fielding side, especially around point. Even if he didn't hit the ball in the middle, he had the fielders slipping and sliding. The ball remained wet. Massie took less than half an hour to put Australia in the lead. He planted his feet and rolled the broad shoulders of his 183-centimetre frame into his shots, primarily on the off. He loved the cover drive and preferred the front foot. Massie often hit the ball wide of his body rather than step back for the cut.

He crashed the ball through and over the field for 55 in just forty-five minutes. Massie had seized the moment and swung the game. It was the only fifty for the contest and the match-winning knock.

'It was the Demon who inspired me,' Massie said. 'His fire con-sumed the England batting. Such an effort needed a batting comple-ment from at least one of us. It was my good fortune to provide it.'

When the pitch dried, the ball spun. Allan Steel broke one past his legs and bowled him. Australia was one for 61. Bannerman hung on for a grim 13 and Murdoch was run out for a little gem of 29, superbly played under the conditions. When the sticky developed its full terror, Australia collapsed. No one else scored more than 7 and the visitors reached just 122. Spofforth, in turn inspired by Massie and W G Grace's thoughtless run-out of Sam Jones when he was innocently farming, did the rest. He took seven for 44 and delivered Australia victory by just 7 runs.

Hugh Massie was of Scottish descent and was born in Port Fairy in 1854. His parents moved to New South Wales when he was three. Massie reached the New South Wales XI at age twenty-two in the 1876–77 season. He came to the attention of Australian selectors when he hammered his way to 56 and 76 against Alfred Shaw's England team in 1881–82. It was enough for him, at age twenty-seven, to make his debut in Murdoch's strong side in the First Test of the season at Melbourne. He opened and made 2 in a drawn match.

No one could recall Massie defending for long. In any innings of duration he was never bogged down. He was either out early or on the attack, in the mould of England's Colin Milburn and Australia's Adam Gilchrist. He earned his keep in the Second Test at Sydney, top-scoring with a blazing 49 in the first innings and a useful 22 in the second, when quick runs were needed in Australia's five-wicket win. He hit 0, 9 and 19 in the last games. Massie's efforts were enough for Murdoch to want him in the squad for the 1882 tour of England. His teammates voted him the man least likely to succeed. Massie gave them grave doubts about their judgment in a game against Oxford in an era when the students were not a chopping block for opposition. He smote a hundred before lunch. It was impressive, but only the passage of time put this innings into perspective. It took no less a player than Victor Trumper to do the same twenty years later—twice—in 1902 in the Manchester Test and then in a game at Bristol. Another twenty-four years on Charlie Macartney did it in the Leeds Test of 1926. Then in 1930 Don Bradman crafted the fastest pre-lunch hundred ever on the first day of a Test, and then followed it up at Scarborough in the same year. Arthur Morris (1948), Colin McDonald (1961) and Bob Cowper (1964) also performed the feat. In all, a half-dozen bats in a century emulated Massie's effort.

In that Oxford innings, he went on to a second century in fifty minutes. His teammates managed just 12 as they watched in awe from the other end. Massie collected 206 in just under three hours. The rest of the team and sundries amounted to 59.

He made fools of his teammates and their pre-tour assessment of him in the only Test when he dashed off his 55, which, with Spofforth's bowling, did most to win the contest for the tourists. In all tour games his aggregate of 1346 from twenty-nine first-class games was second only to Murdoch.

Hugh Massie played in the first three Tests of the four-Test series against Bligh's visiting Englishmen in 1882–83. In the Second Test at Melbourne, he almost repeated his Oval entertainment, with a thrashing top score of 43 in an opening stand with Bannerman of 56. This time England won.

He lost his place after the Third Test but returned to an Australian team in disarray as captain at Sydney on 20 February 1885. Will Murdoch had been sacked after the First Test. Massie, then thirty years old, took over from Horan in the Third and led the side with distinction. In keeping with his batting style, he was aggressive in the field, making bowling changes without fear of later criticism. One move, giving medium-pace round-armer Horan the ball to partner Spofforth, brought early derision but proved tactically brilliant. Horan took six for 40, sliding the ball off Spofforth's footmarks. Australia won by 6 runs.

It was Massie's ninth and last Test. He scored 249 runs at 15.56.

A promising career with the Commercial Banking Company of Sydney forced him to miss the next tour of England and retire from big cricket. His marriage to Agnes, the eldest daughter of his employer's managing director, Sir Thomas Dibbs, was a good career move. When Dibbs retired at 89, Massie took over as general manager. He was sixty. He worked for another decade at the top of the bank, retiring at seventy in 1925. He died at age eighty-four leaving a then fortune of 57,000 pounds.

Hugh Massie demonstrated that a heavy hitter could start a Test innings and succeed.

5

JACK BLACKHAM

11 May 1854 – 28 December 1932

Tests: 35; Captain: 8; Wins: 3; Losses: 3; Draws: 2;
Win ratio: 37.5 per cent

THE PRINCE

The finest sight in nineteenth-century cricket was Australia's first Test wicketkeeper, Jack Blackham, standing up at the stumps to fast bowler Fred Spofforth. Blackham bent his back, with legs straight and apart, and plucked the Demon's deliveries from all angles with mittens that were no thicker than gardening gloves. The keeper's takes were so swift that some batsmen, when stumped, would dispute that Blackham could have taken the ball and removed bails in one action. Spectators, even in club games for South Melbourne, would go just to see Blackham perform. His unmatched skill, intensity, sportsmanship and courage attracted them. Like all keepers he had to have guts to keep so close to the stumps and swinging blades. Wayward balls, bats and bails all collided with Blackham's head, ribs (three cracked), and teeth (three knocked out) through his twenty-year first-class career and seventeen-year Test career, not to mention his fractured fingers and, finally, a battered thumb, which ultimately finished his playing days.

His leadership ability was obvious long before he played for Australia or Victoria. Jack Blackham had a unique advantage standing so close to the wicket. He could sense a batsman's strengths and weaknesses more quickly and better than other fieldsmen. The keeper was often in consultation with a skipper in club games and Blackham, quiet yet obsessive, was never afraid to voice an opinion. He loved winning. Removing batsmen efficiently by his lightning hands or ideas helped that outcome.

John McCarthy Blackham (Jack), the son of wicketkeeper Frederick Blackham, a printer who worked for *The Age* newspaper, was brought up in North Fitzroy and went to Bell Street school with Tom Horan, another future Test captain. Young Jack honed his freakish capacities in endless games against brick walls in the schoolyard. Even then, his agility was eye-catching.

Blackham worked his way up to the Carlton Second XI by the time he was sixteen in 1871–72. He was spotted in a park match between Romsey and a Melbourne Press XI by journalist John Conway, who wrote under the name Censor for *The Australasian*. Conway was the South Melbourne captain who managed the first Australian team to England.

Conway was amazed that the teenager could take deliveries standing up. His longstop had no work to do. Conway spoke to Jack's father and asked if he would like to play in the following season— 1872–73—for South Melbourne, then one of the best clubs in the country. It featured Conway, one of the most influential men in early Australian cricket, and other future Test players Billy Midwinter (eight Tests) and Frank Allan (one Test).

Blackham became South Melbourne's keeper. At seventeen in his first year he played in the final against East Melbourne. An incident in that match modified the game of cricket forever. Blackham was keeping so well that nothing was getting through. The traditional longstop—a position on the boundary behind the keeper—was prowling discontentedly. The player, a leading Melbourne barrister Lou Woolf, said to Blackham, 'I think I should field at fine leg, Jack. I'm getting nothing to do here.'

The keeper and Conway agreed. Blackham was at first apprehensive without his 'safety valve' but accepted it, and he did not concede a run from not having a backstop. After that, Blackham never had a fielder directly behind him, so his team always had an extra man compared with the opposition. Over the 1870s and 1880s, teams in Australia and England copied this development. The convention of a backstop became optional. Eventually the position died out of the game.

Blackham made his first-class debut for Victoria aged twenty, on 26 December 1874 against New South Wales, which also had a first-gamer in the ranks, Fred Spofforth. It was an auspicious beginning. Blackham hit 32 out of Victoria's 149 on a rain-affected wicket and made five dismissals. Two seasons later, in 1876–77, he performed brilliantly against James Lillywhite's England tourists when playing for a Victorian Fifteen. Off the field he settled into a job as a bank clerk, which allowed him leave without pay for 'any first-class matches'.

Soon after this, the lean, 177-centimetre, 68-kilogram Blackham, aged twenty-two, played in the first Test ever, in mid-March 1877. The popular figure was not an automatic choice in the Test team. Conway and captain Dave Gregory had to fight for him. Fred Spofforth wanted Will Murdoch to keep and was prepared not to play if Murdoch wasn't selected. But anyone who had seen Blackham put him ahead of any other keeper. Conway and Gregory stood firm. Spofforth and Murdoch were not chosen.

In only his fourth first-class match, Jack Blackham took three stunning catches, effected a fine stumping and made 17 and 6. His keeping was acclaimed by all observers as a key factor in Australia's win, especially as England was forced to use makeshift keepers, as their star, Edward Pooley, languished in a New Zealand gaol. The English bats were not used to a player of Blackham's quality so close to them. He took five Australian bowlers at the stumps.

In the Second Test in Melbourne less than two weeks later, Spofforth and Murdoch were selected but there was no argument over Blackham, now sporting a gleaming black beard and moustache, keeping.

Australia made just 122, with Blackham promoted up the order to number three (making just 5). When England batted, spectators and journalists wondered whether Blackham would take Spofforth at the stumps. He did. Henry Jupp and Alfred Shaw opened. The Demon twice signalled the keeper that he wished to bowl extra fast—indicating that he should stand back—but Blackham said he would stand up. Spofforth sizzled one down the off side. Shaw drove hard at it with his back foot sliding out of his crease a few inches. Blackham took the ball at stump height and whipped off the bails in one stunning action to dismiss the Englishman. England was two for 4, but recovered to 261. Australia batted better the second time, with Blackham (26) being one of five players to contribute between 25 and 43. The tally of 259, however, wasn't enough. England won by four wickets.

Fast and fearless

Blackham's capacities captivated England on his many tours. In 1882, *The Sporting Times* wrote:

> No observer can name a more proficient operator on the leg side. His facility in taking the ball, any ball, is as gracious as it is unique ... Has he fear? No one has seen it. He stands up [at the stumps]. Does it matter how quick the delivery? No. Yet with all these pointers to finesse, there is no evidence of it. If he is a showman at heart, he hides it well. Jack Blackham is simply better than anyone else.

Blackham played in the first seventeen Tests, but was tipped out of the Australian side in the push for greater pay in 1884–85. He supported the stand by Will Murdoch. Blackham was back in the team for the Fourth Test at the Sydney Cricket Ground as captain for the first time. Australia won by eight wickets.

Even though he lost the captaincy in this season of upheaval, which saw four men—Murdoch, Horan, Massie and Blackham—captain Australia in five Tests, Blackham's performance at the helm was noted by administrators and journalists. He retained his place as keeper, barring injury, for the rest of the decade and was elected captain again after the poor 1890 tour of England under Murdoch. Australia lost both the Tests and sixteen of thirty-four first-class games played. It had just ten wins, one of the smallest returns by Australian tourists. Will Murdoch, it seemed, jumped before he was pushed. He did not return with the team to Australia, but instead remained in England to play for the English team and Sussex.

Lawrence of Australia. Charles Lawrence at age 62 (seated left), in 1890. Lawrence led the first Australian team ever to England in 1868. Also pictured are former cricketers: back row (l–r) George Bonner, Nat Thomson, Charlie Beal and Harry Boyle; front row (l–r) Lawrence, George Moore and Henry Hilliard.

A tactician of tact. Dave Gregory was Australia's first Test captain. His tact held together a group of rugged cricketers from the country's colonies. He was a batsman of grit, but no stylist.

Billy's winning ways. Billy Murdoch was one of the great early Test batsmen with the taste for the big gesture and the big innings. His wit made him as popular with the Australians as he was with the English. He ended up playing for England.

Murdoch's marauders. The 1882 team led by Murdoch was the first to win a Test in England. Back row (l–r): Charlie Beal, George Bonner, Fred Spofforth, Sam Jones; seated (l–r): Harry Boyle, Hugh Massie, Tom Horan, Billy Murdoch, George Palmer, Tom Garrett, Percy McDonnell. Front: George Giffen.

Bloody tourists. The 1893 team to tour England distinguished itself with a bloody punch-up on a train trip from London to Sussex. Jack Blackham (seated centre) and manager, Victor Cohen (standing second from left), didn't have the required control over the squad. George Giffen (seated third from left) was often at odds with his skipper. Apart from Blackham and Giffen, Harry Trott (seated first on the left), Hugh Trumble (seated second from left) and Syd Gregory (front row on right) also led Australia.

The prince. Jack Blackham was the finest keeper of the nineteenth century and a capable and intense captain. His standing up at the stumps to speedster Fred Spofforth was one of the finest sights in the game.

Third man in. Tom Horan, who substituted for Murdoch in his one Test as skipper, had a charmed cricketing life. Highlights included playing in the First Test (March 1877) in which he was third man in, and playing in the thriller at The Oval in 1882.

Massie's mud mastery. Hugh Massie made his name with a slashing second innings opening 55 in the mud of the famous Oval Test of 1882. This knock and Spofforth's great bowling gave Australia the first Test thriller by seven runs and inspired The Ashes.

Dr Blue-blood. Dr Henry Scott was not born to lead. He lost the only three Tests he skippered. But he performed well with the bat, scoring a century at The Oval.

Percy the classicist. Percy McDonnell also failed as a leader with one win and five losses from six starts. This Greek scholar, however, was a batsman of class, especially on England's wet wickets.

Giffen's gift. George Giffen captained in four Tests. He was the first outstanding Australian all-rounder at Test level.

A postie for posterity. Harry Trott, a Collingwood postman, was the first outstanding tactical leader and a good all-rounder. He led Australia to five wins in eight Tests.

Australia's darling. Joe Darling was the first leader to regularly challenge the English team in England and skippered Australia to two Ashes wins in 1899 and 1902. He was a forceful left-hand bat and could defend with the best of them.

Trumble's lofty offies. Hugh Trumble, a popular leader, took the hat-trick in Tests twice with his off-spinners. His height (193 cm) gave him advantages with bounce and turn.

Big scoring Clem. Clem Hill, a big scoring left-hander, captained Australia in 1910–11 and 1911–12, before a punch-up with another Test selector, Percy McAlister.

Noble by name and deed. Monty Noble ranked with Keith Miller as one of Australia's great all-rounders. His performances and leadership gave Australia ascendancy over England in the early twentieth century.

Textbook style. Syd Gregory, a diminutive figure, used quick footwork, timing and a textbook style to make up for lack of centimetres. A dapper and well-liked leader, he was a perpetual tourist to England.

From the front. The 133 kg Warwick Armstrong leads his 1921 Ashes team onto the field in the First Test at Trent Bridge. Australia won the series 3–0, giving it a record eight wins in a row. It took the leadership of Steve Waugh, nearly eighty years later, to beat it.
(Behind l–r: Jack Gregory, Johnny Taylor, Herbie Collins, C E 'Nip' Pellew, H 'Sammy' Carter and Tommy Andrews.)

Gambler's toss. Herbie Collins (right) tosses the coin with England's skipper Arthur Gilligan at Adelaide before the third of the 1924–25 Ashes series. Collins was an astute leader, who only seemed to lose control in one controversial Test—at The Oval in 1926—which he was accused of throwing. The evidence against him was circumstantial. Collins was a stubborn and courageous bat, who never wore gloves in Australia.

Six of the best. Six of Warwick Armstrong's strong 1920–21 Ashes team who won 5–0. Standing l–r: Charlie Kelleway, Jack Gregory, Jack Ryder. Seated l–r: Warren Bardsley, Armstrong, Charlie Macartney. Ryder and Bardsley also captained Australia.

Jack hammer. Jack Ryder took over as captain in the 1928–29 Ashes series during a time when the side was in brief decline, although he performed well himself. He was one of the hardest hitters ever.

Bodyline's combatants. Bill Woodfull (right) led Australia to two Ashes wins in England and series victories over the West Indies and South Africa. The only blemish on his record was caused by Douglas Jardine (right), who resorted to bodyline tactics in the 1932–33 Ashes.

Jack Blackham lined up as skipper against W G Grace, who captained Lord Sheffield's team that toured in 1891–92. The two leaders were keen rivals. They showed respect for each other which didn't, however, stop gamesmanship. Blackham placed fielders close to the wicket to pressure Grace when he was batting. The Englishman objected, suggesting he would injure the fielders. Blackham, wrists resting on hips, told Grace that he would place his own field, not Grace.

Yet their combat never drifted into poor sportsmanship. When England played Victoria, leg-spinner William Cooper enticed Grace down the wicket and he was late in sliding his foot back behind the crease. Blackham made the stumping with ease, but did not appeal with his usual nod to the square-leg umpire. The umpire noted that Blackham hadn't appealed and cried 'not out' to Cooper.

'Why didn't you back me up, Jack?' Cooper demanded between overs.

'Sorry Bill, my mistake,' Blackham replied. 'I was so eager to stump him [Grace] I grabbed the ball in front of the wicket. I just couldn't appeal.'

At home at home

After the 1890 debacle, Blackham's team was more than keen to win in 1891–92 at home. In the First Test in Melbourne, Australia won a tight game by 54 runs, when England managed just 158 in the final innings of the match. Charlie Turner (five for 51) and Harry Trott (three for 52) did the damage. In Sydney, Australia hit just 145 in the first innings. England's George Lohmann took eight for 58. England replied with 307, with Robert Abel (132) becoming the first England player to carry his bat through an innings. Bannerman crawled to 91 in 448 minutes (the slowest ninety recorded in first-class cricket anywhere to that time) and Jack Lyons (134) put on 174 for the second wicket. The painstaking fightback set up Australia for a win. Blackham and Turner combined to have Grace caught for just 5, and England made 157 in its second innings, to be beaten by 72 runs. George Giffen (six for 72) and Turner (four for 46) were the match winners with the ball.

The Third Test in Adelaide, beginning on 24 March 1892, saw England amass 499 (A E Stoddart scored 134) before torrential rain ruined the wicket and the game as a spectacle. Australia could only manage 100 and 169 in reply, giving England a win by an innings and 230 runs.

The two–one series win for Australia ensured that Blackham led the squad to England in 1893—his eighth and last tour. Right from the start, the skipper, given to mood swings that suggested he may have been a manic depressive, had trouble keeping his players together. Discipline was needed on any tour, but Blackham didn't seem to know how to handle the eccentrics and personalities in the squad. For instance, Arthur Coningham, the ex-Queenslander playing for New South Wales, had been chosen to tour to appease Queensland, which had just been accorded first-class status. Coningham was a larrikin and was often absent without leave when required to play. In a game at Blackpool, he became bored with fielding on the boundary and being denied a bowl. So at the fall of a wicket, Coningham gathered paper and lit a fire, pretending to be isolated and cold.

Blackham also fought often with South Australian all-rounder George Giffen over field placings and how the bowlers were used. Hugh Trumble once had to intervene on the field to stop a fist fight between the two. However, Trumble's conciliatory ways couldn't stop an altercation on a 'pleasure' train trip to Sussex on 20 August 1893. Australia had just been soundly beaten at the Oval after drawing the First Test at Lord's. There was ill temper in the tour group, which was accentuated by drinking on the train. A brawl developed in an Australian compartment, which was, according to reports, 'splattered with blood'. The local and Australian press tried to obtain details but the team closed ranks behind Blackham, no matter how disgruntled individuals may have been.

However, incidental comment about the skipper leaked out. Giffen said after the Third Test, which was an even draw, that Blackham had lost a stone in weight through worry during the Tests. Giffen was also the source for stories about the captain hiding his head under a towel when the game was tense, or even going for a hansom cab ride around the ground to avoid on-field drama. This does not seem excessive when compared to the behaviour of certain skippers towards the end of the twentieth century. Yet in the inflexible times at the end of the Victorian era it was frowned upon. Skippers were supposed to be stoic, even under the electrifying atmosphere of a close Test match.

Despite the tour problems and the loss of the Test series one–nil, Jack Blackham was still the best choice for captain to begin the 1894–95 Test series against the visiting Englishmen. The series began well at the SCG in mid-December 1894, with Australia compiling 586 (Syd Gregory 201; Giffen 161). Gregory had a record ninth-wicket stand of 154 in seventy-three minutes, with Blackham crashing 74. England made 325 and was asked to follow on. Blackham injured the top joint of his thumb during England's second innings and had to relinquish the gloves, a rare event for the hardy forty-year-old. He prowled around mid-off with his thumb strapped for the rest of the innings, as the tourists rattled up 437 (Albert Ward 117), in one of the finest fightbacks in history.

Australia was left to score 177 to win. The home team wanted only 64 with eight wickets in hand on the morning of the sixth day. It had to bat on a rain-soaked pitch and lost seven quick wickets. Blackham, a bundle of nerves and in pain, came in last at nine for 162. He made 2 before being bowled by Bobby Peel, who took six for 67. England won by 10 runs, the first time a team following on had been victorious.

Blackham's injury was made worse in a game a week later for Victoria against New South Wales (in which Victor Trumper was twelfth man) and he retired, reluctantly.

Jack Blackham played thirty-five Tests and for most of his career was known as 'the Prince' of keepers. He made sixty-one dismissals—thirty-seven caught and twenty-four stumped—and collected 800 runs at 15.69. In 277 first-class matches he made 449 dismissals (269 caught, 180 stumped) and hit 6394 runs, including twenty-seven scores over 50.

Earnings from his tours of England had allowed him to give up his job as a bank clerk, but his investments turned sour at the end of the nineteenth century. The Victorian Cricket Association arranged a testimonial that granted him an annuity for his services to the country and his colony. Blackham never married, his obsession for cricket overriding the opportunity or the possibilities for taking a wife.

When asked who was the greatest keeper of his era, W G Grace replied, as if surprised that such a question was necessary, 'Why, Jack Blackham, of course.'

But the last word on Jack Blackham goes to a Victorian country umpire. Responding to a 'How was that?!' from the keeper after a lightning stumping off a fast leg-side delivery, the umpire uttered, 'Wonderful!'

6

HENRY SCOTT

26 December 1858 – 23 September 1910

Tests: 8; Captain: 3; Losses: 3

SILVER TALE

Henry Scott could hit a ball as well as anyone in cricket in the 1880s, but he was inclined often to be stodgy, as if there was something unseemly about tearing an opposition apart. Perhaps knowing that he wasn't gifted like Will Murdoch restricted him. Yet his shortcomings in shot production were more than compensated by a supreme confidence of the sort prevalent in born-to-rule stock from Melbourne's early elite class. His grandfather Charles—a captain in the British Royal Marines—hadn't come to Australia on a convict ship or a boat of hardy free settlers. He had sailed his own cutter from England to Port Phillip Bay. Charles Scott bought land in the heart of Melbourne and generated wealth enough to ensure a privileged start in life for his son John, who became secretary of the Melbourne Gas and Coke Company. John married Elizabeth Miller and had five children. All of them were educated at top private schools and Melbourne University.

Henry James Herbert went to Wesley College in St Kilda, and the St Kilda cricket club was quick to spot his abilities. It selected him in its first XI when he was still at school and just sixteen years old. Henry didn't let St Kilda down, topping its batting averages. He made his first-class debut in the 1877–78 season three years later against New South Wales, taking six for 33. Victoria lost, but young Henry carried away a trophy for the best bowling.

However, it was a false start. Victorian players made up half the Australian team, and Scott had to bide his time playing club cricket and sorting out a career befitting his education and background. He started as a bank clerk, then studied civil engineering. After three years of that tertiary course he switched to medicine. At twenty-three, during the 1881–82 season, he slipped back into the colonial team. He consolidated with enough runs to maintain his place, and then notched a fine century in 1883–84.

Scott's timing was good. Selectors put the 25-year-old student in the squad that toured England under Will Murdoch. The trip cut into Scott's medical studies, but he was keen to see the land his grandfather Charles had bravely left sixty years earlier. Determined to imbibe as much of London as possible, he took to riding around in twopenny buses. It earned him the nickname 'Tup' from his less peripatetic teammates.

Henry Scott made his Test debut at a wet Old Trafford in July 1884 and had the dubious honour of being bowled for 12 by Dr W G Grace. After the game the good doctor chatted with the colonial medical undergraduate about his future. Grace recommended a country practice as 'the most rewarding', but suggested that he consider working in London after he graduated in Australia.

Scott retained his place for the Second Test at Lord's. Murdoch won the toss and batted. Scott came to the wicket at six for 93 and accompanied George Giffen (63) in a useful stand of 39. Scott then took control in a fighting knock. England's fielders soon came to understand why he had renown for belting the ball. Grace attempted to stop a scorching drive, injured his hand and was forced to leave the ground. After some confusion in the pavilion, Murdoch emerged as the substitute fieldsman. Henry Scott continued his fine innings of defence and attack. He found a willing partner in last man 'Harry' Boyle, who arrived at the wicket at nine for 160. The partnership reached 69, with Boyle on 26 and Scott, 75, his team's top score.

Scott launched into an on-drive, but it fell straight down the throat of his skipper, who snaffled it.

'It was the only time I was not overjoyed to take a catch,' Murdoch said.

Scott's form had peaked. He notched 31 not out in the second innings—again top score—giving him 106 for once out, a Lord's performance worthy of a lifetime boast, despite the fact that Australia lost. Yet it wasn't quite the real thing. Scott was hungry for a Test hundred in one knock.

In the Third Test at the Oval, he came to the wicket on the first day—11 August—at two for 158, after Percy McDonnell had thrashed a magnificent 103. Scott and Murdoch then put on a 207-run partnership, a record for any wicket in Tests. Scott, perhaps robbed of a century at Lord's by his honest skipper, this time secured the sporting feat of his life, making 102 in fine style. There was more attack and less defence than normal. He even demonstrated an impressive cut.

'I'd watched Grace and Murdoch deliver it [in England],' Scott said. 'So I thought, on such a true wicket, it was worth the risk. The cut was not a natural execution for me.' Scott preferred to drive forward of the wicket.

Henry Scott returned to Melbourne a star in a beaten team and a month after getting off the boat from England was a certain starter in the Tests against Arthur Shrewsbury's team. The series began in Adelaide on 12 December 1884. Scott made 19 and 1 in a losing team. He stood out of the Second Test at Melbourne (won by England) alongside Murdoch in the fight for half the gate receipts, but was restored to the team for the Third Test at Sydney, making just 5 and 4 in Australia's historic 6-run win. It wasn't enough to keep him in the team once the top players returned.

His form improved in 1885–86, and an outstanding 111 against New South Wales was enough for the Melbourne Cricket Club (MCC) to select him as a captain of an Australian team to tour England in 1886. The MCC financed the tour.

The trip was a disaster. The undermanned, injured and squabbling group lost all three Tests and five other matches, although nine games were won. Scott took criticism, as all skippers do when they lose a series.

The Times observed, 'Scott was against the odds all the time and it is perhaps unfair to compare him with Mr W Murdoch. But he did not marshall his troops in keeping with his aspirations [of winning] ... Perhaps he did not know how. He is admired and means well. But admiration is not enough [to win Tests].'

Scott nevertheless created a minor record that made a mockery of those who described him as simply a defensive player. He smote 22 runs—6,4,6,6—in a four-ball over against Yorkshire. It took Don Bradman half a century later to improve on this, with 30 off a six-ball over.

Scott's record in England was impressive. On two tours he scored 2244 runs from sixty-seven innings, including two centuries and twelve fifties. He held thirty-three catches. Scott played eighty-five first-class matches, making 2863 runs at 22.72. He hit four centuries and fourteen fifties, held fifty-seven catches and took eighteen wickets at 27.44. His eight-match Test record was better, with an aggregate of 359 runs at 27.62, but he failed to notch a win as captain in three games in 1886.

He stayed on to complete medical studies and obtain the degrees of Member of the Royal College of Surgeons, and Licentiate of the Royal College of Physicians. Scott returned to Australia in June 1888 and a few months later married Mary Mickle, a Victorian grazier's daughter. He then took Grace's advice about country medicine, taking a post in Scone, New South Wales. Scott became a highly respected rural practitioner, as well as mayor and chief magistrate of Scone.

He died of typhoid in 1910.

Henry Scott was often tackled about the poor tour of England in 1886, but he replied without rancour that he was well satisfied with his career. 'Captaining Australia, scoring a Test century at the Oval and a healthy performance at Lord's,' he said, 'was invariably a record a little better than that of my critics.'

7

PERCY McDONNELL

13 November 1858 – 24 September 1896

Tests: 19; Captain: 6; Wins: 1; Losses: 5;
Win ratio: 16.67 per cent

THE FIRST CLASSICIST

Right from his first Test at the Oval in 1880, Percy 'Greatheart' McDonnell, at just twenty-one years, demonstrated an elegance, grace and force as a batsman that would set a standard for generations to follow. He acquitted himself with distinction, scoring 27 and 43, and rarely looked back.

His London appearance was a 'coming home' for the gifted Percy. He had been born the son of a barrister, Morgan McDonnell, in Kensington, London, a few kilometres from the site of his later debut. Morgan was sent to Melbourne as Attorney-General in a Victorian cabinet in 1864, when his son was four. The handsome, athletic Percy Stanislaus McDonnell was educated at St Patrick's College and Xavier College, where he excelled as a Greek scholar and mathematician. He carried this intellectual refinement onto the cricket field and was snapped up by the Melbourne Cricket Club's first XI at just sixteen years. Percy looked on with hunger at the First Test ever played—in March 1877—and vowed to represent Australia. He made his colonial debut at just nineteen years for Victoria in 1877–78 against New

South Wales. Coming in at number nine, he scored 0 and 0 not out. It was a lean start, but his scoring in club cricket made it a certainty that he would do well if given more opportunities. Percy, a student teacher, was then selected for the 1880 tour of England.

On the rise

Percy's gift, evident from his school days, was the capacity to hit the ball on the rise with power and placement. In a hundred years of cricket, few have had this skill. After McDonnell, those with this enormous hitting asset included 'greats' such as Trumper, Macartney, Bradman, McCabe, Harvey, Greg Chappell and Mark Waugh.

McDonnell was selected for the three-Test series to play Arthur Shrewsbury's England tourists. He continued on steadily at the Melbourne Cricket Ground over the New Year of 1881–82 with 19 and 33 not out, then 14 and 25 in Sydney in mid-February. But it was in the follow-up Sydney Test beginning 3 March 1882 that McDonnell's majestic talent was given a complete showing. He stroked and crashed 147 runs, including a six out of the ground, in the most dominant innings since Bannerman's 165. The rest of the batsmen collected just 99 (70 of this from Bannerman). It was McDonnell's first first-class century and one to remember.

He followed this up with a superb 52 a week later in the Fourth Test at Melbourne, which established him as one of the best bats of the period. He made the tour of England in 1882 but was not chosen in the only Test. The Australian batting line-up of Bannerman, Massie, Murdoch, Bonnor, Horan and Giffen, with Blackham coming in at number seven, was strong enough to keep him out. But not for long. McDonnell returned to the XI at the end of 1882. He replaced Bonnor for the game against Ivo Bligh's England team at the MCG and hit 43 in terrific style. His 3 and 13 in the Second Test at the MCG, which England won, was seen as a mere blip in his steady progress. More worrying was his pair at Sydney in the Third Test in another loss. McDonnell and Hugh Massie were dropped and made scapegoats for the continuing team failure, which was halted by a win in the Fourth Test at Sydney.

Will Murdoch asked McDonnell to open the batting in the three Tests in England in 1884. At twenty-three years, McDonnell was given the responsibility to get the Australian innings going in the manner of

Hugh Massie. In other words, he was expected to go for it from the first ball. McDonnell had a tough task at Old Trafford on a wet wicket, but his quickfire 36 was second-top score in Australia's only innings. The match was drawn. At Lord's in the Second Test, the experiment was unsuccessful. McDonnell was bowled by Peate for a duck, having a go, and he made just 20 in the second innings as Australia went down by an innings and five runs.

Undaunted, Percy McDonnell returned to the Oval, the scene of his original minor triumph in 1880, and slammed 86 not out before lunch on the first day out of Australia's one for 130. This would only be bettered by Trumper in 1902, Macartney in 1926 and Bradman in 1930, who each managed centuries before lunch. Yet observers who saw them all put Percy right up with those three giants of the game in terms of skill, style and dash.

McDonnell went on to 103 before Peate had him caught by Ulyett. He had put on 143 with Murdoch in a partnership that McDonnell dominated, again demonstrating his exceptional talent. Few batsmen in Murdoch's long career outscored him with such purpose.

The Australians returned home by boat in mid-November and were soon playing another Test—at Adelaide in mid-December—against Arthur Shrewsbury's 1884–85 England tourists. McDonnell maintained his form as if playing back-to-back Tests in a week. Again licensed by Murdoch to attack the bowling, McDonnell exhibited a bewildering innings for the opposing fielders. He delivered delicate cuts, glances and dabs. Then, when Shrewsbury moved the field up and attempted to cover the gaps, McDonnell would slide his hands up the handle and launch into lofted drives. He lost Bannerman (2) at 33, Murdoch (5) at 47, and Scott (19) at 95 before Blackham joined him in an onslaught. With his score at 79, McDonnell lofted a ball that might have carried for six had the fielder not knocked it to the ground in attempting a catch right on the long-on boundary. It didn't restrict McDonnell, who reached his second successive Test hundred and his third in all. On 124 he had a dip at the accurate Attewell and nicked one onto his stumps. Australia was four for 190. It was the first-ever Test hundred at Adelaide.

Despite the intensity of McDonnell's innings and Blackham's supportive 66, Australia only reached 243. England replied with 369. McDonnell, on the roll of his cricket career, stroked another superb

83 before Giffen ran him out and stopped him from becoming the first-ever cricketer to hit two centuries in a Test.

End games

Percy McDonnell's fine run came to a sudden halt with the Murdoch-inspired effort to gain more pay. He missed the next two Tests and returned for the Fourth in Sydney. His form had deserted him. He made just 20 and 3.

During the 1885–86 season, McDonnell ended his troubles over leave with the Victorian Education Department by moving to Sydney. It was a useful move for his cricket career at least. Playing for New South Wales against Victoria he made a whirlwind 239 out of 310. It helped him get elected as Australia's captain for the 1886–87 season after England's three–nil thrashing of Henry Scott's team in 1886.

But McDonnell fared no better as skipper. England, under Arthur Shrewsbury, was a strong, balanced side compared with Australia, which lacked batting strength. The tourists won two–nil and returned a year later in 1887–88 for one Test at the Sydney Cricket Ground and won that too. Australia was dismissed for 42 on a rain-affected pitch, and scored only 82 in its second innings. McDonnell's responsibilities as leader adversely affected his batting. He wandered around the batting order from number one to six, and scored 14, 0, 10, 35, 3 and 6, a far cry from his previous efforts.

The rain dogged the combatants wherever they went. In the First Test at Lord's in England in 1888, McDonnell at last had success—on a mud pitch. Rain on day one, 16 July, stopped play until 3 pm. On day two, twenty-seven wickets fell for 157 in just over three hours of playing time. Australia's Charlie (the Terror) Turner (five for 27 and five for 36), bowling off-cutters, and J J Ferris (three for 19 and three for 26) delivering left-hand spin, did more damage than the opposition opening attack, and Australia won by 61 runs.

But that was it as far as McDonnell's winning ways were concerned. Australia lost the next game at the Oval by an innings and 137 runs, and the Third at a very wet Old Trafford by an innings and 21 runs. His record of one win and five losses from six matches reflected the imbalance between the teams in this period rather than any short-comings in his tactical or leadership ability.

Percy McDonnell played nineteen Tests, making 955 runs at 28.94.

The closing of his Test career in 1888 at age twenty-seven marked the opening of another phase of his life when he became engaged in London to Grace McDonald, the heiress to the fortune of a prosperous merchant. They married three years later in 1891. The couple moved from Sydney to Brisbane after being hit by the crash following Australia's land-price boom. McDonnell became a stockbroker, but in his early thirties was troubled by heart disease. It didn't stop him from playing top cricket. The courageous McDonnell captained a Combined XI against the 1896 Australian XI. At thirty-five, and with his disability causing him constant pain, he still managed a score of 65 in less than an hour for Queensland against New South Wales. In 166 first-class matches he made 6470 runs at 23.52.

He died of a heart attack at the beginning of the 1896–97 season, not long after deciding that he would play one more first-class season. Grace was then pregnant with their third child. Despite the way he died, there was no irony in his nickname 'Greatheart'. It was gained from Percy McDonnell's willingness to attack his way out of a corner in a tight match. He was a fighting cricketer of class.

8

GEORGE GIFFEN

27 March 1859 – 29 November 1927

Tests: 31; Captain: 4; Wins: 2; Losses: 2;
Win ratio: 50 per cent

THE FIRST TOP ALL-ROUNDER

South Australia's George Giffen was Australia's first great all-rounder. His talents as a hard-hitting bat and right-arm slow-medium bowler were matched by his strength. Giffen was a robust man, 180 centimetres tall and weighing about 85 kilograms, who played Aussie Rules football for Norwood and South Australia in the off season to keep fit. He had the energy to keep going, sometimes for too long with the cricket ball, especially when captain. Players and observers suggested he often overbowled himself.

In his first Test as captain at Melbourne in early January 1895, vice-captain Hugh Trumble was urged by the other players to suggest George Giffen take himself off. He had bowled in a long spell of twenty six-ball overs in England's second innings.

'Giff, what about a change?' Trumble said diplomatically.

'Good idea,' Giffen replied. 'I'll switch to the other end.'

He ended up bowling 78.2 overs—23.2 more than the next bowler, Turner. Yet Giffen took six for 155. Unfortunately, England won by 94 runs.

This gifted son of a carpenter was a bowler of guile and variety. His stock ball was a slow-medium off-break, but he relied more on different delivery speeds and flight rather than turn. Giffen's action was unique. He started his eight-pace run in by throwing both arms back as if in aerobic or stretching exercises. His run in was rarely the same pace in consecutive deliveries. He troubled batsmen by turning almost side on at the moment of delivery in order to hide his bowling hand. The better bats of the era said he was the hardest bowler to concentrate on when he delivered, such was the contortion of body and arm just before letting go. Batsmen would be watching for the ball coming out of his hand. Giffen gave his opponents the least possible time to make a judgment on what was coming.

He had four main deliveries: the off-break; the top- or over-spinner, which many regarded as his best ball; a slower ball that he tossed above the batsman's eye level, which dipped into a blind spot and caused some uncertain probing; and a well-disguised straight ball, which seemed on occasions to skid low, trapping victims lbw.

Giffen even resorted to cunning to deceive batsmen. He would appear to shorten his run and move in slowly, delivering a faster ball with a last-second heave of his powerful shoulders. Other times he would run in faster with a grimace on his face as if he were going to thunder one in. It would invariably be his slower ball.

George Giffen's all-round ability was evident at fifteen years when he was chosen in 1874 as a net bowler for a visiting England team. At seventeen and twenty he played for South Australia against the tourists. In 1880, Giffen was a pioneer for South Australia in inter-colonial games, travelling the 805-kilometre voyage from Adelaide to Melbourne to play Victoria.

He made his Test debut aged twenty-two at the Melbourne Cricket Ground on 31 December 1881 against Alfred Shaw's England team. Skipper Will Murdoch gave him just three overs (none for 12) in England's first innings of 294, and ignored him in its second innings when W H Cooper took six for 120.

Giffen acquitted himself well with the bat, notching 30 in his only knock. The game was a draw. He was a passenger in his next Test— the Third of the 1881–82 series—in Sydney, making 2 in his only knock. He wasn't able to catch Murdoch's eye in the field. In the Fourth Test he made just 14, but got his best chance with the ball, sending down thirteen overs, including six maidens, and taking two for 17. He sent down 8.3 overs for none for 25 in the second innings.

Giffen didn't fare well with the bat (2 and 0) in the sensational Oval Test on 28 and 29 August 1882. Yet he was not alone—only Hugh Massie reached fifty in the four innings. Giffen didn't bowl. But with Spofforth (fourteen wickets) dominating and on fire, and Boyle backing the Demon up, there was not any call for him. It wasn't until a few months later, at Melbourne in the First Test of the 1882–83 season, that the talents Giffen had displayed in intercolonial games came to the fore at the top level. He hit a strong 36 in his only innings and took four for 38, the best return in England's second innings. Australia won by nine wickets.

Giffen backed this up with four for 89 in his only bowl in the next Test in Sydney. Although he failed to save Australia with the bat, making 0 and 19, Murdoch promoted him to open with Bannerman in the Third Test, with orders to keep the score ticking over. He played according to instruction and was the first wicket to fall at 76, out stumped for 41. Again Spofforth hogged the bowling, sending down 92.1 overs in two innings and taking eleven for 117. Giffen was only required to bowl in the first innings. He took none for 37. England, under Ivo Bligh, won by 69 runs. Batting at number five in the Fourth Test, Giffen justified his position with 27 and 32, but was not favoured by Murdoch with the ball. Six Australians were called on and they all performed evenly, so much so that five of them took two wickets each in England's final innings. Australia won by four wickets.

In what was virtually a trial game for the tour of England in 1884, George Giffen became the first-ever cricketer anywhere outside England to take all ten wickets (for 66) in a first-class innings—an Australian XI versus The Rest, in Sydney. It was enough to allow him to be chosen in Murdoch's touring team.

The fanatic

George Giffen had always been keen on physical fitness. On the boat to England he was the first to volunteer to stoke coal. Others in the squad joined him, much to the appreciation of the ship's furnace workers. They were happy to have these famous cricketers join them in their tough daily labour all the way to England.

Giffen's super condition helped him consolidate his Test spot in the poor three-Test series for Australia (which it lost nil–one). He managed a fine 63 at Lord's and 32 at the Oval in a run feast in which Australia scored 551 (Murdoch 211, McDonnell 103 and Scott 102). He was a useful back-up bowler rather than a penetrative one, taking one for 25, one for 68, one for 36 and one for 18. Overall, his status as a top all-rounder was established under English conditions.

The infamous 1884–85 series in Australia saw his progress interrupted, but he did enough to show that he was the country's best allrounder. He played under Murdoch in the First Test on his home ground at Adelaide and belted a superb 47 in the second innings. This was after his workhorse effort bowling in the first innings, when he took two for 80 off 56.2 overs.

Giffen bowed out of the next two Tests, seeking more pay, only to return under wicketkeeper–skipper Jack Blackham at the Sydney Cricket Ground in mid-March 1885. Blackham brought him on earlier than other captains to replace George Palmer. This decision laid the groundwork for a home-team win when he bowled three and had one caught behind. He took the first four wickets. Giffen went on to take seven for 117 off 52 overs. England made 269 and Australia replied with 309, mainly thanks to a thundering 128 by George Bonnor. Spofforth took five for 30 and Palmer four for 32 to win, dismissing England for 77 on a drying pitch. With these two on target, Giffen didn't get a bowl. Australia won by eight wickets.

In the Fifth Test at the MCG, new skipper Tom Horan demonstrated how much Giffen was regarded around the country as a batsman when he promoted him to number three. He played with a sound defence but Ulyett bowled him for just 13, and dismissed him caught for 12 in the second. Aware of Giffen's enormous strength and energy, Horan gave him twenty more overs than any other bowler in Australia's only turn in the field. He sent down 74.3 overs with thirty-one maidens for a return of two for 131. His tireless effort could not be blamed for Australia's comprehensive defeat by an innings and 98 runs.

In mid-March 1886 George Giffen produced a set of figures with bat and ball in a game against Victoria at Adelaide that placed him among early record holders and demonstrated his steady development in every facet of the game. In the last few days before his twenty-seventh birthday, he became the first player to make 100 runs—20 and

82—and take ten wickets in a match. But his bowling figures were more profound than this record. In the first innings he took nine for 91 off 69.2 (four-ball) overs. In the second he snared eight for 110 off forty-seven overs, taking seventeen for 201 in all.

Giffen toured England in 1886 under Henry Scott. He showed fine form off the boat early in June, taking seven for 20 against Lord March's XI at Chichester. Scott retained the all-rounder at number three in the batting order. Yet it wasn't a successful positioning for him as he scored 3, 1, 3, 1, 5 and 47. He was steady with the ball, taking one for 44, two for 31, one for 63, and none for 96 in Australia's worst record—it lost nil–three—in Tests on tours so far to England.

Giffen proved a mainstay for the tour, heading both bowling and batting averages with 159 wickets at 17, and 1453 runs at 26.

Giffen's gaffe

The unsuccessful tour changed the fortunes of several players, George Giffen among them. He was on the outer for several years, but not out of the headlines. In a game for South Australia against Victoria in December 1889, he refused to leave the crease after being given out. Giffen wasn't known for being a poor sport, but his stubbornness did nothing for his reputation. On 9, facing Hugh Trumble's off-breaks, he had survived an lbw decision. A fielder noticed a bail on the ground and appealed. The umpire at the bowler's end gave him out. Giffen stayed at the crease. The umpire again indicated he was out. Giffen complained that the appeal had been made when the ball was dead. The umpire pointed out the ball was not dead. Giffen would not agree. A rule book was called for. Giffen was found to be wrong, but he still refused to leave the ground. Blackham threatened to lead his team off the field. Then after consultation with the umpires he realised that he had the right to withdraw his appeal 'in the interests of the game's progress'. Blackham withdrew the appeal. Giffen went on to make 85, but Victoria won.

Later, Giffen said, 'After the game, no one regretted my actions more than I did and I was not sorry when Victoria won.'

This incident didn't hasten his return to Test cricket. He was out of the game at the highest level for five years, refusing to tour England twice—in 1888 and 1890—because he felt the team was too weak to be competitive. Giffen preferred to play from a position of strength or at least be competitive. He demonstrated this in 1890 in a game against Victoria at Melbourne, when he scored 237 and took twelve wickets. A year later he topped this with another double century— 271—and sixteen wickets, again against Victoria, also in Melbourne.

George Giffen returned to Test cricket at the age of thirty-two, to play under Blackham in 1891–92 against W G Grace's team. His 2 and 1 in the First Test at Melbourne early in 1892 didn't justify a spot at number 3, but he halted England's middle order, taking three for 75 off twenty overs. Australia won by 54 runs.

Giffen, who was often at loggerheads with skipper Blackham over how often he should bowl and when, performed excellently with the bat, hitting 49 at number four in the second innings. He did even better with the ball, taking four for 88 and six for 72, his first ten-wicket haul in Tests. Australia won two–one and Blackham marched over to England in mid-1893 confident of being victorious again.

It wasn't George Giffen's fault that the tourists didn't quite make it. In the First Test at Lord's in mid-July he made a duck at number three. Yet the mature Giffen was rarely out of a complete game, taking five for 43 off 26.4 overs in a drawn match. In the Second Test at the Oval he was the only Australian bowler to look like breaking through. Blackham, whatever his personal feelings about his teammate, again bowled him more than anyone else. Giffen's hunger to be in the action was justified. He took seven for 128 off fifty-four overs from England's 483 as the long innings was played in rare tropical heat for down-town Kennington. Australia, unusually, was affected by the long stint in the field. It made 91, with Giffen batting at number six notching just 4. In the follow on, he asked Blackham if he could go in at number three, after the early collapse in the first innings. The skipper acceded and Giffen justified his self-confidence, scoring 53 out of Australia's 349. It wasn't enough to challenge the home team, which won by an innings and 43 runs. Giffen's all-round performance was one of the best ever in a losing Test side.

In a drawn Third Test, Giffen began well in both innings but couldn't get past 17. Yet he again had the bowling figures—four for 113 off sixty-seven overs with thirty maidens.

Giffen retained his not-quite-justified spot at number three at the SCG in the First Test of the 1894–95 season and reached his peak in Tests with an attractive 161. His trademark strokes of powerful drives to mid-on and mid-off were in evidence. In this innings, the full face of his bat seemed fuller and bigger than ever, and his high batting grip more pronounced. He let loose with strong cuts and delicate glides to leg that seemed incongruous coming from this muscular figure.

With Syd Gregory making 201 and the tail wagging, Australia rattled up 586. Giffen bowled well in England's first innings, taking four for 75, but was off target in the second, returning four for 164, as the tourists pulled off one of the great turnarounds in Test history to win by just 10 runs.

Once more Giffen was in record-making form with a 41 in his second innings, which gave him 202 for the match and eight wickets, a feat not yet repeated in Anglo–Australian Tests.

Jack Blackham suffered an injury that ended his career, giving Giffen the chance to captain Australia. His penchant for overbowling himself as South Australia's captain carried into his Test career, but not in the first innings, when England was dismissed for 75. Trumble (three for 15) and Turner (five for 32) did the job. Australia replied with 123, Giffen (32) equal top score with Joe Darling. England again fought back with a massive 475 (captain Stoddart 173), and this time Giffen gave himself a bowl. He sent down 78.2 (six-ball) overs and took six for 155. Australia battled hard to make 333 (Harry Trott 95), with Giffen scoring 43, but fell 94 short.

Giffen led a fightback from the front in the Third Test at Adelaide beginning 11 January 1895, top-scoring with 58 out of Australia's 238. He then took the bowling figures of five for 76 off twenty-eight overs, dismissing England for 124. Giffen was again criticised for overbowling himself, but he didn't need to do more than point to the results.

Australian notched 411 in its second innings (Frank Iredale 140, Giffen 24) and then rolled England for just 143. Giffen (two for 74) partnered Albert Trott in his first Test (eight for 43), in giving Australia a win by 382 runs.

At the SCG two weeks later he was fortunate to lead Australia to an easy win. The home team hit 284 and then England was caught on an awful sticky, scoring 65 and 72, to be beaten by an innings and 147. Giffen took the figures—three for 14 and five for 26—in each innings.

George Giffen had now been a dominant figure in the four Tests. There was unprecedented interest as Australians booked trains and boats from everywhere to get to the Fifth Test at the MCG, beginning on 1 March 1895. More than 100,000 watched the five days of play——the highest yet at the MCG.

Giffen again showed his leadership ability by continuing his form with the bat, scoring 57 and 51. He was less effective with the ball, taking four for 130 and one for 106. The latter bowling figures upset the critics when England ended up winning the game by six wickets.

England's Pelham Warner said Giffen was 'a poor captain' for over-bowling himself. Unfortunately for Giffen, the attacks stuck, even though he had led Australia's recovery in the close-fought series. Harry Trott replaced him as skipper for the 1896 tour of England. Never-theless, Giffen had a fair series (which Australia lost one–two) scoring 0, 32, 80, 6, 0 and 1. He returned useful efforts of three for 95, one for 48, three for 65 and two for 64.

At age thirty-seven, George Giffen had come to the end of his career of thirty-one Tests, in which he made 1238 runs at 23.36. He took 103 wickets at 27.1.

But Giffen continued to play in first-class cricket. At forty-one, he took thirteen wickets for South Australia against the touring English of 1901–02. He retired, but after two years came back for a game against Victoria in February–March 1903. Approaching forty-four years of age, he scored 178 runs (81 and 97 not out) and took fifteen wickets for the match. It was a fitting finale against an enemy he ranked with the English, mainly because of the intense rivalry against the Victorians in Aussie Rules during the winter.

In first-class cricket, he played 251 matches for 11,758 runs at 29.54 (with eighteen centuries). He took 1023 wickets at 21.29. Giffen nine times made a hundred or more in games in which he took at least ten wickets. He stands alone as a first-class cricketer who has taken sixteen or more wickets in a match five times. Giffen has the best double in an Australian first-class season, taking ninety-three wickets and scoring 902 runs in eleven matches in 1894–95.

George Giffen never married. He worked for the Postal Service from age twenty-two to sixty-five, and continued to coach boys on South Parkland opposite his home until his death at sixty-eight. Even in his sixties he batted and bowled with an agility that astonished on-lookers. It made them understand why George Giffen was the first great all-rounder to captain Australia.

9

HARRY TROTT
....

5 August 1866 – 10 November 1917

Tests: 24; Captain: 8 Wins: 5; Losses: 3;
Win ratio: 62.5 per cent

THE POSTMAN'S KNOCKS

George Henry Stevens Trott, better known as Harry, was an eccentric one-off. He would put his hat on first after taking a bath. One of his party tricks was hypnotism. Although a teetotaller, he would give a nervous player a well-disguised potent drink to give him the courage to bat. Yet this eccentricity encompassed another dimension as a leader that made him stand out above others. Trott had the gift of intuition. A change in the batting order, a bowling switch, a bold move in the field. Trott never had a set plan. He just made moves as the moment dictated, and usually got them right. His teammates swore by his uncanny ability to make the right move at the right time. In the field, Trott's own bowling helped. Under Australia's harsh sun, he knew how quickly the fittest of men wilted. Trott never demanded long spells from his charges, preferring to keep them fresh. He developed a reputation for breaking partnerships with his tossed leg breaks. But instead of keeping himself on, he might just deliver the one or two overs to take the vital wicket and then throw the ball to his more exalted bowlers. This was as much self-effacement as a sense that another player was better suited to taking the next wicket.

Trott was a postman, a job that kept his 175-centimetre, 70-kilogram frame fit early in his career and made him more appreciative than most of how the heat could sap a person's strength. He reckoned he understood people (and dogs) from his long inner-Melbourne routes, where he was a popular figure. Trott was a character whom everyone liked. He always had a joke or a kind word for whomever he met or knew. His handling of people gained him respect among his cricket-playing peers.

At twenty years he smashed 200 for South Melbourne against St Kilda. This saw him pushed into state cricket, where he acquitted himself well and developed into Victoria's most stylish batsman. He had a good cover drive and was an early expert exponent of the late cut. Trott loved nudging the ball through slips. He would mix and match with drives and cuts. He had a delicate leg glance, which he employed less often. Trott also liked to be on the drive, clipping the ball through mid-wicket. If that area were covered, he would wait and deflect. Early in his career he was picked in club and intercolonial games for his batting first, but he was developing into a handy leg-spinner. He made point his fielding position, exhibiting brilliant reflexes.

Trott's solid form for Victoria saw him selected in an Australian XI to play early in 1888 against New South Wales. He scored a dashing 172 and booked his boat trip for the tour of England that year. Trott batted at number three in the three Tests, scoring 0, 1, 13, 4, 17 and 0, in Australia's one–two loss under Percy McDonnell. Away from the Tests he made more than 1000 runs on tour. Trott's form for Victoria was good during 1888–89 and 1889–90. In February 1890, he married Violet Hodson, and then prepared for his second tour of England in the same year.

Will Murdoch was back as captain, so Trott lost his spot at number three in the first innings of the First Test at Lord's. He came in at number five and made just 12 before being run out for the second time in Tests. Australia made 132, despite J J Lyons (55) scoring the fastest fifty (thirty-six minutes) in Tests for Australia to that point. England replied with 173. Hoping to instil more attack in the batting, Murdoch juggled the order again, slipping himself down to five and pushing Trott to number three once more. It didn't work. Bobby Peel bowled

Trott for a duck and the captain made 19. Australia struggled to 176, thanks to Jack Barrett (67) carrying his bat. England, with W G Grace (75 not out) in fine touch, won by seven wickets.

Murdoch took his number-three spot back for the Second Test (of two) at the Oval. Trott, at number five, top-scored in both innings with 39 and 25 on a rain-affected pitch. He adapted to the tricky conditions better than any player of either side, demonstrating that his style was not simply a capacity to finesse. Trott played forward with soft hands or back for sweet deflections. This touch was reflected during a damp tour, in which he again topped 1000 on tour.

Trott's permanent spot

At twenty-five, Harry Trott was a permanent member of the Australian team. His all-round skills began to emerge at the highest level under the watchful eye of his fellow-Victorian and captain, Jack Blackham. Blackham knew how capable a leg-spinner Trott was from intercolonial and club games.

In the First Test of 1891–92 early in January 1892 at the Melbourne Cricket Ground Australia batted first and the skipper dropped Trott down the order to number seven, placing him as a true all-rounder, rather than a batsman–part-time bowler. Trott made 6 and 23. When England batted, Blackham tossed Trott the ball for ten overs—only his second stint in Tests. He took none for 25. England's second innings was the last of the match and it needed 213 to win. This time Blackham brought his leg-spinner on earlier. In three spells he took three for 52 off nineteen overs with two maidens and was a match winner with Turner (five for 51). In the Second Test at the Sydney Cricket Ground beginning on 29 January, Trott made just 2 in the first innings. Blackham pushed him in to open in the second, where he made just 1. Trott took two for 42 from fourteen overs and none for 11 from five overs. Australia won again, but lost the Third Test at Adelaide, when caught on a sticky after England had amassed 499. Trott took one for 80 off twelve overs on a perfect batting wicket, and then made 0 and 16 on an awful one.

The following year—1893—Harry Trott was again in the team to tour England. In the First Test at Lord's he didn't take a wicket, but in Australia's only innings he stroked a stylish 33. The game was drawn. In the next at the Oval, his high leg breaks were dealt with in

England's only innings of 483. He took none for 33 off six overs.

Australia then batted in what *Wisden* called 'tropical' heat. It should have suited Trott at number three. But his first innings duck didn't allow him to show his prowess in such adverse conditions more associated with Australia than England. In the second innings, Blackham promoted the attractive hitter William Bruce to open and this pushed Trott to number four, where he played his finest Test innings yet, driving and late-cutting his way to a superb 92 out of Australia's 349. It wasn't enough. England won by an innings and 43. In the drawn Third Test at Old Trafford, he was retained at four and made just 9 and 12. He didn't get a bowl.

For the third time, he had scored more than 1000 on tour.

Trott's next Test—at the SCG in December 1894—was against Andrew Stoddart's team, which toured Australia in 1894–95. Blackham experimented with Trott as an opener, but he scored just 12 and 8. He took one for 59 and two for 22 in a game that Australia should have won when it scored 586 in its first innings. England, forced to follow on, won by 10 runs in a magnificent fightback. Blackham's Test career ended when he broke his thumb and South Australian George Giffen replaced him as skipper. Giffen dropped Trott down to number seven again, where he made 16 (run out) and then a top score of 95 as opener in Australia's second innings of 333. It wasn't enough to prevent another England win, this time by 94.

Trott wasn't needed in England's first innings of 75, but was a little loose in England's second innings, taking none for 60 off seventeen overs.

Trott, now twenty-eight and much heavier (85 kilograms) than when he began in first-class cricket, was joined in the Test team by his younger brother Albert (twenty-one years), also a fine all-rounder, for the Third Test at Adelaide in extreme heat. Harry made 48 and Albert 38 not out in Australia's first innings of 238. Giffen bowled himself for half the overs and he and Sydney Callaway took five wickets each while England made 124. The Trott brothers were hardly needed.

In Australia's second innings, Harry edged one into his stumps to be out for a duck, but Iredale (140), Bruce (80) and Albert Trott (72 not out) helped Australia to 411. England then collapsed to the swing and accuracy of Albert Trott, who took eight for 43.

At Adelaide in the Fourth Test beginning on 1 February, Albert

(85 not out) again upstaged his brother. Harry opened and made 1 out of Australia's 284, but took three for 21 when England (65) was caught on a terrible sticky. The wicket was still nigh unplayable in England's second knock of 72. Australia won by an innings and 147.

With the series level, *Wisden* dubbed the Fifth Test at Melbourne as 'the match of the [nineteenth] century'. It attracted big crowds. Even Queen Victoria, according to *The Times*, wished to be informed of the unfolding drama.

George Giffen won the toss and Australia made 414 with the innings nicely jump-started by Harry Trott (42), and maintained by even performances (Giffen 57, Syd Gregory 70, Joe Darling 74, J J Lyons 55). England responded with 385, Archie MacLaren starring with a solid 120. Harry Trott had the best bowling figures of four for 71. Harry also made 42 in the second innings out of Australia's 267.

England needed 296 to win. John Brown decided to attack from the first ball he faced at two for 28. He changed the game in twenty-eight minutes with the fastest fifty yet in Tests. His century took ninety-five minutes—again the quickest yet—and pushed England to a great six-wicket win. The Trotts contributed, Harry with two for 63 off twenty overs, and Albert none for 56.

England's three–two win was a boost for the game in both countries.

A national institution

There were complaints from fellow managers at the Post Office that Harry Trott was away from his job too long, whether touring England or Australia (where a trip to Adelaide, for instance, would mean a round tour of nine days). Yet there was no chance that this strong character and man of good humour would be sacked. When grumbles filtered through to the Victorian colony's postal chief, he responded that 'Harry Trott is a national institution'. Given that Australia was not yet officially a nation, this was much more than simply a supportive statement. No one complained about Trott again, except perhaps his wife, who would have liked to see more of him. Those long tours of England, particularly, where a loved one might be away eight or nine months, put undue tensions on relationships.

But Harry Trott enjoyed them. 'How many posties born in Collingwood', he once remarked, 'ever went so far?' This humility understated his achievement. Trott was regarded by many as the best colonial skipper. He invariably drew more out of his team than rival captains.

Inevitably Trott's own teammates recognised his skills and they had a say in electing him Australian captain. It said much for Australia's early egalitarianism and lack of the social barriers that would long plague England. Better-educated men, including barristers, engineers and bankers, acknowledged without hesitation an individual of superior leadership capabilities.

One of Australia's finest ever left-hand batsmen, Clem Hill, himself an Australian captain, said Trott was the best leader he ever played under. His other captains included George Giffen, Joe Darling, Hugh Trumble and Monty Noble. Trott, Hill noted, was not afraid to try his 'experiments' out in Tests to the point where they were not punts. They were the way he captained and made him unique.

'Trott was that rare bird,' Hugh Trumble said, 'a born leader. His demeanour demanded an easy respect and men followed his directions without complaint. Harry took a personal interest in each player's temperament, his problems and personality.'

Harry Trott became Test captain for the 1896 tour of England and was for the first time at the helm at Lord's on 22 June. About 30,000 spectators attended the opening day, their expectations high after reports of the heroic last Test at the MCG in March 1895.

Trott won the toss and batted. The tourists began poorly with a run-out at 3, then lost Giffen and Trott for ducks. Australia was three for 4 and never recovered. The speed of Tom Richardson (six for 39) and the nagging accuracy of medium-pacer George Lohmann ran through the visitors for 53.

England replied with 292, with Robert (the Gov'nor) Abel (94) batting well and Grace (66) going past 1000 in Tests. Trott brought himself on to finish off the tail, taking two for 13. Australia again began badly, losing two for 3, but then Trott and Syd Gregory came together at three for 62. Instead of playing defensively, these two went after the bowling, as if building a big score for England to chase. The first 100 came in 78 minutes. The second hundred was up in marginally less time and the two put on a startling 221 in 160 minutes. Trott hit 24 fours in his whirlwind 143, a fine effort in his first Test as captain. It demonstrated he had the right temperament for the job and should have been elected years earlier. He was well supported by Gregory, who made 103. Australia's total was 347. England was set 109 and won comfortably by six wickets. Trott and his team lost the game but won the respect of all England.

Harry Trott and his team continued where they left off in the Second Test at Old Trafford, scoring 412 (Iredale 108, Giffen 80 and Trott 53). Trott, backing his hunch that the wicket would turn, surprised by putting himself on to open with his slow leg breaks lobbed into a breeze. Grace and Stoddart thought all their birthdays had come at once. They both moved out of their crease to drive these tantalising, apparent lollipops. Keeper J J Kelly stumped them both in Trott's first two overs.

The temptation was to carry on, but the captain took himself off and brought Hugh Trumble on. Trott ended with two for 46 and England made 231. The home side was sent in again and this time did better, scoring 305, thanks to a magnificent 154 not out on debut from K S Ranjitsinhji, the backfoot-playing Indian star. Australia lost wickets steadily but scraped in by three wickets.

This left the Third Test at the Oval beginning on 10 August as the deciding Test. Trott thought he had a strong chance after an England team pay dispute that saw Lohmann and Gunn drop out. Rain prevented play until late on day one when Grace won the toss and batted. England reached 145 on day two, a good effort considering the conditions, which caused 24 wickets to fall. Australia fared nearly as well with 119 as rain interfered again. England collapsed a second time to be all out for 84. That left Australia 111 to win. Apparently not enough of the team took seriously the English superstition about Lord Nelson's number (111—for one eye, one leg, one arm) and the tourists went down for a shocking 44, giving England a win by 66 runs, and a series victory two–one.

Everyone, Grace in particular, acknowledged Australia had been unlucky to bat on the worst wicket ever seen at the Oval on the third and final day. Trott went home with his fine reputation for leadership intact. His team won twenty of their thirty-four matches with eight draws. No county team beat it.

Once more Harry Trott topped 1000 runs for the tour.

Inspiration for a nation

Harry Trott was now a much heavier 'Friar Tuck' figure of 102 kilograms, 32 kilograms more than when he began in Test cricket. But

until now it had not seemed to affect his performances and he led
Australia in the five-Test series that began at the SCG in December
1897. Trott lost the important toss and England batted on a near-
perfect wicket. The tourists took advantage of it and racked up 551
(Trott one for 73), with captain Archie MacLaren hammering 109 and
Ranjitsinhji scoring a fine 175. Australia replied with 237 and 408 (Joe
Darling 101 and Clem Hill 96). England went on to win easily by nine
wickets.

There were minor rumblings about Trott's leadership, but notably
not from within the home team. Darling, a likely successor, was
another who ranked him higher than anyone he had played under.
Trott's weight was troubling his health, but not his good humour and
he seemed to spectators to be as jolly as ever. He showed how intuitive
a skipper he was by batting and putting Charlie McLeod in as an
opener—a promotion eight places up the order—for the Second Test
at Melbourne, beginning on 1 January 1898. Trott felt McLeod was
Australia's 'form' player of the First Test when he scored 50 not out
and 26 run out (McLeod was a bit deaf and when he left his crease
he didn't hear a no-ball call).

This hunch proved to be a success. McLeod began slowly but
moved on to a sound 112. Hill (58), Syd Gregory (71), Iredale (89)
and Trott (79) lifted the home side's score to 520. England replied with
315 and 150, giving Australia a boosting win by an innings and 55
runs.

The country was again galvanised by interest in cricket. There was
a direct correlation between this sense of 'one nation' on the sporting
field and Australia's steady thrust towards a federation of states, which
was being formulated in the 1890s.

Less than two weeks later, Trott, who was having trouble seeing
through his right eye, had a lean Test with bat and ball. But with
Darling scoring a fine 178, Australia's 573 was too much for England,
which was dismissed for 278 and 282. The win by an innings and 13
runs gave Trott's team a two–one lead with two to play.

The teams reassembled in Melbourne for the Fourth Test in late
January. Trott won the all-important toss again, and batted. Twenty-
year-old Clem Hill, with a magnificent 188, helped Australia reach
323.

Trott, still troubled by his sight, experimented again by opening with his tantalising leg breaks and took an early wicket. His knack was to bowl himself or others for just the right spell. If anything, Trott would underbowl himself. He took two for 33 in three spells. England made 174 and Trott ordered them to follow on. Juggling his bowlers with skill, he made use of his six-strong strike force with intelligence, not allowing anyone to get tired in the heat. Each bowler took one or two wickets. Australia lost just two wickets in reaching the 115 target.

There was rejoicing around the country in the knowledge that Australia, with a three–one lead, could not lose the series. The celebrations were another boost for politicians looking for symbols of nationhood. Victory against 'the mother country' was as good a boost for national aspirations as the founding fathers could hope for.

Buoyed by this stimulating success, Trott and his team refused to succumb to any dead-rubber blues, although for most of the final game Australia looked beaten.

MacLaren won the toss at Sydney and looked like taking the Test away from Australia in a strong century opening partnership with Ted Wainwright. Trott tried everyone, including himself, to break the link. Finally Hugh Trumble combined with the curse of the English superstition to take the first wicket at 111. Then Trott came on and removed his opposite number MacLaren (65) and the ever-dangerous Ranjitsinhji (2) in quick succession to change the game's tempo. England went on to 335.

Harry Trott's condition caused him to struggle in the field and he suffered sunstroke on the first day. He went straight to bed and woke still feeling ill but determined to lead his team again on day two. Australia replied with 239. McLeod made 64 and Trott hit 31, despite near-blindness in his right eye and suffering again in the heat. Tom Richardson took eight for 94, his best figures in his last Test.

England's modest 178 second innings was once more due to Trott's judicious and clever bowling changes. He would never be guilty of waiting for something to happen. Several English batsmen had promising starts only to be brought up short by a telling fielding or bowling change.

Darling, the champion of the series, notched his third century (160) and Australia came from behind to win by six wickets.

Australia won the series four–one, establishing Harry Trott as arguably Australia's best skipper of the nineteenth century. He was captain in eight Tests for a five-win, three-loss record.

Trott's full Test record was twenty-four matches, 921 runs at 21.93; twenty-nine wickets at 39.14.

At thirty-two, and dangerously overweight, Harry Trott's mental health deteriorated alarmingly. Doctors examined him and described 'irrational fears'. They recommended he be admitted to a hospital for the mentally ill, where he stayed for more than two years. When discharged he moved to Bendigo to convalesce. At the beginning of the 1902–03 season he turned up unannounced at Bendigo's practice session and asked if he could have a net. The club's officials were at first concerned about the former Test skipper, who was thought to be an invalid. But Trott showed enough at 36 to be selected. He began making runs and taking wickets. It was a courageous form of self-rehabilitation through his great love for cricket. Fellow players noticed that, as the season progressed, the former hero's humour and form returned.

The next season he came back to Melbourne to play for South Melbourne and was selected—on form—to captain Victoria against England. At age forty-one, four years later in 1908, he played his last game against the old enemy. The match featured such great names as opening bat Jack Hobbs and bowler Sydney Barnes. Trott took five for 116.

Harry Trott's first-class career spread over twenty-three years from 1886 to 1908. He played in 222 matches, scored 8797 runs at 23.52, and took 386 wickets at 25.12. He took 183 catches.

If anything, Trott got better with age. At forty-five, in 1910–11, he topped the batting and bowling averages for South Melbourne. In 1912, after turning forty-six, he toured New Zealand with South Melbourne and averaged 37 runs.

At forty-eight, not long after giving up all cricket, he was shocked to learn that his brother Albert, then forty-one, had been diagnosed with terminal cancer. Albert shot himself. The diagnosis later proved false. The shock caused Harry's health to decline again. He died at fifty-one.

Harry Trott was an initiator on the sporting field. Off it, he showed enormous courage to fight back from severe illness. Harry Trott's legacy was a belief that Australia could dominate in cricket, if it applied itself with daring and intelligence.

10

JOE DARLING

21 November 1870 – 2 January 1946

Tests: 34; Captain: 21; Wins: 7; Losses: 4; Draws: 10;
Win ratio: 33.33 per cent

VOYAGE AROUND A FATHER

Joseph Darling had the sort of look you would expect of an army commander of the nineteenth century: features both refined and strong; eyes that searched for integrity in others; a moustache that refused to sag. Joe was the son of the Scots-born, so-called grain king, John Darling, a wheat-exporting member of South Australia's parliament and social elite. The young left-hander showed his batting prowess early with several centuries in games for Prince Alfred College. At fifteen, he smote 252 against traditional rival St Peter's College. A year later, in 1886–87, he played for South Australia against an Australian XI, and in the winter of 1887, he played Australian Rules for Norwood.

Joe was not academically inclined. His school results were mediocre. His father thought he would be best suited to the wheat business. So Joe was sent to Roseworthy Agricultural College, then to one of the family properties to learn about farm management from the bottom up. This meant labouring in the wheat belt. Joe cropped and lugged bags with the toughest country lads and built strength. He grew up fast, playing bone-crunching bush football in the winters and cricket for local country teams on matting.

Joe's high-scoring performances filtered through to state selectors. He was selected to play for South Australia in 1889–90 but his father refused to let him leave his work. This disappointed Joe. His father argued that 'there was no future in sport' and urged him to establish himself further with experience in the wheat belt.

Joe was disgruntled. He felt the continual pressure to 'achieve' from his rich, professional father, when all Joe really wanted to do was play cricket. Had he been born of less-privileged stock, he would have advanced much more quickly.

At twenty-two years Joe married a Mundoora farmer's daughter, Alice Francis. This move gave him more independence from his dominant father. Joe and his new bride wanted to build their own home and not stay on a Darling family property. Joe argued that he would have to find a business in Adelaide if he were to support a wife and family. His father preferred him to stay on the land, and threatened not to help at all if he took up cricket again. But with Alice's help Joe put a case to his demanding father, which would combine his love of sport with business. He said he would like to open a sports goods store. Darling Senior was sceptical but was persuaded against his better judgment to help finance it. This drew Joe back to the city.

At last Joe could try for the big time in cricket. After establishing himself in the Rundle Street Adelaide sports store for a year, he was selected to play for South Australia in 1893–94. In the first game he faced an initiation ceremony held by Broken Hill ex-miner turned city bricklayer Ernie Jones. After the first day's play, Jones, a big fast bowler, would shower and then challenge any newcomer to a naked wrestle, which would end with the 'loser' dumped on the concrete floor. Jones took on the smaller, yet nuggetty Darling, who was 173 centimetres tall and 82 kilograms. The struggle that ensued surprised the other players, who watched in awe as big Ernie met his match as every wall in the dressing room was hit by 180 kilograms of locked muscle. To everyone's shock, Ernie was unceremoniously dumped hard on his behind. In locker-room parlance, Joe was now top dog, someone to be treated with respect. He would never be challenged like this again.

More important feats were performed on the field and he made a lasting impression on crowds, opposition and Test selectors alike with scores of 117 and 37 not out against England's touring side in 1894.

Darling was selected to play for Australia a year after his debut season for South Australia. His first Test against England at the SCG in mid-December 1894 was a game of mixed fortunes for him and his teammates. Darling, batting at four, ran into a rampant Tom Richardson and had his middle stump uprooted for a duck. He had to look on in anguish as Australia racked up 586 (George Giffen 161, Syd Gregory 201). England then made 325 and when asked to follow on notched up 437. Darling made his mark in the second innings with a fighting 53, but only fellow South Australian Giffen (41) supported him, as Australia scored 166 and fell 10 short, much to the horror of skipper Jack Blackham.

No-nonsense Joe

Australia lost again over the New Year in Melbourne and Darling contributed 32 and 5. In Adelaide he scored 10 and 3 when Australia won by 382.

John Darling watched the game and was as proud as any father of his son's achievement in the big time. Yet he would always choose the moment to remind Joe that he could not make a good living from the game. The sports store was not receiving Joe's full attention because he was travelling the country. His father asked him to consider becoming a farmer again. Joe refused, saying there was always time for a move when his cricket career was over. Darling Senior offered to buy Joe a country property. Joe's answer was to travel to Sydney for the Fourth Test in early February 1895 and score a useful 31 in Australia's 286. England, caught on a sticky, capitulated to Trott, Turner and Giffen, and was beaten by an innings and 147 runs.

Even Darling Senior was now caught up in the national fervour that had built up before the Fifth Test at Melbourne, dubbed by *Wisden* 'the match of the century'. Huge crowds turned up in Melbourne from 1 March 1895. England won by six wickets in a fascinating battle that lived up to expectations. Darling was established as a fine performer under pressure when he top scored (74 and 50, out to Peel twice) in both Australia's innings. His batting impressed those commentators still unsure about the capacities of left-handers to play other than drives and swings onto the on side. Darling presented a very full face of the bat, and continued to demonstrate broad extremes. He could stonewall as well as the most defensive bats or hit the ball as hard as anyone. It would not have surprised anyone if he had scored the slowest or fastest centuries in top cricket.

Darling's prestige and self-confidence allowed him to resist his father's overtures. Joe wanted to represent Australia on a tour of England in 1896 under Harry Trott. His father was not happy but was powerless to stop his 25-year-old son, who was fulfilling long-held dreams.

Darling's preparation suggested he was a most thorough individual. In the last month before leaving, he had groundsmen water a practice wicket at Adelaide in order to simulate English conditions, particularly the infamous sticky dog that previous touring batsmen had found so tough. Darling had spinners and pacemen dish up every kind of delivery. By the time he walked up the gangplank on the boat to England, Darling felt ready for anything the notorious weather, especially early in the season, would present.

It paid off. Joe Darling showed his prowess on wet wickets. But he was asked to open for the series and rarely got going in the Tests, scoring 22, 0, 27, 16, 47 and 0. Tom Richardson, who claimed Darling as his 'bunny', snared him another four times.

Australia lost one–two, but performed well.

Darling's complete tour was nevertheless a success. He hit 1555 runs in thirty-two matches, a record for a first-timer on English wickets.

Wisden commented on Darling during this tour, 'With his upright style and a good straight bat he plays as orthodox a game as a right-hand man.'

Joe Darling was now regarded as the best Australian batsman on all kinds of wickets.

Darling maintained the sports shop, which was doing better after the early years of establishing it. The shop was his lifeline to a cricket career. He continued to perform well for South Australia in 1896–97 and was determined to play for Australia under Trott against A E Stoddart's English tourists in 1897–98.

In the First Test at the Sydney Cricket Ground in mid-December

1897, Richardson, as ever, had Darling caught for 7 out of Australia's 237 in reply to England's 551. The home team was forced to follow on. Darling now showed his true colours in a wonderful fightback, an adroit mixture of solid defence and brilliant attack. He made top score of 101, and became the first left-hander to score a Test hundred. Australia's second innings reached 408. England made one for 96 and won by nine wickets.

The tables were turned in Melbourne at the Second Test and Darling, opening again, made 36 out of 520. Australia went on to win by an innings and 55 runs. It was then on to Adelaide for the Third Test in mid-January.

Darling Senior was in attendance in the members' stand to watch his now-famous son bat. Some family members believed Joe was determined to make a point to his father as he strode out to bat on the first hot morning of the match. The full face of his blade with forward thrusts early in his innings put England on the back foot from the first over. Darling enjoyed mastery over Richardson for the first time as he strode towards his century before tea. At 97 he stepped lustily into Johnny Briggs and sent the ball sailing out of the ground for six. The rules then stated that the ball had to be right outside the arena, not just the ropes, to score six. This was the first six ever without the aid of overthrows. Darling thus became the first batsman ever to score two centuries in the same series. He reached 117 at tea, the highest score by an Australian at the tea break on day one. He went on to 178 (Richardson having him caught behind), top score of the innings of 573. England replied with 278 and 282. The tourists lost by an innings and 13 runs.

Australia now had a two–one lead in the best of five series and the country was mad about Test cricket again. The home team won easily once more at the Melbourne Cricket Ground by eight wickets, Darling making 12 (caught off Richardson once more) and 29. The series was now safe. Nevertheless, reputations were at stake at the SCG in the Fifth Test. England batted first and made 335. Australia replied with 239 (Darling 14). England faltered in its second innings, scoring just 178. That left a last-innings chase of 275 for victory. Joe Darling led the charge with the fastest century ever by an Australian against England. It took him just ninety-one minutes, and included 20 fours (a record not equalled until Arthur Morris hit 20 fours in a century in

1948). Darling became the first player to score three centuries in a series and the first to aggregate 500. He went on to 160 in just 175 minutes and hit 30 fours in all.

Thanks to Joe Darling, Australia came from behind to win by four wickets and take the series four–one. Darling, at twenty-seven years, was a national hero. For the moment, his father was silenced. There were fewer mentions of the need to 'make a serious living'.

Tough Captain Darling

Joe Darling was involved in selection of the 1899 squad, which did not include 21-year-old Victor Trumper, the brilliant young New South Wales stroke maker. In a game at Adelaide between the chosen team and The Rest—a virtual second XI—Darling was so struck by Trumper's ability in making 70 that he called a team meeting to discuss the possibility of the new champion joining the squad for England. It was decided Trumper should be added, but at a fee of 200 pounds taken out of tour profits—half that of the others.

Darling wasn't yet officially the team captain, but he was acting as a leader. On the boat trip his peers elected him skipper. No doubt Trumper voted for him. They knew from Joe's no-nonsense demeanour that it was not going to be a slack tour. He stamped his authority early by saying the drinkers in the team (he was an abstainer) should curb excesses, particularly during games. Big Ernie Jones was made twelfth man for a county game to stop him getting drunk on a day off. He refused to play. Darling called a team meeting that saw Jones facing a team vote to send him home. Darling spoke to him in private and made it clear that if he didn't apologise to the team he would person- ally take him to the next boat bound for Australia. The player also had to promise to curb his drinking and turn up when selected as twelfth man. Jones received the steely eye of the man who had beaten him in the dressing-room wrestle. He understood Darling would carry out his threat. Jones knew that he would be returning to bricklaying earlier than he planned if he didn't do as instructed. Jones agreed to the conditions. He wasn't exactly a lamb for the rest of the tour, but he was never out of order again.

When five players turned up late for a game after thinking it was too wet for play, Darling fined each five pounds. On other tours, this might have caused rebellion. But no one challenged Joe or transgressed again. He didn't run the team with an iron fist so much as a very firm one.

Trumper was the early star on tour, belting brilliant centuries against the counties. Darling showed full confidence in him. When two batsmen were out lbw trying to glance, the captain told the team that if anyone else tried the shot they would be dropped. He made two exceptions: Clem Hill and Victor Trumper. This kind of discipline paid off.

The Australians were in fine form individually and as a unit when the first-ever five-Test series in England began at Trent Bridge on 1 June 1899. Darling's rival captain was Grace, then aged fifty and in his last Test. Darling won the toss, batted and made 47 out of 252. England replied with 193. Darling made 14 from the second innings of eight declared for 230 (Hill 80), leaving England 290 to win. It reached seven for 155 and should have lost but for some alarming bias by an umpire, who called back Ranjitsinhji early in his innings after he had 'walked' when run out. The Indian went on to 93 not out and saved the game for his adopted country. (The same umpire had actually gone up in appeal for an Australian run-out before the English fielders did.) Darling complained to the Marylebone Cricket Club. Its chairman, cricket supremo Lord Harris, told him the umpire would not be chosen for any other Test or tour match.

The game was a moral victory for the tourists and their tails were up for the Lord's Test, beginning on 15 June. England was rolled for 206, with Ernie Jones putting in for his skipper and taking seven for 88. Australia's response was 421 (Darling 9). Clem Hill, in great touch, made 135, but the innings, indeed the game, was stolen by Trumper. He stepped forward to play everything on the front foot, smashing his way to 135 not out.

Joe Darling watched every run of the knock and said it was the best he had seen in international cricket. It paved the way for Australia to win easily by ten wickets.

Right after the game, Darling called a team meeting and proposed that Trumper be given full pay—400 pounds—for the tour, arguing that the young star would do more for gate receipts than any other player. The team voted unanimously for the proposal.

The skipper was asserting his authority everywhere, even suggesting rule changes. He urged cricket authorities to award 6 runs for hits over the fence instead of out of the ground, an innovation that was eventually taken up.

Rain at Leeds washed out the last day of the Third Test, which was drawn, as was the Fourth at Old Trafford and the Fifth at Kennington Oval.

Darling with scores 9, 16, 4, 39, 71 and 6 (run out) was not in top form. But Hill, Noble, Syd Gregory and Trumper, who were batting well, took the pressure off. Still, Darling had an excellent tour, making 1941 in thirty-five games at an average of 41. Australia won the series one–nil. This demonstrated he was the man for the top job. He could handle it and make runs too.

Will against the will

Yet despite his success, Joe Darling's father wanted to impose his will. Darling Senior asked him to give up the barely profitable Rundle Street sports store and do something more suitable to the Darling heritage. His father bought a 10,000-acre sheep station in Tasmania's midlands and gave Joe an ultimatum: work on the property or be cut out of the will.

Joe was disappointed, but reconciled himself to the fact that he had set great batting records in one Test series and had been a victorious captain in another. He was twenty-nine and had a wife and four children to consider. In effect he had achieved his sporting goals. There was little point in standing up to his father with such a choice.

Joe moved his family to remote Tasmania and disappeared from big cricket. He missed the 1899–1900 and 1900–01 seasons and became a full-time farmer again after a seven-year break, but this time farming wool, not wheat. It was a tough, demanding business. The land had to be cleared and the property developed. After two years of diligent application in the wilderness, Joe argued with his father that he had fulfilled his side of the bargain to remain in his will. The property was viable. He had a manager to run it. He wanted to return to big cricket and let it be known in the right circles in Melbourne that he would be prepared to make a comeback.

The Melbourne Cricket Club (MCC) offered Joe the Australian captaincy for the first three of the five-Test series. He grabbed the chance. Australia had become a federation of states in 1901 and he was very aware of the historical importance and honour of leading his country as a nation for the first time.

The not-so-baggy velvet

Joe Darling led his team onto the SCG on 13 December 1901 for the First Test of the twentieth century wearing velvet skull caps. He insisted that the side wear the caps throughout the game. He wanted to present the opposition with the perception of a tight unit, truly representative of the new nation.

Nothing would give England greater delight than to upset Australia's first birthday party. On the first day England captain Archie MacLaren (116) did the spoiling in style and became the first batsman to score four centuries in Test cricket. He combined with fellow opener Tom Hayward in an opening partnership of 154. Australia was reduced to the image of floundering schoolboys as England reached 464.

MacLaren's influence on the Test was profound as his protégé, the almost unknown brisk-medium 'spinner', Sydney Barnes, on debut took five for 65 and reduced Australia to 168. Darling batted down the order at number eight and scored 39. Australia followed on and Darling, encouraged by his first innings form after such a long break from first-class cricket, opened. He was removed by Len Braund for 3. Australia made 172 and was thrashed by an innings and 124.

Australia regrouped for the Second Test at Melbourne. If anything the loss in Sydney galvanised the home team. The pride of a nation, literally, was now at stake.

MacLaren won the toss at the MCG on 1 January 1902 and sent Australia in on a rain-affected pitch. Darling, who was trying to make an opener of Trumper, asked the dasher to go in first. Barnes struck with the second ball of the match and had Trumper caught by Johnny Tyldesley for a duck. Darling showed his prowess on a wet wicket but was caught behind off Colin Blythe for 19, second-top score to debutant Reg Duff's 32 in Australia's 112 (Barnes six for 42).

England fared worse on the afternoon sticky and was dismissed for 61 (Monty Noble seven for 17) in just sixty-eight minutes. Darling changed his batting order to meet the conditions. Other skippers might have held themselves back for an improved wicket on day two, but Darling liked to confront the adverse elements and lead from the front. Had he put anyone else in first, Australia could have been all out for the second time on day one. But he opened with Hugh Trumble and they kept out Barnes and Blythe for ninety-two minutes, pushing the score to 32. However, the spinners held sway in the last twenty minutes and Australia lost five for 16 to be five for 48 at stumps.

Darling's 23 was one of his best-ever performances, given the conditions. He was the only top-order sacrifice. Bowler Bill Howell batted at three and was dismissed by Barnes for a duck. Keeper James Kelly at four was run out for 3 and Ernie Jones was removed by Barnes for 5. The wicket was still poor in the pre-lunch session of day two, but it was drying out.

By lunch time it was ideal for the recognised batsmen. Hill at seven made the first ever 99 in a Test. Trumper at eight made 16, while Duff hit 104 at number ten, the first Australian to score a century in this position against England. Duff's last-wicket stand of 120 with the other Australian first-gamer, Warwick Armstrong (45 not out), put his country on top. It made 353 with Barnes taking seven for 124. This brought his tally to nineteen wickets in two Tests.

England responded with 175, Monty Noble again the destroyer with six for 60. Australia won by 229 runs.

The Third Test at Adelaide now took on a grander importance with the teams locked at one win each with three to play. MacLaren won the toss and batted. England made 388 (Hayward 90 run out, Braund 103 not out). Darling made just 1, but Trumper at last found something like his true form, with 65. Hill (98) and Syd Gregory (55) pulled Australia out of a hole and it reached 321. England was pegged back to 247. This left the home side with 315 to win. No team had ever scored more than 300 in the fourth innings of a Test to win a match. But the tourists were without Barnes, who had a knee injury that had finished his season.

Darling had a team meeting and spoke about challenges being there to be accepted and won. He mentioned that the nation would be expecting them to fight all the way. The captain believed in his team acting as one, and at the expense of upsetting the less flexible in his squad, he rejigged the batting order again, putting form player Reg Duff in to open and dropping himself to number five, behind Gregory.

The opening gambit failed when Duff was out for 4 after treading on his wicket. Trumper was bowled driving at Gunn for 25 and

Gregory fell to him caught for 23. Darling came in at three for 98. He and Hill put on 96 for the fourth wicket before Hill was bowled by G L Jessop for 97 at 194. Australia was 119 short of victory with six wickets in hand.

Trumble joined his skipper and they dug in for a 61-run stand before Jessop struck and had Darling caught by Hayward for 69. Australia was five for 255, still 60 short but with five wickets intact. Noble was then run out for 13 at 287. The game was now tight, with 28 needed and four wickets left. Trumble (62 not out) and Armstrong (9 not out) steered Australia home for a four-wicket win.

England's lure

Joe Darling had fulfilled his agreement with the MCC. He went back to farming in Tasmania, while the Australians under makeshift skipper Hugh Trumble won the next two Tests by seven wickets and 32 runs, giving it a four–one rubber win to mark the beginning of Tests in the twentieth century.

At thirty-one Darling decided to embark on another tour of England in 1902. It was the wettest summer in years. Trumper had taken Darling's advice about practising on wet wickets before the tour and it had paid off for him (2570 runs, eleven centuries on tour), but not in the first two Tests.

At the first Test ever at Edgbaston, Birmingham, Australia was caught on a saturated wicket and dismissed for 36. Trumper top scored with 18, while Darling made third-top score of just 3. Australia scrambled out of the game with a draw against a team with the strongest batting line-up England ever produced. Every player had scored a first-class hundred.

The Second Test at Lord's was almost completely washed out and also a draw. The only 'win' for Darling was his doubtful strategy to unsettle Ranjitsinhji, where he placed five men on the leg side and had his bowlers deliver leg theory. Darling placed himself at short leg and Syd Gregory at short-fine leg. Both were out of the batsman's view. When the bowler ran in they shifted their positions, never ending up in the same spot. It had unsettled the Indian in an earlier game in which he had been caught by Gregory at short-fine leg after the fielder had moved. This made the batsman tentative about playing his great on-side shots. In the Tests he was bowled for 13 by

Armstrong and for 0 by Hopkins. Ranjitsinhji lost confidence and was dropped.

Despite making a duck in each innings, Darling led the tourists to a 142-run win at the Third Test early in July 1902, held for the one and only time at Bramall Lane, Sheffield. Hill made 119 in Australia's second innings after Trumper had dashed off a brilliant 62 in fifty minutes (50 in forty minutes) and presaged things to come in the Fourth Test at Old Trafford, beginning on 24 July.

Darling won the toss and batted. Trumper slashed and drove his way to a magnificent 103 not out before lunch, the first time this had been done in a Test. He and Duff put on an opening partnership of 135 in eighty minutes, the first hundred coming in a record fifty-seven minutes.

Darling came in at four for 183 and, inspired by Trumper, smashed two glorious sixes out of the ground, the first time this had ever been done in a Test in England. He then hammered 51. Australia made 299. England replied with 262 (Stanley Jackson 128). The tourists faced a damp wicket in their second innings and Darling, coming in at four with the score at 9, stopped a complete rot with a fine top score of 37. His 54 partnership with Gregory (24) allowed the team to scramble together 86. England needed 124 to win.

English skipper MacLaren told Darling at the Australian dressing-room door, 'I think we've got you, Joe.'

'We've only got to shift a few of you,' Darling replied, 'and the rest will shiver with fright.'

Darling may have been thinking of 1882 when a fired-up Spofforth secured a win by 7 runs.

England began well with an opening stand of 44. At four for 92 it had just 32 to win with six wickets left. But then it lost five for 24, with Trumble taking three. Last man in, Fred Tate (father of Maurice), was not at the striker's end with three balls to go. Wilfred Rhodes was facing. Darling moved every player in to stop the single. Tate had to face left-hander Jack Saunders. He edged a four. England now needed 3 to tie and 4 to win. Saunders bowled him, giving Australia the tightest win yet in a Test.

The series was Australia's, two–nil, with one to play at the Oval. This time England was set 263 to win. It looked all over when Saunders rocked the home team, putting it at five for 48. But Jessop

(104) came in and played the innings of his life. England reached nine for 248 and Hirst (58 not out) and Rhodes (6 not out) steered England home by one wicket.

Darling was content with the two–one series win. His squad only lost two games for the tour. It won twenty-three and drew thirteen. *Wisden* noted, 'Darling has the rare power of being able to keep a whole team up to something approaching his own standard.'

Comeback compliant

On the way home, Australia played its first three Tests against South Africa, winning two–nil. Darling's form slipped. Scores of 0, 14, 6, 4 and 1 caused him, at thirty-two, to consider giving up Test cricket. He went back to his sheep station and missed the 1903–04 Test series in Australia, led by Monty Noble, against Pelham Warner's team. England won three–two.

But Joe Darling couldn't resist making a comeback. He played for South Australia in 1904–05 after not batting in a first-class game for two years. His form was good and he was chosen to lead Australia to England in 1905. The tourists this time had a weak bowling side, and Darling resorted to defensive leg and off theory in three of the Tests. The hope was more that the batsmen would become frustrated and lash out for a catch to one of the seven men placed on one side of the wicket. In the Third Test at Leeds, Charlie McLeod sent down sixty overs, mostly of off theory. Armstrong delivered 77.3 overs of leg breaks and top spinners, most delivered wide of leg stump. The Yorkshire crowd at Headingley was angered by Darling's tactics, which killed the game as a spectacle. In England's second innings Tyldesley played a superb knock of improvisation to reach 100. Many of his shots were made to the opposite side of the wicket planned by the 'theory' bowler.

England won two Tests and three were drawn. Darling's own Test form was fair, with scores of 0, 40, 41, 5, 2, 73, 0, 57 and 12 not out for an average of 33.

Joe Darling played in thirty-four Tests, making 1657 runs at 28.57. He retired from first-class cricket at thirty-six after the 1906–07 season.

In first-class cricket he scored 10,635 runs, including twenty-one centuries, at 34.52. His highest score was 210 (in 270 minutes) against Queensland at Brisbane.

Darling stayed on his Tasmanian property for thirteen years until 1920, but never lost interest in big cricket. His concern after retirement was the rights of other players. He pushed for testimonial matches for retiring players and proposed a long-service fund out of Test profits.

In 1921, aged fifty, Darling became a member of Tasmania's parliament. He had fifteen children, and his eight sons all played some form of cricket in Tasmania. Late in 1945, Joe Darling, aged seventy-five, suffered gall bladder problems. On 1 January 1946, Don Bradman, who had not played big cricket for seven years, returned for South Australia in a game against the Services XI and stroked a brilliant, chanceless century in ninety-five minutes. Aware of this, Joe Darling expressed the hope that Don Bradman would make a comeback. Darling died soon after surgery on 2 January 1946.

Joe Darling's sustained success as captain lifted Australian cricket to a new level in the Golden Age of the game before the First World War. He proved a flexible, fearless leader, who always thought of the team's success first.

11

HUGH TRUMBLE

....

12 May 1867 – 14 August 1938

Tests: 32; Captain: 2; Wins: 2;
Win ratio: 100 per cent

DOUBLE HAT TRICKER

Tall, phlegmatic off-spinner Hugh Trumble took over as an interim captain in the 1901–02 series against England when Joe Darling honoured his commitment to return to his Tasmanian sheep farm after three Tests. Trumble was equal to the task. He retained his leg-pulling humour and led his team thoughtfully in two Test wins, coming from behind both times.

At Sydney in mid-February 1902 he took three for 65 off thirty-eight overs with 18 maidens in England's 317 first innings. Trumble opened the batting, presumably to protect batsman Reg Duff, but only made 6. An even performance lifted Australia to 299. Then Saunders and Noble ran through England, taking five wickets apiece. Australia won by seven wickets. Trumble and his team were heroes, securing the series.

In the Fifth Test at Melbourne, Australia was rolled for 144. England's MacLaren and Jessop got away to a flier, smashing 50 in twenty minutes. Trumble brought himself on and quickly removed them both. He ended with five for 62, the best figures, and England was held to 189. Clem Hill (87) helped Australia to 255 in the second innings, with Trumble coming in at seven and producing a useful 22. England had 211 to win. Trumble again struck vital blows early, removing Jessop (16), Tyldesley (36) and Hayward (16). His three for 64 complemented Monty Noble, who did the rest, taking six for 98. England made 178 and was beaten by 32 runs.

The series went to Australia four–one.

Trumble took twenty-eight wickets at 20.04, and his figures were second only to those of Monty Noble, who took thirty-two wickets at 19. He also made 169 runs at 24.14, proving his usefulness as a batsman as his career progressed. At Melbourne in the Second Test he took a hat trick to finish the game, which Australia won by 229 runs.

Hugh Trumble's cool handling of his troops was a factor in tight-contest wins. He had the gift of exploiting the weaknesses of opposition batsmen. This was accentuated when he was skipper, as was his honed skill of setting fields. In both games he also developed a superb knack for changing his bowlers at the right time. He either managed a wicket-fall or bottled up a troublesome attacker.

Despite his success, he would never captain his country again. Joe Darling returned to lead the Australians to England in 1902. When England toured in 1903–04, Darling went bush again, and Monty Noble took over until the sheep farmer, who had now added cattle to his expanding property, made another comeback to lead the team to England in 1905.

Hugh Trumble was the son of Northern Irish immigrant William Trumble, who settled in Melbourne and became a civil servant. William was a cricket fanatic who bowled leg breaks for South Melbourne, one of the country's most famous and successful clubs. He set out a pitch in their Kew home and taught his three sons to bowl line and length. This was Hugh's strength, along with his height of 192 centimetres. Hugh got bounce and turn off a length that often left a batsman in two minds about going forward or back. Those endless practice sessions before school and after his father came home from work enabled him to boast that he could land a ball on a dinner plate if it was placed at a perfect length.

Trumble played for Victoria first in 1887 and then made his Test debut in England in 1890. He took just two wickets at 22 and was noted more for his height and gawky, 'camel'-like (as Pelham Warner called him) looks than his exceptional bowling skills. In the 1893 tour, he took six wickets at 39 runs in three Tests, which was again a modest return, but after that he became one of the most effective spinners in the world. In his next series—in England in 1896—he took eighteen wickets at 18.83. His best performance was at the Oval in the Third Test when he took six for 59 and six for 30. He proved a fine performer on wet or dry wickets throughout that third tour, snaring 148 wickets. Trumble had one of the best slower balls ever seen. It had an unnerving dip. He took wickets with it regularly. His awkward bounce upset batsmen, and he varied his deliveries with in-swingers.

Wisden named him one of the five cricketers of the year for 1896, and commented on his agreeable nature, 'whether on the winning or losing team', which was another way of saying he was a fine sportsman. No longer did he suffer jibes about his looks or lanky awkwardness. The experienced observers were impressed by his ability. W G Grace said that he was 'the best bowler Australia has sent us'.

Hugh Trumble had to pay more for his wickets in Australia, yet his figures still reflected exceptional reliability and fair economy. In the 1897–98 series he took nineteen wickets at 28.16 and made 181 runs at 36.33.

C B Fry noted in 1899, 'I should fear in England this summer— not his bowling arm, spinning finger, deft as they are. It is the head, best in the side, that makes the difference for the Australians.'

Trumble took fifteen wickets at 25 and had a good series with the bat, scoring 232 at 38.67, with a top score of 56. He also took seven catches, more even than the keeper. For the tour he took 142 wickets and made 1183 runs. Only George Giffen had done better.

Hugh Trumble married Florence Christian in March 1902 before making the trip to England, which served as their honeymoon. He broke his right thumb, an injury that extended their postnuptial celebrations in England in May. Florence was pleased by the break. She called it 'lucky', because she saw more of her Hugh than she had planned during an often wet, sometimes beautiful English spring.

Despite the lay-off, Trumble came back to be a key in Darling's successful 1902 tour squad, taking twenty-six wickets at 14.27 in just three Tests, a feat yet to be bettered.

Trumble retired at thirty-six, but after England won the first of the five-Test series of 1903–04, he was persuaded to make a comeback. In four Tests he took twenty-four wickets at 16.58. He ended his Test career at the Melbourne Cricket Ground during the 1903–04 series with the most dramatic and memorable farewell performance ever by a bowler: he took a hat trick in front of his adoring home crowd. His innings figures were seven for 28.

Trumble played thirty-two Tests, taking 141 wickets—all against England—at 21.79. He made 851 runs (four fifties) at 19.79, figures that belied his effectiveness in several Tests. He took forty-five catches and was usually the top catcher apart from the keeper. In first-class cricket he took 929 wickets at 18.46. Trumble made 5395 runs at 19.47.

Until Trumble retired from big cricket, he was a bank clerk, but with more time on his hands, he studied to become a bank accountant. He was secretary of the Melbourne Cricket Club between 1911 and his death in 1938, a period during which the MCG grew into a mighty stadium capable of holding crowds of 70,000.

Trumble and Florence had two daughters and six sons.

He ranks as one of Australia's greatest Ashes bowlers. But the most important words on his career are credited to his son Robert:

> What the scorebook can never show, but what remained a
> memory of those with whom he had played, was the
> unblemished record of a courteous and chivalrous
> opponent in the field, and, off it, a team-mate of unfailing
> gaiety and kindness.

12

MONTY NOBLE

....

28 January 1873 – 22 June 1940

Tests: 42; Captain: 15; Wins: 8; Losses: 5; Draws: 2;
Win ratio: 53.33 per cent

NOBLE OBLIGATIONS

Many ranked Montague Alfred Noble the best all-rounder Australia ever produced. He was an upright bat with various speed gears to match conditions, and a menacing off-spinner, who could deliver a fierce medium-pace off cutter. He played baseball in the winter and learned the thumb and forefinger grip that imparted swing through the air. Noble was nigh unplayable on a wet wicket.

Monty Noble was an unusual captain, regarded by some as one of Australia's greatest ever. He managed the delicate balancing act of being strict disciplinarian while maintaining his popularity among his players. Off the field he liked a drink and to smoke a pipe, but during Tests he abstained from both, and asked his players to do likewise. On the field, he didn't miss anything. Once Charlie Macartney spoke to admiring women near the fence. Next ball he was in slips and feeling humiliated, not a common sentiment for that great player. Noble was against appealing unless it was a serious question to the umpire. He was not interested in gamesmanship, only fair play to the point of eccentricity. Once a New South Wales batsman called to

Noble, his batting partner, 'Come on, he'll drop it,' as a fielder hovered under a catch. When it was spilled, Noble walked up the wicket and had quiet words to the offending batsman. On another occasion a batsman jumped the fence to get to the wicket in a tight club game between Paddington and Mosman. Noble, Paddington's skipper, and his batting partner, told the player to go back and come through the gate. 'Mosman', he explained, 'is giving us every chance to make the runs, if we are good enough.'

One of eight sons of a grocer turned publican from Surrey, the 185-centimetre, 81-kilogram Noble first played for New South Wales in 1893 at age twenty on a tour of New Zealand. A year later he played in a New South Wales Colts eighteen against Archie MacLaren's visiting England team of 1894–95 and dashed off 152 not out.

Monty Noble waited three more seasons to be chosen for the Test team under Harry Trott. It was at the Melbourne Cricket Ground on New Year's Day 1898. He was embarrassed doing 'the leave' to a Tom Richardson in-swinger that bowled him for 17 out of Australia's 551. Trott threw him the ball early and the new man's spin encouraged Ted Wainwright to have a heave and be caught by Ernie Jones. Noble finished with one for 31.

In England's follow-on, on a worn wicket, Trott wasted only a few overs with pace before bringing on Noble and fellow off-spinner Hugh Trumble. Noble this time bowled Wainwright and a few runs later captured the prize wicket of Ranjitsinhji, then Tom Hayward and William Storer. His four quick wickets reduced England to five for 80, and the tourists were headed for a big innings loss. Noble's figures were six for 49 off seventeen overs. There had been hardly a better start in Test cricket. Analysis after the match put his success down to the baseball-style swerve through the air that had been seen by few Englishmen.

In the next Test at Adelaide, Australia again started with a mammoth 573. Noble batted solidly for 39 until shouldering arms again to another Richardson in-swinger. He was bowled once more. If he were embarrassed in Melbourne, he was humiliated here. 'I wished the earth could have swallowed me up,' he told friends after play. 'I think I'll be dropped after this.'

But Monty Noble, twenty-four, had underestimated his importance as a new spinning talent. His confidence lifted when he took a good catch to dismiss Ranjitsinhji off Trumble before the talented Indian got going. Trott tossed him the ball in England's first innings and said, 'See if you can repeat your Melbourne effort.'

Noble took three for 78. In England's follow-on, Trott, the fine tactician from whom Noble learned most as a skipper, opened the bowling with him. Noble picked up Jack Mason in his first over for a duck. Trott used all his bowlers in tight spells and brought Noble back as the wicket deteriorated. He dismissed the stumbling block, Archie MacLaren, caught behind for 126 off a well-concealed quicker ball that the England captain misjudged. Noble then wrapped up the tail, taking five for 84 with off cutters and spin into a strong Adelaide headwind. Australia won again by an innings, with Noble bringing his tally to fifteen wickets in his first two Tests. Only a handful of bowlers had started so well in the history of Test cricket.

Noble finished the four 1897–98 Tests in which he played with nineteen wickets at 20.26, and made 106 runs at 26.5, an auspicious all-rounder's debut series.

On being Noble

Monty Noble's career changed his life and also his profession. Despite being a sudden 'name' in Australia's biggest sport, his employers at a city bank were begrudging about time off. Noble, being Noble, agreed that he wasn't doing his share. He wanted no special privileges, so he decided to study dentistry, a profession that would allow him to act as his own boss.

Noble was chosen to tour to England in 1899 with Joe Darling's team. Although he took vital wickets in the five Tests, it was with the bat that Monty Noble shone out in his second series. He began well at Trent Bridge, justifying his captain's faith in him with 41 and 45, batting at four. At Lord's he backed up the dash of Trumper (135 not out) and drive of Hill (135) with a rock-like 54, before Rhodes snared him for the third time in three starts. Noble managed a pair at Head-ingley in the Third Test. He was run out in the first innings and avoided further embarrassment from Rhodes by surrendering to Jack Hearne in the second. This aberration was quickly followed by infamy at Old Trafford in the Fourth Test when he made a stodgy top score of 60 not out in the first innings. When Australia had to follow on, Darling did the sensible thing and put his new snail in to open. Noble crawled to 89 before attempting his first drive in several hours. Hearne gratefully swallowed the catch, but by this time Noble's efforts had helped Australia dodge defeat. He was booed off the field. But his skipper and teammates slapped him on the back for saving his team and carrying out strict instructions to stay at the wicket in order to let the other more adventurous bats make the runs. He went on to make 9 and 69 not out at the Oval in another draw.

Australia won the series one–nil. Noble took just thirteen wickets at 31.23 and found the slower English wickets with far less bounce not much to his liking. Yet his batting figures of 367 runs (the top Australian aggregate) at 52.43 were second only to Clem Hill (301 at 60.2) and far ahead of Trumper (280 at 35). The 1899 tour established Noble as the best all-rounder since George Giffen, and with the potential to do better.

The chance for Noble to make his name as Australia's number one all-rounder came at the beginning of the new century in the 1901–02 Ashes series against Archie MacLaren's side. He received a setback in the First Test at the Sydney Cricket Ground, batting at four, where he made 2 and 14. He was given a pasting off England's bats and returned his worst figures yet, one for 91.

At Melbourne on New Year's day, exactly four years after his debut Test at the same venue, Monty Noble took seven for 17 on a wet wicket and skittled England for 61. He was literally unplayable. After Trumble had sent back the first three Englishmen, Jessop and Gunn decided that it was impossible to play either spinner from the crease or on the back foot. They launched themselves at Noble. Kelly stumped them both. This left the tourists' dressing room in turmoil. There seemed no way to counter these bowlers on such a wicket. They bowled unchanged. Ball after ball speared in from the off, spinning or shooting at the stumps. Noble took the last seven wickets in 7.4 overs, a wicket an over. In England's second innings he took six for 60, giving him the extraordinary figures of thirteen for 77, the best per-wicket return in a Test. Australia won by 229 runs and avenged the drubbing in the First Test at Sydney.

Noble encountered a different proposition in Adelaide in the Third Test, taking three for 58 and none for 72, but thanks to Trumble with the ball (six for 74) and Hill with the bat (98 and 97) Australia won by four wickets.

At the SCG—Noble's favourite ground—he found batting form and made 56. He took 3 for 78 in England's first innings, and in its second innings was once more the destroyer, this time on a Sydney turner, taking five for 54.

The Fifth Test at Melbourne was a similar story. He took one for 80 and six for 98. He snared thirty-two wickets at 19 for the series, and together with Trumble formed the best spinning double in cricket. Only Grimmett and O'Reilly, two leg-spinners thirty years later, would perform as well.

In England in 1902 he had a moderate Ashes, taking fourteen at 21.93. His batting was a disappointment. His record of 129 runs at 18.43 was not up to his previous England tour. Yet still he played a vital part in Australia's win at Bramall Lane, Sheffield, taking five for 51 and six for 52 in an unofficial man-of-the-match effort. Australia won the series two–one. The highlight of the tour was Noble's 284 against Sussex in a 428-run partnership with Warwick Armstrong.

On the way home via South Africa Noble had mixed form, scoring 53 not out in the First Test at Old Wanderers, Johannesburg. In the Second Test at the same venue he suffered his worst belting in Tests, going for 75 off fifteen overs. Yet he still took three wickets and figured in Australia's first win. The tourists won this series two–nil.

Lofty leader

With Joe Darling turned farmer again, Monty Noble, now thirty-two, was appointed captain after playing twenty-two Tests in 1903–04 for an Ashes series in Australia. He received the news on the morning of the First Test at the SCG on 11 December 1903 and promptly went out and made his highest Test score—133 out of 285. Unfortunately, it wasn't enough as the amateur, R E 'Tip' Foster made two more than that by himself. England wound up to a massive 577. Noble maintained some dignity throughout the onslaught, taking three for 99 off thirty-four overs, the best Australian figures in an attack left in tatters. Australia, through Trumper (185 not out) fought back with 485, but England went on to win well by five wickets.

After England had won by 185 runs at Melbourne to lead the series two–nil there were cries for Noble to be replaced. But Joe Darling was busy on his remote Tasmanian property dipping sheep and building up his cattle numbers. It was too early or too late for him to return.

Besides, Joe was confident that Monty Noble 'could still lead Australia to a series victory'.

He wished both sides good luck and went back to crutching. Rumours abounded that Darling would turn up in Adelaide to watch his former squad in the Third Test. If he was there, he stayed out of sight.

As predicted, Noble led a fightback from the front, scoring a fine double of 59 and 65. If anything, he underbowled himself as he had at Melbourne. Yet Australia won by 216 runs. The home team was back in the hunt for the Ashes. But despite an outstanding double of seven for 100 in England's first innings at the SCG in the Fourth Test, and a rearguard 53 not out (top score) in Australia's second innings, the home team went down by 157 runs. Duff, Trumper, Hill and the team could not stay with the captain in his quest for a long-shot win. Australia had lost the series and rendered up the Ashes, causing more than just Hugh Trumble to have a long face. Noble rallied the team for a final fling in the dead rubber of March 1904. He took four for 19 on a wet track and England was all out for 61 in pursuit of Australia's 247. The tourists never recovered and were beaten by 218 runs, thus giving England a three–two series win.

Noble hit 417 runs at 59.57 and took sixteen wickets at 20.5 in a losing side, thus demonstrating again his true standing as an all-rounder. In most observers' eyes now, Noble had surpassed George Giffen as Australia's finest all-rounder. If anything, the added burden of the captaincy had lifted his ratings.

Noble's leadership skills in the 1903–04 series were given a chance to develop. Among other things, he was one of the first-ever skippers to leave cover open, inviting batsmen to drive. Mishits and gully catches were prevalent. Over the next century most skippers would use this ploy at some time, especially with spinners operating and exceptional drivers at the crease. Noble learned from Harry Trott how to preserve his bowlers, and rarely let anyone go longer than five overs in a spell. Noble was also said to give a nip of whisky, brandy or rum to bowlers at tea before a spell late in the day. But batsmen were disabused of this practice, although some did like a dram or two, more for courage.

Noble kept a tight rein on his troops. The Macartney incident, where 'the Governor-General' ended up in slips after chatting to a woman over the fence, was not isolated. There were other examples of players being invited to catch the next train home if they flirted with female admirers during play. If a player missed a clap of attention from the skipper, he would receive a reprimand. Noble was a master at keeping his players alert and focused. He never let a bowler set a field without his approval and the odd adjustment. Even the more experienced bowlers bowed to his judgments, often fine calibrations from previous observations of the batsman. Noble was said to have a prodigious memory of the strengths and weaknesses of every batsman he opposed, even at club level.

He also exuded an extreme confidence that bordered on arrogance, especially when going out to bat. He once told Syd Gregory, next man in, to 'relax; get ready for a long wait'.

Noble often said, 'I can feel a long stay coming on.' It was usually the case. His fellow players regarded this not as bravado, but inspiration. No matter who was bowling, Monty would see them off. It was his way of saying, 'We are in control, if we put our minds to it.'

In 1905, Noble struggled in Joe Darling's losing team. He was thirty-two and past his prime. But he could still produce bursts of his best. Against Sussex (the county he slaughtered in 1902) at Hove he belted 267 and took six for 39.

Dental deliverance

In 1907–08 when Monty Noble resumed the captaincy he led Australia to a resounding four–one victory. England under Frederick Fane lost by two wickets at Sydney in the opening game. For once, Noble had little impact, as Australia fell to eight for 219, chasing 275 for victory. Noble retired to a room where he couldn't watch the game. He may have been one of the coolest operators ever on the field and while batting, but when everything was outside his control, he became the arch-pessimist and quite sick at his impotence.

Fortunately, Gerry Hazlitt (34 not out) and Albert (Tibby) Cotter toughed it out for a gallant ninth-wicket stand of 56. Their skipper was thrilled and relieved.

England felt not cheated but hard done by. It fought back in the Second Test at Melbourne, and despite Noble's fine double of top score (61) and second top (64), England won by a solitary wicket. The tourists gained enormous satisfaction from going one better than the

Australians at Sydney, with a last wicket winning stand of 39 by Sydney Barnes and Arthur Fielder.

Noble had opened in the second innings at Melbourne after being one of the last out in the first innings. He decided to experiment there in the Third Test in an effort to combat Sydney Barnes. England's finest bowler (arguably ever) got him for 15 in the first innings, but was seen off in the second when Noble made a sound 65. Hill, batting down the list at nine after suffering heatstroke fever, made a courageous 160, and Australia posted 516 (R J Hartigan 116) in its second innings, coming from behind. England crumbled for 183 and Australia won by 245 runs.

Monty Noble, now turned thirty-four, was a shell of his former bowling self, deferring to Warwick Armstrong as the key spinner, and Macartney.

At Melbourne in the Fourth Test on a rain-affected track Noble returned three for 11 off six overs. His last wicket was Jack Hobbs (57), probably the greatest player of spin on an adverse wicket ever. Looking back on his career, Noble said that bowling Hobbs in this game was one of his finest achievements. 'The batsmanship displayed was magnificent,' Noble noted.

The skipper played a big part in the game, making 48 as opener in the first innings. Australia won by 25 and took a stranglehold on the series of three–one. The Ashes were back in Australia.

Noble opened again in the Fifth Test at the SCG and made 35 and 34. The home side struggled and was 144 runs down after the first innings. Trumper, relieved of his duties as opener, made 166, batting at three in the second innings. Australia made 422 and ran out the winner by 49 runs. Noble contributed with the key early wicket of Fane.

The stats were indicative of Noble's steadiness with the bat, even in the arduous, new task of opening. He made 396 runs at 39.6. Comparisons can be odious, but over the series he was again more important than Trumper, the best bat of the era, who made 338 at 33.8. Noble, however, showed his decline with the ball, taking just eleven wickets at 27.18. Age was catching up with him at the bowling crease, although it seemed he used himself too modestly.

At thirty-six, Noble's contribution with bat and ball was limited, but he still led Australia to another Ashes win (two–one) in England in

1909. His astute captaincy in juggling Frank Laver, Bill Whitty, Bert Hopkins and Charlie Macartney was an important factor in Australia's two decisive wins at Lord's in the Second Test and Headingley in the Third.

In Tests, Noble made 1997 runs at 30.26 and took 121 wickets at 25.

He retired after the series to take up dentistry full-time. One of his patients, Bill Ferguson, went to him (in 1905) to have his teeth filled, but was really after the job of Australia's baggage manager and scorer. Years later, Ferguson sent his sister Ellen to Noble for dental work. They ended up getting married and having four children.

At forty-six, just after the First World War, Noble made a mini-comeback to help restart first-class cricket, which had gone into a long hibernation during the international conflict. Even in his maturity Monty Noble could play the game well. He made 52 against Victoria and took seven wickets.

In first-class cricket Noble made 13,975 runs at 40.74 and took 625 wickets at 23.11. He hit 37 hundreds, including seven doubles.

Noble joined the Sydney Cricket Ground Trust and organised the building of a stand, which was later named the M A Noble, the first stand to be named after a former great cricketer. In 1926 he toured as a journalist with the Australian Ashes team under Herbie Collins. Then he began to make phantom radio broadcasts in Sydney of matches abroad, armed with telegraph information and crude sound effects, such as the pencil tap on the desk to simulate willow on leather, and canned applause.

Noble performed on and off the field as if honour-bound to live up to his name. Apart from maintaining the highest standards of fair play and sportsmanship, he was at least the best all-rounder Australia produced until the advent of Keith Miller after the Second World War. Coupled with his outstanding captaincy, most observers who witnessed teams of the late 1800s and early 1900s ranked Monty Noble as the best cricketer of that era.

13

CLEM HILL

18 March 1877 – 5 September 1945

Tests: 49; Captain: 10; Wins: 5; Losses: 5;
Win ratio: 50 per cent

FIRST MOUNTAIN OF RUNS

Clement Hill made his name not as a captain but as the first of the heavy-scoring batsmen of the generation before the super-scorers of the 1920s and 1930s, Bill Ponsford and Don Bradman. Hill's leadership record was unremarkable. He followed Monty Noble and skippered Australia for the first time at home in the 1910–11 series against an undermanned South African team, winning four–one. A greater test of his ability at the helm came the following season in Australia against a strong English team led by Johnny Douglas. The visitors lost the first game and won the next four. It marked a decline in Australian cricket after a long period of ascendancy. When a dispute occurred between the Board of Control, which ran cricket, and Clem Hill, Hill's mediocre record as captain weakened his position. He was forced to resign. But not before one of the most ignominious incidents in Australian cricket history.

During the 1911–12 Ashes series, Hill led six rebel players who objected to the board selecting the manager for the 1912 tour of England. The team had experienced this before in 1909 when

Victorian Peter McAlister, aged forty, was appointed vice-captain to Noble. McAlister then wasn't up to Test standard and others felt he had taken the place of a younger, better player. Matters came to a head when skipper Hill wired McAlister, a national selector, asking for the inclusion of 25-year-old Charlie Macartney in the Third Test at Adelaide. McAlister suggested he drop himself if he wanted Macartney in.

When the selectors gathered in late January 1912 in Sydney to pick the team for the Fourth Test at Melbourne, McAlister was critical of Hill's captaincy. Australia was down one–two, with two Tests to play. Hill was angered. By nature he was a guileless, pleasant individual. The comments about his leadership pushed him too far. He reminded McAlister how star all-rounder Warwick Armstrong would not play in any of the games in 1909 when McAlister captained the side in England while Noble rested. Armstrong, a fellow Victorian, had been protesting against McAlister's inclusion in the tour party. 'Did you ever win [as acting-captain] except against the second-rate games?' Hill asked rhetorically.

McAlister replied that he was a better captain than Trumper, Armstrong and Hill together. 'You are the worst captain I've ever seen,' McAlister added.

At that point Hill, a trim, square-shouldered 175 centimetres, got up and moved around the selection table, confronting McAlister, a skinny 183 centimetres. 'If you keep on insulting me,' Hill said, 'I'll pull your nose.'

'You are the worst captain I've ever seen,' McAlister repeated as he rose from his chair.

Hill threw a half-slap, half-punch, striking his tormentor's face.

'You struck me when my hands were down,' McAlister protested.

'My hands are down now,' Hill said, putting his hands behind his back.

They grappled with each other for several minutes. Hill recalled: 'Mr Iredale [a selector] and [board secretary] held him [McAlister] back, and as I went out he called out that I was a coward. But as the others prevented him from leaving the room, the matter ended.'

And so, prematurely, did the 34-year-old Hill's career. He resigned as a selector. It became clear that the board would send its own mana-ger on tour. This forced Hill into retirement after the 1911–12 Ashes was completed, and lost one–four. The others who backed Hill in demanding that the players select the 1912 England tour manager— Armstrong, Trumper, Cotter, Ransford and Carter—also missed the tour for the first tri-nation competition, between South Africa, England and Australia. (The weakened Australians lost nil–one in three games against England and beat South Africa two–nil.)

It was an unfortunate end to a fine sixteen-year career as a Test cricketer. Hill played forty-nine Tests and made 3412 runs at 39.22. He hit seven centuries and 19 fifties, with a highest score of 191. Hill's first-class career demonstrated even more that he was the first of the big-scoring batsmen. The left-hander played in 252 matches, scoring 17,213 runs, including forty-five centuries and 83 fifties, at an average of 43.57. His highest score was 365 not out against New South Wales, demonstrating that he could go on into the big innings that Bradman and Ponsford commandeered twenty and thirty years later.

Big early signs

Clem Hill's hunger for the big innings was first appreciated when he hit 360 for Prince Alfred College against St Peter's College in Adelaide. His score beat Joe Darling's record of 252 for the same school. Yet even before he clocked up this massive schoolboy score he played for South Australia against Western Australia at just sixteen years.

His father, John, had made the first hundred ever at the Adelaide Oval. John Hill must have thought that, by producing eight sons (and eight daughters), at least one of them would carry on the cricket gene in a big way. Clem did. He was chosen in South Australia's Sheffield Shield side at seventeen, against Victoria, in the 1894–95 season. He made just 21, but it was enough for Jack Blackham to announce, 'Clem Hill will develop into a great left-hander.'

Hill was chosen to tour England in 1896 after topping the South Australian averages, with 56.37 in 1895–96. This included 206 at Sydney versus New South Wales, which was captained by Tom Garrett, a Test selector, who tried everything, including leg theory, to slow him up as he advanced his team's score with 154 out of the final 197. Hill countered by moving across his wicket to play cross-bat shots on both sides of the wicket. Another factor was a blistering 150 not out for South Australia against Stoddart's touring English team early in 1895. Stoddart praised the knock and predicted a Test career.

That career began for Hill at nineteen at Lord's in the First Test of 1896. He made 1 and 5. In the next two Tests he failed again with 9, 14, 1 (run out) and a duck. But when the two sides lined up again in Australia in 1897–98, Hill, now twenty, was a more mature player after five years of interstate experience and his first England tour. He had an ungainly grip, low on the handle, and the wide-legged stance of a baseball slogger, but his stroke play was attractive. He now had a wide range of shots on the on and off, including a good cut and an efficient cover drive. The grip reduced the power of his driving, but he made up for this by jumping down the wicket. His fast footwork allowed him to add strength to his forward-of-the-wicket shots and to penetrate the field with good placement.

George Giffen early on advised Hill to cut back his hooking. It took the gutsy left-hander some time to face the fact that although hooking got him runs, it often cost him his wicket. At first he was loath to take Giffen's advice. Hill loved taking on the quicks. But discretion became the rule in his batting as he followed the greater inclination to make big scores. The hook was finally put away in 1897–98. It paid off. He scored 19, 96, 58, 81, 188, 0, 8 and 2. The 188 was made in the Fourth Test at the Melbourne Cricket Ground on 29 January 1898. Hill was in at one for 1 and couldn't find someone to stay with him until Hugh Trumble arrived at the crease at six for 58. Hill reached his 100, with Trumble digging in. The score was 142. After tea, Hill told his older partner he would have a go. Trumble instructed him to continue with the same balance of vigilance and attack. The partnership reached 165 when Trumble was out for 46.

The score was seven for 223. Hill went on to 182 not out after batting a few minutes short of a full day of five hours. He fell, caught to Jack Hearne the next morning on 188 when he was hungry to go on and set up more records. As it was, his score was the highest in Ashes Tests for someone under twenty-one years. It turned out to be the innings of his life, considering the circumstances, where others had fallen around him. Australia made 323 and went on to win by eight wickets. Trott's team won the series four–one and Hill (452 runs at 56.5) was only outranked in runs scored by Joe Darling (537, average 67.13, three centuries) at the peak of his career.

Clem Hill continued with this steady output in the next Ashes tour of England under Darling in 1899. He scored 52 (run out), 80, a superb 135 at Lord's, 34 and 0. He missed two Tests and the rest of the tour after having surgery on a nose growth. Hill topped the Test averages with 301 at 60.2.

His exceptional consistency continued in the next series in Australia in 1901–02, the first Ashes contest of the twentieth century. His scores—46, 0, 15, 99 (the first ever in Tests), 98, 97, 21, 30, 28 and 87—gave him an aggregate of 521 at 52.1. This made Hill the most reliable batsman in Australia's first twenty-five years of Test cricket.

Hill slipped a little in England in 1902 but still topped Australia's aggregates (258, including a fine 119 at Bramall Lane) and averages (36.86) in a side that had Trumper, Darling and Noble. Trumper was the most brilliant bat in the side, but Hill was the better man if you were playing to win a series. Joe Darling always was. His side won two–one.

Clem Hill remained in form on the first trip to South Africa on the way home from England in 1902. In the three Tests he scored 76, 142, 6, 12, and 91 not out. Again with 327 runs at 81.75, he outgunned Armstrong (281 at 70.25) and Trumper (239 at 47.8).

At twenty-six, he struggled in the 1903–04 home series against England, which Australia lost two–three under Monty Noble. Hill scored 276 at 27.6, with a top score of 88.

Early in 1905 Clem Hill married Florence Hart in Tasmania and two weeks later in February was on a liner bound for England and his third Ashes tour. He had a second successive mediocre—by his earlier standard—Test series, scoring just 188 at 20.89. Australia under Joe Darling lost nil–two.

Hill's climb back

At thirty, in the 1907–08 Ashes series, Clem Hill returned to the form of his younger days, with 360 runs at 36. This included a magnificent 160 under trying conditions at Adelaide in the vital Third Test. Hill was ill with sunstroke in Australia's second innings, which began 78 runs behind England. The series to that point had been tight, both sides having won one game. Captain Noble dropped Hill from number three to number nine. He came in at seven for 180 with the game and the Ashes swinging England's way. Australia was 102 runs behind. Hill, who was not well enough to field in England's first innings, and

Queensland's Roger Hartigan then combined for one of the great Test recoveries.

Hill vomited several times in the Adelaide heat. But he refused to give up. 'Clem's courage was an inspiration,' Hartigan said after the game. 'There is no doubt that his determination lifted me for a stronger effort.'

Hartigan was under more pressure from the boss of his Brisbane auctioneering company, who wanted him home to oversee hide sales. But Hartigan's batting to save his country caused the company to relent. He was allowed to see out the game. Hartigan and Hill took the match into the fifth day with a long, gutsy partnership of 243. Barnes finally removed Hartigan (116) for the innings of his life. Hill went on, despite suffering for the second day. With the score at 501 and the lead 423, Hill, near collapse, was out caught off John Crawford, for a magnificent 160. It had taken him a day and nineteen minutes—319 minutes in all—and ranked as his second greatest knock, after his 188 a decade earlier on 1 January 1898. Australia went on to win the game and the series.

Clem Hill felt compelled to miss the 1909 tour of England, which would have seen him away from his family for nine months. He was elected captain against the first visiting South African team in 1910–11. The tourists' bowling lacked penetration and the Springboks were not a battle-hardened group. Most played less cricket and were not as experienced as their Australian counterparts. The disparity led to a batting bonanza. Hill was able to have one more great Test series, scoring 425 at 53.13, which placed him third behind Trumper (661 at 94.43) and Warren Bardsley (573 at 63.67). South Africa's Aubrey Faulkner was also dominant, with 732 runs at 73.2.

Hill began the series determined to dominate the tourists from the First Test at the Sydney Cricket Ground. It helped that he won the toss for the first time as skipper (it was his thirty-ninth Test). He came to the wicket at 52 and joined fellow left-hander Warren Bardsley (132) in a run spree. Hill slammed his way to 100 in just ninety-eight minutes, one of the swiftest ever, and the two batsmen put on 224 in just two hours in front of a packed and enthralled Sydney crowd. Hill went on to his highest Test score of 191, which he accumulated in just 200 minutes. The Australians compiled six for 494 (100 runs an hour, five an over) in the best day's Test cricket, from a batting perspective, yet seen. This blistering start helped Hill return to something like his former consistency with follow-up scores of 39, 0, 16, 55, 11, 100 and 13. Despite the opposition standard, it was a fine effort considering he had the added responsibility of being captain and dealing with the Board of Control, which had a strained relationship with the players.

Hill's form during the 1911–12 Ashes series in Australia (274 at 27.4, with a top score of 98) was not strong enough for him to assert authority with the board, especially as the team slipped into a sequence of four consecutive losses.

Hill was thirty-five when forced into retirement. He returned at forty-three after the end of the First World War to play for South Australia and made 66, and played in benefit matches for George Giffen at forty-six, and then off-spinner Bill Howell at forty-seven in 1924, when he made 40 for an Australian XI against New South Wales.

Clem Hill retired from all cricket after thirty-two years. All his runs were made on uncovered wickets (Australia began covering wickets in poor weather in 1926). His massive figures stood out among Australian batsmen until after the First World War. Even when considered within the entire history of Australian cricket, he ranks with the biggest accumulators in first-class cricket.

Clem Hill's love of horse racing led him to being a stipendiary steward and handicapper in Adelaide. In 1937, aged sixty, he was made the Victorian Amateur Turf Club's handicapper at Caulfield in Melbourne, where he and his wife and two daughters took up residence. At sixty-eight, he was thrown from a tram in a Collins Street traffic accident. It led to his death.

Clem Hill's outstanding success at the two sports in which he participated was in part due to his genial nature and straightforward manner. Coupled with his skills, discipline and application, he was an admirable character. His approach to batting paved the way for the mightiest run-plunderers of the twentieth century.

14

SYD GREGORY

....

14 April 1870 – 1 August 1929

Tests: 58; Captain: 6; Wins: 2; Losses: 1; Draws: 3;
Win ratio: 33.33 per cent

POCKET DYNAMO

Sydney Edward Gregory became captain of Australia for the 1912 tour
of England, the toughest time to lead the side in the 35-year history
of Tests. At forty-two he was well past his prime and had inherited a
side torn by the dispute between the Board of Control and the players.
There were also internal politics, where the unpopular board was
under threat by the Melbourne Cricket Club (MCC), which had been
keen to once more control Australian cricket. To make matters worse,
Gregory couldn't control his team off the field, where there were
continual problems with drunken behaviour throughout the tour of
England, Ireland, Canada, the United States and New Zealand. From
every port reports of unruly exhibitionism and brawling filtered back
to Australia. The problems began before the tour left Australia when
six players—Hill, Armstrong, Trumper, Ransford, Cotter and Carter—
dropped out because the board would not let the team appoint its own
manager. Gregory was left with almost a second XI to captain in the
triangular competition with England and South Africa. Australia easily
accounted for South Africa two–nil. The trouble began when the
weaknesses of the tourists were exposed against a strong English team

featuring Jack Hobbs, Wilfred Rhodes, C B Fry, Frank Woolley, Johnny Douglas, F R Foster and Sydney Barnes. Rain ruined the first two Tests, but Australia was thrashed by 244 runs in the decider at the Oval. This lowered the esteem of a divided, problematic squad. Gregory, who scored just 72 runs at an average of 12 in the six Tests, lost all authority, although he tried in vain to keep the trouble makers in check. The big drinkers in the team—Jimmy Matthews, who claimed a hat trick in each innings of the First Test versus South Africa, keeper 'Barlow' Carkeek, and batsman Dave Smith—roistered their way across England and the world.

It was a harrowing, dispiriting end to Gregory's fine career of fifty-eight Tests, in which he had scored 2282 runs at 24.54, including four centuries. In first-class cricket he played 368 matches, scored 15,192 runs at 28.55, and hit twenty-five centuries.

Pedigree positive

Syd Gregory was short (164 centimetres), usually no drawback for a batsman, and came into the game with a strong cricketing pedigree. His father, Ned, who helped lay out the Sydney Cricket Ground and design its scoreboard, had played with his uncle Dave in the first Australian XI in 1877. Young Syd played for Waverley Club in his late teens and was first picked for New South Wales in 1889–90. He entered the Test team for the first time in England in 1890 at age twenty, just thirteen years after his father and uncle. His beginning was inauspicious: four innings for just 15 runs at 5. But he excelled in fielding, and this alone allowed him to keep his place in the Test team. Cover point was his speciality. His close-to-the-ground saves had all England marvelling. He was fearless. Even W G Grace's vicious cuts had trouble getting past him. If they did, Gregory's magnificent throwing of up to 110 metres brought regular applause. He could hurl a ball with his tiny frame further than any other Test cricketer.

The dapper, moustachioed Gregory, a postal clerk, had paid his way to England and recouped 400 pounds, which was four or five times what he was earning as a postal clerk. Nevertheless, he was advised not to give up his day job. He was failing to score well. He managed just one Test—the Third at Adelaide in the 1891–92 Ashes—and made 3 and 7. He was selected to tour England again in 1893 and, anticipating another bonanza, left the postal service. Unfortunately the team's ordinary tour, which was marred by internal brawling, was a financial failure. Gregory came back with nothing. He returned with not much more on the Test batting ledger, making just one good score—57 at Lord's. He was a disappointment again, with an aggregate of just 75 in five innings, for an average of 15.

The apotheosis of Little Tich

It wasn't until the glorious 1894–95 Ashes in Australia that the modest Gregory, now twenty-four, demonstrated that he was more than a neat fielder and dresser. Coming in at four for 192 at the SCG in the First Test, he proceeded to cut and drive off the back foot. After he reached 50, he became audacious with that rare speciality, the front-foot cut, which required the sharpest eyes, or an ability to acutely judge the length. Being short, he had to improvise and be a fraction more discerning when deciding on his shots. He also 'cribbed' occasionally, by cheekily batting a foot forward of the crease to other than the spinners. Gregory always batted on the simple basis that if the bowler let the ball go high in the 'arc' of his delivery it would pitch full, allowing the little man to push forward to meet the ball. If the ball was let go late in the arc it would be short and he could rock onto the back foot to cut, hook, pull or drive.

In this innings—one of the greatest played in the nineteenth century—his judgment worked better than ever before in a Test and he treated the Saturday crowd of 24,000 to the innings of his life. He gave one chance—at 131—when he edged a delivery to the keeper, who spilled a tough catch. Gregory partnered George Giffen (161) in a 139-run stand early in the innings. But the most astonishing link was with Jack Blackham (74), who came in at number ten with the score at eight for 409. They put on a startling 154 in seventy-three minutes for the ninth wicket. Gregory cut loose. His wagon wheel of shots had more spokes than ever before. His innings included every stroke in the manual. He didn't shirk hooks or pulls, which came with a rush in his last fifty. This fleet-footed flurry allowed Gregory to become the first batsman ever to score a double hundred in a Test in Australia. He was out caught on 201, after a scintillating 270 minutes. The big crowd rose to the little man who had reached the summit of

the most coveted mountain in cricket, but in the manner of an entertaining dancer, not a dogged climber. They cheered him all the way
up the pavilion steps.

After people had retrieved their hats, one was passed around the
ground. More than one hundred pounds was dropped into it, about
what he would earn at the post office in a year. He was most grateful
but no more than the crowd, who reckoned they had had their money's
worth and then some.

Syd Gregory couldn't quite find that incredible form again until the
final and deciding Test, when he got near it with a top score of 70 in
the first innings and 30 in the second. His 362 for the series at 40.22
at last justified the selectors' faith in him.

Butts, bats and cuts

Gregory put the 100-pound windfall into an enterprising men's shop,
which doubled as a tobacconist and hairdresser's, while carrying a
range of sports goods. The shop was well located in Sydney's King
Street in late 1895. Little Tich Gregory's popularity augured well for
its prosperity. Early in 1896, at twenty-five, he married Maria Sullivan,
just before his third tour of England and the United States.

In the First Test at Lord's he played another 'blinder' in a tremendous fightback with captain Harry Trott (143). Australia was routed
by Tom Richardson in the first innings for just 53. England replied
with 292 and then had the tourists three for 62, before a partnership
of 221 in double-quick time. Gregory made a chanceless 103 with 17
fours.

He was no fool. He would rather go for his shots in a calculated
attempt to entertain. Such feats pulled the crowds back to watch the
Australians. His dashing play and fine return for the tour—he topped
the averages with more than 30—meant he did more than any player
to ensure the tour's profitability. (He had an average of 30.33 from an
aggregate of 182 in the Tests.)

Australia lost the series one–two, but each player went home with
400 pounds in his pocket. Gregory, at twenty-six, had some more
capital for investment after his retirement.

He matured as a batsman in the next series—1897–98—in
Australia with an even run of scores—46, 31, 71, 52, 0, 21 not out,

21, 22 not out—for an aggregate of 264 at a 44 average.

Meanwhile, off the field, his hard-earned investment in the triple-purpose store faltered. He got out of one partnership and started another, drawing 250 pounds a year for himself, which was better than his pay as a postal clerk but still not a huge salary.

He toured England again in 1899 under Joe Darling and saved his country in the final Test at the Oval with 117, this time in a rearguard fight in poor light against fast bowling from Bradley and Lockwood. This helped his Test returns (188 at 23.5) in Australia's one–nil series win.

This tour, in turn, saved Gregory's business. He made 700 pounds and this money was used to pay off debts run up when his partner over-stocked with sports goods. Gregory took on a third partner in order to raise funds and move from King Street to Pitt Street.

Back on the field, he did better in the 1901–02 series, with an average of just under 30 (29.89 from a 269 aggregate) in an era of uncovered wickets, where 30 was equivalent to a fifty average a genera-tion later. This fine effort was undone on the long tour (March to December), accompanied by his wife and four-year-old son, of England and South Africa in 1902. Gregory played in eight Tests for a miserable aggregate of 129 runs and an average of just 10.75. Far worse was the shock of coming home to a bankrupt business. The shop was closed. A trustee was in charge of the stock. His partners had let the business collapse. At thirty-three, Gregory took a clerical job with the Water Board.

By the fingernails

Syd Gregory now clung onto his cricket as an extra means of prestige and some income. His form held and he was chosen for the 1903–04 series in Australia against Pelham Warner's team. Despite a magnifi-cent 112 (a century in 127 minutes) in Adelaide, he was dropped from the final Test at Melbourne, after thirty-nine successive games for his country. His average of 23.63 from 189 runs was not enough to carry him with impunity any more. But he was still chosen for the team to tour England under Darling in 1905. He lasted three Tests, but with just 94 runs to his credit at 23.5, the years—he was thirty-five—seemed to have caught up with him.

The trip yielded around 700 pounds, most of which was eaten up

by debts and medical expenses for his wife. He was discharged as a
bankrupt on his return to Australia in late 1905, by which time his
previous saviour—his batting—was in jeopardy. New South Wales
dropped him for the 1906–07 season.

The pocket dynamo's career appeared over. Yet he was selected in
late 1907 for a testimonial match and cracked 94 in 123 minutes of
superlative batting that reminded onlookers of the Gregory of a decade
earlier. He then crunched 201—his equal top score—against Victoria,
followed by 126 for an Australian XI versus The Rest. Midway through
the 1907–08 series against England, the national selectors were now
forced to consider him again. He was brought back for the Fourth Test
at the Melbourne Cricket Ground A big factor in his return was a
recommendation from his skipper in the state and national teams—
Monty Noble. He had batted with him in several big innings and
knew first-hand how the tiny champion had regained touch. He hit just
10 and 29 at Melbourne but struck form in the Fifth Test at Sydney,
with a top score of 44 in the first innings and second top score of 56
(Trumper dominated with 166) in the second. This gave him an
aggregate of 139 at 34.75—figures more in keeping with Gregory at
his best.

Weight of experience earned him his seventh tour of England in
1909, and he took on the demanding role of opener with courage,
scoring 222 runs at 24.67, with a top score of 74 run out in his last
innings of the series, which was won by Australia two–one. Gregory
had set himself to make a century in that last knock, feeling that at
thirty-nine he was playing his last Test in England.

Gregory wasn't chosen for any of the five Tests against the visiting
South Africans in 1910–11 but was slipped back into the team for the
final Test of the 1911–12 season against England. This was to tune
him up for the tour of England in 1912. When a dispute blew up
between the players and the Board of Control, the board turned to
Gregory, the most experienced tourist in Australian cricket history, to
be the makeshift skipper.

Through no fault of his own, he presided over an awful tour in every
way. It left him with a poor record as Australian captain, but Syd
Gregory is remembered for his cheerful courage in the face of adversity
in life and on the field. He was also a talented batsman, who would
have entertained at the highest level in any era.

15

WARWICK ARMSTRONG

....

22 May 1879 – 13 July 1947

Tests: 50; Captain: 10; Wins: 8; Draws: 2;
Win ratio: 80 per cent

THE UNSINKABLE

Warwick Windridge Armstrong was Australia's equivalent to Dr W G Grace. Both started tall and lean, and ended their careers bulky. They were imposing, authoritative figures. Their captaincy records were similar, with both leading their country to eight wins. Armstrong had an 80 per cent win ratio, with eight wins and two draws from ten Tests as leader, while Grace had a 61.54 per cent win ratio with eight wins, three losses and two draws from thirteen times as England's captain. Both were successful as all-round cricketers, with Armstrong securing the stronger international impact and figures (Armstrong: fifty Tests, 2863 runs at 38.69, eighty-seven wickets at 33.6, forty-four catches; Grace: twenty-two Tests, 1098 runs at 32.29; nine wickets at 26.22, thirty-nine catches).

Armstrong began his senior sporting career for South Melbourne in Australian Rules football and cricket at nineteen in 1898. Being 190 centimetres tall and weighing 94 kilograms, he was able to play key football positions. He had outstanding endurance and was a straight-ahead player, who was not averse to delivering the 'shirt front', where a player hit an opponent with hip and shoulder fairly, always within the rules. If his name hadn't been Armstrong, it might have been his nickname. He could move his lean frame with surprising speed and agility, something he carried onto the cricket field in batting, fleet-footed ball chases and long stints bowling his accurate leg spinners. An unfortunate legacy of his football was an injured knee, which seemed to restrict his movements increasingly as he matured. It caused him embarrassment later in his career against spinners, who had him propping at the crease.

At twenty, Armstrong switched to the Melbourne Cricket Club, which employed him. In his first game for Victoria in 1899–1900, he made 118. Two years later, in 1901–02, he played his first Test at the Melbourne Cricket Ground against Archie MacLaren's team. MacLaren won the toss and sent Australia in on a fearful 'sticky'. Armstrong came to the wicket with the score at seven for 85. He defended well in an impossible situation and remained 4 not out from Australia's 112. England fared worse, making just 61. Armstrong came in at number eleven in the second innings with the score at nine for 233, joining Reg Duff, who was also on debut. Armstrong was happy to play second fiddle to the powerful New South Wales bat and they put together a match-winning last-wicket stand of 120. Duff got to 104 before L C Braund bowled him. Armstrong had batted stoutly and without any sign of nerves, scoring 45 not out. England's second innings' response was 175, giving Australia a win by 229 runs.

Armstrong made 9, 9 not out, 55, 17 not out and 20 in the remaining games in a winning team under Joe Darling. His batting returns—159 at 53—were flattering but indicative of a new star all-rounder who had the right temperament for the highest level. With Hugh Trumble and Monty Noble dominating Australia's bowling, Armstrong was not getting much of a chance to show his skills as a leg-spinner. His strengths with the ball were line and length, delivered off a longish run for a slow bowler.

Armstrong's Test performances in England in 1902 were more sobering. He scored 97 runs at 13.86 and took just two wickets at 61.5. Yet his 1087 runs at 26.51 and eighty-one wickets at 17.4 on tour caused *Wisden* to predict a most viable future for the 23-year-old. It named him one of its 'Five Cricketers of the Year'. Armstrong's season highlight was an innings of 172 not out in a sixth-wicket partnership of 428 (Monty Noble went on to 284) against Sussex.

On the way home he demonstrated his all-round skills by taking his first wickets (two for 24 off seven overs) against South Africa at Johannesburg in the First Test, and making 59 batting at number four in the second innings.

His confidence high, Armstrong went on in the Second Test, making 49 run out in the first innings and 159 not out in the second innings, in which he carried his bat. The latter happened to be Australia's winning score. He ended the three-Test series with 281 runs at 70.25, and those two wickets at 64.

Apart from a 48 in the first innings of the First Ashes Test of 1903–04 Armstrong had a poor Test series. He was dropped after three matches (125 runs at 20.83; two wickets at 79 runs). Big Warwick, not for the last time, took it out on the students—this time of Melbourne University—in a club game for Melbourne, belting 438 in 395 breathless minutes of power hitting. At a time when club cricket performances made headlines, Armstrong was reminding everyone of the weight he could put behind his bat.

Form spill-over

This form spilled over into 1904–05 when Warwick Armstrong scored 460 state runs at 57.5 and took fourteen wickets at 26. A blistering innings of 200 versus Queensland at the MCG secured his trip to England in 1905. It wasn't Armstrong's fault that Darling's team went down nil–two in the five-Test series. He hit 252 at 31.5, with a top score of 66 in a most consistent effort. Armstrong took sixteen wickets at 33.63. His form for the tour was first rate. Armstrong achieved the rare double of 2002 runs at 48.82 and 130 wickets at 17.6. He took five wickets in ten innings and ten wickets in two matches.

In the match against the Gentlemen of Lord's he hammered 248 not out, then the third-highest knock at cricket headquarters. Never had the Gentlemen been treated to such batting abuse or contempt. There was a 273-run partnership with Darling in just 160 minutes. At one point, the Gentlemen's captain, H C McDonell, had his three best fielders deep in the covers spaced nine metres apart in a vain attempt to stop Armstrong's drives going through.

His top score was 303 not out in 315 minutes (299 balls) against Somerset at Bath. Local folklore for decades held that this was the most power-laden innings ever seen in the county. Two balls (later auctioned for charity) were so misshapen that they had to be replaced.

Wisden said of his batting:

> The great batsman of this [1905] eleven [it included Trumper, Darling, Hill, Syd Gregory, Duff and Noble] was Armstrong. In form nearly all through the tour, he struck the happy medium, being brilliant without recklessness and safe without overcaution. In point of style he has improved out of knowledge since he was here in 1902. All the clumsiness that marred his fine natural powers has disappeared.

Joe Darling instructed Armstrong to use leg theory (copied from Braund, the Surrey and England bowler), the precursor to bodyline, in the First Test at Nottingham, and the Third at Leeds. Deliveries slid down the leg side with the field dispersed. Scoring dropped to one or two singles an over, and this forced 'economy' helped the team compensate for an attack that lacked penetration.

Writer Sumner Reed commented, 'Armstrong was once positively, or if you will, negatively, mean with the ball, but on this tour we have seen another dimension to his bowling. As usual, he was tight. But he also took wickets. This imposing figure was more dangerous to England than ever.'

Armstrong continued with strong performances with bat and ball over the next two Shield and club seasons. When the Englishmen under Arthur Jones arrived for the 1907–08 season they were confronted with a bigger, and bigger-performing, Armstrong than 1905. His weight had increased to more than 110 kilograms. Big hundreds at every level of the game were now expected from him. In the 1907–08 Tests he topped aggregates and averages for both sides (410 at 45.56), and took fourteen wickets at 25.79. He was remarkably consistent with the bat, doing well in every Test with 7, 44, 31, 77, 17, 34, 32, 133 (at the MCG), 3 and 32.

Warwick Armstrong belted another four centuries during the season, all big-occasion performances: 110 at Sydney versus New South Wales (his fourth hundred against that state); 231 versus Queensland at the MCG; 117 for Victoria versus England; and 146 not out for the Australian XI versus the Rest of Australia, in March 1908.

As the big man approached thirty during the 1908–09 domestic season, his leg-spinning matured. In two trial games that would decide who would be part of the tour side going to England in 1909, he took five for 37 and six for 59. In the main Shield game for his state he belted his fifth century against New South Wales, 171 at Sydney in 244 minutes. Next to Trumper, Armstrong was Noble's first choice for the touring side. He achieved another fine double—1451 runs at 43.96 and 113 wickets at 16.38. These figures included three centuries and nine five-wicket hauls, plus thirty-three catches, the most by any one player. Armstrong's input was greatest of all the tourists under Monty Noble in terms of the results—thirty-nine games, for thirteen wins, four losses and twenty-two draws.

In the 1909 Tests, which Australia won two–one, Armstrong's batting fell away, with 189 runs at 23.63, but his bowling—fourteen at 20.93—reflected his development, which was normal for leg-spinners, after eight years in top cricket. He took six for 35 off 24.5 overs with eleven maidens in England's second innings on the third day of the Lord's Test. Australia won the game by nine wickets.

Armstrong contracted malaria in Penang on the way home, which disrupted his 1909–10 domestic season. He lost a lot of weight and played only a handful of state games, while not turning out for a single club match.

A year's rest saw him return for the 1910–11 season. After his first experience versus South Africa in 1902, Armstrong looked forward to taking the Springboks on again. He found their bowling to his liking, hammering 410 runs at 51.25. Once more he demonstrated a consistency rarely found in the annals of Test batting by scoring 48, 75, 29, 30, 48, 48 run out, 132 at the MCG, and a duck. Noble used him as more of a stock bowler (eleven wickets at 46.09 from 184 overs). Only left-arm fast-medium Bill Whitty (thirty-seven at 17.08 from 232.3 overs) and fast man Albert 'Tibby' Cotter (twenty-two at 28.77 from 194.5 overs) bowled more.

In the poor one–four series loss of 1911–12 against England Armstrong continued his batting run of useful scores, totalling 324 for an average of 32.4. His nine wickets cost 37.11.

Despite being thirty-two and slightly weakened by the lingering effects of his illness, Armstrong showed he could still mount a big innings with his score of 250 versus South Australia. It was the highest score by a Victorian and a record that would last fifteen years. (Bill Ponsford broke it in December 1926 by hitting 352 out of a massive score of 1107 versus New South Wales).

Armstrong was a signatory to the infamous Clem Hill letter of 25 January 1912, which threatened the withdrawal of six players unless the team—and not the 1905-formed Board of Control—could appoint a manager. Armstrong was thus left out of the 1912 tour of England, where his huge performances on three previous visits had been vital to Australian success.

This temporarily closed his Test career. He fell into dispute with the Victorian selection committee over his captaincy of the state in 1912–13. He resigned when he was not allowed to lead the state for the entire season.

He married a Gundagai grazier's daughter, Aileen O'Donnell, in 1914 and they had a son.

Warwick was back captaining the state in 1914–15. He was appointed captain of Australia for the first-ever direct tour of South Africa. But the First World War intervened. The tour was called off. Armstrong instead led Victoria to a Sheffield Shield win. All first-class cricket ceased for four years and while the Shield was not resumed in 1918–19, interstate matches were organised. Armstrong, now thirty-nine and more troubled by his early-career knee injury, celebrated by crunching 162 versus South Australia in 183 minutes of force-hitting at the MCG.

The big ship as leader

Warwick Armstrong exhibited no major fall off in form with bat or ball at Shield or club cricket in 1919–20. This led to Armstrong being asked to skipper Australia the following season against Johnny Douglas's 1920–21 tourists, the first such squad in almost a decade. The Big Ship, as Armstrong was known throughout the cricketing world, led his tyro squad to a five–nil Ashes victory, the first time this had been achieved. Despite his forty years, he reached his best ever form with the bat, beginning with a chanceless 158 in the Australian second innings of the First Test at Sydney. It was top score for the match. Australia won by 377 runs and then followed up in Melbourne with a huge win by an innings and 91 runs. England had an experienced side with some of its finest players of the era in its company— Jack Hobbs, Wilfred Rhodes, Patsy Hendren, Frank Woolley, Johnny Douglas and Percy Fender. Yet it lacked bowling penetration. Its reliance on off-spinner Ciss Parkin (sixteen wickets at 41.86) and Fender (twelve wickets 34.17), a good county leg-break trundler, allowed Armstrong and a feast of Australian batting (Warren Bardsley, Herbie Collins, Jack Gregory, Charlie Kelleway and Charlie Macartney) to flatter their Test figures.

Armstrong slammed—he preferred to hit fours rather than run— his way to 121 at Adelaide in the Third Test.

The cricket world was shocked when he was dumped as captain of Victoria mid-season. It was part of an ongoing war between Armstrong and certain officials, including Ernie Bean. It began in the early 1900s and was exacerbated by events in 1912. Warwick's style upset officialdom, which in turn endeared him to the press and public. He could be brusque and blunt. He spoke his mind. If he didn't get his way, he would be cantankerous. This, plus his ability and imposing stature, caused him to be a formidable, implacable enemy. He had, or would have preferred, a dictatorial approach.

The state kafuffle had no impact on Armstrong's performance in the Tests. In the Fourth at Melbourne, he came to the wicket in Australia's first innings at a critical moment, with Australia's score five for 153, chasing England's 284.

A story, no doubt promulgated by Armstrong's supporters, had Bean, a teetotaller, 'gloating' as the captain strode out to bat. What ensued, it was said, drove the official to drink. Armstrong launched his huge frame at the bowling and restored Australia's innings in a big partnership with Johnny Taylor (77). Armstrong suffered a recurrence of malaria during the innings, but battled on to 123 not out in front of an appreciative crowd, in what was to be his farewell Test at his beloved MCG.

Armstrong's batting aggregate for the series was 464 for a 77.33 average. Only Collins (557 at 61.89) scored more.

During the series, he used himself as a back-up with the ball (nine wickets at 22.67 off 102 overs), mainly because he could call on the best leg-spinner Australia had yet produced in Arthur Mailey (thirty-six wickets at 26.28 from 244.1 overs). But their relationship on the field was strained. It was Mailey's way to 'buy' his wickets by pitching up and tempting batsmen to hit out. Catches, stumpings and plenty of runs were the result. Armstrong resented this 'profligacy' with the ball. The problem arose in the First Test where Mailey returned six for 200 off forty-eight overs, more than 4 runs an over. Armstrong didn't let Mailey bowl in Melbourne in the Second Test and was rebuked by the selectors, despite Australia's two massive wins. The skipper threw Mailey the ball in the Third Test at Adelaide where Mailey's match figures of ten wickets for 302 off 61.3 overs was an even worse economy of nearly five runs an over. This was hard for Armstrong, who had been miserly with the ball all through his career and prided himself on not being hit. Directing the field for a gambler such as Mailey annoyed him. The captain wanted defensive fields. The leggie wished for inviting gaps.

The issue was still contentious in the Fourth Test at Melbourne when Mailey took four for 115 off 29.2 overs in England's first innings. It ended amicably in the second innings when Mailey took nine for 121 off forty-seven overs and sealed the match after Armstrong's 123 not out had set his team up for a win.

At forty-two years, Armstrong had grown to 155 kilograms. He wanted to lose weight on the boat trip to England in 1921, so he and the fast bowlers in the squad stoked fires each day, taking a leaf out of the fitness books of former tourists. However, Warwick was the same weight when the boat docked in England, but claiming more muscle than fat. Whatever the ratio, cricket writer Ray Robinson summed him up in his book *On Top Down Under*, saying that any ball Warwick hit or any deckchair he sat on was never the same after the experience.

Armstrong led a strong team for the Ashes, including Ted McDonald, the quick who originated in Tasmania and played for Victoria under Armstrong. The captain, in a powerful position after his crushing win over England, fought the Board over McDonald's inclusion. It nearly cost him his leadership. He won the right to skipper the tourists by one vote. 'I believed that he and Jack Gregory would form the most lethal fast combination ever seen in England,' Armstrong remarked years later. 'They were needed to combat England's expected strong batting line-up. I didn't say I wouldn't go without Ted, but I put my case as persuasively as I could. It was a case of rising above state politics for the country's good.'

McDonald and Gregory took forty-six wickets between them and were instrumental in Australia's three–nil series win. The team also sailed through the entire season under the 42-year-old leader with just two losses. Armstrong's own form was variable, mainly due to recurring bouts of malaria, yet he still achieved the double—with 1213 runs at 41.82 and 100 wickets at 14.44. In the Tests, he hit 152 at 30.4 and took eight wickets at 26.5. He lifted his rating in the important Third Test at Headingley with a first innings score of 77, and bowling returns of two for 44 and two for 6. It was a fine all-round effort, which went a long way towards the 219-run win and the retaining of the Ashes.

Once appointed leader, Armstrong asserted himself through the tour. He complained about three-day matches against the universities of Oxford and Cambridge, saying he wanted only two-day games. This was granted but not before protest from the British establishment, most of whom emanated from these institutions. Worse, when a young Oxford law student, Douglas Jardine, was 98 not out at the end of the second day's play, Armstrong refused to give him an extra over in order for him to reach a coveted century. Jardine saw it as a slight from the 'colonial'. It was not forgotten.

Armstrong caused another stir at the 1921 Imperial Cricket Conference by suggesting that umpires should not be appointed until the first day of a Test. He reckoned that because their pay was meagre 'it would be wise to remove them from [betting] temptation'.

England's cricket supremo, Lord Harris, said he could find no evidence of betting on cricket. 'People don't do it,' Harris told the Australian leader.

'You don't think so, my Lord?' Armstrong replied, sucking on a pipe. 'If you'd like 500 pounds on the next Test, I can arrange it for you.'

In the final Test at the Oval, Armstrong became fed-up with England playing for a draw in its second innings, following its first innings score of eight for 403, and Australia's 389. He placed himself at long-off. When a piece of paper blew near him, he picked it up and pretended to read it.

Later Arthur Mailey asked him why he had done this.

'To see who was playing,' said Armstrong.

England, South Africa and opposition states were never in doubt when Armstrong was on the field.

Warwick Armstrong continued to play until the end of the 1921–22 season. In December of 1922 he retired from his employment with the MCC and joined the Scotch whisky company, Peter Dawson. He wrote about cricket for newspapers after his retirement and in 1935 moved to Sydney to become general manager for James Buchanan's whisky operations in Australia.

Warwick Armstrong led Australia to eight straight wins and never lost a Test while at the helm. He created a standard for assertiveness and a will to win that few have come near. This plus his record that placed him among the three best-performing all-rounders (along with Monty Noble and Keith Miller) in Australian history, made Warwick Armstrong a formidable cricketer.

16

HERBIE COLLINS

21 January 1888 – 28 May 1959

Tests: 19; Captain: 11; Wins: 5; Losses: 2; Draws: 4;
Win ratio: 45.45 per cent

COOL-HAND HERB

Did Herbie Collins throw a Test match? That question has exercised many who played in or witnessed the Fifth Ashes Test at the Oval in 1926. In that game England won the toss, batted and made 280. Australia responded with 302, with captain Collins making 61 in 233 minutes in a painstakingly slow but important partnership with Jack Gregory of 127. Suspicions arose when England batted a second time on the third day after a heavy thunderstorm hit London overnight. The wicket was a sticky and the home team would have been happy making 150 and a lead of around 130. It was turning so much that it would have been tough, even for the great English opening pair, Jack Hobbs and Herbert Sutcliffe. But they were let off the hook. Collins insisted on keeping inexperienced off-spinner Arthur Richardson on at one end for forty-one overs, bowling on leg stump with a packed leg-side field. The bowler had taken just two for 193 so far in the Tests. The skipper had the option of using the very skilled Arthur Mailey (leg spin) and Charlie Macartney. But at a critical time, Collins ignored them. The openers couldn't believe their luck. They made a stand of 172, with Hobbs making 100, and Sutcliffe 161.

England reached 436 and then Australia collapsed in an inept display for 125 (Collins, 4) in its second knock, giving England a win by 289 runs.

It was a timeless Test. There had to be a result, always a good betting option. Given that England had won one of the last nineteen games against Australia, a punter could have received long odds against the home team securing victory.

Hunter 'Stork' Hendry, who was in the touring squad, was ill but present at the game. He remained convinced that it was thrown yet could provide no proof. Former captain Monty Noble expressed his suspicions in private and was critical in public of Collins's tactics. There was also concern about his incessant betting, which sometimes lasted long into the night, even during a Test. Yet the evidence against the Australian skipper remained circumstantial. He returned home with his bank balance apparently intact, but Collins was not conspicuous for his consumption after the tour.

The national selectors would have been aware of rumours about the tour and they may well have suspected him. Even though he wished to continue as captain after that 1926 series (lost nil–one), and his record was good (five wins, two losses and four draws), he was ostracised. Suspicion grew because of Collins's penchant for excessive gambling and losing. He seemed to be often in debt and looking for a way out. He was a mug punter, albeit a big one who had the occasional win. Because of this, the game at the Oval remained in contention. Did he or didn't he? No one could tell from Herbie Collins's face. It remained inscrutable after years of experience playing poker, at which he was a dab hand.

The poker-faced minimalist

The son of an accountant, Herbert Leslie Collins grew up in Darlinghurst and played for Paddington under Monty Noble. Despite the flamboyant style of his hero, Victor Trumper, Collins developed as a defensive, minimalist bat who had no power in his drives. He was an unruffled accumulator, who took longer than usual to impress New South Wales selectors. He made the state side at twenty-four in 1912–13, and in an early game against Tasmania made 284 and hit 598 for the season. It was enough to see him selected in Edgar

Mayne's team that was to tour the United States and Canada in 1913 But the war intervened. Collins enlisted as a trooper in the Light Horse reinforcements and was shipped to Palestine and France in 1915. There he volunteered for the dangerous job of driving ammunition trucks to the front line. During the war, his love of gambling developed into an addiction. He became an 'expert' at betting on everything from two-up and cards to races and sport.

Collins was only a lance corporal after four years of service, but his leadership skills were appreciated by his cricketing peers—several of them with higher ranks—when they elected him captain of the Australian Imperial Forces team of 1919. It beat a full-strength, Test-standard Marylebone Cricket Club team at Lord's and lost only four of twenty-eight matches on its tour of England, which was meant to boost the national morale after the ravages of war. It also lifted and enriched Australian cricket. Collins made 1615 runs and scored five centuries, as well as taking 106 wickets.

Eighteen months later at thirty-one, the trim, 173-centimetre tall Collins began his Test career under Warwick Armstrong against England in the 1920–21 Ashes in Australia. In the First Test at the Sydney Cricket Ground he opened. After a couple of early dropped chances, he was run out for 70. His second innings was a chanceless 104, making him the fifth (and oldest) Australian to score a century in his first Test. Collins went on to an impressive string of scores in the series—64, 162, 24, 59, 32, 5 and 37—for the best aggregate of both teams: 557 at 61.69.

Australia won five–nil, and Collins was part of the squad that soon after took the boat trip to England for the 1921 season.

He made just 17 in the First Test at Nottingham, which Australia won by ten wickets, but broke his thumb catching Ernest Tyldesley at point and missed two Tests. He came back for the Fourth Test at Old Trafford and defended stoutly for 289 minutes for just 40 when Australia collapsed for 175 in its chase of England's four for 362 declared. His stonewalling saved Australia from defeat and kept Armstrong's unbroken record intact.

Herb Collins's impregnable look and cool demeanour helped when he became captain in South Africa in 1921 when Warwick Armstrong was ill. He lifted for the occasion at Durban in the First Test after a mediocre season in England (71 runs at 23.67) curtailed by injury. He was thirty-three and this was his ninth Test. He scored 31 and 47 in a drawn game.

He was bristling with confidence at the Old Wanderers ground, Johannesburg, on 12 November, where he had captained the Australian Imperial Forces in 1919. Then he hammered 235 and took five for 52 with his slow left-armers. Opening again, he linked with Jack Ryder (56) for a 113-run second-wicket partnership, then a 209-run third-wicket link with Jack Gregory (119), who lashed his century in just seventy minutes. Collins, known for his lack of stroke play, advanced by nudges and deflections, mainly behind square leg. But on a placid pitch and against yeoman trundlers, he unfurled late cuts and square cuts en route to 203 in a day, the first double century against the South Africans in South Africa.

This game was also drawn. In the third, he made 54 from Australia's 396 (Ryder a smashing 142), which was one run short of an innings win.

After leaving home in March 1921 an ageing cricketer who had probably missed his chance for prolonged glory because of the war, he returned a victorious skipper of a Test series with a future as the national team's leader.

At the barrier

Herb Collins's success as captain and batsman in South Africa meant that age was no barrier to his later Test career. He led Australia against Arthur Gilligan's Ashes team in 1924–25. Collins won the toss in the First Test at the SCG and lost opening partner Warren Bardsley at 46. He was joined by Bill Ponsford on debut. Maurice Tate, bowling medium-pace swingers, was causing trouble. Collins met the nervous young Ponsford mid-wicket and said he would 'take Tate until he's off'. The newcomer, watching from the other end, said later, 'He [Tate] was formidable, getting great pace off the pitch from his deceptively short [seven-metre] run up. The ball was swerving late from leg and off. I was most grateful to Herbie for taking this until I was settled in. I doubt I would have scored a century but for his selfless approach.'

Collins (114) and Ponsford (110) put on 190, which led to Australia's solid 450. England replied with 298. Collins was aware that with England's powerful batting line-up, led by Hobbs, Sutcliffe, Woolley and Hendren, Australia would have to amass another big score to win. He opened with 60 and was backed by Arthur Richardson (98) and Johnny Taylor (108).

Australia's second innings of 452 left England with 605 to win. A 110-run opening stand by England's finest ever opening pair, Hobbs (57) and Sutcliffe (115), worried Collins. England went on to make 411—the best final innings effort to that time—but it still lost by 193 runs.

Collins led Australia to an 81-run win at the Melbourne Cricket Ground in a high-scoring game, with Sutcliffe hitting 176 and 127. In the Third Test at Adelaide, another that was allowed to go into a seventh day, Australia had two wickets to get and England needed 27 runs at the end of day six. Collins was approached at the team hotel by 'a well-known racing identity', who offered him one hundred pounds to throw the game.

Collins suggested to Arthur Mailey that they throw the visitor down the stairs. The man left in a hurry. The next morning Australia scraped in by 11 runs to take the series, so it could not be construed that Collins had acted improperly on this occasion. But the question does arise: why did the racing crook approach Collins in the first place? And with such a huge (for the time) offer? Was it known in racing circles that he was a man who would punt on anything, even cricket?

The home team went on to a four–one Ashes win.

Collins had an ordinary series after the opening game, making 294 at 29.4.

In his final series in England in 1926 Collins was ill with neuritis and played just four innings, in which he hit 90 at 22.5. Australia lost the Ashes nil–one.

Herb Collins proved to be a laconic, thoughtful captain, who knew how to handle the different types of characters under him with equanimity. His love of betting, which he encouraged in his players, endeared him to them, even though several lost much more than they made. Somehow the mug punter mentality galvanised the squad. They had fun being losers together off the field, but usually winners on it. Even on the unproductive tour of 1926, the squad was a happy one.

Betting even began on the boat over, with Collins putting money on a ribbon-snipping competition. In England, no race meeting was ever left unscathed by the Australian team members, who were often seen poring over guides during matches. Baccarat and poker games went long into the night almost every night and there were no restrictions during big matches. Many of his men had been hardened by war. Nine of them were single and lusty for nightlife.

Collins's hunting grounds around the world, according to Arthur Mailey, who had a high regard for his captaincy, 'were the racetrack, the dog track, a baccarat joint at King's Cross, a two-up school in the Flanders trenches and anywhere a quiet game of poker was being played'.

In nineteen Tests Collins scored 1352 runs (four centuries) at the high average of 45.07. In first-class games, he played 164 matches and hit 9924 runs (thirty-two centuries) at 40.01. He also took 181 wickets at the remarkably good return of 21.38.

Collins became a bookmaker after cricket. His inveterate gambling caught up with him. He made two punting fortunes and lost them. In the early 1930s, he looked for work away from the racetrack but with little success and had trouble making ends meet for himself and his invalid mother. The New South Wales Cricketers' Fund assisted him and he found work as a stipendiary steward. Yet there was little appeal for him. He invariably punted all his earnings.

In 1940, at fifty-one, he married 24-year-old Marjorie Paine. In 1941, he joined the second Australian Imperial Force and had a job as sergeant at Victoria Barracks. This took him back to his addiction. He became a commissioning agent for enlisted men putting money on at the track. He and Marjorie had a son, Lawrence. They divorced after a thirteen-year marriage.

Herbie Collins was a successful captain and notable as a batsman for being one of the few from the pre-First World War era to lift his Test average above 40. His scoring capacity set a standard for others to aspire to in the 1920s.

But his memory as a sporting leader is tainted, fairly or unfairly, by his love of the bet and the doubt over that Oval Test in 1926.

17

WARREN BARDSLEY

6 December 1882 – 20 January 1954

Tests: 41; Captain: 2; Draws: 2;

THE FASTIDIOUS FIGHTER

Warren Bardsley was forty-three when he was appointed captain of Australia to replaced the ill Herb Collins for the Third Test of the 1926 Ashes series in England. He may have been old and with no future as a leader, but he had the respect of all the players, not least because of his performance in the previous Test at Lord's. Then he had become the oldest man to score a century against England. What's more, the left-handed opener carried his bat to 193 not out in a demanding 398 minutes, in which he faced a hostile Harold Larwood. It was Bardsley's highest score in forty-one Tests and put him in a good frame of mind for the great honour of leading his country.

There had never been a better prepared cricketer in fitness and technique. This showed in his captaincy. He had long been fastidious about everything from the pitch to the slope of the oval; from the impact of the light to the efficiency of the sightscreen. When he came to flip the coin for the first time on a damp Headingley oval he was ready for whatever eventuated. It was a good thing. He lost the toss to Arthur Carr and was out first ball, caught off Maurice Tate for a duck. No amount of readiness could have avoided the bitter disappointment this conscientious performer must have felt. Bardsley was said to be 'wedded' to the game for his long first-class career spanning twenty-three years.

Bardsley looked on with mixed feelings as Woodfull (141) and Macartney (151) thwarted Hobbs' strangulating tactic by putting on 235 for the first wicket. The new Australian captain was thrilled that the two batsmen had provided an auspicious start for his leadership, but uneasy that he had not performed better himself. Australia went on to 494 (Arthur Richardson 100 run out).

England replied with 294. With the game cut short by the weather, Bardsley had no choice but to send England in again. That great opening combination, Hobbs (88) and Sutcliffe (94), ruined his chance for first-up glory as a skipper by putting on 156. England was three for 254 at the end of the drawn game.

Bardsley was competent in the use of his varied, fine spin attack of Grimmett, Mailey and Macartney (slow, left-arm orthodox), but lacked inspiration, which was understandable. It was his first Test. Throwing the ball to Jack Ryder on a spinner's wicket, or trying Tommy Andrews, would have seemed extravagant to this intelligent yet conventional cricketer.

Bardsley won the toss at Old Trafford in the Fourth Test. Despite the rotten Manchester weather, which allowed ten balls to be bowled on the first day, he did not make Carr's blunder of sending the opposition's powerful batting line-up in to bat. Carr went down with tonsillitis after the first wet day curtailed play and Hobbs took over as England skipper on the second, becoming the first professional ever to do so. He soon showed a difference in approach as Woodfull and Macartney (dropped fourth ball) settled in, by setting a negative leg theory field of seven men to Fred Root's in-swingers.

The pattern of play was similar to the previous Test. Bardsley managed 15, and again sat back to watch Woodfull (117) and Macartney (109, his third century in successive Tests) put on 192 for the first wicket. Australia went on to 335. England was five for 305 in reply. It was another draw.

Herb Collins had recovered from neuritis in time to lead Australia in the Fifth Test, which England won by 289 runs. It gave the home team the series, one–nil.

Bardsley hit 231 at 57.75, mainly thanks to his historic knock at Lord's, which gave him the top average for the less than satisfactory, rain-damaged series, with its four draws. Nevertheless, he went home and retired with a fine Test record intact. In forty-one matches he had hit 2469 runs, including six centuries, at 40.47. He went on for another two domestic seasons for New South Wales and finished his first-class career with 17,025 runs (fifty-three centuries) at 49.94, one of the best averages of the first quarter of the twentieth century. His 7866 runs on four trips to England were the most by a tourist until Don Bradman, on his fourth tour, passed him and went on to 9837.

Textbook stylist

Warren Bardsley, the son of a Dubbo, New South Wales, school-teacher, had a striking stance. He held his 175-centimetre frame more erect than anyone in the game to that point, and also held his bat straight. His footwork was quick and shrewd, for he never telegraphed his intentions by early movement at the crease. Bardsley had a good range of strokes. Strong wrists and muscular forearms allowed him to drive well, and be confident on the back foot.

Writer A G 'Johnny' Moyes said Bardsley 'never was a stylist' like Trumper, Kippax or Jackson, yet he still had 'style, and he stroked the ball fluently, following the textbook slavishly—right leg across the wicket, bat straight, and with a good follow-through. He moved correctly in defence and knew the most difficult of all things—which ball to leave alone, especially on a biting wicket'.

Bardsley was an early fitness fanatic and was regarded as eccentric for it. A vegetarian, he didn't smoke or drink. He would be up at 6 am for practice at Glebe's Jubilee Oval, and in the winter he played football there, all before breakfast. He walked five kilometres to his job in the Crown Law Office in Macquarie Street, Sydney. At lunchtime he boxed in a city gym, which gave him aerobic conditioning and fast footwork. He was never without a skipping rope on tour and carried a cricket ball everywhere, which he squeezed for wrist strength.

After work he either went to practice or returned to the gym. His teammates regarded him as an obsessive, but Bardsley said it would allow him to play first-class cricket until he was fifty. He didn't quite make it but did play grade cricket until then. His outstanding conditioning over the years did permit him to play on at the highest level into his forties without a discernible drop-off in form or fitness.

Bardsley nearly always opened the batting. He began his career on fast wickets with Trumper and ended it with Bill Woodfull, facing from 1909 to 1926 great England bowlers such as Hirst, Rhodes, Barnes, Foster, Larwood, Tate, Blythe, Brearley and Parkin.

Wisden said of Bardsley after the First World War, 'No left-handed batsman [in the post-war era, 1919–1926] has possessed greater skill in scoring all round the wicket.'

Harsh heroic lessons

Warren Bardsley made several centuries playing for Glebe in club cricket before making the state side at twenty-one. He came to prominence at twenty-five in 1907–08 against the touring England Ashes team, making 108 for New South Wales. A year later he made 264 in a trial game of Australia versus The Rest, and this allowed him to book a trip to England for the 1909 Ashes under Monty Noble. He found his best form in a game against Essex, but was deliberately run out for 219 by Victor Trumper. Victor reminded him later in the dressing room that others wanted to have a hit in the run-up to a Test. It was a tough lesson for the meticulous opener, who had trained himself never to throw his wicket away. Trumper also happened to be his hero.

Bardsley struggled in the Ashes matches until the deciding Fifth Test at the Oval, when he became the first man to hit two centuries in one game—136 and 130. Both innings lasted 225 minutes. In the second knock he was in an opening stand of 180 with Syd Gregory (74).

He led the batting for the tour ahead of Trumper, Armstrong, Ransford, Syd Gregory, Macartney and Noble, with 2180 at 46.39. Bardsley held this form for more than a year until he faced the South Africans during the 1910–1911 Australian summer. Then he scored 132 in the First Test at Sydney and followed with 85, 14, 54, 58, 82, 15, 94 and 39 for an aggregate of 573 at 63.67. He experienced a slump in the following Australian summer against England, hitting just 129 at 16.13, but struck form in the triangular series in England later in the year, 1912, with 121 at Old Trafford and 164 at Lord's, both against the South Africans. He hit just 51 at 17 in three innings in limited chances against England but returned 341 at 113.67 against

South Africa. The combined aggregate for the six-Test series of 392 runs at 65.33 was the most prolific of the three teams. His tour too was strong. He hit 2441 at 51.98.

However Bardsley had to wait eight years, until 1920–21 for another chance at Test level, this time under Warwick Armstrong. Bardsley turned thirty-eight during the season and was consistent with four fifties in an aggregate of 311 at 38.88. It was enough for another tour of England a few months later where he maintained his steady output in the big games with another three Test fifties in an aggregate of 281 at 46.83, which was the top average for the Australians. Seven half-centuries in ten Tests in nine months indicated he had lost little since his peak a decade earlier.

Bardsley played on for Glebe until he was fifty in 1932. Once 'divorced' from the game that was his whole life, he married Gertrude Cope, forty-five, in 1945 at age sixty-two.

A week before his death at seventy-one, Warren Bardsley was at a lunch attended by Douglas Jardine and the then prime minister, Bob Menzies. Jardine complimented Bardsley, saying it was a fine feat to average more than 40 in forty Tests, especially the way he had made his runs. Menzies, a cricket lover, told Bardsley that he would go down in history and be remembered by people when poor politicians were forgotten.

These comments pleased Bardsley a great deal, and were fitting tributes. Warren Bardsley had played determinedly, with distinction, skill and cool courage at the first-class and Test level for nearly a quarter of a century.

18

JACK RYDER

8 August 1889 – 3 April 1977

Tests: 20; Captain: 5; Wins: 1; Losses: 4;
Win ratio: 20 per cent

THE VICTORIAN HAMMER

Jack Ryder took over as captain during the 1928–29 Ashes series in Australia, when the national team's fortunes were at a low ebb. This hard-hitting batsman from Victoria was thirty-nine and past his peak. Ryder had never been secure in Test cricket. But the taciturn Ryder lifted for the occasion and did not allow his own game to fall apart under the pressure exerted by a powerful England team. Led by Percy Chapman, it included George Geary, Wally Hammond, Patsy Hendren, Jack Hobbs, Douglas Jardine, Harold Larwood, Maurice Leyland, Herbert Sutcliffe, Maurice Tate and Jack White. They formed the backbone of one of the most talented and tough squads ever to tour Australia from any country. Ryder headed the Australian aggregates with 492 at 54.67, just pipping the reliable Bill Woodfull (491 at 54.56).

He presided over an ageing team in decline. The great fast bowler Jack Gregory broke down in the First Test and retired. Ryder was forced to rely on his top-class leggie, Clarrie Grimmett. Grimmett took twenty-three wickets but suffered from overbowling and no support against England's best ever batting line-up next to Peter May's team in the 1950s. Grimmett's wickets cost 44.52 runs each. His main support was from Victoria's Don Blackie, forty-six, with his off spin, which netted a useful fourteen wickets at 31.71. This negligible attack allowed Hammond to belt 905 runs at 113.13 and four other bats to average more than 50. It led to a lot of leather chasing and a one–four drubbing.

The 1928–29 Ashes would have been a complete disaster for Australia but for the opportunities the Tests presented for the introduction of new blood. One debutant was the brilliant Archie Jackson, who catapulted onto the Test scene with a magnificent 164 at Adelaide in the Fourth Test. Another making his first appearance ever in Tests was Don Bradman, who, from that series on, would for two decades dominate the game like no other player in the history of cricket.

Jack Ryder was a conventional skipper who perhaps lacked the shrewdness, lateral thinking, daring, inspiration and 'sixth sense' required for greatness. He didn't display imagination in the 1928–29 series, but there was little he could do with such a meagre attack. He made an error in not supporting Bradman after he failed in the First Test at Brisbane with scores of 18 and 1. But in fairness, he needed pace bowlers more than anything else. So he asked the selectors for them rather than supporting the new young 'star'. It led to Bradman, twenty, carrying the drinks as twelfth man at the Sydney Cricket Ground in the Second Test. 'He did a good job too,' Ryder remarked later, 'but I had the impression he didn't want the position again.'

The selectors were timid. Apart from the youthful Don, the average age of the team at Sydney was thirty-five. Instead of going for more youth the selectors fell back on experience. The upshot was two thrashings in the first two Tests. In the Second, Ryder scored 25 out of Australia's 253. England's response was 636, with Hammond hitting 251. Ryder came out firing in his second innings, as if intent on taking the game from the tourists as quickly as possible. A half-century in thirty-six minutes was the result. But at 79 inevitably the mayhem was over, when he was caught off Larwood. Australia reached 397. England only had to score 15 to win and lost two wickets doing it.

Ryder was given Bradman back for the Third Test, along with two young all-rounders, Ron Oxenham and Ted a'Beckett. The selectors had received a clear message from the press, which reflected strong public opinion. A youth policy had to be invoked.

It nearly paid off in the Third Test at Melbourne, when Ryder hit a strong 112 in the first innings, aided by Bradman (79) and a'Beckett (41). This innings was vintage Ryder in front of a supportive, urging Melbourne crowd, who loved the 185-centimetre, 85-kilogram heavy hitter from the sports-mad and tribal Collingwood. Ryder's batting style left much to be desired. At times he looked flat-footed as he stood and delivered. He gripped the bat handle high in the manner of a tailender intent on quick runs in a short stay. But Ryder had a very good eye. He could defend as well as the next man, and hit harder than most players in history. His gift was to pick the right ball to crunch. It worked in 1928–29 and might have led to two wins instead of one if Bert Oldfield hadn't run out Bradman (58) in the final innings of the match. Australia lost by 12 runs.

Despite the setback Australia was on a winning roll, which led to a win in the final Test at Melbourne. This time, when Bradman joined Ryder, who was a notoriously bad runner, they were circumspect between the wickets. An unbroken partnership of 83 (Ryder 57 not out, Bradman 37 not out after 123 in the first innings) delivered a five-wicket win. Ryder could fairly say that he had skippered Australia out of one of its worst slumps and put it on the road to being competitive again, quite a turnaround in one series.

He was one of three selectors for the coming tour of England in 1930. He felt the other two, Richard Llewellyn Jones and Dr Charles Dolling, would select him. They told Ryder during a Victoria versus New South Wales match in Sydney that they had not chosen him. It was one of those cruel decisions that selectors felt compelled to make from time to time. Ryder was bitterly disappointed. Yet he took the dumping with courage, hitting a century off New South Wales bowling on the day the decision had been taken against him. There was protest in Victoria, but Ryder remained dignified and would not be drawn into criticism of his co-selectors and their choices for the fifteen-man squad. Even as a later radio commentator and journalist he remained mute on the subject of his 'dismissal'.

Jack Ryder went out of Test cricket with a superb average of 51.63 from 1394 runs with 3 hundreds in twenty Tests. This record was substantiated by his first-class career. Ryder scored 10,499 runs at

44.29. He hit twenty-four centuries for Victoria with a highest score of 295 against New South Wales. Ryder was also a useful medium-pace swing bowler, taking 237 wickets at 29.8.

Jack Ryder's career began at Collingwood at seventeen in 1906-07. He made the state side at twenty-two and was a regular for the next twenty years. Ryder came into national consideration at twenty-five when he blasted 242 against South Australia during the 1914–15 season. He was also taking bags of wickets with his then medium-fast swing. The slow-talking, laconic Victorian was one of a few players who could honestly claim that if the First World War had not eventuated he would have had an even more illustrious Test career. With first-class cricket suspended in 1915, Ryder, a bootmaker by trade and a boot salesman by profession, took time out to get married to Fan Smith. They had two children.

When Tests resumed in 1920–21 Ryder was thirty-one during the five–nil sweep by Warwick Armstrong's strong team. He was selected for the 1921 tour of England but couldn't break into the Test side which won three–nil. Yet he could claim to be a member of a squad that only lost two games in that highly successful tour.

He struggled on the lower, slower England wickets. Ryder's game was based on powerful driving on the front foot, especially on the on-side, and he struggled against England's county bowlers, who relied on swing and short-of-a-length, wear-the-batsman-down tactics on softer pitches. Batsmen who could play back did better.

Free of such conditions in South Africa on the way home, Ryder was second in the aggregates (334) and first in the averages (111.33). He had four out of four fine knocks—78 not out and 58 at Durban in the First Test; 56 at Old Wanderers in the Second; and 142 at Newlands in the Third.

When England toured Australia in 1924–25, Ryder, thirty-five, strained his back bowling for Victoria and the injury kept him out of the first two Tests, which Australia won. He came back for the Third at Adelaide and arrived at the crease when the score was five for 118 in the first innings. It was soon six for 119. Tommy Andrews joined Ryder and Australia looked likely to collapse for about 150. Then a bizarre run of injuries changed fortunes. Tate, who had bowled Australian captain Herbie Collins for 3 and had trapped Johnny Taylor lbw for 3, limped off with foot blisters. England skipper Arthur Gilligan soon followed him, not long after dismissing Ponsford for 31. Gilligan had strained a thigh muscle in his eighth over. Ryder and Andrews, with luck on their side, set about restoring the Australian innings. Ryder was severe on 'Tich' Freeman, the talented little leggie from Kent. Australia's score mounted to 253, when Andrews (72) was bowled by Roy Kilner. Ryder plundered on and took control of the game, driving with tremendous power on a good Adelaide wicket conducive to his front-foot lunges. He reached a century—his second in successive Tests three years apart—and then stepped up a notch. On 145, Ryder hit one low chance with enormous force to mid-on fielder Freeman, who collapsed in pain, his wrist badly bruised. Freeman became the third bowler to leave the field. His figures of one (Jack Gregory, bowled for 6) for 107 off eighteen overs reflected Ryder's pulverising.

Last man in, Arthur Mailey, arrived at the wicket at nine for 416, with Ryder on 161. Ryder had instructions from Collins to go for everything. He obeyed, realising that message conveyed two meanings. Collins wanted at least half an hour to bowl at England before stumps and hitting out was the only way Ryder would get near a double hundred. The chance for this came rarely in the average Test batsman's career. Ryder launched at everything and reached 201. Mailey (27) then deliberately had himself stumped with the team score at 489.

Ryder's unconquered first innings was followed in the second by another hard-hitting knock of 88, making him the first Test player ever to hit a double century and fifty in the one Test. It demonstrated that Jack Ryder, a late developer, whose career had been foreshortened by the war, was hungry for big cricket. Despite his back injury, he was strong and fitness conscious. He didn't drink or smoke and did extra running to stay in condition.

Jack Ryder ended the 1924–25 series with 363 runs at 72.6. He sent down forty overs for four wickets at 33.

English conditions again troubled Ryder on the tour of 1926. In four Tests he managed just 73 runs at 24.33. Back in Australia for the 1926–27 season he was involved in a massacre of New South Wales bowling at the Melbourne Cricket Ground. On Christmas Eve 1926,

New South Wales was dismissed for 221. Christmas and Boxing Days were rest days. Play resumed on 27 December and Victoria hit one for 573. Woodfull made 133. Ponsford was 334 not out and 'Stork' Hendry 86 not out at stumps. Ponsford was out next morning (day three) for 352 and Ryder came to the wicket with the score on two for 594. He thumped 295 in Victoria's record score of 1107. He hit 33 fours and 6 sixes, which had never before been done on the huge MCG.

Ryder retired from state cricket after the 1931–32 season aged forty-two years. His last innings was against Queensland at Brisbane, where he made 71 before being bowled by new Aboriginal pace sensation, Eddie Gilbert.

At fifty-six Ryder was appointed a national selector at the beginning of the 1945–46 season. He joined Don Bradman and Edmund Dwyer in choosing Australia's first post-Second World War team, which toured New Zealand and played one Test in March 1946. Ryder remained in this non-paying position for another thirty-eight years until the age of eighty-four in the 1973–74 season, a period of monumental service to the game in Australia.

By the beginning of the twenty-first century, seventy years after being forced out of Test cricket, Jack Ryder was just one of five Australians who had played twenty or more innings and held his average above 50. He was the first ever. The others were Don Bradman, Greg Chappell, Allan Border and Steve Waugh. It puts Ryder's good eye, powerful hitting and cool demeanour into perspective. Jack Ryder is in an exclusive category of high-calibre performers.

19

BILL WOODFULL

22 August 1897 – 11 August 1965

Tests: 35; Captain: 25; Wins: 14; Losses: 7; Draws: 4;
Win ratio: 56 per cent

THE PRINCIPLED PRINCIPAL

Bill Woodfull, who had a distinguished life as a courageous opening bat, a highly principled Australian captain and a headmaster, was defined by one comment during the bodyline dispute, cricket's most publicised incident.

'There are two teams out there, Mr Warner,' Woodfull told England's manager at Adelaide during the Third Ashes Test of 1932–33. 'One is trying to play cricket and one is not.'

'Plum' (Pelham) Warner, a former captain of England and very much an establishment man, was stunned. He had come into the dressing room when Woodfull, Australia's captain, was out after a torrid time facing England's speedster Harold Larwood. Woodfull, lying on a massage table, had suffered fearsome blows in the chest and shoulder during a spell in which England delivered bodyline, a then-legitimate style of bowling designed to either injure or dismiss batsmen.

'It is too great a game for spoiling by the tactics your team is adopting,' Woodfull added. 'I don't approve of them. It might be better if I do not play the game.'

This final remark indicated Woodfull was considering not letting his team play on. It was a seminal moment in the history of cricket. Woodfull, a guileless man of high moral principles, would not let his bowlers attempt to retaliate with similar methods. England's tactics, directed by its captain, Scottish-born lawyer Douglas Jardine, were not in the spirit of the game as understood by its guardians since its inception.

Leo O'Brien, Australia's twelfth man, was in the dressing room and witnessed Woodfull's confrontation with Warner. Seconds later O'Brien told Australian opening bat Jack Fingleton ('word for word' according to O'Brien) what had been said. Fingleton, a journalist by profession, supposedly informed a fellow correspondent, Claude Corbett. Corbett asked Woodfull and Warner to verify the quote. Woodfull refused to comment. Warner admitted it was correct.

The Australian press ran the story. England's press, ill-informed and 20,000 kilometres away, editorialised and accused Woodfull of being a 'squealer'. This was as ignorant as it was wrong. The opener had shown the highest courage and application during the fateful series.

Some urged Woodfull to retaliate by choosing bowlers such as Victoria's bruiser, Laurie Nash, who could deliver bodyline at England. But Woodfull would have none of it. A tit-for-tat use of these intimidatory tactics would destroy cricket. The main problem was the field placing. Up to eight men were on the leg side. Five or six of them were close to the batsman, crouched like toy soldiers, waiting for the mishit catch. This left the batsman limited options against Larwood, who was unerringly accurate during the 1932–33 series. If the batsman responded by hooking, he would soon either be hit or would give a catch. The result was endless bruising and lost wickets.

Woodfull made a mockery of the squealer remark through the bodyline series, especially in that Adelaide Test. Despite being struck in the chest by Larwood in the first innings, he defended for an hour, making 22. He began the second innings, amidst mounting tension, with Australia needing 532 to win. Woodfull batted with a set jaw and dead-straight bat, as if determined that no ball would get through him. He would be there at the finish, come bodyline or bedevilment. He used a short backlift, which diminished the opportunity of anything sliding under his blade, to push forward in defence or to pinch a single. Woodfull's style was ungainly but effective. For much of his career before that 1932–33 series, he had been known as the unbowlable. Very few bowlers, from junior grades through to Test cricket, had managed to hit his wicket.

In the last innings at Adelaide he lost Fingleton bowled by Larwood for a duck, leaving Australia at one for 3. In came Don Bradman in a headstrong mood. He was soon swinging at Larwood with success. He saw him off. Later, Jardine set a bodyline field, much to the crowd's anger. Bradman countered by using his unorthodox slugs into the off-side field. It worked. Woodfull was steadfast and hopeful at the other end. But instead of settling down after the 'victory' over Larwood, the young Bradman continued with a rush of blood against left-hander Hedley Verity and was caught for 66 in seventy-three minutes. Woodfull was disappointed that he hadn't told his superstar to settle down after the initial burst. The captain knew that Bradman, with his unquenchable capacity for runs, was the only player in the team who could have mounted the individual double or triple century needed to win. A sad procession of wickets followed as all but Woodfull capitulated. Australia was dismissed at nine for 193, Oldfield being unable to bat after Larwood had fractured his skull in the first innings. This delivered a 338-run win to England and Jardine, for he was the master of these tough, merciless yet successful tactics.

Woodfull carried his bat to be 73 not out. It was his highest score in a series aggregate of 305 for an average of 33.89, a fine performance given the extraordinary circumstances. In all he batted for nearly twenty hours in the Tests and faced more of the onslaught than anyone. Woodfull's approach was to wear down the aggressors, scoring about 30 runs a session. But with no other batsman except Bradman with any sustained counter-tactic, Australia went down one–four in the series.

Woodfull led by example and cared for his men. In one innings he told a jittery Bill O'Reilly, who had no pretensions to be a batsman against England's bodyliners, 'Listen carefully, Tiger, I want you, above all, not to get hit.'

'What a relief,' O'Reilly wrote later. 'Could any shivering batsman ever have been presented with a more reassuring exit (from the dressing room) than that? I have always been quick to offer him my undying gratitude for those few kind words in my biggest moment of crisis.'

Woodfull was the benevolent leader with all his subordinates, dispensing relief like this at moments of crisis, quiet rebukes for indiscretions on and off the field, and well-defined directives.

In the end Woodfull's wisdom and stand against bodyline was justified. After English batsmen had received the tactics from the West Indies and their county opponents, it became clear, even to those born-to-rule stubborn heads of the 1933 Marylebone Cricket Club, where bodyline would take the game. If it persisted, each country would produce its red-leather thugs, trained to fell opponents in acts that would be copied up and down the grades of cricket everywhere, with deadly results. Feverish protest by English batsmen being struck led to the tactic effectively being outlawed by 1934.

William Maldon Woodfull received his early moral and cricket training from his father, Thomas, a Methodist preacher from Maldon in central Victoria, who was transferred to Collingwood. Thomas laid out a backyard pitch, fenced it with wire netting to stop wayward balls smashing neighbours' windows, and bowled to Bill every spare hour in the summer. He taught Bill a strong defence and asked his son to be patient. Just like the right opportunity in life, the right ball to hit came along for those who waited. But young William Maldon had a trait that no training could bring—temperament. It helped him through a bout of rheumatic fever in his mid-teens that weakened his strong frame and threatened his cricket career.

Woodfull, broad-shouldered and tallish at 180 centimetres, became a country teacher, and regularly hit big scores from 1916–17 to 1919–20. In 1920–21, the second season of first-class games after the First World War, he made the Victorian Colts and hit 186 not out against South Australia. This pushed him at twenty-three straight into the state Second XI, where he made 227 against New South Wales. These two big strides took Woodfull into the first-class arena at twenty-four, where he remained until his retirement from big cricket in 1934. He scored 153 run out versus Western Australia in his first season, 1921–22.

In this period he studied an arts degree at night while teaching at Williamstown High. The Australian team seemed impregnable and

Woodfull was making sure he had good professional training, whether or not he moved up in the cricket world. Vacancies at the top of the Test order appeared on his first tour of England in 1926. In his third Test innings—in the Third Test at Headingley—Woodfull opened, lost his partner Warren Bardsley for a duck and then embarked on an innings that cemented his place in the Test side. He put on 235 for the second wicket with Charlie Macartney (151) and went on to 141, before Tate bowled him. Woodfull followed that up with the top score of 117 in his next innings, in the Fourth Test at Old Trafford. His first Test series netted 306 runs at 51. Only Bardsley and Macartney—two of the biggest names in the history of Australian cricket—did better.

Woodfull was on top for the tour itself, topping the aggregates and averaging 57. He was the first player to do this on his initial tour. *Wisden* chose him as the first of its 'Five Cricketers of the Year'. Woodfull toured New Zealand at the end of the 1927–28 series and hit a career best of 284 versus New Zealand in an unofficial Test at Auckland.

On returning from England, Woodfull, now twenty-nine, married Gwen King, whom he had first met when she sang in the choir at his father's Albert Park church. They had three children.

Woodfull started the 1928–29 Ashes series with a duck, then followed up with 30 not out, 68, 111 run out, 1, 107, 1, 30, 102 and 35, for an aggregate of 491 at 54.56. Jack Ryder (492 at 56.67) did a fraction better. In the middle of all this Woodfull crashed 275 not out for Victoria against England. Its bowlers were thoroughly sick of him during the season. In all he batted about thirty hours against the visitors. England's bowlers must have had nightmares about that forward push or deflection for runs.

It was enough for selectors to realise that he was rock-like, reliable material in all seasons on any style of wicket. This, plus his rectitude and popularity with his fellow performers, made him right for Test leadership. But when his friend Jack Ryder was pushed aside in early 1930, Woodfull was at first reluctant to take over as captain for the tour of England. He felt he was letting a teammate down.

One of the selectors, Richard Llewellyn, tried to talk him around. 'Jack's not been selected to tour,' he told Woodfull, who had experience captaining Victoria. 'Someone has to lead.'

It wasn't enough. The Victorian XI manager, W L Kelly, tackled the problem another way by persuading Woodfull to nominate for a board ballot for the captaincy. Dr Charles Dolling, from South Australia, nominated Vic Richardson. Woodfull won the ballot and thus led the most youthful fifteen ever to tour England. Eleven had never played there before.

Woodfull opened the tour with a fine hundred under the Cathedral at Worcester, only to be happily overshadowed by Don Bradman, who carved out 236 not out in 275 minutes. Grimmett took nine for 86 in the county's two innings and Australia went on to win by an innings and 165 runs. England had been caught napping. After the Hammond-led slaughter of 1928–29 in Australia, the tourists were expected to be easy pickings. It had been said, not for the first time, that they were 'the weakest squad ever to come to these shores'.

After Worcester, critics took stock. Australia had a very solid opener–captain not known for capitulation. It had the best leg-spinner in the world in Grimmett. Then there was Bradman, who was now not quite quality 'x' in England. Yorkshire's fine all-rounder Wilfred Rhodes saw his innings at Worcester and told a friend he had just watched 'the greatest batsman the world had ever seen'. The pronouncement proved accurate. Woodfull had a secret weapon worth not one, not two but three top Test batsmen. Bradman accumulated 974 at 139.14 in the Tests.

Woodfull had a poor First Test at Trent Bridge, but made up for it at Lord's, first in a terrific opening stand of 162 with Bill Ponsford (81), then with 231 with Bradman (254). Woodfull hit 155 and was 26 not out in the second innings when Australia won by seven wickets, thus squaring the series. At Leeds in the Third Test, he contributed 50 to a second-wicket stand of 192 with Bradman, who was en route to sporting immortality with 309 not out in a day. Rain robbed the game of more than a day's play and Australia's chances for another win.

At Old Trafford more foul weather didn't even allow the completion of two innings. Still, Woodfull was steady at the beginning, scoring 54. He gave his country another fine start (54 again) in the deciding Fifth Test at the Oval. Australia only needed one innings of 695, with Bradman (232) the match winner again.

Woodfull's series was good with 345 runs at 57.5—figures that were second in aggregate and average to only Bradman. The skipper went home a satisfied Ashes winner. A few months later, he led his team to

a four–one series win over the first ever West Indies side to visit
Australia. He unselfishly dropped himself down the list to number six
to allow Archie Jackson to slot in as opener with Bill Ponsford. The
experiment didn't work. Jackson was ill and never reached anything
like his potential. Woodfull was uncomfortable down the order and
when he was finally put back at the top, he hit 83. His tally was a
modest 204 at 34.

Woodfull opened the entire series against the first South African
team in 1931–32 and returned his best figures yet—421 runs at
70.17, with a top score of 161 at the Melbourne Cricket Ground in
the Third Test. Again, he was second only to Bradman (806 runs at
201.5).

In 1932–33, the aggressive Jardine caused Woodfull's experience
to turn sour, and throughout 1933 bodyline bitterness looked set to
cause a postponement of the 1934 tour of England. But agreements
that such tactics would not be repeated caused Woodfull to agree to
take on the 1934 assignment of restoring goodwill in the game.

Only once did the tactic resurface, in a game against Nottingham-
shire. Bill Voce, one of the bodyline exponents in 1932–33, delivered
it in Australia's first innings. Woodfull told the county's secretary that
if Voce tried it again in the second innings, he would take his team
back to London. Voce was off the field with a claimed 'leg strain' for
the rest of the game.

Woodfull had a poor 1934 series for him, scoring 228 at 28.5 with
a top score of 73. Yet it didn't matter. Woodfull was there to lead, while
Bradman (758 at 94.75) and Ponsford (569 at 94.83) made enough
runs, and Grimmett (twenty-five wickets at 26.72) and O'Reilly
(twenty-eight at 24.93) took the wickets. Australia won back the Ashes
two–one.

Woodfull retired after this triumphant series, having played thirty-
five tests (twenty-five as captain) for 2300 runs at 46 with seven
centuries. He was even weightier in 173 first-class matches, amassing
13,392 runs (forty-nine centuries) at 65, the third best average by an
Australian after Ponsford (65.18) and Bradman (95.14).

The only criticism of Woodfull's captaincy was his caution. He
tended to delay declarations. His experience during bodyline caused
him to stack his 1934 team with batsmen and leave the tough job of
dismissing England to Grimmett and O'Reilly, who bowled 730 overs

between them. Only Tim Wall was a back-up to the spinners, but he had a poor series, taking six wickets at 78.67.

Yet this prudence was outweighed by the clear-thinking, common-sense decisions he made with limited resources that were concentrated on the superb spin combination of Grimmett and O'Reilly. Woodfull showed his skill in the way he handled them. He had no choice but to use them more than he would have liked, but he still managed to spell them judiciously. It helped that both bowlers loved being on and rarely lost control through fatigue.

Woodfull's outstanding leadership capacities centred on the team's wellbeing. He set high standards with his moral and physical courage, and this influenced his players, a varied bunch. Some, like him, were teetotallers, but he was tolerant of the drinkers, as long as they kept the socialising within sensible bounds and were fit for selection. He was unselfish and patient on tour, inspiring his men to do their best for him. Woodfull behaved like a benign headmaster (he became one at Melbourne High School), who was aware of each player's personal life, problems, hopes and aspirations. The players and their families appreciated this. It built great trust in him as a captain.

20

VIC RICHARDSON

7 September 1894 – 29 October 1969

Tests: 19; Captain: 5; Wins: 4; Draws: 1;
Win ratio: 80 per cent

VALIANT VIC

If popularity and fun off the field were the yardsticks for good leadership, Vic Richardson would be ranked high in Australia's pantheon of captains. Those accompanying him to South Africa for the 1935–36 series, which Australia won four–nil, voted it the 'happiest' tour they had ever been on. While contentment in a squad might appear irrelevant to success, in fact the two usually went hand-in-hand. It was no coincidence that under Richardson Australia went undefeated on the tour, winning thirteen out of sixteen matches, ten of them by an innings. This had never been done before, and although South Africa was weak due to injuries and the death of one of its better players, Tests still had to be fought and won on foreign soil. There was always the chance that a big game would be lost because players had become disinterested or homesick. Or perhaps they had had a too convivial night. Only a strong captain like Richardson could keep most players up to the mark most of the time. The skipper also had to keep the morale up for the lesser tour games.

Richardson had a poor series himself, scoring just 84 at 16.8, but it was his skill as an organiser, coordinator and captain that counted when he, like Bill Woodfull before him, had the mighty double of Grimmett (forty-four wickets at 14.59) and O'Reilly (twenty-seven at 17.04) to call on. It didn't matter that he had only one other effective option (Ernie McCormick, fifteen at 27.87). The South Africans were out of their depth facing the two best leg-spinners in the world.

Sturdy for Sturt

Victor York Richardson was seventeen when he started work in Adelaide's Produce Department and began his club cricket with Sturt at eighteen. This 'Collingwood six-footer'—at 181 centimetres and weighing 76 kilograms—spent the winters as a fleet-footed Sturt halfback flanker, who played what would be called 'rebound' football in the modern era. Richardson was more an attacking player than defender, with a penchant for running off his opponent and drop-kicking the ball into the forward line. Vic's dapper moustache and suave looks matched his on-field dash, which saw him often in the centre, where he didn't have to worry about his opponent. This style was also apparent in his cricket. He liked to attack and enjoyed opening, where he was in the play and could attempt to dictate it from the first ball. His batting, like his football, was fearless. He was the type who relished taking on a big opponent or a bruising fast bowler.

Richardson's ugly stance and grip was a clue to his intentions. The right or bottom hand held the bat as low on the handle as possible, which was the classic cutter and hooker's position. It caused him to bend his right knee and hunch his shoulders. Yet what he lost in appearance by his stance and grip he gained in effectiveness. They allowed him better control to wield the willow square of the wicket. Richardson loved nothing better than hooking a fast bowler off the eyebrows early in an innings to let him know, as he would say, 'who was boss'.

Like Warren Bardsley, Richardson was a fitness junkie sixty years before it became mandatory at state and Test level. During his twenties, it wasn't unusual for Richardson to play, train or compete at a different sport almost every day of the week. Cricket and football, depending on the season, would be accompanied by baseball, lacrosse, basketball, golf (off a 12 handicap), swimming and gymnasium workouts.

Richardson was twenty at the outbreak of the 1914–18 war and could claim that the conflict robbed him of a chance of an early break into first-class cricket. He had to wait until he was twenty-four in 1918–19—when he married Vida Knapman—to represent his state in a limited competition. He scored 72 and 48 in his first game for South Australia against Victoria at the Melbourne Cricket Ground and two games later in 1919–20 scored 134.

At twenty-seven in 1921–22 he progressed to captain of South Australia and at the end of the season he toured New Zealand, making 112 in an unofficial Test at Auckland. In 1923, at twenty-eight, he was elected skipper of the state football team, and in all took part in three premierships for Sturt. This was on top of representing South Australia at baseball, which helped him become one of the best all-round fielders ever, whether catching close to the wicket or moving fast in the covers. During this energetic decade he also won two state handicap tennis doubles championships.

A dapper thirty-year-old with a filmstar-like black moustache, Vic Richardson finally cracked the Test team in 1924–25. He made his first appearance at the Sydney Cricket Ground against Arthur Gilligan's team, along with three other debutants, Arthur Richardson (no relation) and Bill Ponsford for Australia, and Tich Freeman for England. Vic Richardson made 42 and 18, but it was in the Second Test beginning at Melbourne on New Year's Day 1925 that he made an international name for himself.

Herb Collins won the toss and batted. Richardson came to the wicket at four for 208 after Bill Ponsford and Johnny Taylor had put on 161 for the fourth wicket. Richardson began playing his strokes from the first ball he faced, keeping the pressure on his opponents. He gave just one chance, with a mishit hook at 67, and continued on to score a century in 178 minutes.

Johnny Douglas was brought on with the second new ball. Richardson proceeded to hit 21 (4, 4, 4, 4, 2, 3) off one over, a record for the MCG. At 135, and with a double century a distinct possibility because of his total control over the bowling, he drove deep in the MCG outfield for 3 off Maurice Tate. A misfield close to the wicket saw Richardson call for a fourth run. Percy Chapman, one of England's finest ever fielders, underhanded the ball into the stumps, running out Richardson for 138.

Australia went on to 600 (Ponsford 138) and needed all of them, as Hobbs and Sutcliffe put on a 283-run opening stand, which helped England make 479. Richardson made just 8 in Australia's second innings of 250, which led to an 81-run win when England managed 290 in its second innings. Richardson only managed 4 and a duck in the Third Test at Adelaide, which in a competitive batting environment was not enough for him to retain his place. Series figures of 210 runs at an average of 35 were not strong enough in the period following the First World War, with plenty of talented rivals, including Collins, Arthur Richardson, Johnny Taylor, Bill Ponsford, Jack Gregory, Jack Ryder, Warren Bardsley, Alan Kippax and Tommy Andrews, all fighting to secure a Test spot.

Despite his up and down experiences at the top of cricket, Richardson took some solace after the 1924–25 series when, at thirty-one, he was inducted into the American Hall of Fame as the best Australian athlete of 1925. This was for his performances in a wide range of sports. He was also rewarded with a job as a representative of Spaldings, the sports goods manufacturer.

Happily hooking Harold

Vic Richardson didn't get another chance to make a claim for his Test spot until a month after his thirty-fourth birthday in October 1928, when he slammed a magnificent 231 in 313 minutes at Adelaide for South Australia against Percy Chapman's team. One shot—a hooked six off Harold Larwood—above all stayed in the mind of selector Dr Charles Dolling, who now had useful ammunition to push for his fellow South Australian at the selection table. When Larwood ran through Australia at Brisbane, taking six for 32 and two for 30, and the home team was humiliated with a 675-run loss, Dolling had a persuasive argument for Richardson's selection. His double hundred was not a flash in the pan against England. He had made runs against the tourists ever since they began arriving again after the war. Not only that, he appeared to have Larwood's measure, and he was a natural choice to open, having been a regular starter of South Australian innings. Dolling had his way. Richardson was selected along with Otto Nothling, twenty-eight, and Don Blackie, forty-six. Any idea of a youth policy was shelved. Don Bradman, twenty, was dumped after one try-out. Charlie Kelleway (ill from food poisoning) and Jack Gregory (retired after a troublesome knee cartilage collapsed) were unavailable.

Richardson began well but was bowled by Larwood for 27 in the first innings in the Second Test at the SCG. Tate had him caught for a duck in the second innings. Australia lost by eight wickets.

The selectors, realising that this series was as good as lost, now did an about-face and took the youth policy off the shelf. Bradman was selected again. Richardson was retained for the Third Test at Melbourne, but Larwood had him twice for just 3 and 5. He was dumped to make way for the dashing twenty-year-old Archie Jackson at Adelaide, who justified his inclusion by making 164.

Richardson's series of 35 runs at 8.75 was not enough for him to hold a regular place in 1928–29, but he was still close to selection—thanks to loyal support from Charles Dolling—as tour skipper for 1930. It was testimony to the harmony he generated among his peers, and his leadership skills, so well displayed for South Australia. In the end, Jack Ryder was forced out and replaced by fellow-Victorian Bill Woodfull, with Richardson as Woodfull's deputy. Despite his ordinary 1930 Test series of 98 runs at 19.6, and being dropped (for Jackson again) from the deciding last Test at the Oval, Richardson helped keep the team morale high.

Richardson was not selected in the 1930–31 series against the West Indies or the 1931–32 series versus South Africa. But, at thirty-eight, he was returned to the Test team for the bodyline series of 1932–33. His bluster matched his courage as he took on Larwood, Voce and Bowes, with whom he had had several titanic duels. But Larwood was at his peak and more accurate than in the previous two Ashes series. On top of that he and the other bowlers could use that notorious ring of close-in leg fielders. Like all his fellow batsmen, except for Bradman, who was still reduced to fifty per cent of his best, Richardson failed to counter them. Yet it wasn't through lack of thirst for the fight.

After three Tests in which Richardson had managed five starts in six innings (49, 0, 34, 32, 28, 21), he put up his hand for the toughest job of all in this series—opening—after Bill Ponsford and Jack Fingleton had failed to make headway. Woodfull thought it was worth a try at Brisbane in the Fourth Test. In hot conditions, Richardson saw himself in and then launched an attack at the flagging Larwood, hitting him out of the firing line. He and Woodfull put on 133 for the opening stand. It took keeper Les Ames, standing up at the stumps to Wally Hammond, to get rid of Richardson, stumped for a fine 83.

In the second innings, he saw Larwood off again. This time it was spinner Hedley Verity who had him caught for 32. Australia lost by six wickets. Larwood more than squared the ledger in these encounters with Richardson by snaring him early for a pair in the Fifth Test at the SCG. England won again, by eight wickets, and took the series four–one.

After the successful 1935–36 season, Richardson, now forty-one, lost the Test and state captaincy to Don Bradman, twenty-eight, who had moved to South Australia. In nineteen Tests Richardson scored 706 at 23.53.

He went on for one more season under Bradman at State level and then retired from first-class cricket at the end of the 1936–37 season. In 184 matches he scored 10,727 runs at 37.63.

Vic and Vida Richardson had a son and two daughters, then twelve grandchildren, including Ian, Greg and Trevor Chappell, who all played Test cricket.

At forty-seven, Richardson ended his cricket career at Sturt in 1941 after thirty seasons, and then joined the RAAF after Vida died. He was posted to India and finished the war with the rank of squadron leader. He moved from a pre-Second World War position with insurance group, Australian Mutual Provident Society, to a rewarding post-war career as cricket broadcaster. He married Peggy Chandler after the war and she accompanied him when he did ABC radio broadcasts with England's former skipper Arthur Gilligan of the first post-war Ashes Tests in Australia in 1946–47.

Vic Richardson made memorable the line, 'What do you think, Arthur?'

He was a cheerful, unorthodox and enterprising leader, who liked to lead from the front with forceful batting.

Victor victorious. Vic Richardson led the Australian team undefeated through South Africa in 1935–36. It was his last series.

Bradman the Great. No tactician or strategist ever led a team better than Don Bradman led his cricket team. The Don dominated the game from 1928 to 1948. Here, he is on his way to 138 in the First Test at Trent Bridge in 1948—the Ashes summer in England in which Australia did not lose one of 34 matches.

On the front foot. Bill Brown got Australia off to a positive start in the post–World War II era by leading Australia to a win in New Zealand, March 1946.

The humorous hooker. On and off the field, Lindsay Hassett did things in style. His quick footwork at the wicket and in front of a microphone kept Australia on top for five years after the Bradman era.

The face of pace. Ray Lindwall is ranked as one of Australia's top speedmen. He was an underrated skipper who led Australia only once. His toughness and endurance ensured victory.

Heart-to-heart. Lindsay Hassett (left) and Ian Johnson (right) at a South Melbourne Club game in 1953. Hassett's heart-to-heart talk inspired Johnson to get back on the Test side and become captain.

Leadership and brains trust. The Australian team that toured South Africa in 1957–58 had five players who at some time led their country. Ian Craig and Neil Harvey (standing fourth and fifth from left), were captain and vice-captain respectively on the tour. Richie Benaud (standing first on left) and Bob Simpson and Barry Jarman (front row, first and second from left) were the other future captains.

The Arthur Boyd of cricket. Arthur Morris, one of cricket's great artists with a blade, stamped his authority on post–World War II cricket to such an extent that he was always part of the leadership. He captained Australia twice.

Harvey in a hurry. Neil Harvey hooking in an interstate game in 1951. Harvey was unlucky not to have led Australia more than once (at Lord's in 1961). His aggressive style, knowledge and popularity would have seen him lead with distinction.

At the peak of his powers. Brian Booth in his best batting form at the Fifth Test in Sydney vs South Africa. He scored 102 not out and 87. Booth displayed the highest sportsmanship as skipper.

Instruction from The Don.
Don Bradman advises an attentive Bob Simpson in late 1965. Simpson made an extraordinary contribution to Australian cricket over four decades as a player, captain, and coach.

Taking a dive. Barry Jarman at MCG practice in 1959. Jarman skippered once in 1968 and helped Bill Lawry's team retain the Ashes.

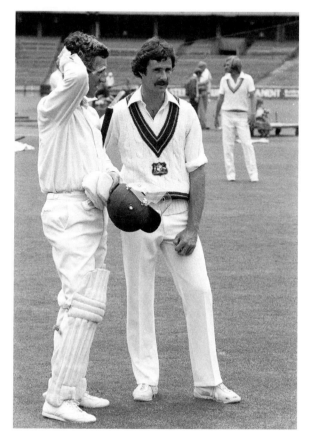

Not quite at the gallop. Graham Yallop (right) was appointed leader of virtually a second XI during the short World Series Cricket period. Mike Brearley (left), one of the most astute leaders England ever produced, had the advantage at the selection table in the 1978–79 Ashes in Australia.

Winners are grinners. (l–r): Ian Chappell, Bill Lawry, Bob Simpson and Richie Benaud in 1976. These four captains all led Australia to the top of world cricket.

21

DON BRADMAN

27 August 1908 –

Tests: 52; Captain: 24; Wins: 15; Losses: 3; Draws: 6;
Win ratio: 62.5 per cent

DONALD THE DOMINATOR

Donald George Bradman took on the captaincy of Australia in his twenty-ninth Test and applied the same integrity, skill, aggression, intelligence, shrewdness and efficiency to leadership as he did to making himself the best batsman of all time. Like most captains, his performances, statistically at least, improved once he took on the top job. Bradman's average while captain in his last twenty-four Tests (101.51) was higher than in his first twenty-eight games (98.69). He scored fourteen centuries while skipper, a better rate than his fifteen before that.

His win ratio record of 62.5 per cent (fifteen wins from twenty-four games) is the best of all captains who led Australia in twenty Tests or more until the year 2000. He was skipper in five series. Four of them were won decisively. Two of the five teams he led—in 1936–37 and 1938—were among the weakest in Australia's Test history, but for one factor—Bradman.

His leadership was the most successful and astute in history. Yet his advantage was himself. When the big match- or series-winning innings was needed, Bradman would deliver it. He was worth two of the best batsmen in history. The combined averages of the Chappell brothers, Ian and Greg, or the Waugh brothers, Steve and Mark, don't amount to Bradman's 99.94 in Tests. He was worth an extra batsman, giving Australia the equivalent to another Harvey, McCabe, Walters, Macartney or Border.

In 1936–37 and 1938, particularly, he could have led Australia's second XI and the series result would have been the same. He won one series and saved another. After the Second World War, when he led three stronger sides against England in 1946–47 and 1948 and India in 1947–48, the distance between Australia and the opposition was huge. At forty, Bradman's output remained more or less the same, with a better batting line-up around him and a far better, more rounded bowling array to throw at the opposition.

After a rotten start in his first series as captain in 1936–37, in which Australia lost the first two games to England, he scored 270, 212 and 169, to dominate victories in the last three Tests. In the drawn (one all) 1938 Ashes he scored a century in each of the three Tests in which he batted. In the last game at the Oval, Wally Hammond let England bat on to a record seven for 903. He feared that Bradman, given two innings, would make a huge score in at least one of them. The game ended in anticlimax when Bradman tore ankle ligaments in the field and did not bat.

He had more control over events and the environment he worked in than any other skipper in history. Bradman only experienced three match losses over five series. Two of those were his first games as leader when the weather, not the opposition, beat Australia, which was caught on sticky wickets. The third loss was that game at the Oval in 1938. Then Bradman didn't have Bradman to score a double or even a triple century to force a draw.

There was never a more shrewd leader than 'the Don'. He supported Bill Woodfull when he opposed Jardine's bodyline tactics. When he became skipper, his attitude was more flexible. He included bowlers in his line-up who could intimidate the opposition. In 1936–37 South Melbourne's paceman, Laurie Nash, bruised and upset England's batsmen in a game versus Victoria. Nash was then selected in a squad of thirteen for the final and deciding Test. England protested his inclusion. At a private lunch over the issue of Nash's possible inclusion in the eleven, England skipper Gubby Allen told Bradman that he didn't want a bumper war, but that he 'would really turn it on' if such a conflict began. Bradman reminded him that Australia's speed line-up was more lethal than England's, without suggesting that Nash would be selected. Bradman assured Allen that he would adhere to 'the spirit of the game' in how pace was used. In other words, Australia would not resort to a barrage of bumpers. Allen went away relieved by Bradman's 'promise'. But then he became apprehensive when he learned that Nash was still in the squad when it was reduced to twelve. On the day of the game, Nash was selected to play. The move played on the minds of the Englishmen, who were concerned that the wild and unruly Nash, a sort of mean, 1930s version of Merv Hughes, might unleash his brutal 'throat balls'.

As it turned out, he was wayward and hardly used the bumper. Yet his selection helped in the psychological battle, which went some way towards Australia's win by an innings and 200 runs. The English bats were tentative against him and Nash took four for 70. His wickets included opener Charlie Barnett (the first English wicket to fall), Les Ames and, significantly, Gubby Allen, whom he had caught behind for a duck. Nash also bowled the accomplished Joe Hardstaff for a duck in the second innings—his only wicket—for 34 runs.

Don Bradman's mind was sharp and sagacious. On the boat to England in 1948, he discussed tactics with his main weapon, fast bowler Ray Lindwall. Lindwall would be used in an attempt to destroy England's trump, Len Hutton, who had scored 364 and taken Bradman's Ashes record score of 334 during that mammoth construction of seven for 903 in 1938. Bradman wanted Lindwall confident and prepared for the Tests. He didn't want him to be a spent mental force before the Test matches as Ernie McCormick had been in 1938, when he was no-balled thirty-five times in his first game at Worcester.

Lindwall had a suspect 'drag' of his trailing leg when bowling, which made him liable to no-balling. Bradman told him to concentrate on passing the umpires in the opening games. Taking wickets was of secondary importance until the early umpires passed his 'drag'. The captain told him his place in the Test team was assured, no matter what his figures were early in the tour. Lindwall did as instructed and was 'passed' by the umpires. He went on to play a significant part in the Tests.

Bradman also let Lindwall bowl bouncers at Hutton at Lord's. The star opener was troubled and dropped prematurely by selectors after failing in three of his four innings of the first two Tests. By the time Hutton was restored to the Test side, Australia had retained the Ashes.

In the Third Test, Lindwall felled Compton (en route to 145). When Australia batted, Bill Edrich then bowled five bouncers at Lindwall, hitting him once. When Edrich came to the wicket in England's second innings, Bradman told Lindwall not to bowl any bouncers. The captain allowed intimidation, but would not cross the line into a bumper war that would 'not be in the spirit of the game'. Bradman was also aware that the media would pounce on the swapping of throat balls.

There was evidence of more subtle use of psychology in the way Bradman handled Lindwall in 1948. The bowler strained his groin in the First Test. Bradman gave him a tough physical examination at Lord's before the Second Test. He passed but Bradman, who knew all about leg injuries and recovery times, was sceptical.

'Leave me out on form if you want to,' Lindwall said, 'but not fitness.'

Bradman picked him. When he bowled he pulled up during the follow-through of his first delivery. Lindwall tried to hide his discomfort. Bradman, who never missed a trick on the field, pretended he hadn't seen anything. Lindwall did everything to cover up his problem, including taking wickets—five of them—for 70.

Years later, on prompting from Bradman, Lindwall admitted he had hurt his groin again with that first ball.

'Why didn't you say something at the time?' Lindwall asked.

'I noticed that you were trying so hard to hide it from me,' Bradman explained, 'and I reckoned you might bowl better if you thought I didn't know about it. I wasn't far wrong, was I?'

Bradman was also the pragmatist's pragmatist. He more than once rearranged the batting order to preserve his own wicket and those of his key batsmen, when his team had to bat on a poor wicket. He had no time for the heroic skipper, such as Joe Darling, who would go in first on a sticky to set an example to his men. Invariably, this was a suicide mission. By contrast, Bradman dropped himself down the list to avoid the worst of the wicket. The strategy worked, the classic case

being the Third Test of the 1936–37 series at the Melbourne Cricket
Ground. Bradman sent in bunnies 'Chuck' Fleetwood-Smith and Bill
O'Reilly to open, and Frank Ward, a third man with no batting pretensions, at number three. He dropped opener Jack Fingleton to six,
himself to seven and further protected Stan McCabe at eight and Len
Darling at nine. Australia lost three for 38, four for 74 and five for 97.
Bradman (270) then joined Fingleton (136) on a dried out, flat wicket
for a mighty partnership of 346. Australia went on to win by, not coincidentally, about the size of the Bradman–Fingleton link.

'Some were unkind enough to suggest that my purpose was to avoid
batting on a wet wicket,' Bradman remarked. 'Of course it was; but only
because such avoidance was *necessary in the interests of the team.*'

The interests of the team were a win. Had Australia lost that game
the Ashes would have been lost. Bradman's mind, unfettered by vanity,
the need to preserve an average, fear of failure, or bravado, speared
right to the heart of the matter. He had to give his best batsmen a
chance on a better wicket.

Bradman was not known for his nurturing skills. But he did
dispense advice, sometimes gratuitously usually when asked. Bradman
kept it simple, often getting to the point in a word or two. If an individual absorbed what was said and acted on it, he was better for it. In
1948, Neil Harvey, the nineteen-year-old 'baby' of the squad, had a
shaky start to the tour. He was too nervous to ask Bradman himself
for advice, so he prevailed on his Victorian friend Sam Loxton to
intervene with 'the boss' and find out what he should do to improve
his batting results.

Bradman told Loxton to tell Harvey to keep the ball along the
ground.

The teenager was baffled. Was that it?

'That's what the boss said,' Loxton said, with head tilted and a
shoulder shrug.

A bemused Harvey took the advice. Bradman's reasoning as ever
was pertinent. There was nothing wrong with Harvey's batting at all,
and Bradman regarded him highly and as without any weaknesses.
To confuse him with unnecessary science about stroke play on
low, slow wickets, which he knew anyway, would be superfluous and
counterproductive. To say nothing at all might lower the young
man's confidence. Bradman's minimalist edict caused Harvey to

concentrate on a basic. His scores improved. He was selected for the Fourth Test and scored 112 in his first ever Ashes match and helped Australia to one of the great wins in history. No observer could recall any lofted shots from the teenage star.

During the 1970–71 season, Bradman met a youthful Dennis Lillee at a function just before his first Test at Adelaide. There was much media and paper talk about Lillee being selected as a counter to the aggressive fast bowling of England's John Snow. Lillee was not quite sure what his approach should be.

The 62-year-old Bradman took the new demon bowler aside and said, 'Forget all the newspaper talk about bowling bumpers. Concentrate on what you've done. It's got you into the Test side.'

'It was a good, logical piece of advice,' Lillee remarked in his book *Over and Out*. 'It relaxed me for the huge job ahead.' Lillee was twenty-one and the responsibility of opening the bowling for Australia was bigger than anything he had shouldered before. He said that his chat with Bradman eased his inner tensions but put him deeper in awe of the man himself.

Lillee bowled brilliantly in his first effort, taking five for 84, and never looked back.

Also during the 1970–71 season, Bradman came into the dressing room after play in a Shield game and asked Ian Chappell what happened to his hook shot. 'You used to be a good hooker,' Bradman remarked.

Chappell had put away the hook shot on Bob Simpson's advice early in his career. Bradman picked his mark well. He was aware that Ian was an aggressive type, who deep down loved the shot. Not using it was thwarting his natural instinct and character. Without it, he had struggled to counter the South African speedsters such as Peter Pollock the season before and, in 1970–71, England's John Snow. Chappell had his brother fire baseballs at him on a concrete pitch until he had conquered the shot. He used it for the next decade and had an effective counter-punch to the world's speedmen.

When Bradman was a state selector he advised a young Greg Chappell to change his grip (to something more like Bradman's), reminding him that the last player so advised had ignored him. 'He's not playing first-class cricket any more,' Chappell was told. Bradman suggested Chappell would be better able to play strokes all round the wicket, especially through the covers, if he employed the grip Bradman had used himself.

Greg went into the nets that day and worked on the new grip, in which his two hands formed the letter V on the bat handle. He never looked back and became the most successful batsman since Bradman himself.

In 1999, Steve Waugh, worried about Sachin Tendulkar, asked Bradman for advice on how to dismiss the Indian star in the upcoming series against India during 1999–2000. Bradman said he couldn't say until after he had seen Tendulkar during the season. Advice after that would be too late. Bradman probably didn't wish to enter the contest. A guess would be that he wanted to keep the monumental battle between the world's best bat (Tendulkar) and the two best bowlers (Glenn McGrath and Shane Warne) on an even keel.

Within his means

Don Bradman's amazing ability to make big scores at will and on average with twice the capacity of the best of the rest in history, has been discussed by everyone interested in cricket, including kings and philosophers. Australian expatriate Brian O'Shaughnessy, regarded as England's best and most radical modern philosopher, in his book *Consciousness and the World*, dwelt on Bradman when examining human skills and the power we have over our limbs to achieve goals using those skills.

O'Shaughnessy said, 'I was using Sir Donald as an example in which the distinction was almost negated—so great did his power of choice seem to be.'

The philosopher also noted:

> The great batsman Donald Bradman signalled his arrival in England, in 1930, 1934, 1938, with innings of 236, 205, 258; and at the age of thirty-nine in 1948 relented to the extent of notching a mere 107. Each of these innings was played at Worcester, they were the first first-class innings in each tour, and he made four tours in all. And yet cricket is supposedly noteworthy for its marvellous 'uncertainty'! But this was the man who hit over 300 in a day in a Test match against the truly great bowling of

Larwood and Tate, and without taking any risks. And it
was he of whom Constantine wrote, on witnessing his 254
in the Lord's Test Match in 1930: 'It was like an angel
batting.' Indeed it was Bradman who said of McCabe, who
played three innings of genius in Test matches, that he
had the impression that he 'played beyond his means'. And
it is entirely credible to claim that he did, and that
Bradman did not do this. After all, we are talking surely of
the greatest sportsman who ever lived.

O'Shaughnessy here touched on the distinctions Bradman had over
other batsmen in regard to willpower, determination and singlemind-
edness, along with outstanding powers of concentration. These innate
capacities were evident long before he played Test cricket. They were
well developed by the time this son of a country carpenter was
seventeen during the 1925–26 season. He slammed 234 for country
New South Wales Bowral against Wingello. Wingello's key bowler
was twenty-year-old leg-spinner Bill O'Reilly, who was then on the
verge of state selection. Later in the season Bradman hit 300 in a final
against Moss Vale. A year later he scored 320 not out.

Over the next twelve years until 1939, Bradman scored another
seven triple centuries (including one quadruple and excluding one
near miss, 299 not out versus South Africa in 1931–32) in all forms
of cricket, making nine in all. The scores were 452 not out for New
South Wales versus Queensland in 1929–30; 369 for South Australia
versus Tasmania in 1935–36; 357 for South Australia versus Victoria
in 1935–36; 340 not out for New South Wales versus Victoria in
1928–29; 334 for Australia versus England in 1930; 304 versus
England in 1934; and 303 for Kensington versus Glenelg in 1939.

More important than these mind-boggling achievements was the
manner in which he acquired runs. While he was a fast, entertaining
scorer by nature, these big innings at all levels of the game were often
scored at better than a run a minute and a run a ball. Invariably the
team he was playing for was set up for a win thanks to the rapidity with
which he built those mountainous innings. He also scored thirty-
seven double centuries in first-class cricket in much the same manner.

Don Bradman treated all bowlers at all levels in country, club, first-
class and Test matches with the same respect, never slackening off to

become blasé or arrogant when batting against lesser lights. And never did Bradman become the billionaire batsman by playing 'beyond his means', except when he considered his job done for the team. He threw his wicket away in about a quarter of the innings he played by having a go at everything, attempting to get out. Making a not out for the sake of averages never entered his cool, calculating and creative mind. He even occasionally made sure a particular bowler took his wicket, if he felt him worthy of it!

At about 170 centimetres, Bradman was not tall, with a trim figure weighing 65 kilograms. No athlete had better coordination of brain, eye, hands and feet. His handling of late cuts, all drives, the hook—every shot in the book and some not—was testimony to his extraordinary skill. More important still was philosopher O'Shaughnessy's point. No sportsman ever had better control or power over all his innate physical and mental attributes. If he wanted to make a double hundred, he would. If he wanted to win a game or a series, or lead an undefeated team through a long tour, he could organise his mind to achieve the goal.

Yet at eighteen, when he tried out at the Sydney Cricket Ground number two ground nets early in the 1926–27 season, he was dismissed by every Test and state selector, except for one, as a flawed country kid. No Sydney club even bothered to try him out. Bradman went home to Bowral and crunched 170 not out in two hours against Exeter. His raw genius could not be ignored. There had always been big scorers in country cricket, but never from someone so young and consistent. He had to be tried out at the state level.

By early in 1927 he had been on a rollercoaster of cricket games for Bowral, in the Country Week tournament, Sydney's St George club, and the New South Wales Second XI. Bradman's talent was showcased, and he developed with the experience of each walk to the crease. One by one he was ticking off standards he could cope with. The innings in 1926–27 that meant most to him and his career was his first game with St George against Petersham. He hit a run-a-minute 110, facing ninety-seven balls, before being run out. There were no more jibes about up-country bumpkin batting directed at this youth ever again. He was now doing to top city bowlers—Petersham had two Test bowlers, Sam Everett and Tommy Andrews—what he had been doing in the country.

He ended the 1926–27 season with a magnificent 320 for Bowral. He moved to Sydney to work for a real estate agent and broke into the New South Wales Shield team in 1927–28. He signalled his intent, confidence and future by hitting the world's best spinner, South Australia's Clarrie Grimmett, for 2 fours in the first over he faced. Bradman went on to score 118 in three hours. It was clear after these two initial seasons that this player thrived on adversity, challenge and big-name competitors. He began by destroying young Bill O'Reilly (whom he later deemed to be the greatest bowler he ever faced) in their first encounter. He then conquered Grimmett when they were first pitted against each other. He clipped centuries in his first club and state games, and ended 1927–28 with a Shield average of 46.22, second only to Alan Kippax.

Don Bradman's rapid progression was unstoppable. He made the Test side at age twenty against Percy Chapman's touring team in 1928–29, stumbled on a Brisbane sticky with 18 and 1, and was dropped for the Second Test in Sydney. He came back at Melbourne for the Third Test, scoring 79 and 112. The verve, temperament and courage in the way he constructed his first Test century told everyone that the expectations of a nation might well be fulfilled. England just scraped in for a three-wicket win at Melbourne and were lucky to win by 12 runs at Adelaide in the Fourth Test. Bradman made 40 and, had he not been run out for 58 in the second innings, Australia would have won the game. In the Fifth Test at Melbourne his 123 and 37 not out completed Australia's irresistible drive towards a Test victory.

Bradman had hit 468 in four Tests at 66.86 for the series. He was on the way. His success saw him pick up a job with Mick Simmons sports goods store. Bradman was thankful for work in the Depression, but disliked the front-of-store glad-handing and public relations he had to do. It wasn't him. Making runs was.

In 1929–30 he hit his world-record 452 not out versus Queensland. He would happily have gone on to 600 if New South Wales skipper Alan Kippax hadn't declared. This launched Bradman onto the boat for England in 1930. He hit the ground running with 236 not out in 276 minutes in the first tour game versus Worcester. The 21-year-old—at the peak of his physical powers—never looked back. His next major conquest was against Percy Fender's Surrey. Fender had been Bradman's sternest critic, saying he would not be effective in England.

His flaws and tendency to include unorthodoxy would see him undone, Fender propagandised before the Tests. Fender had no idea—no one did—of the mental force that he was attempting to thwart with psychological warfare. He would have been better to avoid giving Bradman a reason to perform at his peak. In response, Don Bradman hit 252 not out off 238 balls in 270 minutes. Only the rain stopped him from going on to 400, a score that his skipper Woodfull would have happily endorsed. He could see what a huge psychological advantage his young champion was giving the tourists. All observers felt Fender did more scurrying after balls than any other fielder. Bradman said it was an optical illusion, while admitting that the innings gave him some satisfaction, considering Fender's earlier comments. Bradman's assault on the counties produced 1000 runs before June.

In the First Test of 1930 at Trent Bridge, Tate bowled him for 8 in the first innings. Australia was set 429 to win in the final innings, a task that would have appeared impossible, but for the tourists having big-scoring Bill Ponsford and Don Bradman in their batting order. At one stage, with Bradman on 131, Australia looked as if it might pull off the greatest chase in Test history, but then Walter Robins bowled him with a tremendous wrong 'un. It caught the young champion on the back foot and in two minds. If the cricket world could have seen inside Bradman's mind after this dismissal it might have seen something of what was to come in this series and for nearly the following two decades. Bradman's indecision in that one moment gave him nightmares, literally, for the rest of his life. He hated the idea of making even a split-second error. He was tormented by not forcing a win for his country. But instead of dwelling on the mistake, he made the correction in his memory bank, left it to his subconscious to stew over for another eight decades and willed himself to do better in the next Test at Lord's.

He hit 254, which was, he felt, technically the finest innings he ever made. Bradman measured his performances by the number of errors he made. Not even the shot that got him out, a hard, low cover drive, brilliantly caught by Chapman, was a false one.

In the Third Test at Leeds, he hit 309 not out in a day, a feat never eclipsed at the highest level, and went on to 334. He broke Reginald Foster's Ashes record of 287, and was dropped once at 273, a hard chance behind. This and one mishit caused him to downgrade this knock compared to his 254 at Lord's, even though England had Larwood in its line-up. The speedster was belted out of the attack four times during a day's play. It was the worst humiliation—one of several from Bradman—Larwood ever experienced. He didn't forget it.

While Bradman didn't rank his 334 as his best, it was enough for an Australian soap manufacturer living in England, A E Whitelaw, to give him 1000 pounds for the effort, which was equivalent to twice his tour salary.

Myth and reality

In the final Test at the Oval, one of cricket's great myths was born. Bradman began the fourth morning on 130 not out and performed one of the most dazzling sessions of tenacious, skilled batting ever in Test cricket, scoring an unconquered 98. The track was wet and Larwood was getting the ball to lift alarmingly. Archie Jackson was felled. Bradman was hit on the forearm and fingers. Larwood later claimed it was the first time he had seen him flinch. Much later in retirement Larwood elaborated and said, yes, anyone would have flinched when hit by the deliveries that day. Larwood was pleased that he was able to strike Bradman. He had failed to do it until that game. 'Bowling to Australia's batsmen is like potting pheasants,' Larwood said. In other words they were slow and easy to hit. He added, 'But with Bradman it was like trying to trap a wild duck, his movements were so swift.'

Larwood had struck his wild duck, causing him to flinch. The speedster felt good about doing it at last and told everyone, including England's captain, Douglas Jardine. The comment long detracted from Bradman's mighty performance at the Oval, in which he twice drove, hooked, pulled and deflected Larwood out of the attack in that one morning session.

Bradman went on to 232 in that innings and ended with 974 runs at 139.14 for the 1930 series. He scored 2960 first-class runs at 98.66 for the tour, and 3170 at 99.06 in all games.

He strode from strength to strength, scoring 447 at 74.5 from just six innings in the 1930–31 series versus West Indies, and 806 at 201.5 versus South Africa in 1931–32. Established, settled and with some money in his bank account at last, Bradman married his childhood sweetheart, Jessie Menzies, on 30 April 1932.

The Marylebone Cricket Club and Douglas Jardine, reading Bradman's 'telephone numbers' in the two years following England's drubbing in 1930, realised that a plan would have to be devised to shoot this wild duck down. Otherwise, Larwood's fear that he would face further humiliation under Australia's hot sun and in front of partisan crowds, would come true. If Bradman could crash 974 in England, what would he do in Australia on pitches he had used to amass unassailable records?

The Larwood 'flinch' remark became Douglas Jardine's propaganda tool and justification for the introduction of bodyline in the 1932–33 Ashes series. Bodyline was a method of bowling designed to destroy Bradman as a batting force. The tactic worked in the short-term, reducing the star bat to 396 runs at 56.57, statistics that brought him back from his 100 average to that of the other best batsmen in history. But with bodyline outlawed by 1934, Bradman hit 758 runs at 94.75 in the Ashes in England, including a 304 at Leeds. Despite a life-threatening illness brought on by peritonitis, which fatigued and troubled him on the first half of the tour, Bradman emerged as a force again in the final two Tests and won the series for Australia. Even with his illness, he hit 2020 runs at 84.16 and topped the tour averages.

In 1935 he and Jessie moved to Adelaide. He took up a six-year contract in which he was to be trained as a stockbroker.

Recuperation caused him to miss a tour of South Africa in 1935–36. He used the domestic season to build his strength and establish his credentials as a captain, leading South Australia in the Shield. Bradman amassed 810 runs at 90 in the 1936–37 Ashes series, his first as captain, and in the drawn Ashes of 1938 he scored 434 at 108.5, after beginning that tour with another 1000 runs before June. His tour statistics read 2429 runs at 115.66, including a record thir-teen centuries.

He joined the armed services in 1940 and was made a lieutenant but debilitating fibrositis caused him to be invalided out. Jessie worked overtime during this period, bringing up two young children and looking after her ailing husband. After the war he began his own stockbroking firm, again with Jessie's help, and made a comeback to cricket, captaining Australia against the visiting England team in 1946–47. Bradman, now thirty-eight, may have lost a little in his batting skills, but it didn't show in his statistics—680 runs at 97.14. Australia won three–nil.

The fibrositis recurred from time to time and his continuing at the top level was a season to season proposition. He led Australia against India in the 1947–48 home series, winning four–nil. Bradman notched 715 runs at 178.75. Despite breaking down with fibrositis in the last Test at Melbourne, he decided to tour England one last time in 1948.

English cricket writer and broadcaster John Arlott thought that no military commander ever planned a better campaign than Bradman's management of the 1948 tour. He turned forty during the season, and hit 508 at 72.57 in Australia's four–nil win. His team went through the entire tour undefeated in thirty-four games, and almost all of them came under his influence as a leader and batsman. He scored 2428 runs at 89.92, hitting eleven centuries. It was the first time he didn't score a double century on tour or in a season, but it was not through any reduced ability. Bradman decided before the tour began that he would rarely go on much beyond the century mark unless necessary. Double hundreds were out. He feared the exertion would bring on a prolonged bout of back pain associated with his fibrositis.

Bradman ended his 52-Test career, scoring 6996 runs at 99.94 with twenty-nine centuries, including ten doubles and two triples. He played 234 first-class matches, and scored 28,067 runs at 95.14 with 117 centuries including thirty-seven doubles. He scored a century on average every third innings. Two-thirds of his centuries were chanceless.

On retirement in Adelaide he became the first Australian cricketer to be knighted, and was at different times chairman of the Board of Control. Bradman was a selector of Australia's Test side from 1934 (on tour) until 1971 and also a long-serving state selector. He was married to Jessie for sixty-five years until her death in September 1997.

Despite being one of the most popular figures in Australia's history, he had his detractors and critics. No one with his genius, quest for perfection, directness, individualism and fame could slide through to his tenth decade without attracting opposition. It began in the 1920s when he first emerged on the international stage. The English soon made him a target. They were frightened of him. Some Australians attacked. They were jealous. Others, including former captain

Warwick Armstrong, found fault when it wasn't there with both his batting and his captaincy. Even later in his life some commentators developed a little industry of spurious beat-ups, knowing that there was always a taker for a lazy blitzkrieg on 'the Don'. It sold papers.

Over the years, the more he avoided the media, the more the media followed him. He became like a curio to be placed in a museum, open all hours. But Sir Donald Bradman at ninety yearned for privacy. He wrote to friends after his wife died asking for this precious, long-denied commodity 'for what little time I have left on earth'.

Bradman's old acquaintance, the late, long-serving English journalist E W Swanton, wrote of him, '[Bradman] has been, if any man ever was, a victim of his fame.'

His choice of profession, stockbroking, and later, investment advice and professional directorship, dictated discretion. He behaved accordingly, but could never control the media frenzy surrounding him, more than fifty years after he stopped playing.

Bradman's bluntness was refreshing.

On his ninetieth birthday, after he had met with Shane Warne and Sachin Tendulkar, a media pack waited outside his front door. One well-meaning journalist asked him how he was 'feeling' on the big occasion.

'How am I feeling?' Bradman asked in reply. 'I'd be feeling a lot better if there weren't so many cameras out here.' He turned and walked back into his house.

Bradman's experience of the Fourth Estate was not always negative. He used his experience as a journalist to write two outstanding books on the game: his autobiography, *Farewell to Cricket*, and *The Art of Cricket*.

At the end of the twentieth century, almost every media outlet made lists of the world's and the nation's greatest sportsmen. Bradman took every award in Australia and some in England. London's *Daily Telegraph* named him second only to Muhammad Ali as the top sports performer ever. *Time* magazine went further and named Bradman as one of the top 100 people, from all walks of life, of the entire century. Australia's only other 'representative' was American Rupert Murdoch.

Bradman was also chosen as captain of Australia's team of the twentieth century by twenty experts from home and abroad.

But the award that pleased him most was being named as one of

Wisden's five cricketers of the twentieth century. One hundred cricket experts and commentators were asked for their best five. Every one of them chose Bradman. Ninety chose Sir Garfield Sobers, followed by Sir Jack Hobbs (30), Sir Vivian Richards (25) and Shane Warne (27).

Sir Donald Bradman has said for thirty years that the West Indies' Gary Sobers was the best all-round cricketer who ever lived. English critics like to put W G Grace in the number one spot. But no one could get near Bradman for his batsmanship and, after the 1948 tour, his supreme all-round leadership skills. He was the greatest cricketer ever.

22

BILL BROWN

....

31 July 1912 –

Tests: 22; Captain: 1; Wins: 1;
Win ratio: 100 per cent

AN OPENER OF STYLE

Bill Brown strode to the wicket in front of a packed Lord's with opening partner Jack Fingleton to begin the chase after England's massive 494. It was 1938. The Ashes contest was the only regular issue challenging Adolf Hitler and Nazi Germany for front-page news, as Europe braced itself for inevitable conflict. Brown, the team's batting stylist, put his head down. He always did at Lord's, cricket's spiritual home. In his first innings there on the previous tour in 1934, he had scored 105.

The crowd had seen Wally Hammond mount a magnificent 240 in 367 minutes, and it now waited for not Australia's but Don Bradman's reply. The purists wanted to see a brilliant answering century from the master. But not a double century. That would dent England's chances.

At 69, Fingleton was out. The crowd craned their necks towards the pavilion. Bradman emerged to thunderous applause. Some over the years begrudged Bradman being the centre of attention always, wherever he went or played. But not Bill Brown. He was happy to be playing Test cricket and doing his own thing with the bat, which at times was exceptional and always classy. Besides, he liked his captain and appreciated his genius. If Bradman could top Hammond's effort, which he usually did, Brown would love to be there to contribute to a fighting reply.

But to Brown's and a big section of the crowd's disappointment, a big Bradman double was not forthcoming. Left-arm spinner Hedley Verity caged then removed Bradman for 18 when he chopped the ball onto his stumps. The biggest scorer in history was out. The responsibility was on Brown and the rest of the line-up to dig a little deeper.

The score was two for 101. Stan McCabe came in, batted like a millionaire and was out for 38 in thirty minutes. It was three for 152. Lindsay Hassett then joined Brown in a partnership of 124 in one hundred minutes. Brown was more cautious in his stroke play than the critics would like to see. But this day, he was not restricting himself to gentle leg deflections and delicate late cuts. Intermingled with his sound defence, Brown was being the 'real' Brown by standing to his full 176 centimetres and driving with style on both sides of the wicket. He was letting flow the very correct skills that his teammates knew he had. They had seen this form now and again in Tests, county and Shield games. Somehow, a little of that Bradman aggression had transferred itself to the opener. He was taking the initiative on a huge occasion, which was even bigger than anyone realised. War would ensure that this would be the last Ashes contest at Lord's for a decade. Brown marked the occasion by moving to his century in 193 minutes. Then Hassett was out for 56. Jack Badcock was bowled for a duck. Barnett came in and stayed with Brown (140 not out) until stumps, with Australia on five for 299.

On day three Brown carried his bat to 206 not out in 375 minutes from a score of 422. In the end it wasn't far behind Hammond's rate of accumulation. Considering the respective bowling line-ups, Brown's innings was a better one. In fact, it was the finest performance of a distinguished career.

William Alfred Brown, the son of a Toowoomba, Queensland, farmer, first played Shield cricket for New South Wales at twenty during the 1932–33 season, which was marked by the bodyline controversy. In his only encounter with the Marylebone Cricket Club tourists he acquitted himself well, scoring 69 and 25. In 1933–34 Brown made 154 versus Queensland in his seventh first-class game. In his thirteenth match, he made a brilliant 205 against Victoria. Through the season, Brown opened with Jack Fingleton. At the end of it, there was only a place for one of them to tour England in 1934. They had performed more or less at the same standard. Bradman had batted at number three in the same New South Wales side during the season. The national selectors asked Bradman who he would choose out of the two of them. Bradman chose Brown, suggesting he would bat better on English wickets.

Brown played his first Test at Trent Bridge, scoring 22 and 73. He then made a name for himself with his first Test hundred at Lord's and ended the series with a respectable 300 at 33.33. He followed this with 417 at 59.57, with a top score of 121 in the South African series of 1935–36. Brown had a setback with injury in the home series of 1936–37 against England. He could only manage two games, scoring 95 at 23.75, with a top innings of 42.

Brown moved to Queensland, where he had been born, for the 1937–38 season. He and Fingleton were both chosen to tour England in 1938, and Bradman's analysis that Brown was better on English wickets proved correct. Fingleton managed 123 runs at 20.5 during the series. Brown hit 512, the highest aggregate of either side, at 73.14.

Australian writer Johnny Moyes put Brown's success in England down partly to lack of harassment from spectators there. 'He could plan his innings [in England],' Moyes noted, 'and pursue that plan to the end without being urged to "have a go". A placid chap was Brown, and he liked to play in peaceful surroundings. When on the job he was as emotionless as a stoic.'

At Trent Bridge in 1938 Brown was allowed to proceed without hindrance from 'Hillite' hoons to compile 133 in the second innings, and with Bradman (144 not out) he saved the Test. His unconquered 206 put Australia back in the game at Lord's. Brown's 69 at the Oval in the first innings was a fighting knock in Australia's hopeless cause of chasing 903, without Bradman.

Brown's best season was 1938. He was again second only to Bradman in the averages for the tour, compiling 1854 at 59.57. This form carried through into Australia's domestic season in 1938–39, where, now state skipper, he scored 1057 for Queensland, with another carrying of his bat for 174 not out versus South Australia at Adelaide.

In 1940 at twenty-eight he married Barbara Hart, a shipping company receptionist. During the war he was a pilot officer in the RAAF. When hostilities ceased, Brown had the honour of leading Australia against New Zealand in the first post-war Test at Wellington on 29 and 30 March 1946. In his side was a wealth of leadership talent, proven and potential, in Keith Miller, Lindsay Hassett, Ian Johnson and Ray Lindwall. New Zealand won the toss and batted on a rain-affected pitch. Brown's toughest task was deciding who should be given the ball to do the destruction.

New Zealand made 42 (Bill O'Reilly, in his last Test, five for 14; Ernie Toshack, in his first Test, four for 12). Australia replied with eight for 199 declared. Brown top-scored with 67 and New Zealand was removed for 54 in its second innings. Towards the end of it, Brown resorted to tossing a coin to decide which two ex-airmen who would bowl—Colin McCool or Ian Johnson. Australia won by an innings and 103 runs.

In 1946–47 any further chance of national leadership was thwarted by Bradman's return to Test cricket. An injured thumb kept Brown out of the series versus England. He returned against the Indians in 1947–48, and began slowly with 11 and then 18, when he was run out sensationally while backing up too far. Indian left-hand spinner Vinoo Mankad stopped at the wicket and whipped off the bails. It was the second time in a month Mankad had done this to Brown. The verb 'to Mankad'—as in 'he was Mankaded'—became part of the language.

The transgression of not backing up properly and losing his wicket unnecessarily saw Brown dumped for the Third and Fourth Tests. He came back for the Fifth at Melbourne. He was run out for 99, a well-crafted knock that assured him a place in the mighty Invincibles squad to tour England in 1948. Unfortunately for Brown, two other fine players, Sid Barnes and Arthur Morris, had entrenched themselves as the opening pair. Brown was tried down the order, but the move didn't come off. He had only three innings for a return of 73 runs at 24.33, but there was some satisfaction in having two of them at Lord's, where he scored 24 and 32.

Brown's total in twenty-two Tests was 1592 at the top-drawer average of 46.82. In first-class cricket, he had 189 matches for a total of 13,838 runs at 51.44. He hit thirty-nine centuries.

There followed a troubling short period as a Test selector where he was abused and harassed for not making sure the national side included Queenslanders.

During the 1999–2000 season, Australian captain Steve Waugh invited Bill Brown, a popular speaker on the cricket circuit, to address his team before the Second Test against Pakistan at Hobart. Every player found Brown's words and presence inspiring.

Johnny Moyes described Brown's batting career as having 'quality. Even when slow, he never wearied, as some do, because his style was cultured and free from jarring faults.'

23

LINDSAY HASSETT

28 August 1913 – 16 June 1993

Tests: 43; Captain: 24; Wins: 14; Losses: 4; Draws: 6;
Win ratio: 58.33 per cent

THE TALENTED ELF

Lindsay Hassett had the toughest captaincy act to follow in the history of cricket—that of Don Bradman. But the little Victorian with the big, playful demeanour handled it all in his own, very individual way without any sense of inferiority to the master.

Hassett was a beautiful batting stylist, quick on his feet with a wide range of shots. He turned on some superb knocks for Victoria, but tended to freeze up here and there in the Test arena. He didn't always bat in keeping with his character or skills.

Lindsay Hassett was sporting and very much in charge. Observers at times found it comical to watch him waving men twice his size around in the field. But, as with his predecessor, there was no question about who was boss. Like Bradman, Hassett also had the verbal skills for any moment—a crisis on the field, giving urgent instructions in the pavilion, or a witty speech at a function.

Both had a quick wit and both liked the odd risqué joke. But the two men differed in their style and humour. Hassett tended to be a clown, even an up-market larrikin, while never losing the respect of his players. Always lurking was his desire, under any circumstances, to be the impish joker, which made him an ideal touring companion. Hassett never allowed anyone—particularly himself—to be depressed on the team's travels.

All class and clown

Arthur Lindsay Hassett was the sixth son of a real estate agent. He was educated at Geelong College, where he excelled at cricket, football and tennis. His leadership skills were evident early and he invariably led his Australian Rules and cricket under-age teams right through to the first XI and XVIII. In 1931, at age seventeen and in his final year at school, he was Victorian Public Schools Tennis Champion. He was too light to go further in Australian Rules, so was left with a choice of tennis or cricket for higher accolades. Cricket won when, also at seventeen and playing for Victorian Country while still at school in the 1930–31 season, he made a brilliant 147 against the touring West Indies. After that, tennis was relegated to a fun, social activity.

It was widely suggested that Hassett was destined to play Test cricket. Anyone who ever even watched him in the nets had no doubt he would make it. He lacked nothing in courage. His footwork to spinners rivalled even the Don's and he was able to handle Bill O'Reilly, who presented the toughest examination of batsmen in the 1930s. Hassett's late cut, always a sign of class, was superb.

Hassett broke into the state side at nineteen, in 1932–33, the same year as Bill Brown, but he couldn't hold his place. It was four years— in 1936–37, when he was twenty-three—before he became a regular for Victoria.

In 1937–38 he was chosen in D G Bradman's XI against V Y Richardson's XI. This game was a testimonial for Clarrie Grimmett and Victor Richardson. It was also a trial for the coming tour of England. Hassett only made 13, before Grimmett, in fine touch for the game, dismissed him. But it didn't matter. A good season for Victoria had secured him the second-last batsman's spot in the squad to tour England in 1938. Hassett was ranked behind Fingleton, Brown, Bradman, McCabe and Badcock, and ahead of Sid Barnes.

The diminutive Hassett was chosen for the first four tour games and scored 43, 146, 220 not out and 57, enough form to secure a spot in the Test side. He began badly at Trent Bridge with 1 and 2, but lifted for Lord's with 56 and 42. The Third Test was washed out without a ball being bowled. Hassett hit 13, 33, 42 and 10 in the last two Tests for a 199 aggregate at 24.88. The 33 at Leeds was a cool final innings knock in a heated moment that did most to bring Australia its only Test win, by five wickets. Hassett's complete tour was more impressive. He notched 1589 runs at 54.79.

Just as important was his aid to team morale throughout the long tour. He never lost a chance for a practical joke. After a convivial evening at Grindleford, in the Derbyshire Hills, he waited until roommates Stan McCabe and Bill O'Reilly were asleep before smuggling a goat into their room. They awoke the next morning to bleating and strange smells.

At twenty-six, in 1940, just when he had approached his peak as a batsman, the Second World War intervened and he enlisted as a gunner in the 2/2nd Anti-Aircraft Regiment. He was sent to Egypt and Palestine in 1941. A year later, while on leave in Australia, he married Tessie Davis, whom he had met earlier working for a Geelong accountant. In 1944 Hassett, thirty, like tens of thousands of other Australians, was brought back from Europe and the Middle East to defend Australia from the Japanese, who were coming down through New Guinea. He was serving at Port Moresby when the enemy was stopped less than 50 kilometres away at Ioribaiwa Ridge.

In 1945, Lindsay Hassett began to think about playing for Australia again. He was appointed captain of the Australian Services XI and took part in the five Victory Tests against England as well as other games against India.

Hassett played in the first post–Second World War Test at Wellington under Bill Brown in March 1946 and, at thirty-three, was in the Australian side for the resumption of the Ashes series in 1946–47. In the opening game at Brisbane, he figured in a 276-run partnership with Bradman, making 128, his first Test century. Hassett was at an age when most players contemplated retirement. But, cheated by the war, he was determined to play on as long as he could. In that second series, he nearly doubled his average to 47.43 from a 332 aggregate.

Hassett's improvement continued in the next series against India in 1947–48, when from the same aggregate—332—he came away with an average of 110.67, second only to Bradman (715 at 178.75). His highest score was 198 not out at Adelaide in the Fourth Test.

His record, maturity (age thirty-four), and experience as a skipper in the Victory Tests in 1945 and as captain of Victoria, made him an ideal vice-captain to Bradman for the 1948 tour of England.

He was the life of the party on board ship and in every port. When the Australians were in Egypt en route to Europe they saw an Arab ruler at their hotel. 'He has 198 wives,' their guide told them.

After the players had digested this, Hassett remarked, 'Another two and he's entitled to a new ball.'

In England, some of the team were at a reception at a stately home of a wealthy host. Over dinner, the host's well-endowed wife, who was wearing a low-cut dress, asked if Hassett had seen the pyramids.

He stood up, leaned across the table and ogled her cleavage. 'I think we may have missed the best of them,' he said.

On another occasion Hassett, Keith Miller, Bill Johnston and Ian Johnson were being chauffeured back to London after a black-tie dinner in Surrey. It was midnight. They had only gone a few kilometres when Hassett asked the driver to call in at the next mansion. The driver obliged, taking them down a long driveway to a two-storey home.

Hasset rang the front-door bell, waking the household.

A window on the top storey was thrown up. A gentleman inquired, 'What the hell are you doing?'

'Just thought we'd pop in,' Hassett said.

The man at the window suddenly recognised the cheeky intruder.

'Are you Lindsay Hassett?' he asked. The Australians had made an enormous impact on England throughout the summer and most knew them by sight.

'Indeed I am.'

'Wait there.'

A butler ushered the four revellers in. Port and cigars were offered. The unprepared host, who happened to be a cricket fan, entertained them for two hours. Hassett heard later that their host dined out on the intrusion for years afterwards.

Hassett's love of a good time didn't affect his 1948 performances. He scored 310 at 44.29 in the Tests, including 137 in Australia's first innings of the series at Trent Bridge. It was a slow knock, partly due to England's bowling of leg theory—deliveries down the leg side. Yet it helped give Australia a psychological advantage early in the series, which it never surrendered.

Hassett's tour figures of 1563 at 74.42 were second to Bradman. Only Ponsford and Bradman ever did better in England.

Wisden named Hassett as one of its Five Players of the Year in 1948. Bradman's notes concerning his vice-captain for the 1948 tour in his *Farewell to Cricket* said that he was a great player and a valuable lieutenant as vice-captain. Bradman judged Hassett's knowledge of the game and views on tactics as 'extremely sound'. He complimented his stroke making and thought him capable of taking charge with the bat at critical moments. Bradman also noted that Hassett was prepared to risk his wicket in Australia's interests. He saw Hassett as sound in defence under almost all conditions. Bradman liked his forcing shot off the toes in front of square leg, the best of all his shots, including the drive and the cut, at which he was also proficient. He also ranked Hassett as a fine fielder either on the fence or at short leg.

Leader of the post-Bradman era

Such a glowing report card for a deputy may well have helped Lindsay Hassett's election to the Australian captaincy. He led his country for the first time to South Africa.

Hassett began the Tests in style with a century (112), in his first innings as captain, and ended it with 167 in the last Australian innings. His aggregate was 402 and he averaged 67.

Hassett also demonstrated a shrewdness as captain. He prolonged South Africa's second innings on a rain-affected pitch at Durban, stretching it out with delaying tactics, defensive fields and instructions to Miller, who was spinning the ball prodigiously, to bowl straight. South Africa scored its last nine runs in more than an hour. Australia began its second innings with a target of 336 to win on a wicket that was drying out, but still dangerous to bat on. In the last one hundred minutes of the third day, Australia reached three for 80. Harvey (151 not out) batting at five and Sam Loxton (54) at six did most on the final day on a better wicket to give Australia a five-wicket win.

It became the tradition that the more adventurous team members would attempt off-field conquests on the African tour. One player was rumoured to have spent the night with three women. Hassett saluted him the next morning at breakfast, saying, 'Congratulations. You're the only man ever to take a hat trick with two balls.'

The happy tourists went home with a four–nil series win. It was a fine start to the post-Bradman era without the great player–captain's presence after two decades of dominance.

A broader examination of Hassett's ascension came in 1950–51 when Freddie Brown's England team toured Australia. The Australian team was weaker than the 1948 line-up without Bradman, Sid Barnes, Ernie Toshack and Colin McCool, and with Don Tallon's keeping skills on the decline. Yet England didn't seem any more powerful than in the last Ashes.

Australia was bundled out on a good wicket in the First Test at Brisbane for just 228, then England, not for the first time, was caught on a sticky. Brown declared at seven for 68, forcing the Australians in on the worst of it. The home side collapsed to be seven for 32.

Instead of hanging on for as many runs as possible, Lindsay Hassett walked onto the field and waved to the England skipper.

'What's happening, old boy?' a perplexed Brown inquired.

'I'm declaring,' Hassett said.

'Oh, I see,' Brown replied and turning to the wicket added, 'You want us in on *that* again.'

Hassett nodded and said, 'It's your move, old chap.'

England had seventy minutes to bat before stumps and another day to score the modest 193 to win. Instead of playing safe, it attacked and lost six for 30 by stumps.

The next morning, the wicket had dried out. It looked good. England had 163 runs to get with four wickets in hand. Hassett made great play of pointing out imaginary spots on the pitch. He crowded the batsmen, bluffing them into believing the life that was there previously remained. Brown placed his two best bats, Denis Compton and Len Hutton, at eight and nine respectively. Hutton and Godfrey Evans came to the wicket to start the morning. Evans and Compton soon popped up catches expecting balls to rise when they didn't. Hutton realised it was a good track and batted without fear, reaching 62 not out. But it was too late. England reached only 122 and Australia won by 70 runs.

Australia won the series four–one, the loss being in the last Test at Melbourne. Hassett was one of five batsmen to average in the 40s (40.67 at 366), highlighting for the first time how important Bradman had been in Ashes contests since 1928.

Against the West Indies in Australia the next season, 1951–52,

Lindsay Hassett led another four–one series win. He was the only player of both sides to average more than fifty (402 at 57.43).

In 1952–53, South Africa challenged for a series win for the first time, but the series ended two all. Hassett, now thirty-nine, maintained his form, hitting 346 at 43.25, but he was leading a team in decline after the heights reached in 1948.

This was apparent a few months later in 1953 when England, relieved at facing Australia without Bradman for the first time at home since 1926, won the series one–nil. England hadn't won the Ashes since the bodyline series of 1932–33, twenty years earlier.

In congratulating England skipper Len Hutton at the Oval after the home team had secured the only win of the series, Hassett was the sporting joker to the end. He had bowled the second-last over of the game, when it was as good as finished.

'England deserved to win,' he said, 'if not from the first ball, at least from the second-last over.'

Away from the microphone, Hassett was congratulated for his speech by several in the winners' camp.

Hassett then showed a different face which demonstrated he was just as upset about losing as the next leader. 'Thank you,' he said and then added tartly, 'It [the speech] wasn't bad, considering that Tony Lock chucked half the side out.'

Slow, left-arm spinner Lock, who took five for 45 in Australia's second innings, had a suspect action, especially with his quicker delivery, which was in evidence almost every ball in Australia's second innings. Hassett was more than irritated that Lock wasn't called in this game and in earlier encounters. (Lock was later unofficially warned about his action. A few years later he cut the faster delivery altogether.)

Despite Australia's poor series, Hassett never lost his humour. While dining at the Park Royal Hotel with other players, a waiter spilled a peach nelba dessert on Hassett's jacket. The waiter apologised profusely and asked Hassett if he wished to have his jacket cleaned. Hassett at first declined. The waiter continued to fuss about. Hassett relented and while removing his jacket noticed a spot on his trousers, not related to the tumbling dessert. With the aplomb of a silent movie actor, he pointed to the spot, and motioned for the waiter to wait. Hassett then removed his trousers, folded them and handed them to the astonished waiter. The Australian captain went on eating his meal in his shirt, tie and underpants, much to the mirth of his companions. The waiter returned with the cleaned clothes while the players were finishing their cognacs.

Hassett's 1953 Ashes returns of 365 at 36.5, were again the best for the Australians. He scored 1236 at 44.14 for the tour.

Lindsay Hassett realised at forty that his time had come. Australia needed new blood and was facing a period of transition. His forty-three Tests had yielded 3073 runs at 46.56 with ten centuries. In first-class cricket he had scored 16,890, with fifty-nine centuries from 216 matches at an average of 58.24.

Lindsay Hassett's fun-loving, urbane style made him one of Australia's finest ambassador–captains. As well, Hassett's fine winning record as leader, in addition to Bradman's during the immediate post-war era between 1946 and 1953, enabled Australia to dominate world cricket. Lindsay Hassett was also one of the classiest stroke makers ever.

24

ARTHUR MORRIS

19 January 1922 –

Tests: 46; Captain: 2; Losses: 2

THE ARTIST

Left-hander Arthur Morris had a distinguished career as Australia's best opening bat but not as captain. Like Don Bradman in his first two outings as skipper, Morris was unlucky. Unlike Bradman, he didn't have another twenty-two games as leader to improve his record.

A leg strain kept Lindsay Hassett out of the Third Test against the West Indies at Adelaide in 1951–52, and this allowed his deputy, Arthur Morris, to take over. Australia had won the first two games. Morris won the toss and decided, bravely, to bat on a rain-affected pitch. Frank Worrell bowled him for 1, which started a rot that led to Australia being out for 82. The West Indies didn't fare much better, making 105.

Morris wisely rearranged his batting order for the second innings, opening with Ian Johnson and keeper Gil Langley. The number ten, Geff Noblet, was at three, with Doug Ring (usually nine) at four. The new order allowed Australia to push its score up to 255. Ring surprised by reaching 67 run out. Morris batting at five made 45 before spinner Alf Valentine, who troubled him often, bowled him.

The West Indies made the runs required with six wickets to spare on day three, the first Christmas Day of Test cricket. It was Australia's second loss in twenty-nine matches since the war. Hassett returned for the next game and Morris was his able deputy again in a one-wicket win for Australia.

When Lindsay Hassett retired, Victoria's Ian Johnson was elected captain of the national team instead of the popular Keith Miller, who had taken over from Morris as skipper of New South Wales. Morris nevertheless kept the Australian vice-captaincy for the 1954–55 Ashes.

Len Hutton sent Australia in at Brisbane in the First Test. Morris, dogged on day one, then dashing on day two, notched 153, and with Harvey (162) set up an unassailable total of eight for 601. England replied with 190 and 257, giving Australia a win by an innings and 154 runs. Johnson was injured and Morris took over for the Second Test at the Sydney Cricket Ground in mid-December 1954.

Morris won the toss but, mindful of his earlier miscalculation as leader, sent England in. It seemed he'd made the right decision when England was dismissed for 154. But Australia didn't quite capitalise and only made 228. Peter May took his time over his first century against Australia (104 in 298 minutes) as the tourists climbed to 296. Speedster Frank Tyson, who had been felled by a Lindwall bouncer, came back hard for several ferocious spells and took six for 85. Australia's second innings at 184 left it 38 short.

Rain one game and freakish speed by Tyson in another had put paid to Morris's opportunities to lead his country again. Yet his misfortune did not detract from the honour, which had capped off a brilliant career.

Quick rise to the top

The son of a school teacher, Arthur Robert Morris was a good all-round sport at school who was inspired in the early 1930s by the champions playing for New South Wales—Bradman, McCabe, Kippax and O'Reilly. At just fifteen in 1937, he was in St George Second XI. A year later he was in the firsts playing under one of his heroes, Bill O'Reilly. The spinner told him to give up his left-arm tweakers and to concentrate on batting. One day, without warning, O'Reilly put the solidly-built, 178-centimetre sixteen-year-old in first. Morris never looked back. Two years later, at eighteen, he cracked the state side and began magnificently with a century in both innings (148 and 111) against Queensland.

His career was rudely interrupted by the Second World War. In 1941, the nineteen-year-old enlisted in the Australian Imperial Forces, which saw him stationed in Australia and New Guinea. In these wilderness years he played more rugby than cricket. He was overjoyed when hostilities ceased in 1945. Morris returned to a clerical job at the Sydney Town Hall, but soon found a position as a motor parts distributor that allowed him more time off for cricket. In 1946–47, a 98 for New South Wales versus Queensland, and injury to opener Bill Brown, saw Morris, now twenty-four, in an Australian XI versus England. It was a trial game. Morris (115) and Bradman (106) put on a 196-run partnership.

Bradman thought Morris had the skill and temperament for Test cricket. Soon afterwards Morris was in the Test team under Bradman playing against England. He began slowly with 2, 5 and 21, but in the second innings of the Third Test at the Melbourne Cricket Ground he hit a fine 155 in six hours. Neville Cardus wrote that Morris had a 'loose' technique. Bradman told the opener to ignore the criticism and to keep doing what he was doing.

Morris did. In the next Test at Adelaide he scored a century in both innings (122 and 124 not out), matching Denis Compton's 147 and 103 not out in the same game. This feat placed Morris, in only his fourth Test, in a special class. He seemed to be capable of excellence in all conditions and situations. It showed in his figures of 503 runs for the 1946–47 series at an average of 71.86. Big Alec Bedser, the mighty England medium-pace swing bowler, was said to have his measure. But Bedser was not taking Morris's wicket before he had scored plenty of runs. (Morris's final career figures suggested Bedser was not the bogy he appeared, despite dismissing him twenty-two times. Morris's overall Test average was 46.48. In innings in which Bedser bowled to him, his average was just over 61.)

Morris's rise continued in the next Test series versus India in 1947–48, when he scored 209 at an average of 52.25 and with one century. But it was enough to gain him selection for the tour of England in 1948. Not only that, Bradman valued his thoughts so much that Morris joined Hassett as a selector on the tour.

Now twenty-six years old, Arthur Morris followed his skipper's lead by starting well, with a fine 138 in four hours in the opening game at Worcester. He was less efficient in the First Test at Trent Bridge, scoring 31 and 9. But at Lord's in the Second Test, the real Morris emerged. Once more he announced himself with a century—105—and 62. In the next match against Gloucestershire at Bristol he slammed a mighty 290 in 300 minutes, putting paid to any chance spinner Tom Goddard had of replacing Jim Laker in the England team.

Morris scored 51 and 54 not out in the Third Test at Manchester. In the greatest form of his career, he went on to two big innings that rank with the best in Ashes Tests. At Leeds he made 182 in a 301-run stand with Bradman (173 not out). This was in a successful chase of three for 404 on the final day of the Test.

With the 1948 Ashes lost to England, that country's leading critic, Cardus, now gushed praised over Morris, calling him 'masterful, stylish, imperturbable, sure in defence, quick and handsome in stroke play. His batting is true to himself, charming and good mannered but reliant and thoughtful'.

If Cardus hoped this might help cause the champion to slacken off in the final Test at the Oval, he would have been disillusioned. Morris scored 196 (run out) and held Australia's innings of 389 together. While all the talk and headlines centred on Bradman's duck in his last ever Test innings, Morris played the finest innings of his Test career. Morris finished the historic 1948 Ashes series with 696 runs at 87 with three centuries and three fifties.

Bradman retired and Morris was billed as Australia's top bat when he arrived home. He lived up to this rating, scoring 1069 runs at 66.81 in 1948–49, which gave him a sensational year of cricket. He played thirty games for forty-six innings (three not outs) and accumulated 2991 at 69.56. In this golden period he scored thirteen centuries and nine fifties. It meant a good start for him and his teams on average of one every two innings. Few openers in history could claim such a run of brilliance and consistency in a twelve-month period.

There was more to come.

Arthur Morris toured South Africa in 1949–50. After another slow start in the Tests he hit centuries in the Fourth and Fifth Tests. His aggregate was 422 at 52.75. Morris's tour record continued as it had in 1948–49. He totalled 1411 runs at 58.75 and kept his extraordinary form running over an eighteen-month period. Morris was approaching twenty-nine and seemed to be making up for the half-decade he'd lost due to war from the age of nineteen to twenty-four.

An inevitable drop-off in form came in 1950–51 against the visiting English team. His performances in the first three Tests were 'ordinary' but he revived in the Fourth Test at Adelaide with a strong 206 out of a 371 total. This innings had to be set alongside his 182 and 196 in the 1948 series. It was his seventh Ashes century. But Morris's aggregate of 321 at 35.67 was a sign that he may have been past his best.

This was confirmed in 1951–52 versus the West Indies, when he collected just 186 at 23.25. The guile of spin twins Alf Valentine and Sonny Ramadhin caused Morris more trouble than Bedser. They snared him five times from eight encounters and Morris was dropped for the first time since his Test cricket career began in 1946. He lifted his rating in 1952–53 for the series against South Africa, scoring 370 at 41.1, with a top score of 99. Coincidentally, Australia struggled (two wins all) for the first time in a series since the war.

In the 1953 Ashes contest in England, the national side continued its decline, and lost the series nil–one. A more cavalier Morris managed 337 runs at 33.7. On the tour he met and fell in love with an English showgirl, Valerie Hudson. They married soon afterwards.

England returned to Australia in 1954–55 with its strongest post-war side yet. Tyson and Bedser proved a handful and Morris managed 223 runs at 31.86. If his 153 in the first innings was taken from the aggregate, the figures looked poor.

Yet his career was not spent. He was selected to tour the West Indies soon after the Ashes contest. Morris stroked a brilliant 157 against Jamaica, giving him the distinction of scoring a century on debut in four countries—England, South Africa, the West Indies and Australia. It said much about Arthur Morris's mental application. He missed the last two Tests through illness and managed a respectable 266 at 44.33, which was close to his average in forty-six Tests of 46.49.

The West Indies series marked the end of Arthur Morris's Test career. When his wife fell ill he retired early. She died in 1956.

In all Morris had 79 innings with an aggregate of 3533 and hit twelve centuries. He had 162 first-class games, in which he accumulated 12,614 runs at 53.67, with forty-six centuries.

Arthur Morris joined British engineer George Wimpey for a few years before taking up a public relations job in Sydney with security group Wormald. He was a trustee of the SCG for twenty-two years. In 1968 he married Judith Menmuir. In the late 1980s the couple retired to live at Cessnock in the Hunter Valley. In 1998, Arthur Morris and other members of the 1948 Invincibles were fêted around Australia to mark that great team's fiftieth anniversary. It was special for Morris. He had been the side's dominant player on tour. In 1999–2000, Morris received another great accolade when he was chosen in the Australian 'Team of the Century'.

Arthur Morris showed that magnificent batting artistry could begin a Test innings. He is ranked as one of the finest openers of all time.

25

IAN JOHNSON

8 December 1917 – 9 October 1998

Tests: 45; Captain: 17; Wins: 7; Losses: 5; Draws: 5;
Win ratio: 41.18 per cent

THE SPIN DIPLOMAT

When discussing his captaincy, Ian Johnson would always point to his success in the West Indies and India rather than the two failed Ashes contests at home in 1954–55 and away in 1956. Losses to England in the mid-twentieth century received more publicity. They are better recalled than the jubilant tours to far-off lands that allowed Johnson to end with two more Test wins than losses. There was no TV or radio coverage of games in Barbados and Bombay. In Georgetown in the Third Test versus West Indies in 1955 Johnson took a career best of seven for 44 with his floating off spinners, which won the game. Such a feat in Australia against a powerful batting line-up boasting Clyde Walcott, Everton Weekes, Frank Worrell and Gary Sobers would have seen Johnson fêted as a hero. But with no mass-media eyewitness of his performances as a player and skipper, the memories of the 1954–55 lost Ashes predominated. When Australia was beaten for the Ashes again in 1956, the humiliation of the weak batting perfor-mances reflected on the captain, no matter how much events were pushed out of his control. Johnson's triumphant two–nil win in

India—never an easy assignment—on the way home from England did little to salvage the image of a beaten side in need of regeneration.

Ian William Johnson's father, Bill, a Melbourne wine and spirit merchant, taught young Ian the fineries of off spinning when he was in his early teens at Wesley College. One particular ball, spun from the palm rather than the fingers, collected plenty of wickets and earned Johnson praise from Don Bradman, who regarded him as one of the best off-spinners he ever faced.

Ian made the South Melbourne seconds at fifteen and the firsts at sixteen. The famous club was also home for Keith Miller and Lindsay Hassett. Johnson's action—high-jumping and looping—was distinctive. The lean, 178-centimetre bowler could spin the ball best on Australia's harder pitches. Johnson put 'grunt' into each ball a half-century before Shane Warne's exhalations signalled energy expended. Like Warne, who spun the ball the other way, Johnson used flight as a weapon. He was less inclined than most 'offies' to hurry balls through low for fear of being belted. Johnson would rather gamble on bite and turn once the ball hit the deck from greater elevation. It was successful at home, in South Africa and the West Indies, but less so in England, although Johnson on tour always took wickets.

Johnson made the Victorian side to play Tasmania in 1935–36 at just eighteen and remained a state player for the next five seasons, without chance of advance. His spinning was less prodigious than the fine array of leggies around in the 1930s. He was ranked behind Clarrie Grimmett, Bill O'Reilly, 'Chuck' Fleetwood-Smith and Frank Ward, and missed the 1938 tour of England.

Then war intervened and changed his life dramatically. In 1941, aged twenty-three, Johnson joined the RAAF and flew Beaufighters with 22 Squadron. A year later he married Lal Park (the daughter of Dr Roy Park, who played one game for Australia). Ian and Lal later had two sons Bill and Bob. In 1944 Johnson was a flight lieutenant seeing action in the south-west Pacific.

After the war, at twenty-seven Johnson was selected for Australia to play New Zealand in the Test match of March 1946. He made 7 not out and didn't get a bowl in a team that also featured Hassett and

Miller. They were also with him when he made his Test debut against England in 1946–47 at Brisbane. Johnson made a spirited 47 and felt at home. Not only were two friends in the team, he had known Don Bradman for more than a decade. Ian's father, Bill, who died in 1941, had been a national selector with Bradman. Young Johnson had come to know the great man well.

In four games in 1946–47 Johnson took ten wickets at 30.6, with a best performance at Sydney in the Second Test when he took six for 42, including Len Hutton's wicket. Johnson, who could bat a bit, also collected 106 runs at 21.2. He maintained his bowling form against India in 1947–48, taking sixteen wickets at 16.31, including four for 59 and four for 35 at Melbourne in the Third Test.

It was enough to get him selected for the 1948 tour and he played in the first four Tests for meagre returns, seven wickets at 61. The only consolation was that he took Hutton's wicket twice before the England champion could take control of an innings. But Johnson was considered a success on tour, for he formed an important part of 'General' Bradman's grand plan to go through the entire fixture of thirty-four games without a loss. The captain needed Johnson to do the donkey work in the county games so that he could rest his speed attack of Lindwall and Miller. Johnson delivered more balls than anyone but Bill Johnston and took eighty-five wickets in twenty-two games.

Johnson did better on the tour of South Africa in 1949–50 under Lindsay Hassett, where the harder wickets suited him better. His best effort was at the First Test in Johannesburg, where he made 66 in Australia's only innings and took five for 34 in South Africa's second innings. Overall he took a creditable eighteen wickets at 24.22.

He had a mediocre series against England in Australia in 1950–51, taking just seven at 44.43. His best performance was with the bat— 77 at Sydney in the Third Test. He had another lean time in the next season at home against the West Indies, taking only eight at 32.75.

Hassett's heart-to-heart

Ian Johnson, at thirty-four, was not chosen for the 1953 tour of England. When Lindsay Hassett returned from that failed campaign he retired. At a dinner after practice at South Melbourne, at the commencement of the 1953–54 season, Hassett asked Johnson what his plans were. The spinner had none. He didn't think he would make it back into Test cricket. Hassett told him not 'to die wondering' about a comeback.

'There's no reason why you couldn't be a candidate for the captaincy,' Hassett said. He reminded Johnson that he was thirty-six when appointed skipper. 'You've got no major injury worries. You could go onto until you're forty. But you've got to have the desire. You must be fit and want it.'

Johnson listened without saying anything.

'But of course, if you don't want to be captain . . .' Hassett said.

'I do want it,' Johnson said with conviction.

After this heart-to-heart, Johnson was inspired to make a supreme effort to get super-fit. He trained hard, especially with sprints and boxing with South Melbourne footballers. He had a good season with Victoria and captained it with distinction. The betting was on recent New South Wales skippers Arthur Morris and Keith Miller to captain Australia against England in 1954–55, especially as they had been on the Ashes tour of 1953. But Miller was not in favour for reasons never fully explained, despite the fact that he was indeed a highly regarded leader of his state.

Ian Johnson was chosen not only to play for Australia but to lead the Australian team. The move seemed inspired when Australia had a runaway victory at Brisbane in the opening Test. Johnson was injured and couldn't play in the Second Test, which England just won. Johnson returned for the Melbourne Test. He was unfortunate to run into a rampant Frank Tyson (seven for 27 in the second innings) on a cracked pitch. Tyson destroyed Australia, which went down by 128 runs. The home team never recovered. Tyson had the side bluffed and struggling in the Fourth Test at Adelaide, which England won. The Fifth was drawn. Johnson had fair all-round figures, making 116 runs at a flattering average of 58, while taking a steady twelve wickets at 20.25.

The one–three series loss might have led to the skipper being sacked, but the following tour to the West Indies in early 1955 needed a diplomat at the helm. England's recent tour had seen riots at George-town, where bottles had been thrown. It was thought that the English leadership could have handled it better.

Johnson, who had already instigated post-match, on-the-record chats with journalists, did the same in the West Indies.

Johnson won the toss at Sabina Park, Kingston, in the First Test. Australia batted attractively, but for some time into the second day. The crowd grew restless. Johnson, himself not out on eighteen, declared at nine for 515. As he was walking off, he and his partner, Bill Johnston, were mobbed by small boys. One insisted on talking to Johnson. Instead of ignoring him, Johnson picked him up and carried him towards the pavilion, engaged in conversation. The crowd cheered. It was a far cry from the more aloof image presented by the English players. This, along with other gestures, endeared the Australians to the West Indians. There was also excellent off-field fraternity, especially with poker games among the players that went well into the night.

After winning the first game, the Australians were on top in the drawn Second Test at Trinidad, where Morris, Harvey and Colin McDonald each scored centuries, and Johnson 66. The Third Test at Georgetown was so decisively won by Australia, thanks to Johnson taking seven for 44, that the locals didn't get a chance to disrupt a close finish, even if they had wished to. The Australians' demeanour, thanks to the tone set by their urbane, ever-gracious skipper, and the evident friendliness on and off the field with their West Indian counterparts, allowed the visit to a potential trouble-spot to go smoothly.

Trouble at mill

In the Fourth Test at Bridgetown, Barbados, there was trouble of a different kind. Australia made a whopping 668 with Miller (137), Lindwall (118) and Archer (98) all in attacking touch. Then the West Indies were reduced to six for 147. Miller, on his own volition, dropped his pace about 15 kilometres and bowled slow-medium swingers into a cross wind. In one over he induced a nick behind from Weekes (44) and the dangerous Collie Smith (2).

Two players who Johnson thought would be more suspect to pace, West Indian captain Denis Atkinson, and Clairemonte Depeiza, were in and handling Miller's medium pace with apparent ease. The always cogitating bowler was working towards an error from one of them. Johnson asked Miller to bowl fast. He kept delivering at a reduced rate. The captain demanded pace. 'Give me some speed, Keith,' he said.

Miller refused.

The Australians had a 'chat' at the top of the bowler's mark. 'I'll say who bowls and what they bowl,' Johnson remarked. He took Miller off and put Lindwall on. But the speedster was a little fatigued after his batting. He was loose. The batsmen attacked and were on top by stumps. The timing on the switch from Miller to Lindwall seemed wrong.

Miller, who thought he should have been captain for the tour, insulted his skipper in front of his teammates as they filed from the ground. 'You couldn't captain a team of schoolboys,' was one hostile put-down.

Johnson waited until most players had left the shed. Then he invited Miller 'outside' to settle the matter in the time-honoured manner of a punch-up. Miller, a much bigger man physically, realised his attacks had gone too far. He declined the offer. They continued to argue the issue back at their hotel. It simmered. The next day both men were more subdued as they set about trying to break what had become an unlikely but worrisome partnership. It reached gigantic proportions—347 and a seventh-wicket Test record. Miller (two for 113 off twenty-two overs) was off the boil and dispatched to all corners of Kensington Oval. Lindwall, also not at his best, took one for 96 off twenty-five. Benaud (three for 73) finally removed Depeiza for 122, and Johnson (three for 77) had his counterpart Atkinson for 219. The West Indies made 510. Australia made 249 in its second innings. Johnson top-scored with 57 but perhaps erred again by batting too long and making the chase (408 to win) too difficult. The West Indies were in trouble at six for 234 when the game finished in a draw.

In the final Test the differences between the captain and his brilliant all-rounder appeared settled. Miller was motivated. He turned on his best displays with bat and ball for the tour. Delivering pace and swing as directed this time, he took six for 107 in West Indies' first innings. When Australia batted he scored 109, backing up Archer 128 and Harvey 204.

Australia won by an innings and 82 runs, giving it and Johnson a three–nil triumph against a strong side away. Johnson had his best series, making 191 at 47.75, and taking fourteen wickets at 29.

It was enough to ensure that, at thirty-eight, Johnson would lead Australia to England for another Ashes battle. But important things had changed by mid-1956. England had developed into a powerful,

well-balanced combination with its finest batting line-up in twenty
years, and a formidable group of bowlers, including the lethal Surrey
spin twins, Jim Laker and Tony Lock. Lindwall broke down on tour and
was never fully fit. The wickets prepared were well below Test standard
and suited England's spinners far more. This led to Australia's bats,
especially its star, Neil Harvey, underperforming. Harvey averaged
just 19.7, while only one Australian, opener Jim Burke, averaged 30
(30.11), in the worst returns ever for a touring team. No one scored
a century in the Tests.

Laker and Lock helped Surrey beat Australia before the Tests. It set
a pattern. The tourists seemed in the hunt after drawing the First and
winning on a seamer's wicket at Lord's. But the twins demolished them
in the Third and Fourth Tests at Leeds and Manchester. Laker took a
world-record nineteen for 90 on an Old Trafford dust bowl. He was
more effective with his off-spin, pushing the ball through lower and
faster than Johnson. (On the figures of their careers, Johnson
performed better than the England star on bouncier pitches.)

Australia went down one–two. Johnson averaged just 7.63 from 61
runs, and took only six wickets at 50.5.

Yet it wasn't quite the end for Ian Johnson, who led the psycho-
logically battered Aussies on the home-coming tour via the subcontinent. Australia was humiliated by Pakistan on matting at Karachi,
making just 80, which took nearly a day in the slowest batting in
history. It was the first Test ever played between the two countries.

Johnson took his unhappy squad on to India for a three-Test contest. The captain, with a top score of 73 in the First Test at Madras,
and aided by an in-form Lindwall (seven for 43 in the second innings)
did most to secure an innings win. Johnson missed the drawn Second
Test at Bombay through injury but was back in charge for the Third
at Calcutta. Australia won by 94 runs thanks to Benaud, who took
eleven for 105.

The Australians won the series two–nil, allowing Johnson, now
approaching thirty-nine, to go home on a better note, although the
crushing by England a few months earlier was upmost in the minds
of Australian cricket followers.

Ian Johnson retired after forty-five matches, managing the double of 1000 runs—exactly—at 18.52, and 109 wickets at 29.19. In first-class cricket he played 189 matches, scoring 4905 runs at 22.92, and taking 619 wickets at 23.3. These returns in both Tests and first-class cricket rank him as the best off-spinner in post–Second World War cricket.

Throughout his captaincy, Ian Johnson put a positive spin on events. In down moments in Australian cricket, his diplomatic, courteous style did much for his country's image. Despite the negative public perception—engendered by Ashes losses—of teams he led, the records show that he was a more successful skipper than most.

Johnson was also one of the best off-spinners Australia ever produced. His Test figures would class him as good in any company, and his first-class returns placed him high in the list of Australian slow bowlers, ahead of more illustrious performers at the Test level, such as Richie Benaud and Shane Warne.

26

RAY LINDWALL

....

3 October 1921 – 22 June 1996

Tests: 61; Captain: 1; Draws: 1;

THE POETIC KILLER

Raymond Russell Lindwall's chance to captain Australia came at Brabourne Stadium, Bombay, under trying conditions. It was the Second Test against India in October 1956. Not only was it exceedingly hot but his was a patchwork team of crocks. The tour skipper, Ian Johnson, as well as Keith Miller and Ron Archer were injured and out. Alan Davidson had a stomach upset. Fellow paceman Pat Crawford strained his hip, while John Wilson pulled a muscle. Richie Benaud had a fever and couldn't bowl for part of the game. Only Lindwall himself, and medium-pacer Ken Mackay, were happily upright and ready to bowl.

'I was a captain without bowlers,' Lindwall recalled. 'Burke and Harvey made centuries, enabling me to close with seven down and a good lead (of 272). Over 1000 runs were scored in the game but the bowlers could not average five wickets a day.'

Somehow, Lindwall's forceful captaincy managed to squeeze efforts out of all his walking wounded. India scored 251 in its first innings. But in the home team's second dig, the Australians could only remove half the side. The game fizzled to a draw. Lindwall, then thirty-five and the greatest Australian pace bowler of the immediate post-war era, had proven to be an inspiring leader. In another era, he might have been the player to cause a break with the convention of never appointing a speedman as captain. But like his pal Keith Miller Lindwall missed out. The bowlers had to be content with showing their leadership talents at the state level. Lindwall did that with distinction for Queensland for the last five years of his first-class career.

Ray Lindwall's outstanding cricket career began at the Sydney Cricket Ground when he was eleven years old. He watched in awe as England's Harold Larwood mowed down Australia's finest with bodyline bowling in the 1932–33 season. Young Ray raced home and practised running in like Larwood, copying the smooth action. He varied the style to suit himself over the years, but it was that initiation to fast bowling that led him to be an outstanding pace bowler.

The Marist Brothers at two Catholic schools—Kogarah and Darlinghurst—helped him refine his bowling and outstanding batting. Lindwall was a natural athlete, destined to play Rugby League as well as Test cricket. Later at St George, the uncompromising but astute Bill O'Reilly nudged him further along the road to stardom by ordering him to lengthen his run and let rip with the ball. O'Reilly made Lindwall bat last, which affronted the teenager. But the wily old spinner knew what counted most if you wished to play Test cricket. A youth had to make up his mind early to develop one skill above all others. By all means he could grow as an all-rounder. But the best way into the state side and then Test team in the middle of the twentieth century was to shine at one and worry about the secondary skill later.

O'Reilly was thinking first about what was best for St George. It needed a speedster to tear in and put the wind up batsmen so that the leg-spinner could come on and remove the shaken batsmen left. This just happened to be the best route forward for Lindwall. His batting was good, but he may or may not have held his place up the ranks as a batsman.

Ray Lindwall was demonic with the ball. But it was controlled, intelligent demonology. His bumper was lethal. He delivered it with a slightly round-arm action that caused it to zero in at the batsman's throat rather than sail over his head. His yorker was nigh unplayable. Lindwall concentrated on a magnificent out-swinger for the first decade of his first-class career. After a season in the Lancashire League in the mid-1950s, he came home with a terrific in-swinger. No great batsman of the era knew how to handle him. Bradman only faced him in two innings in a Testimonial match at the Melbourne Cricket Ground in December 1948, when he made 123 and 10 and was not dismissed by the paceman. But everyone else—all the greats of the 1940s and 1950s, including Harvey, Morris, Walcott, Worrell, Weekes, May, Cowdrey, Graveney, Hutton and Compton—were uncomfortable and never felt 'in' against him.

The death of his father, a Water Board employee, caused Lindwall to forgo university and take an office job in 1940. He made the state side at the beginning of the 1941–42 season at age twenty, but his career was stopped before it started. War broke out. Lindwall joined the army in the ack-ack and fortress signals unit, which was sent to New Guinea. He was fortunate not to be killed when the Japanese bombed Port Moresby. But he was unfortunate to catch tropical dengue fever and malaria. It didn't stop him being picked for New South Wales in 1945–46 when Shield cricket resumed after the war.

Despite being weakened by those diseases, Lindwall, the promising youth before the war, was now a war-hardened man. It showed in his bowling. Described as 'poetic' because of his run up and rhythm, he now had a 'killer' instinct, which was more than a cliché when used to portray his powers with a hard leather ball. With encouragement from O'Reilly, he used the bouncer judiciously and enjoyed softening up or intimidating batsmen. Bradman had a look at him and made sure he was in the Test side against England in 1946–47. The Australian skipper was delighted to have a class speed weapon at his disposal for the first time. Lindwall took eighteen wickets at 20.39. He also crashed a terrific even 100 in the Third Test at the MCG—one of the fastest ever in Ashes cricket—-scoring 160 at 32 for the series.

Lindwall performed at the same level against India a year later, taking 18 at 16.88. He and Keith Miller, who was also never shy about delivering bouncers, formed a menacing pace duet, the best for Australia since the brief ascendancy of Jack Gregory and Ted McDonald in the 1920s. Bradman nursed Lindwall throughout the

1948 tour, making sure his leg-drag wasn't no-balled, and did all he could to ensure his spearhead was fit for the Tests. Lindwall pulled a groin muscle in the First Test, but like all sportsmen who played physical contact sport at the top (Lindwall played first grade Rugby League in 1942), he knew how to 'carry' an injury. He did this and dominated the series with the ball. Lindwall 'neutralised' England's star bat Len Hutton, taking a then fast-bowling record of twenty-seven wickets at 19.62.

But Lindwall's best effort occurred during the final Test at the Oval, when he took six for 20 from 16.1 overs. Bradman ranked one spell after lunch on day one as the 'most devastating' and 'one of the fastest' he ever saw. England was blasted out for 52. Morris with the bat and Lindwall with the ball did most to deliver Bradman and Australia a four–nil win in the series, which had been the first Ashes encounter in England following the end of the Second World War.

On tour in South Africa in 1949–50, Ray Lindwall was ill and injured and did not live up to expectations, taking 12 wickets at 20.66. At twenty-nine in 1950–51, he fought back for another Ashes encounter and contributed to Australia's fifth successive post-Second World War series success, taking fifteen wickets at 22.93. The following year he was in a bumper war with the West Indies. Some considered it the most hostile bowling since bodyline, but such comparisons were odious. Lindwall didn't use eight men on the leg-side. Nevertheless, it heralded an era when all opposing countries would seek pacemen with a bit of devil in them.

Lindwall secured twenty-one wickets at 23.04 and made 211 runs at 26.37 in the 1951–52 series. He had now been dominant and Australia's best bowler in six series wins in the period 1946–52.

Lindwall took his wife Peggy (whom he married in May 1951) to England, where he played a season with Nelson in the Lancashire League. While there, their first child, Raymond Robert, was born.

Lindwall returned to Australia for the 1952–53 season versus South Africa and kept up his high returns, with nineteen wickets at 20.16. But at thirty-one, he was now finding it tougher to overcome injuries, particularly to the knee and groin, and recurring bouts of the fevers that had troubled him after the war. Still, he lifted for the Ashes contest of 1953, taking twenty-six wickets at 18.85 to match his fine performances on the last England tour in 1948. It was not Ray

Lindwall's fault that Australia was in decline after the series loss of nil–one. He maintained his dominance for the eighth successive series.

Lindwall ran into inevitable criticism after the next Ashes series in Australia, in 1954–55, which was lost one–three. Now thirty-three, Lindwall took only fourteen wickets at 27.21. Even his old mentor, Bill O'Reilly, turned on him and called for his dumping in favour of a younger player. Some were drafted in beside Lindwall and his sparring partner, Miller, but the old-stagers still produced in the early 1955 series against the West Indies. Both took twenty wickets, Lindwall at 31.85 and Miller at 32.05. This was a terrific performance, considering the mighty batting line-up to which they delivered. Apart from the three Ws—Weekes, Worrell and Walcott—there were the up-and-coming young Gary Sobers and Collie Smith.

Lindwall also scored a dashing 118 at Bridgetown (his first 50 in sixty-nine minutes), which boosted his aggregate to 187 at 37.4. (Miller hit 439 at 73.17.) While he was on tour, Peggy gave birth to their second child, Carolyn.

At thirty-four, during the 1956 Ashes in England, injuries and slow spinners' pitches caused Lindwall to hit a wall for the first time in his illustrious career. He took just seven wickets at 34. Things didn't improve for him on the way home when Australia played Pakistan on matting at Karachi. But in India in three Tests he showed his toughness in trying conditions by being one of the last bowlers standing. On pitches again far more conducive to spin than pace, he took twelve wickets at 16.58, which was second only to leg-spinner Benaud, who took twenty-three at 16.87.

At thirty-six, Lindwall was finally dumped for the 1957–58 series in South Africa. It came as a shock. He lived for cricket. He considered he was still the best Australian fast bowler. But the selectors, going for youth, thought his time had come. Lindwall followed the South African series with interest. He noted that only Alan Davidson among the pacemen, with twenty-five wickets at 17, was worthy of selection in front of him. Throughout the long winter of 1958 Lindwall trained like a young boxer, with skipping rope, bike, running and exercises. This gallant effort was rewarded during the series against England in 1958–59. He came back for the last two Tests and broke Clarrie Grimmett's Australian wicket-taking record of 216. Limited opportunities saw him take seven Test wickets at 29.86. Yet the season's figures of forty wickets at 20.55 demonstrated just what an effort the 37-year-old champion had made.

It was enough for his final Test tour—of India and Pakistan. At thirty-eight, Lindwall lifted his wicket tally to 228 at 23.03. His run tally was 1502 at 21.15. This made him the first player ever to score 1500 runs and take 200 wickets in Tests.

Ray Lindwall played 228 first-class matches, scoring 5042 runs at 21.82 with five centuries. He took 794 wickets at 21.35.

He and Peggy settled well into a florist business in Brisbane and he put something back into the game by coaching and serving as a Test selector in the early 1980s.

Ray Lindwall ranks with Dennis Lillee and Glenn McGrath as the best of the Australian pacemen in the history of cricket.

27

IAN CRAIG

....

12 June 1935 –

Tests: 11; Captain: 5; Wins: 3; Draws: 2;
Win ratio: 60 per cent

PROMISE UNFULFILLED

The bar was set way too high for New South Wales and Test batsman Ian David Craig when, at seventeen, he was spoken of as the 'next Don Bradman'. He was the first to be so ordained or cursed in a long line that only ended in the late 1960s when observers and historians began to analyse the figures since Bradman retired. No one could get near his batting average and string of phenomenal performances. Not only that. No one had come near him before, during or after his career. But wait a second. Not even Bradman was fast-tracked into Test cricket at seventeen, as Craig was. Not even Bradman was asked to captain his country at twenty-two, as Craig was. At seventeen, the Don was unknown outside Bowral. He was playing his first full cricket season after giving away tennis. At twenty-two, Bradman was a superhero who had every batting record worth having. Yet no one would have expected or wanted him to lead Australia. That opportunity came to him at twenty-eight. Then he was a veteran of nearly a decade at the top of the game, who had played under two experienced Test skippers from whom he had learned much.

Ian Craig was expected to be both *Bradman* and *captain* at twenty-two. It was an impossible demand on one count and a tough one on another.

Yet when the young man was first handed the reins on the tour of South Africa in 1957–58, just about every Australian cricket supporter was cheering him on, agonising over his failures and fluttering with possibilities when he gained even a moderate score.

What precipitated the rush and positioning? Well first, young Craig looked the goods in his early teens. At sixteen, while still at North Sydney High School, he scored a century for Mosman. He was fast-tracked into the New South Wales team, more on the promise than performance and still a sweet sixteen-year-old in the 1951–52 season. In his first state game, versus South Australia, he made 90. The next season he played for New South Wales against South Africa and stroked 213 not out and became the youngest player ever to score a double century for New South Wales. That's when the comparisons with the Don began to be made everywhere in earnest. Bradman, three years retired and playing golf, was missed. Wistful and wishful thinking predominated up and down the country. Keith Miller suggested it was expecting too much to label Ian Craig this way. But his wise words fell on deaf press ears. The name Bradman had sold papers for twenty-five years. The population was hungry for a champion like Bradman. A master's apprentice to be watched on the way up was terrific copy. And there was no doubt the new kid could bat. He was neat and graceful at the wicket with a tendency to leg-side shots. Even descriptions of his unorthodox grip had a Bradman-like resonance.

The national selectors, perhaps swept away by public fever and expectation, yet mindful of that recent double hundred, took a deep breath and gambled on him for the Fifth Test versus South Africa at the Melbourne Cricket Ground The crowd of 47,000 people rose to him and cheered him all the way to the wicket in his first ever Test innings. Craig was seventeen years and 239 days. Harvey en route to a magnificent double hundred was his partner. The score was three for 269. Craig, with leg glances and late cuts nudged his way to 53. The new ball was due. Craig slashed it to cover and was caught. The Melbourne crowd fell silent. It had been willing him to a century. When he disappeared from view, the Bradman link was voiced again.

Hadn't he failed in his First Test? Sure he had, scoring 18 and 1 against England at Brisbane in 1928. So a fifty was considered excellent. Craig came out in his second innings and scored 47, giving him an even 100 for the match. There was an omen in that for the dreamers.

It was enough for him to be selected for the 1953 Ashes tour after just ten first-class games. He was the youngest player ever to be sent to England. He felt the gaze of millions of critical foreign eyes focused by media fever to expect another Boy Wonder as they had in 1930. Then it happened. Ian Craig flopped. He couldn't handle pace or spin or English pitches. In twenty-seven innings he had a top score of 71 not out. His name dropped out of the headlines. His confidence reached rock-bottom.

The English continued to be polite. The Queen met him at Lord's soon after his eighteenth birthday. 'I understand this is your first visit to England?' she said.

'Yes, your Majesty,' Craig replied, 'and unless my batting improves it will be my last.' The Queen smiled.

'I certainly hope not,' she said, and probably meant it. But so did Craig.

He missed the Test series of 1954–55 to finish his pharmacy studies and national service duties. But he did enough in the 1955–56 season to secure a tenuous last place in the team to tour England again in 1956. Food poisoning put him out of action until the Second Test was over. Dwindling options caused tour selectors to cross their fingers and pick him for the Fourth Test after the Laker–Lock spin combination had murdered Australia at Leeds in the Third Test. Laker trapped Craig for 8 in Australia's first innings score of 84. In the second innings he came in at two for 55 to join the gutsy Colin McDonald (89). They put on 59 for the third wicket. Craig scraped, pushed, probed, glanced, missed and defended his way to 38 in 270 minutes spread over several rain-affected days. Australia was thrashed.

The team toured Pakistan and India on the way home. Craig had five innings: 0 and 18 on matting in Pakistan, and 40, 36 and 6 in India.

In the 1956–57 season the selectors knew they had to replace the old brigade led by Ian Johnson and find a new captain. Instead of choosing Neil Harvey, then still only twenty-eight, Benaud twenty-seven, or even Ray Lindwall, thirty-six, they decided on a youth policy and selected Ian Craig, twenty-two, to lead a team for a short tour of New Zealand. He didn't return the sort of batting figures that said he had a big future in Test cricket. But it was enough for a further gamble on Craig, who, it seemed, had become a permanent risk full of 'potential'.

By the time he was selected to lead the Australians to South Africa there was no more talk of Craig being another Bowral Boy. It was more reasonable to think of him as a right-handed Neil Harvey. Someone who could stay at the top for a decade and end with a very good average. Not a hundred, but 40 plus perhaps. Craig was personable, level-headed, educated and able to handle himself in any company. All these things became important on tour, especially in England, where he would be expected to perform in maybe twenty-five to thirty matches and make endless after-dinner speeches. The pressures were enormous. The hopeful judgment was that he could meet these demands.

Expectations were revived when the slight, rather fragile-looking 63-kilogram, 173-centimetre Craig began the African tour with a fine century against Rhodesia (Zimbabwe). Everyone liked and respected Ian Craig. He was sincere and unassuming. This generated harmony on tour among the players. Harvey, who had every right to expect to be captain after more than a decade at the top, could have been forgiven if he had caused problems for the tyro skipper. But he didn't. On the contrary, 'Harvs' got behind him as vice-captain and was more than helpful. It didn't help that the team manager had a heart attack so that Craig had to do two jobs for the first few weeks of the tour. But he handled everything manfully, without complaint. Despite illnesses and false starts even in his short career Craig had never been a whinger.

In the First Test, the youngest Test captain until that point in history, Craig handled his relatively new attack of Ian Meckiff, Alan Davidson, Ken Mackay, Lindsay Kline and Richie Benaud with tact and intelligence. He only scored 14 and 17 himself, but he led well. Benaud's 122 saved Australia from defeat.

In the Second Test, Jim Burke (189 in 578 minutes) and Colin McDonald (99) set the game up for Australia with an opening stand of 190. Kline finished it off with a hat trick. Craig was bowled for a duck but, although it concerned him, he had the big prize of his first Test win. Not even the Don managed that until his third game at the helm. And even the Don struggled with the bat in his first two games as skipper.

In the Third Test, Craig found touch with a fine 52 on a fiery pitch. Everyone breathed a sigh of relief and forgave the second innings duck. The game was drawn.

In the Fourth Test at Johannesburg, he juggled the order, sending the in-form Benaud in at number four, and dropping himself one place to number five. It was a little thing, but gave glimpses of his self-less, thinking approach. He wanted a flexible team, ready to sacrifice. Best to show the way. The move worked. Benaud belted a century and then took nine wickets in the two innings. Craig made just 3. But Australia won by ten wickets. He was forgiven again.

In the Fifth Test he failed twice more with 17 and 6, yet Australia won and he came home triumphant with a three–nil series under his tight belt.

The cold analysis of his series—103 runs at 14.71—and his tour average of 36.9 caused the realists among the selectors to face the fact that the experiment with a youthful leader was not working. Fate solved the problem. Craig contracted hepatitis during the winter of 1958. His light frame became frail. In two games he scored two ducks for New South Wales, the second being against Peter May's strong line-up in Australia to defend the Ashes in 1958–59. Craig felt he wasn't yet fit. He retired for the season. Richie Benaud took over and led Australia to a four–nil victory.

Unless Craig came back in spectacular fashion he would not regain the captaincy or his batting spot. There were moments when that early promise was glimpsed again—especially in showing courage against the really quick bowlers of the time such as Ian Meckiff and the West Indies' Wes Hall. But he needed the big innings gesture—a double hundred—to show he could do it after all. It didn't come. He was playing for the most competitive state and among a plethora of big-scoring batsmen, including Norm O'Neill, Neil Harvey (who had moved from Victoria), Brian Booth and Bob Simpson.

Craig might have struggled to keep his place had he not retired at twenty-six. He played eleven Tests, scoring 358 runs at 19.89. He appeared in 144 first-class games, making 7328 runs at 37.96, including fifteen centuries.

Ian Craig vanished from public view, happy to carry on his distinguished professional life as an executive of the Australian subsidiary of Boots, the giant British-based pharmacy chain. The fact that he made the transition with grace and determination to move on to a 'normal' life said much about his character. He married Rosslyn Carroll. They adopted a boy (Andrew) and had a boy (Jonathan) and a girl (Alexandra) of their own. Craig became a director then chairman of the Bradman Museum at Bowral where he lived. He was for three years a member of the NSWCA Board. He served for a total of 18 years on the SCG Trust from 1968 to 1996.

If ever there was promise unfulfilled in cricket, it was with Ian Craig. Yet he said he had no regrets. He would have done it all again. After all, he had played for and captained his country. The record shows that he was a successful captain, who led Australia through a series undefeated, and on foreign soil. Very few achieved that. And the statistics lied. He was a gifted, brilliant bat. Had Ian Craig been a first-class player today when he could have earned a big income as a contracted ACB player, he may have had another decade at the top instead of opting early for an outstanding working career. Given the extra time, most likely he would have recovered to fulfil his promise as a great Test player and captain.

28

RICHIE BENAUD
....

6 October 1930 –

Tests: 63; Captain: 28; Wins: 12; Losses: 4; Draws: 11; Ties: 1;
Win ratio: 42.86 per cent

THE ATTACKING ALL-ROUNDER

Richie Benaud's 1961 Ashes series had been woeful for nearly four Tests. Ailing with a damaged shoulder, he had taken six wickets at 45 runs each. He had made 38 runs in four innings at an average of less than 13. The Australian captain had not led his team to a win. At the beginning of the final day of the Fourth Test on 1 August everything was on the line. As the chips lay on that final morning, Benaud looked likely to lose the Test, the Ashes and his career.

The scorecard said that Australia was six for 331 in its second innings—just 154 ahead. The next morning it lost three quick wickets, including Benaud lbw to David Allen for 1. Australia was nine for 334. Big Garth McKenzie joined Alan Davidson. The lead was 157, with one wicket intact. England would have almost all day to get the runs. It was all over, almost. Then the tourists were given some hope. The final wicket partnership reached 20. Back in the pavilion a despondent Benaud was praying for a 200 lead. He and the rest of the team reckoned this would give them a semblance of a chance—something to defend.

Allen, brilliant in the morning in removing Ken Mackay, Wally Grout and Benaud, had conceded just two runs in nine overs. Davidson, the powerful, long-armed left-hander, decided that the pat-ball type of game, which he had endured so far, must end. He slammed Allen for 6, 4, 4, 6—20—in an over. They were all terrific shots. He reached his half-century. England's captain, Peter May, brought on Fred Trueman, the finest speedster of the era. Davidson greeted him with a slashing cut to the boundary. Australia was 400. The lead was well over 200.

Benaud was ecstatic. His champion state teammate had given Australia just a sliver of hope. This had turned into a glimmer by the time McKenzie was out for 32, leaving Davidson not out 77 and Australia all out for 432. The last pair added 98 in one of the best fighting partnerships ever, given the state of the game.

Australia led by 255 runs. England had 230 minutes to beat that lead. It would have to motor at 68 runs an hour, which was reasonable considering its powerful batting line-up.

England was none for 20 at lunch. Benaud, with leg spin, and Davidson, with medium-pace swing, were on at the commencement of the second session. They were doing as much containing with accuracy as attacking. Davidson removed Geoff Pullar, caught off a lollypop of a slow bouncer for 26. Imperious Ted Dexter came to the wicket. He crashed 76 in quick time. England was one for 150. It had 106 to make with a session and twenty minutes to get them.

Benaud, who had been in the front line as Dexter attacked, had taken none for plenty. In one last desperate gamble, he was bowling round the wicket, a radical move for the time. He was attempting to hit the rough outside the right-hander's leg stump. Dexter tried a forcing shot off the back foot and nicked the turning ball to keeper Grout. It was two for 150. Benaud had grabbed one back. England's best post-war bat, Peter May, came to the wicket. He ignored the first delivery. Benaud ran wide of the wicket for the next delivery and heaved the ball at those footmarks. May, a brilliant technician and stroke player, went to sweep. The ball bit and spun back forty centimetres past May's bat and legs, cannoning into leg stump.

Grout threw his hands high and yelled, 'Bowled, Richie!'

May, down on one leg, looked at his wicket, Grout and the umpires. He thought the keeper must have broken the stumps. He couldn't believe he had been bowled. A nod towards the pavilion from the umpire conveyed the shocking news to May. Benaud and his team embraced. May and Dexter were the batsmen Australia had to remove to have a chance.

England was three for 150. Tea was approaching. Benaud could now apply real pressure.

Brian Close came in for many comical swings and misses. He connected and hoicked Benaud for six. Moments later, he tried to lap the leg-spinner to the square-leg fence. The ball went straight to Norm O'Neill behind the square-leg umpire. The crowd groaned and fell silent. The Aussies embraced their skipper. He had removed three wickets in a couple of overs. England was now four for 158, still 98 short of victory. That Davidson–McKenzie partnership of 98 now had a deeper significance. Had it not happened, the game would have been lost.

Benaud then bowled the stubborn Raman Subba Row (49) with a top-spinner, the last ball before tea. The fielding team ran to each other again. Benaud had introduced the Aussie 'embrace'. Members everywhere tut-tutted, but it was a sign of the genuine passion, perhaps rooted in his French ancestry, that he brought to cricket.

The Australians left for the break with the score at five for 163. Benaud had bowled unchanged since lunch, wheeling in with his shirt unbuttoned and a distinctive action to deliver with a huge heave and rotation of his right shoulder. Just five weeks earlier fibrositis in the joint had stopped him from playing in the Second Test at Lord's.

After tea, England played for a draw. Only its bowlers were left. Benaud removed two. Ken Mackay and Bob Simpson took one each. With the score at nine for 201 Davidson bowled Brian Statham. Benaud leapt high. His return of six for 70 had won the match, the Ashes and immortality. In the space of less than a session he had gone from flop to fable. Benaud had bowled fifty overs in the match before taking a wicket. But he hadn't given up. It may have left the English gasping. But for anyone who knew Richie Benaud and his history, this magnificent comeback was a thrill but not surprising.

Richie Benaud had been recovering from adversity and winning throughout his career. He was a fighter.

Bowling bloodlines

Richie's father Lou, a leg-spinner, who taught in country New South Wales, took twenty wickets in a game for Penrith Waratah Club. This was before Richie was born. If the capacity to spin the ball from the leg wasn't in Richie Benaud's blood, then his father's enthusiasm for leg spinning was contagious from an early age.

Young Richard Benaud developed as a hard-hitting batsman and spinner for the Paramatta High School, then the Cumberland Club. For most of his early career and even when he began playing for the state in 1948–49 he was viewed more as a batsman who could bowl spin, rather than a spinner who could bat.

More telling than any of his outstanding performances with bat or ball for Cumberland (he averaged 41.66 with the bat in 1948–49) was an incident in a game for New South Wales Second XI versus Victoria. A bumper felled him when he was attempting a hook. The blow fractured his skull just above the right eye and left a dent half the size of the ball. He was operated on to remove some bone and straighten it out. Benaud didn't play again that season. An experience like this would have curtailed or finished other cricketers' careers. But Benaud came back the next season to play for his state. There was no helmet protection. Instead of ducking bouncers, he made sure he was in position before he hooked. But hook he did for the rest of his career, taking on the fastest bowlers at Test level. There may not have been anything definitive in his performances in those early years, yet that incident was a pointer to his courage and determination to reach the top.

In 1950–51, in his first season of first-class cricket, he took five for 270 and made 250 from eight innings with a top score of 93. In 1951–52 at twenty-one, he hit his first century (117), against South Australia. Steady form with bat and ball saw him fast-tracked into Test cricket.

Benaud played in the Fifth Test of the series versus West Indies, scoring 3 and 19, and taking one for 14. His solitary wicket was spinner Alf Valentine. Australia won and took the series four–one. In Shield cricket for 1951–52, Benaud produced 340 from ten innings and took thirteen at 42.84. He had improved, but only incrementally.

He would have to perform better. His batting was aggressive and becoming more effective. He had all the strokes and wasn't afraid to be unorthodox. Yet his results so far were not going to secure him a permanent Test spot in the top six. Benaud just wasn't taking enough wickets to justify choosing him as a bowler alone.

Benaud worked on all facets of his game and managed to play in four Tests against South Africa. In the Third Test at Sydney a flashing cut from John Waite hit Benaud, unsighted by the sun, in the mouth. An upper denture was smashed to pieces. Benaud was sent to hospital and didn't field again in South Africa's innings. But he did bat, sporting a bandage over his mouth. He was lbw for a duck, but that was insignificant compared to the signals he was sending out about himself. Three years earlier he had been struck down by a bumper. He had come back from that and now he had returned from another nasty 'hospital' blow. Benaud fielded and bowled in South Africa's second innings and took two for 21.

Soon afterwards, he was married to Marcia Lavender, still with a bandage over several stitches. You literally couldn't keep this good man down.

In the series he made 124 at 20.66, with a highest score of 45. He took ten wickets at 30.6. It was a fair all-round effort without setting the world on fire, but it was enough to gain him a trip to England in 1953, where he had a poor three Tests, averaging just 3 from five innings. His two wickets cost him 87 runs each. Yet the tour figures were more encouraging. He made 728 at 27.7 and took fifty-seven wickets at an excellent 22.23 runs each. Benaud took away two outstanding performances. Against Yorkshire, he hit 97 and took seven for 46. He also slammed 135 (including a then first-class record of eleven sixes) in 110 minutes at Scarborough against a strong England XI.

These efforts demonstrated to selectors, but most importantly to Benaud himself, that he was capable of brilliant things at the first-class level. The experience in England lifted his rating. In the 1953–54 Sheffield Shield season he scored 665 at 60.45, including three centuries: 158, versus Queensland at Brisbane; 144 not out, against Queensland at Sydney; and 112, playing Western Australia at Sydney. He also took thirty wickets at 27.73.

At twenty-three, Benaud had consolidated at the state level. In the 1954–55 Ashes he played in all Tests but had another lean time, scoring 148 runs at 16.44, and taking ten wickets at 37.7.

Early in 1955, he gained more joy from the birth of his first son, Gregory, but a week later was on his way to the West Indies for a five-Test series. There Benaud at last realised his potential at the highest level. He scored 246 runs at 41, with a highest score of 121 in the last Test at Sabina Park. It was his first Test hundred and he brought it up in seventy-eight minutes, then the third-fastest century ever scored in a Test. He hit 2 sixes and 15 fours. Benaud also topped the bowling averages, with eighteen wickets at 26.94 in Australia's three–nil series win.

Benaud continued this good batting form into the next domestic season, 1955–56, with 587 runs at 41.92, while his first-class bowling returns were 44 wickets at 21.61.

He was on the boat to England again in 1956. His overall figures for the tour were an improvement on 1953. This time he scored 871 runs at 34.84 with one century—160 versus Worcestershire—and took sixty at 22.28 (which were close to his previous figures.) But the Tests (lost one–two) were a disappointment for him and the entire team. He scored 200 at 25 and took eight wickets at 41.25. Yet Benaud, in his most readable book, *Anything But an Autobiography*, saw the Lord's Test as a turning point. Before the game, one of the game's finest writers, Neville Cardus, ranked him as a player to watch—a champion in the making. He noted that Benaud looked good in the nets 'defending seriously, scrupulously behind the ball; and his strokes, when he liberated them, were clean, true, strong. His reactions were swift and natural.' Cardus added that Benaud was twenty-five years old and looked every inch a cricketer. The writer predicted he would confound the critics who had written him off. (There were plenty in England in 1956—a fact that in later Ashes encounters would be a terrific spur.) Buoyed by this vote of confidence from such an illustrious critic, Benaud crashed a magnificent 97 in 113 balls. It was full of hooks and drives and helped the Australians to their only Test win of the otherwise miserable series.

There was more cheer on the way home in India, where Benaud starred with the ball in a three-Test series, taking a remarkable twenty-three wickets at 16.87. In the first innings of the First Test he took seven for 72. In the final Test he took six for 52 and five for 53, giving him his best returns in a Test of eleven for 105.

Setbacks and sensations

Richie Benaud had wished to follow his hero, Keith Miller, as captain of New South Wales. But the national selectors had anointed Ian Craig, and he took over the New South Wales captaincy. Benaud was disappointed, but nevertheless gave his full support to Craig during the 1956–57 domestic season and on a tour of New Zealand. Benaud maintained his all-round form, averaging 30 with the bat in twenty-one innings in Australia and New Zealand, while taking seventy-two wickets at 21.65.

While in New Zealand, a Christchurch chemist, Ivan James, gave Benaud a remedy—calamine lotion and boric acid powder—for his split and bleeding spinning fingers that had nagged him for years. The remedy and instructions saved his career. It was another turning point and Benaud was forever grateful for the advice from the pharmacist. Now free of the problem, his performances with the ball lifted in 1957. In the same year his second son, Jeffrey, was born.

With strong performances behind him in the West Indies and in India, Benaud, now twenty-seven, reached a peak in South Africa in 1957–58. In the Tests he scored 329 at 54.83, with two centuries, and took thirty wickets at 21.93.

In the First Test at Johannesburg he was a star with the bat, hitting a powerful yet restrained 122, as Australia fought back after South Africa's big innings of 470. Benaud then was successful with the ball (four for 95 and five for 49) in the Second at Cape Town.

In the Third Test at Durban he returned five for 114 in South Africa's only innings. Back at Johannesburg for the Fourth Test, Ian Craig sent Benaud in at number four, the highest he had ever batted. The all-rounder didn't let his young skipper down. His even 100 was top score in Australia's 401. Then he turned it on with the ball, taking nine wickets in the two innings (four for 70 and five for 84).

In the Fifth Test at Port Elizabeth Benaud produced another good double—43 and 6 not out, and five for 82 in the home side's second innings.

When Ian Craig ruled himself out at the start of the 1958–59 season, it seemed that Neil Harvey would captain Australia against the touring England side. Richie Benaud was a long shot. He had been captain of Central Cumberland for several seasons but this was a big step up. Everyone was guessing and Harvey seemed the logical choice.

As in the choice of a pope, no rationale would be proffered by the selectors or the ACB, which had the final say after a vote. The decision would have nothing to do with the two candidates' shortcomings. They had none. Any choice would have more to do with something outstanding in the chosen one's make-up as perceived by the Don and the other two national selectors. Harvey had not helped his cause by moving from Victoria (for employment purposes) to Sydney to play for New South Wales. It put him in direct contention for the job of skippering New South Wales with Benaud and Craig. He had not reckoned on the possibility of being skipper. It would take him a season or two to settle in Sydney and play for his new state.

The smoke came up from the Australian Cricket Board (ACB) headquarters chimney and the announcement was made. Richie Benaud would be the twenty-eighth Australian Test cricket captain. His magnificent efforts in South Africa had had a big influence. Neil Harvey was unlucky. He would be deputy to Benaud after filling that spot under Craig.

Benaud broke the news over the phone to Harvey, who accepted the disappointment with grace. 'I'll be playing for you, Rich,' he told his new captain. With men of such character running the national side, it was likely to do well. And it did: Australia won the Test series four–nil. Benaud, Harvey and the team were thrilled, after three successive Ashes defeats. Benaud had had another outstanding series and was far and away the best bowler, taking thirty-one wickets at 18.84. His batting (132 runs at 26.4 with a top score of 64) was only fair, but something had to give. He couldn't expect a repeat of the South African series with bat and ball, considering he was captain as well.

Benaud, a journalist by profession, handled everything with skill, including the media. There were plenty of contentious issues, especially over accusations that Australia's team contained 'chuckers'. It was clear that Benaud was a born leader in every respect with the capacity to extract the best from most of his players most of the time. No one felt excluded by Benaud's style. That toughness displayed after his head was bashed in a decade earlier formed the raw base to a fully developed cricketer and captain. The selectors, always an easy target, like the ACB, umpires and politicians, got it dead right.

Benaud's capacities were again put under the microscope on the toughest tour of all—to both India and Pakistan—for eight Tests from November 1959 to the end of January 1960. He had to counter all the horrors of the mid-twentieth-century tour of the subcontinent. Dodgy food, poor hotels, awful transport, strange umpiring decisions, extreme heat, injuries, stomach sickness and homesickness were just some of the challenges that a team, and particularly the skipper, had to deal with. Harmony and purpose were paramount. Benaud imposed them both. He pushed the strong, cajoled the sensitive and inspired everyone.

And he excelled with the ball. Benaud took eighteen wickets at 21.11 in Pakistan and twenty-nine at 19.59 in India. He was brilliantly supported by his left-hand pace weapon Alan Davidson, who backed up Benaud's forty-seven wickets with forty-one of his own. Harvey and O'Neill led the batting superbly.

The team came home with two series wins: two–nil against Pakistan and two–one against India. Again, as with Ian Johnson's success in India in late 1956, the Australians' efforts were underestimated. The lack of TV or radio coverage limited appreciation of this well-oiled machine that handled tough, different conditions in their stride.

Observers, who had taken no notice of this digging deep in Asia, tipped the talented West Indies to thrash the Australians in 1960–61. Certainly the Caribbean stars presented Benaud with a third mighty challenge inside two years. Bradman, as chairman of the ACB and the supremo of Australian cricket, asked Benaud's permission to speak to the team in Brisbane on the eve of the First Test. Bradman asked the team for brighter cricket. The 1958–59 Ashes had been hard-fought but dull overall for the average fan. Connoisseurs would always turn up. But the game would die if the mass of sports fans turned away from the game. Bradman's words, gently put but forthright and honest, were well aimed. This home unit was bristling with talent and fortitude, and now battle-hardened. They had to lift their rating against the frightening pace of Wes Hall; the wiles of spinners, Ramadhin and Valentine; the all-round brilliance of the greatest cricketer on earth, Gary Sobers; and the dashing batting line-up of Conrad Hunte, Cammie Smith, Rohan Kanhai and Frank Worrell.

The titanic struggle pulled back huge crowds to cricket. Over 90,000 turned up on the Saturday of the Melbourne Test over the New Year, rivalling even the massive crowd that had burst the Melbourne

Cricket Ground during the Melbourne versus Essendon Australian Rules 1959 Grand Final a year earlier.

The first Test tie in history—at Brisbane—had set up the series. Bradman was seen here and there in the pavilions, his permanent half-grin more of a ready smile than people had seen for years. Thanks to Benaud and his counterpart, Frank Worrell, cricket was back as the biggest drawcard in Australian sport. Benaud returned twenty-three wickets at 33.87, which were fine figures considering the opposition. The skipper elicited incredible performances from Davidson, who was the stand-out bowler of either side in a stand-out series that some dubbed the greatest ever. He took thirty-three wickets at 18.55. O'Neill (552 at 52.2) and Bob Simpson (445 at 49.44) delivered with the bat.

Australia won two–one.

Media magnet

Buoyed by this extraordinary success, Richie Benaud prepared himself with confidence for the last big challenge of his career—taking the Ashes in England in 1961. He had been part of the teams that had been crushed there in 1953 and 1956. The pain of those defeats was seared into his competitive mind. While playing against the brilliant West Indians was a career highlight, beating the 'Poms' at home was his number-one dream.

At thirty, he did this with a two–one series win, and at the absolute crunch delivered the coup de grâce himself. Then followed a wonderful domestic season for New South Wales, which dominated the Shield competition. Benaud had a fine summer, heading the first-class wicket-takers, and the averages with 47 at 17.97.

There was more to come, including a drawn Ashes series in Australia in 1962–63 against Ted Dexter's team. It was a tight, concede-nothing affair. Benaud's injured shoulder was not allowing him to bowl with the same freedom of previous years. He took seventeen wickets 40.47, his best effort being six for 115 from forty-two overs in the first innings of the First Test at Brisbane. Benaud compensated for this reduction in his returns with the ball by stepping up with the bat. He hit 227 at 32.43, including scores of 51, 48 and 57. These innings were valuable in a close series.

He captained Australia once more, in the First Test of the 1963–64 series against South Africa. It was to be a mixed but memorable game for the skipper. He scored a speedy 43 to bring him to 2013 runs and make him the first player ever to reach the double of 2000 runs and 200 wickets in Tests. Less appetising was the fate of Ian Meckiff, a loyal team member for most of the past six years. He was called for throwing by umpire Colin Egar. The double-jointed left-handed quick was taken off and never bowled again. Apart from this sad and sour moment in Australian cricket, the captain had a good game personally, scoring 43 and taking five for 68.

The match was drawn. Benaud chatted with Bradman during proceedings and told him he thought he should stand down as skipper. He was not going to England for the 1964 Ashes. The shoulder wouldn't take much more. He was thirty-three. It was time to hand over to a new man, Bob Simpson. Benaud then broke his fingers in a club match and missed the Second Test at Melbourne. Australia won by eight wickets. He returned to play under Simpson, making 43 and 90. He could still deliver with the bat and as a bowler. He took three for 55 and was as accurate as ever.

Two Tests later he was able to take four for 118 off forty-nine overs. It showed he could still command respect from opposing batsmen. But Benaud had made the decision. It was over. His last series' statistics saw him score 231 at 33, and take twelve wickets at 37.42. In all he played sixty-three Tests, scoring 2201 runs at 24.46, and taking 248 wickets at 27.03. In first-class cricket he played 259 matches, scoring 11,719 runs at 36.5, while snaring 945 wickets at 24.73.

Surgery techniques of three or four decades later would have added another three to five years to Benaud's life at the top of the game. Nevertheless, he had a mighty career as an all-rounder and captain. He never lost a series of the six in which he captained from 1958 to 1963.

There was plenty for life after cricket for Benaud. A casualty of his life on the road and stretches away from home was his first marriage, which ended in divorce. At thirty-six, he married an English woman, Daphne Surfleet.

There could never be a substitute for the thrill of playing but Richie Benaud made a smooth transition into TV commentary following training with the BBC. His background in daily Sydney journalism also helped. Benaud could script something as quickly as anyone. And he adapted well to the visual medium. He delivered clearly and succinctly. He kept his body still and wasn't too busy in front of the camera, a no-no when a commentator is appearing in someone's living room every other day. (The frenetic ones were switched off, but the low-key presenters were left on and became part of the furniture.) Benaud didn't have the urge to fill dead air, although he had to. He developed a dry style that could always see the off-beat, even comical side of media presentation. He learned never to make obvious comments to accompany the visual. 'Oh, he's dropped it,' were words that never fell from Benaud's pursed lips. He always constructed another dimension to the visual. When action replays became easily facilitated, he picked out something dramatic or interesting that had not been seen—another angle. It could have been his motto.

In the mid-1960s he began a four-decade career as a TV commentator all year round. British viewers of the BBC became familiar with him as did Australian viewers of the Nine Network. Benaud involved himself in the Kerry Packer experiment to take over cricket in the mid-1970s. When that was over, Benaud went on, summer after summer. When the BBC lost the rights to Broadcast TV to Channel Four in England late in the late 1990s, viewers, including well-known cricket-lovers such as Mick Jagger and former British prime minister John Major, protested that Benaud would not be on their screens. Channel Four just had to contract him, even after it announced it would be looking for 'fresh blood' to comment on cricket to make it more accessible to a younger audience.

Richie Benaud did nothing. He didn't lobby or write a protest letter to *The Times*. He didn't have to. He'd become an institution, not Australian, but British. The establishment made sure he was still the main face of cricket in Britain. It was a compliment to him from many fans who had never even seen him play. He made laid-back look frenetic. Yet behind that tinder-dry wit was a professionalism that made it look all so easy. What the fans didn't see was that Richie Benaud, the anchorman, worked very hard at delivering seamlessly without glitches. He was there in the morning to prepare the opening presentation and last in the evening to do summaries. He applied himself to his second love—TV presentation—with the same verve, drive and skill that he had applied to cricket.

Richie Benaud ranked as one of the best all-rounders ever to play the game for Australia. He is also placed high in the list of talented leg-spinners, from Arthur Mailey to Shane Warne. And he was a captain out of the top drawer. No one in the post-Bradman era is ranked higher.

29

NEIL HARVEY

....

8 October 1928 –

Tests: 79; Captain: 1; Wins: 1;
Win ratio: 100 per cent

THE COMPACT CAVALIER

Robert Neil Harvey was thirty-two when injury to Richie Benaud gave him his chance to captain Australia. It was the Lord's Test of 1961. England won the toss and batted in the second game of what was the heavyweight title in world cricket. England had not been beaten in the last eighteen games. Its last loss was in Melbourne in early 1959. Australia had swept all before it, including England, since 1956. In effect, England was challenging again and this time it had an advantage. It had beaten Australia in England in the last two series of 1953 and 1956. Yet this was also its disadvantage. The Australians, particularly Benaud and Harvey, captain and vice-captain, had experienced those defeats. They had felt the lash and humiliation of being beaten by the 'Poms'. In 1953 England had broken Australia as a post-war force. More galling had been 1956. The Australians batted on substandard Test wickets that would not do for a primary school match. Laker and Lock destroyed the tourists.

The First Test of the 1961 series had been drawn at Edgbaston. There, Harvey had begun brilliantly with his twentieth Test hundred of 114. Now he had to lead the side. Low-key, always in charge of himself, 'Nin' (as he was nicknamed) relished the challenge at the home of cricket. It turned out to be The Battle of the Ridge on a fiery, two-paced wicket.

'It made batting to the fast bowlers a nightmare experience,' Harvey wrote in his book, *My World of Cricket*. 'The ridge was no figment of the imagination—it definitely existed at the Nursery End . . . throughout the game balls bounced off it at the oddest of angles and heights.'

(The wicket was dug up after the game and the ridge was found to be the top of a drain that had been laid twenty years earlier.)

So Harvey had first use of his bowlers on this most dramatic of strips. In the dressing room before they came out to field, Davidson said: 'Best of luck, Nin. I'll try to pull out something special for you today.'

England made 206. The dynamic Davidson delivered more than he promised, taking five for 42. No English player, except for opener Raman Subba Row (48) could handle the treacherous conditions.

Harvey came in at two for 6 to join Bill Lawry and faced England's top speed combination of fiery Fred Trueman and deadly accurate Brian Statham. The two left-handed batsmen found forcing shots impossible. It took exceptional skill and courage to reach stumps intact at two for 42.

Harvey and Lawry carried on in the second morning until 81, when Trueman had Harvey caught for 27. Lawry continued on tenaciously, taking many belts on the body from the shooting deliveries. He reached 130, an innings that would rank, given the degree of difficulty with the ridge, as one of the great fighting innings of all time. Australia made 340, a lead of 134.

England replied with 202. No one in the powerful English line-up, which included Ted Dexter, Peter May, Colin Cowdrey and Ken Barrington, four of the country's finest ever bats, could cope as Lawry had. Garth McKenzie was the destroyer this time, with five for 37.

Australia then collapsed to be four for 19. Harvey, caught behind off Trueman for 4, said to the grim-faced, in-coming Peter Burge, 'Keep playing your shots, Pete.'

Pete took heed. He smashed 37 with pulls and hooks to take Australia home by five wickets. In the battle of the heavy punchers of world cricket, Australia had gone one up with three to play. And Neil

Harvey in his one and only Test as skipper had had a win at Lord's, with cool confidence and aplomb. He would later retire with a one hundred per cent strike rate as captain.

Sailing high with the invincibles

The temperament Neil Harvey displayed in that Lord's Test and whenever he captained was evident at an early age. So was his enormous skill. He made the Fitzroy district team at fifteen. At eighteen in 1946–47, now an apprentice fitter and turner, he made the Victorian team. He was the first of the fine post-war players to not have his cricket career interrupted by international hostilities. In fact, the war helped his career. National selectors were looking for talented youth to blend in with the experienced players of the pre-war 1930s. Harvey, compact at 171 centimetres tall and weighing 66.5 kilograms, fitted all criteria. He was left-handed in a right-hander's world, but it helped. There would always be a place in Bradman's team for the sake of balance if the leftie had the talent and temperament. Harvey had both. He announced his credentials with 154 against Tasmania. He was inspired by his brother Mervyn, who made the Test side as an opener against England during the season. Mervyn only made 43 in his two knocks, but his younger brother by ten years thought it was not such an impossible hope that he too might make it to the top.

A year later, Bradman and his co-selectors gave Harvey the nod at the Test level against India. It was a trial for the 1948 English tour. If Harvey did halfway well, he would be on the boat for England. He began with 13 at Adelaide in the Fourth Test in the shadow of Bradman's dashing 201 and the fine double display by India's Vijay Samuel Hazare, who made 116 and 145.

Harvey didn't think he had done enough for selection in front of a home crowd at the Melbourne Cricket Ground in the Fifth Test. But the gifted, callow youth didn't know the mind of his skipper, who knew talent when he saw it. Bradman thought Harvey was the best batsman to come forward in a long time. He made sure he got a second chance.

The youth, set down as number six, didn't think he would bat on the first day, 6 February 1948. Bradman was in and batting beautifully. But he had an attack of fibrositis on 57 and retired hurt rather than aggravate the problem and put his tour of England in jeopardy. Harvey was in and in touch from the first ball he faced. The next afternoon, in front of an appreciative Melbourne Saturday crowd, he reached 95. Lala Amarnath bowled a shortish ball. Harvey turned it forward of square leg and it went close to the big scoreboard boundary, the longest square of the wicket in the world. He and his batting partner, Ray Lindwall, ran five—a rare first-class event. It was even more rare to reach a century this way. But there it was. A large audience stood and cheered in acknowledgment of a young champion on his way to a sensational career. The spectators who saw that innings felt they were watching someone special. Harvey went on to 153.

Neil Harvey was selected for the 'Invincibles' team to tour England in 1948. He found the going tough early as the 'baby' of the squad at nineteen. He finally cranked up against Lancashire at Manchester, scoring 36 and 76 not out in late May. Soon after in early June at Hove against Sussex he scored 100 not out. Harvey had to wait until the Fourth Test at Leeds before he was selected in his first Ashes Test. He was still several months short of twenty years when he made 112 from 183 balls. He scored four centuries on that 1948 tour in twenty-two innings for an aggregate of 1129 at 53.76, a fabulous beginning for one so young.

Harvey then toured South Africa in 1949–50 and fulfilled the promise he had shown at the MCG and in England by dominating a Test series soon after his twenty-first birthday. There was good cause for comparing him with Bradman. No Australian since he eclipsed the cricket world had such an impact. In the Tests he hit 660 at 132. His scores were 34, 178, 23 not out, 2, 151, 56 not out, 100, and 116. Four centuries in those eight innings were accompanied by another five hundreds on tour. He batted in every condition and demonstrated an ability to rip an attack apart or defend for a long dig. He was number five in the line-up but it was just a matter of time before he would be moved up the order.

While in Johannesburg he met Iris Greenish. They married four years later in Melbourne and had a son, Robert, and a daughter, Anne.

During the 1950–51 home series against England Harvey came down to earth a little with a mere 362 at 40.22. It was hardly a failed series, but he didn't score a century. He had some trouble with Alec Bedser, who was the only bowler to get him out in the first three Tests. A year later he scored just 261 at 26.1 at number four against the West

Indies. Spinners Alf Valentine (left-arm finger spin) and Sonny Rama-dhin (off- and leg-breaks) troubled him. He had never experienced such a combination.

Harvey had not scored a Test century for nearly three years when the South Africans toured Australia in 1952–53. He relished facing them again and scored a massive 834 at 92.67 in nine innings, batting mainly at number three. His scores were 109, run out 52, 11, 60, 190, 84, 116, 205 and 7. This surpassed Bradman's 806 (at 201.5 from five innings) against South Africa in 1931–32.

Harvey toured England again in 1953, and in a losing side per-formed creditably with 346 at 34.6 and a top score of 122 at Man-chester. The tour returns, however, were outstanding. He hit 2040 runs at 65.8, with ten centuries, which put him up with Bradman and Trumper for a tour performance.

When England toured Australia in 1954–55 he was eager to make amends for his mediocre (for him) effort in England in the Tests. He came out of the blocks with 162 at Brisbane and then 92 not out on a Sydney greentop, an innings worthy of double century status, consid-ering that Statham and 'Typhoon' Tyson were on song in this innings as they fired out Australia for 184. After those two fine innings, Harvey fell away, to record an aggregate of 354 at 44.25. England won the series three–one. Harvey was now Australia's top bat in a side that had come down from the heights of the immediate post-war period 1946 to 1952.

He consolidated as Australia's number three in the West Indies early in 1955 with scores of 133, 133, 38, 41 not out, 74, 27 and finally a magnificent 204 at Sabina Park. His tally was 650 from seven innings at an average of 108.33. Harvey was restored as one of history's heavyweight bats.

But pathetic conditions of bad weather and even worse pitches in England in 1956 saw him reduced to just 197 runs at 19.7, with a top score of 69 at Headingley. Australia was mowed down by spinners Jim Laker and Tony Lock.

His confidence was restored on the tour of India on the home journey, when he made 253 at 63.25, with a top score at Bombay of 140. Spinning on fair wickets or matting held no terrors for this great dancer. He loved moving to the pitch of the ball, and was the best batsman in the world doing it. In a period where coaches in England

and some in Australia ordered players to stay at home and play from the crease, Harvey was a beacon of hope for risk takers who didn't wish to be bogged down. There was no better sight in cricket than Harvey, twinkling his toes with that one–two–one balletic movement down the wicket for a cover drive. Not since Bradman had anyone shone so outstandingly at this alleged unorthodoxy.

Harvey was also a sensational fielder, especially in the covers. His background in baseball gave him a whipping, fast throw. Almost nothing got past him at cover in twenty years of any form of cricket. One of the crowd-pulling attractions in the game in the late 1950s was he and Norm O'Neill prowling the covers to Benaud, Davidson and the other bowlers of that era.

The loyal deputy

Neil Harvey skippered Victoria, but at twenty-nine was overlooked for the national captaincy in favour of Ian Craig, just twenty-two. With hindsight this was a wrong turn for selectors as Craig, despite success-fully leading Australia through South Africa in 1957–58 (in which Harvey had a poor series with just 131 runs at 21.83), dropped off the scene through illness.

Neil Harvey reached thirty and began to worry about his life after cricket, a common affliction for most cricketers of the time, who were not earning a living from the game. After serious thoughts of moving to South Africa in 1958, Harvey stopped selling sports goods in Melbourne and moved to Sydney to take up a better-paid job with a glass and diningware company. Necessity then conspired against his opportunity to captain Australia. While he was settling into Sydney, Craig, weakened over the 1958 winter by hepatitis, dropped out of big cricket. That left the captaincy open. After meetings that must have agonised the Australian Cricket Board (ACB), Harvey was bypassed, even though he been seconded to captain an Australian X1 versus England before the Ashes of 1958–59. Richie Benaud was chosen.

Harvey, ever the vice-captain bridesmaid, showed exceptional character despite the huge disappointment and got behind Benaud as he had Craig. Australia won the 1958–59 series four–nil. Satisfaction at regaining the Ashes after three successive defeats overrode any negative feelings that Harvey may have had. He was thrilled to be a big part of the Australian victory, scoring 291 at 48.5, which just happened to be close to his career average. His 167 in the Second Test at Melbourne was the dominant batting performance of the game and the series.

Harvey set off again as Benaud's deputy in November 1959 for eight Tests against Pakistan and India. He was a mainstay of the batting, returning 273 at 54.6 versus Pakistan in three Tests, and 356 at 50.86 versus India in Five Tests. He hit two centuries against India, but his finest knock was a stunning 96 at Dacca against Pakistan on matting. While Fazal Mahmood ran through his teammates, Harvey sparkled and drove his way to one of his finest ever innings. In trying conditions on an unfamiliar surface his sheer class with the bat emerged.

Victorious now as vice-captain in series against South Africa, England, Pakistan and India, Harvey and his new leader had to face their biggest challenge yet, the West Indies in Australia in 1960–61. Australia won two–one.

Despite having a poor series—143 at 17.88 in eight innings, Neil Harvey, now thirty-two, was deputy to Benaud again for the 1961 Ashes tour of England. This was Harvey's last big challenge. He had experienced the highs of winning in 1948, and the lows of losing in 1953 and 1956. Now he wished to square the ledger and experience a winning last tour of England. Australia won two–one, with Harvey captaining one of those wins and Benaud the other. Harvey's aggregate was a commendable 338 at 42.25. Only Bill Lawry, in the series of his life, did better. On tour, Harvey notched five centuries. His aggregate was 1452 at an average of 44.

Harvey turned up for one last hurrah against England in Australia in 1962–63, for an aggregate of 395 at 39.5, including a top score of 154 at Adelaide.

At thirty-four, and while still capable of outstanding performances, Neil Harvey retired from cricket after fifteen years at the top. After settling into the Test team in 1948, he had never lost his place. In seventy-nine Tests, Harvey scored 6149 runs at 48.42, with twenty-one centuries and sixty-four catches. He played in 306 first-class games, scoring 21,699 runs at 50.93 with sixty-seven centuries.

After a twenty-year first marriage Harvey divorced and later—at forty-seven—married Barbara McGifford. Harvey's work career extended into a successful business distributing tupperware, kitchen and cosmetic products.

In 1998, he enjoyed the accolades showered on the 1948 Invincibles for their fifty-year anniversary. Harvey said that the older players—he was the youngest—taught him all about life on that incredible tour.

During the 1999–2000 season he was named in the best Australian team of the twentieth century. This was the crowning accolade of a great career. He was placed between Don Bradman and Greg Chappell in the batting order. It was the finest tribute of all.

30

BOB SIMPSON

3 February 1936 –

Tests: 62; Captain: 39; Wins: 12; Losses: 12; Draws: 15;
Win ratio: 32.5 per cent

BATSMAN, LEGGIE, SLIPPER, CAPTAIN, COACH

Bob Simpson had a complex. He had scored more than forty centuries in first-class cricket without making one in Tests. After twenty-nine matches—seven of them as captain—and fifty-one innings, he won the toss in the Fourth Test at Manchester in the 1964 Ashes and batted. If ever there was a chance to 'crack the ton' it was here, on a flat, fair batting track. He had plenty of time too. Australia was leading one–nil in the series. If it forced another draw then the Ashes, retained in the drawn 1962–63 series, would remain with the Australians. As skipper Simpson could dictate how long his team batted. The plan was to bat as long as possible, even into a third day.

Simpson and Bill Lawry began with a solid, stolid opening stand of 201, before Lawry was run out for 106. Soon afterwards Simpson, who had moved gingerly through the 90s, reached his first Test hundred. 'No one could describe the feeling of relief that flowed through me when the magical three figures went up on the scoreboard,' Simpson reflected after his belated triumph. 'I don't know of any player who was on the international scene as long as I without scoring a century.

I was feeling a bit silly about it by this stage.'

Once the barrier was broken he set about making bowlers—they just happened to be England's—pay. He batted on into the 'zone' that he was familiar with as a multi-double centurion in state games. In 1959–60, opening for Western Australia at Neil Harvey's suggestion, Simpson had scored 98, 236 not out, 230 not out, 79, 98 and 161 not out—902 runs at an average of 300.66. Big scores became a habit for Simpson—outside Tests. The 'zone' territory, where few have gone, was familiar to him. Now, as he built this innings beyond the century, he recalled all those other big knocks. They kept him going. So did the knowledge that with each run and over he was edging himself towards captaining an Australian team that did not lose the Ashes. 'Not losing' became buzzwords. Instead of taking a risk and going for a win, he was securing a draw first.

But he needed partners. Ian Redpath (19), Norm O'Neill (47) and Peter Burge (34) came, did a little job and went. Then the quiet, unassuming Brian Booth arrived at the crease on day two. Together, Simpson and Booth were able to build a big link of 219 runs before Booth (98) was out.

Simpson reached 265 not out by stumps on day two. He had got another one back, if you thought of a double hundred as two centuries, and was well into his third. He woke on day three, Saturday, 25 July, not to plaudits from the papers, but attacks. He was killing cricket, one paper said. He was sending spectators out of the ground, another remarked. They would have been English spectators, not Australian, but the point was made.

Bob Simpson came out on day three and belted everything, scoring another 46 in forty minutes, and leading Australia to eight declared for 656. The captain's score of 311 was just the third triple century by an Australian in England. The others—304 and 334—were both made by Don Bradman. Only one Englishman, Len Hutton with 364, had scored a triple century anywhere against the ancient adversary. Later, Bob Cowper in 1965–66 with 307 in Melbourne, would join the unique Ashes triple centurion club. It would include just four members in the long history of cricket.

The huge score set up an opportunity for another English player—Ken Barrington—to attempt to break in. He reached 256 and his membership was rejected. The game fizzled to a hideous run-laden draw. But Bob Simpson didn't lose any sleep over it. He had made his long-awaited breakthrough. In so doing he had ensured that the Ashes stayed with Australia for another series.

Fly slipper

The son of a Scottish printer and soccer player, Robert Baddeley Simpson was a child cricketing prodigy, like Ian Craig, who emerged in New South Wales's ranks around the same time. Simpson played for New South Wales as twelfth man a week before his seventeenth birthday in late January of 1953. He fielded in that game. Captain Keith Miller put him straight into the slips. This broke convention. You didn't put a twelfth man in a close catching position. But Miller wanted to win. He knew this kid from Marrickville could take a brilliant slips catch. He already had freakish abilities and had made a speciality of the position. The lad was so gifted with sight and finger coordination that he could amuse others with his ability to catch flies. It proved a useful occupation more than once on Australian fields.

Like Craig, Bob Simpson was nursed along early as a potential Test-standard, right-hand batsman. He didn't have a classic style. There was a tendency to play chest on, which may have restricted his ability to drive either side of the wicket, although Simpson was never short of these strokes when he felt the inclination to make them, especially on the leg side. He had a strong defence and could play brilliantly square of the wicket.

Simpson was in his twelfth game for the state late in the 1954–55 season when his promise seemed on the way to fulfilment. He stroked his way to 98 against Len Hutton's England touring team with impressive, unruffled style.

Hutton tested Simpson at that score with gamesmanship, by taking his team off the field when it began to drizzle. The umpires stayed on with the batsmen. An ABC radio commentator at the time remarked, 'I'd heard rumours about the English aversion to water, but this makes cats look like happy surfers!'

When the light rain abated, the umpires beckoned the unusually sensitive English team back on the field. Simpson, fearing further delays, went down the wicket to spinner Johnny Wardle and was stumped. It riled the nineteen-year-old that he let impatience rob him of a prized century against Hutton's tough, talented squad.

Bob Simpson looked on as Ian Craig was fast-tracked into Test cricket while he struggled to hold a place in a strong New South Wales team. After four seasons to the end of 1955–56 he took a gamble and moved to Western Australia, changing his occupation from accountancy to sports journalism with the *Daily News*. The stocky 179-centimetre 21-year-old decided he had to build a platform of good performances. There were enough during the 1956–57 season for him to just make the national team to tour New Zealand under Ian Craig. Simpson was then picked to tour South Africa in 1957–58. The Western Australia move paid off when he was selected for his debut Test in the first of the series against South Africa at Johannesburg in December 1957.

Search for the fifth man

Bob Simpson began with a solid 60 before spinner Hugh Tayfield trapped him lbw. His following six innings left him with an aggregate of 136 at 22.67. Simpson wasn't satisfied with these returns. His restless drive to reach the top was predicated on two factors. First, he had to have opportunity, which he created for himself by his move to Western Australia. Second, once the chances at Test level were offered, he had to perform. Luck, the tough-minded 22-year-old realised, was no substitute for a technique that would lead to performance. Instead of accepting the fate of a poor series, or pointing out that he had done better than Craig, Simpson sought advice on how to do better. He couldn't approach his skipper, who was having his own trouble with form. Instead he turned to the team vice-captain, the genial Neil Harvey, who would always be generous with advice if approached. Harvey went to the nets with him and explained he was playing too chest on, particularly in back-foot defence. This was leading to other problems. Later, when the rare chances arose, Simpson asked Don Bradman for tips and received helpful pointers. The young batsman was never going to die wondering whether he could improve technically. He worked hard in the nets and made a conscious effort to try modifications in the middle in club and state games.

In 1958, during the off-season before Peter May's team arrived for the 1958–59 Ashes series, Simpson married twenty-year-old Meg McCarthy.

He lost his Test place to Norm O'Neill for the Brisbane First Test.

O'Neill, who had missed the tour of South Africa, had amassed a string of scores with his powerful style during the 1957–58 domestic season. But Peter Burge, not O'Neill, failed at Brisbane. Simpson, who was running hot with his better technique in state games, was back in for the Second Test at Melbourne.

Expectations were high for Simpson's return, after he had earned his place again with high first-class scores. But Peter Loader trapped him lbw for a duck in his only innings. Such was the competition for a Test spot, Simpson was dumped for Les Favell in the musical chairs effort to find a player at number five after Burke, McDonald, Harvey and O'Neill, whose places were all secure. After number five came the outstanding all-rounders Ken Mackay, Benaud and Alan Davidson. The selectors could afford to tinker with five: there were solid batting buffers either side of it. They even dispensed with a fifth batsman altogether in the Fifth Test in Melbourne in order to accommodate a four-man pace attack of Davidson, Ian Meckiff, Ray Lindwall and Gordon Rorke.

Simpson, in a bitter disappointment, was pushed out of contention after one failure. He buried the feeling by becoming a professional for Accrington in the Lancashire League. He earned 950 pounds. The experience on English wickets was invaluable. It was another career move that would later pay off for him. Simpson had to adjust to different conditions, which he did with zest, scoring 1444 at 103. Not even the great Gary Sobers, also playing as a professional that year, could better this record.

But while the local League's followers realised that he was an outstanding cricketer who could bat brilliantly, bowl a mean leg-break and catch like no one had ever seen in such company, no Australian selector witnessed his development. He was left out of Richie Benaud's squad to tour Pakistan and India in 1959–60.

Study of the Australian team provided only one spot where Simpson could force his way back: opening. Jim Burke had retired and it was up for grabs. Neil Harvey suggested he should try. It was time for re-invention at the top of the order for Western Australia. Again, Simpson put his head down, knowing that the national selectors would be watching him, or at least be alert to his efforts. He showed aptitude as an opener, constructing big double hundreds against New South Wales and Queensland. Even though the opposition was sub-Test standard, these performances were hard to ignore.

They tipped him back into the Test side as an opener against West Indies for the sensational 1960–61 series. Simpson and Bill Lawry had to face the frightening speed of Wes Hall. There was also the all-round skill of Gary Sobers, who delivered medium-pace and spin, and the wiles of spinners Alf Valentine, Sonny Ramadhin and Lance Gibbs.

The challenge was the making of 23-year-old Bob Simpson, Test cricketer. He started with a courageous 92 at Brisbane and collected 445 runs at 49.44. His quick eyes and hands allowed him to evade the short stuff. In the final innings of the series, he dared to take on Hall in a bold counterattack. It was electrifying for the big crowd at the Melbourne Cricket Ground. With every shot they wondered whether this new reckless Bob Simpson would be out as he up-and-undered, hooked and drove. He crashed 18 off Hall's first over. His first 27 came from fourteen balls. Hall was taken out of the attack. When West Indies captain Worrell banished his big champion to the deep, Simpson was cheered and clapped by the crowd, who appreciated the importance of winning this round in a titanic, last-innings battle to win the series. Australia was chasing 258 runs late on the second-last day. Colin McDonald made just 11 before being out in the opening stand of 50. Simpson went on to 92, before off-spinner Gibbs bowled him. It was the game's top score. Simpson's inventiveness and courage gave the Australian innings just enough impetus to scrape in by two wickets, with O'Neill (48) and Burge (53) assisting. The win gave Australia the series two–one.

Bob Simpson, formerly a fringe player, had created the chance to be a permanent Test team member.

Opening salvos

No one counted on the success of Bill Lawry on the 1961 tour, and his great form created a quandary for selectors, but it was a welcome one. He had to be in the Test team. Colin McDonald, who had held down the opener's job with distinction and courage for some years, would stay. The only solution was to drop Simpson down to number six. He made 76, 0, 15, 2 and 3 before Benaud put him back opening with Lawry in the vital Fourth Test at Old Trafford. There he made 4 and 51. In the Fifth Test at the Oval he made 40, giving him an aggregate of 191 at 23.88. But his usefulness to the side was greater than these figures suggest. He took seven catches at slip and took seven wickets at 32.71, including four for 23 in England's first innings at Old Trafford. He was a capable leg-spinner and a back-up or change bowler with whom Benaud could create permutations.

Bob Simpson was dissatisfied with his batting, which would make or break his career. McDonald's retirement after the tour, however, took pressure off his place in the team. It meant Simpson had one of the opener's spots for the 1962–63 Ashes series, in which he did well in every Test, scoring 401 at 44.56 with a top score of 91. In ten innings he hit 4 fifties. He and Lawry had not quite synchronised their scoring for steady opening partnerships, but they were persevered with against South Africa in 1963–64. Simpson scored 361 at 40.11, and the combination got Australia off to a 'good' start—at least 50 runs—in half their partnerships.

Simpson took over as captain of Australia from the Second Test in Melbourne.

Led by Simpson, Australia defended the Ashes in 1964. Simpson hit 458 (distorted by his 311 at Old Trafford) at 76.33. Again he and Lawry were out of sync. They reached 50 only twice together. Yet individually they did well. They got it right four times out of six starts later in the year in the 1964–65 tour of Pakistan and India. In the one-off Test against Pakistan, Simpson showed his skill, versatility, concentration and determination when he hit 153 and 115. Simpson, with 292 at 48.67, eight catches at slip and six wickets at 25.17, showed that he was in control as skipper, slipper, leggie and batsman in the drawn series versus India.

He led Australia in its next round of Tests, this time against the West Indies. He and Bill Lawry found the going tough on several grounds that were without sightscreens. These made facing Hall and Griffith treacherous, especially as the latter used a blatantly crooked elbow to bowl his brutal bouncers and spearing yorkers. Apart from being an obvious 'chucker', Griffith had a long drag of his trailing foot that brought him more than a metre closer to the uneasy batsmen. Simpson protested to West Indian cricket supremo Sir Frank Worrell, 'Chucked out! How would that look in the record books?'

Simpson and Lawry didn't crank up together until the Fourth Test at Bridgetown, when they put on a record 382-run opening stand.

Simpson made 201 and Lawry 210. Simpson was Australia's second-best performer for the series, making 399 at 49.88. Only Bob Cowper, with 417 at 52.13, gave a more even performance in a series that Australia lost one–two. Simpson added to his importance to the team by taking eleven catches at slip. No one had ever performed better in this vital fielding position. It was an amazing effort considering that he had to run the team as well. But it heightened his concentration. He was in the game all the time and even sent down 111.5 overs of leg spin for a return of five for 263.

A broken wrist and chickenpox kept Simpson out of two Tests against England in 1965–66, in which Brian Booth filled in as captain. In his three Tests, Simpson hit 59 and 67 at Melbourne in the Second Test, and 225 in the Fourth Test at Adelaide. His aggregate was 355 at 88.75. Australia and England won one Test each in a drawn series.

Simpson led Australia to a second series loss (one–three) against South Africa away in 1966–67, even though he performed up to his own high standard, with 483 runs at 48.3 and a best score of 153.

When the Indians toured Australia in 1967–68, Bob Simpson decided after the Second Test that he would retire from Test cricket. His scores of 55, 103 and 109 made it propitious timing. He was going out at his top. Simpson didn't expect to be dropped for the Third Test, but the selectors were keen to give others a trial for the 1968 tour of England. They brought Simpson back in the Fourth Test of the series at Sydney for a final curtain call. When everyone wished him a hundred he made three and 20 run out. But Bob Simpson could not be kept out of the action in his farewell, taking three for 38 in the first Indian innings. In the second, on a turning wicket, he took a career best of five for 59 and snared three catches, therefore taking a hand in eight dismissals. His 'final' series figures were exceptional. He made 294 at 58.8—his second-best figures ever—and took thirteen wickets at 16.38. He also took seven catches. All this was done just short of his thirty-second birthday and in front of a true home crowd.

Answering the calls

'Simmo', as he was mostly called, didn't move too far away from the game. He became a public relations man, and an early cricket 'manager', looking after players' extra earnings in promotion and advertising.

At a time when cricketers struggled to keep playing and earn enough to survive, he was welcomed. He also wrote a book that was the opposite of good PR and not welcomed by some. His resentment against 'chuckers' boiled over in *Captain's Story*. Ian Meckiff, who had suffered from being cruelly drummed out of the game for alleged throwing, was aggrieved at Simpson's words. He sued for libel. The case was settled out of court after five years of litigation. Simpson had to apologise and make a settlement. Unsold copies were pulped.

Simpson kept fit and played grade cricket for Sydney's Western Suburbs. Then came World Series Cricket (WSC) in the mid-1970s. Kerry Packer and a heavyweight team of advisers, including Richie Benaud and Bob Cowper, attempted to take over the game by creating their own competition. They contracted most of the world's top players. This left the conventional teams' player ranks depleted. A decade after he retired Bob Simpson, at forty-one, was lured back by the Australian Cricket Board (ACB) to lead the team of tyros. It was an Australian second XI, except for Simpson and Jeff Thomson. In a heroic comeback, Simpson hit the top score of 89 in the First Test against India at Brisbane, then 176 (in 390 minutes) and 39 run out at the WACA in the Second Test. Australia won both games, then lost the next two. The skipper steadied the ship in the final game with 100 and 51, giving Australia a three–two series win. His aggregate was 539 at 53.9. It was as if time had stood still. Simpson, still a fit 76 kilograms, had led Australia to two successive series wins, both against India.

It was much tougher in the West Indies a month later in early 1978, where bumpers, bottles (at Sabina Park), and tempers flew. Australia went down one–three as the seriousness of Packer's actions sank in. Simpson scored 199 with an average of 22.11. His foray back into the big time made his Order of Australia appear very well earned.

Simpson wanted to go on and lead the country against Michael Brearley's touring England team in the next Australian season of 1978–79. He was fit and ready. The players supported him. But the ACB, in a split board decision, voted him out and replaced him as leader with Graham Yallop, twenty-six. It was all over for Bob Simpson, but not quite on his own terms as it had been the first time.

Yet his unexpected little burst of extra captaincy over ten Tests in an incident-filled six months brought him gains. He scored his sixtieth first-class century against Barbados. He became, at nearly forty-two, Australia's oldest century maker on home soil.

In all, Simpson played sixty-two Tests for 4869 runs at 46.82, which included ten centuries, and another twenty-seven half-centuries, which were especially significant given his usual position as opener. He also took 111 catches at a better rate than anyone in Test cricket, approaching two snaffles a Test. Simpson's bowling brought him seventy-one wickets at 42.27. At the first-class level he hit 21,029 runs in 436 innings at 56.22. Apart from those 60 hundreds, he hit 100 fifties, another indication of his importance at the top of the order. He took 349 wickets at 38.07, suggesting that he could have been a more productive spinner if he had put more time into it. But it was understandable that he did not, with his duties as skipper, batsman and slips fielder taking precedence. His 383 catches demonstrated his importance in the field. Even if he had had a poorer batting record, he might still have kept his place for his importance next to the keeper alone.

Retirement from playing was not the end of Simpson's direct association with the Test team. When Australia fell into a post-WSC hole in the mid-1980s, Simpson came back as team coach to assist Allan Border in his arduous fight to restore Australian Test cricket to number one. Simpson presided over the regimes of Border and Mark Taylor from 1986 to 1996. He brought fielding and fitness drills to the Australian squad that gave it a strong base for its development in the more vital areas of batting and bowling. In his time as coach Australia won the one-day World Series in 1987; four Ashes campaigns; and took over the world Test crown against the West Indies early in 1995. Simpson could claim to be a strong part of Australia's revival. Not even a dangerous blood clot in his leg in the West Indies could keep him from celebrating Australia's ascendancy, when Mark Taylor held the Frank Worrell Trophy aloft after the final victory at Sabina Park. Taylor, in appreciation of Simpson's part in the long climb back to the top of cricket, took the winning ball to him in his hospital room.

Simpson's departure in 1996 was again not of his timing. But there had to be an end somewhere to Simpson's enormous influence over Australian cricket. It had begun when he emerged as a sixteen-year-old for New South Wales in 1953 and officially ended when he was sixty in 1996, a mighty span of forty-three years of close association with the Test team. No one in Australia's history had a longer direct impact.

Bob Simpson was an astute captain. As a batsman he ranked with the best openers in history and as slips fielder he had no peer.

31

BRIAN BOOTH

....

19 October 1933 –

Tests: 29; Captain: 2; Losses: 1; Draws: 1

THE QUIET ACHIEVER

Brian Booth became captain of Australia for the First Test against England in the 1965–66 season and handled the job with quiet certitude. While there was the usual build-up of team meetings and events before a Brisbane game—usually the venue for a series opener—there wasn't much for the stand-in to do. Bob Simpson, out with a broken wrist, handled the media.

Brian Booth did the right thing by calling the toss correctly and batted despite the poor weather at the Gabba. Rain reduced day one to 111 minutes of play. The game was washed out on day two. Booth, coming in at number five, resisted for half an hour on day three before spinner Fred Titmus caught and bowled him for 16. The score, with Bill Lawry defending well, was four for 125. The lean, 181-centimetre Booth, calm whatever was happening, retired to the pavilion, delighted to watch Lawry (166) and debutant Doug Walters (155) put on 187 runs for the fifth wicket. Booth declared at six for 443. Booth juggled his spinners well, using various combinations, to reduce England to 280 all out (leg-spinner Peter Philpott taking five for 90) and a follow-on.

Time ran out with England on three for 186 in its second innings.

There was excitement in the game, with Doug Walters doing well enough to be hailed, unfortunately, as the 'new Bradman'. But there were no dramas. There weren't likely to be any with Brian Booth at the helm. Booth captained the way he batted—all class and no sweat. Booth was apparently stress-free. His profession as a physical education teacher kept his light 66-kilogram frame in excellent condition. He didn't booze or smoke. Another factor in his demeanour was a higher calling, beyond games with balls and implements with which to strike them (he also played hockey for Australia). Booth was an Anglican lay-preacher. There was always a community welfare project to be part of. Brian Booth had the big picture in mind. That was one reason he was a player and leader of the highest principles. Cricket was just a game, no matter how bowlers snarled or batsmen sulked and complained. Sure, he played to win, but fairly, always. He was one of the last Test players to walk when he knew he was out.

When Simpson caught chickenpox, Brian Booth was back as leader for the Third Test of the series. This time he made 8 and 27. Australia lost by an innings—a rare event in the 1960s—and that put it one down with two to play. The selectors made changes. Out went Booth, Bob Cowper, David Sincock and Peter Philpott. In came Simpson, Keith Stackpole on debut, Ian Chappell and Tom Veivers. Australia won by an innings and nine runs, making the series all square. Booth never played for Australia again, after twenty-nine Tests.

Soon after his dumping, Booth received a letter from national selector Don Bradman, which summarised official and unofficial feelings about him. It read:

> Dear Brian,
> Never before have I written to a player to express my
> regret at his omission from the Australian XI. In your case
> I am making an exception because I want you to know
> how much my colleagues and I disliked having to make
> this move.
>   Captain one match and out of the side the next looks
> like ingratitude, but you understand the circumstances
> and will be the first to admit that your form has not been
> good.

I sincerely hope that your form will return quickly and in any event assure you of the highest personal regard in which you are held by us all and our appreciation of the way you have always tried to do everything in your power to uphold the good name and prestige of Australia.

Yours sincerely,
Don Bradman

Booth may have found this a minor consolation at the time. But with the passage of time, Bradman's heart-felt, direct words put Booth's contribution to cricket, and the way it should be played, in illuminating perspective.

Brian Charles Booth was the son of a market gardener of Bathurst, New South Wales. He captained Bathurst High School at cricket and then went to Sydney to study at Sydney Teachers' College. At nineteen, he began with St George's first-grade team. At twenty-one, he was in the state team during the 1954–55 season. He played against Hutton's tourists, and after coming in at three for 12 as a last-minute inclusion in the New South Wales side, made 74 not out.

In this innings and whenever he batted, Booth stood tall at the crease and played all his strokes, especially the cover drive and cut, with gentle authority. If slather and whack was your desire as a spectator, then Booth was not your man to watch. He played for those wishing to see perfect, gracious execution. His stroke play seemed effortless and all timing, a bit like Mark Waugh's in the 1990s. Booth's stance was more square on than Waugh's, but he had that same kind of correct defence. He also liked to skip to the spinners, yet was rarely stumped in his career. He was not a thumper, but could score as quickly as any heavy hitter on a smash and grab raid. If fast runs were needed, Booth never lost his poise. He simply upped the tempo.

Booth's cricket career was interrupted in 1956 when he played hockey for Australia in the Olympics. He jumped back into the New South Wales team and in his fifteenth first-class cricket game scored his first century.

In 1958, at twenty-four, he married Judith Williams, whom he had met at teachers' college. Their first daughter was born in 1961. While he did not create a run of scores like his contemporaries at the state level, he was consistent and a batsman of such class that he was picked for the Ashes tour of England in 1961.

Booth made his debut in the pivotal Test of the series at Old Trafford. He had to face Trueman, Statham and Flavell on a greentop that had the ball flying. He was given the traditional bumper first ball, but it didn't get up. Booth was struck and hurt. After composing himself, he received the traditional follow-up: a spearing yorker. He survived and went on to an impressive second-top score of 46, displaying a fine array of strokes. He was in an important mini-stand with Bill Lawry when runs were at a premium. In the Fifth Test he was at the wicket with the score at four for 211. O'Neill (117) and Burge (181) had set up a big score with power. Booth came in and polished off their efforts with a neat innings. When his skipper Benaud asked for quick runs, Booth went after them and was caught at 71. Most observers agree that had he been left to go at his normal pace he would have reached a century.

That came in his next Test in style. It was at Brisbane in the First Test of the 1962–63 season, also against England. He scored 112 at an entertaining rate in a game where no one else reached three figures, despite thirteen other innings reaching fifty. Booth repeated the feat with 103 in his second innings of the next Test at Melbourne. England's skipper, Ted Dexter, studied him at Brisbane in between chasing his strokes, and in the Melbourne game used boring leg theory against him, with five men on the leg side. Titmus directed his deliveries accordingly.

Booth was consistent through the series, making 404 runs at 50.5.

In 1963–64, he was in at three for 88 in the First Test at Brisbane. Peter Pollock took one look at this mild, thin individual and decided he would soften him up. Five bouncers followed in two overs. Booth withstood that and then delivered the innings of his life, 169 runs of exquisite stroke play that had the connoisseurs applauding.

'More Grace than the Princess of Monaco,' one paper said in review.

'We didn't mind the leather chasing,' South African captain Trevor

Goddard remarked, 'when he played so charmingly.'

Booth, now thirty, had made a late start to Test cricket mainly because of his sidetrack into Olympics hockey, something that not even his love of cricket could prevent. Now he was making up for lost time as if he knew that his Test life was ordained to be short. A broken finger kept him out of the Second Test, but not the Third and Fourth, in which he scored 75, 16, 58, 24. At Sydney in the Fifth Test he dominated Australia's batting in both innings, with 102 not out and 87. In four Tests he tallied 531 runs at 88.5, an outstanding return. He hit five first-class centuries during the season, in an aggregate of 1180. It was his finest summer of cricket.

This ensured he was booked for his second tour of England in 1964 as a popular vice-captain, where he scored 210 at 42—close to his career average—with a top score of 98. In 1964–65, he went on tour to Pakistan and India and, apart from a couple of fifties, had a mediocre time. Booth was on the tough tour of the West Indies, where his average didn't emerge from the 20s. Nevertheless, he did clip a courageous 56 in the First Test at Sabina Park and a strong 117—in his 'most satisfying' innings—in the Second Test at Port of Spain in late March 1965. He and Bob Cowper (143 run out) put on 222.

Facing Hall and Griffith in the West Indies was a test too far. Helmets were thought of but discarded as 'not being cricket'. But times had changed. Ever since Lindwall and Miller had shell-shocked the West Indians in the mid-1950s, they had been organising revenge. Now it had come. Helmets would be needed sooner or later.

When Booth didn't perform for a fourth series in 1965–66 Bradman and the other selectors had no choice but to drop him. But at least he had managed to captain his country. In that sense it was a fitting way to go out, even if it had not been of his own volition.

Brian Booth played twenty-nine Tests in all, tallying 1773 runs at a good 42.21 average, with 5 hundreds. Booth continued playing for New South Wales for another three seasons, retiring at thirty-five. In first-class cricket he had played 183 matches, scoring 11,265 runs at 45.42, with twenty-six centuries.

Booth carried on teaching, preaching and community work. His

Test star was a shooter compared to many of his contemporaries. Yet he could look back with pride at having represented his country at the highest level, and at the Olympics. If this mild-mannered, cheerful and modest teacher was being graded, he would get high marks for everything he did on the field. Few matched Brian Booth's style. As a captain, none played with more fairmindedness and sportsmanship.

32

BILL LAWRY

....

11 February 1937 –

Tests: 68; Captain: 26; Wins: 9; Losses: 8; Draws: 8;
Win ratio: 28.88 per cent

PHANTOM OF THE BROAD BLADE

In his first Test as captain, at Brisbane during the 1967–68 series versus India, Bill Lawry did everything right. He launched Australia's innings with 64 and 45 in partnerships with Ian Redpath of 76 and 116. When India batted, he juggled his unpenetrating attack with intelligence and got the best out of them. Yet still Lawry received plenty of abuse from the Brisbane crowd.

There was some prejudice against Bill Lawry brought on by a decade of watching him bat. Lawry, the left-hander, could attack when he liked. He was a powerful, gutsy hooker. A familiar sight was seeing the hunch-backed, tight-shoulder shot as he swivelled through it. He had the traditional left-hander's penchant for the on side, but usually in first-class cricket he had plundered it more slowly and monotonously than the average punter could stomach, especially as Lawry's powers of concentration allowed him to be around for a long time— sometimes a day or two. He saw his job as pushing Australia or Victoria off to a good start. More often than not he defended his way forward. It was Bill's way and he was steadfast.

He also accepted the abuse. It was a lot less painful than a ball in the chest from Fred Trueman, or one on the shoulder from Charlie Griffith. Once, when a predecessor, Jim Burke, was heckled at Melbourne, he offered his bat to the abuser. It was Lawry's sentiment too but, unlike Burke, he would never have reacted with such a gesture. Lawry would simply pretend he didn't hear a negative comment. Or maybe he didn't. Few had his concentration at the wicket. It resembled a trance at times, especially when he had decided to 'put up the shutters', see an opposing bowler off or bat through an innings, which he did five times.

In his first match at the helm he was accused of giving his fellow Victorians more than their share of the bowling. 'Hey Lawry,' someone called. 'Give Gleeson a bowl—his grandmother lives in Geelong.' After New South Wales paceman Dave Renneberg had warmed up for three overs, another spectator yelled, 'Hey Renneberg, just tell Lawry you were born in Victoria.' The bowling figures showed that Lawry didn't favour his fellow state players. The two Victorians, Bob Cowper and Alan Connolly, sent down 87.6 overs. The other four non-Victorians, Ian Chappell (South Australia), Dave Renneberg (New South Wales), John Gleeson (New South Wales) and Eric Freeman (South Australia) sent down 122. But Lawry did give Cowper the longest spells in the last innings of the match when the ball was turning. In India's first innings Cowper had the best figures, with three for 31 off fifteen. Sensing Cowper was 'hot', Lawry asked him to send down 39.6 in India's second dig. Cowper took four for 104, making the important breakthroughs to dismiss M L Jaisimha (101) and C G Borde (63).

It was a matter of judgment. Lawry put his faith in the 'Wallaby' Cowper and his off spin. Australia won by 39 runs.

In the final Test of the series—the Fourth at the Sydney Cricket Ground—the scenario was much the same. Lawry scored 66 and 52 in opening stands, this time with Cowper, of 61 and 111. In the Fourth Test India chased 395 to win. In the Fifth, it was 342. This time Lawry had Bob Simpson, the skipper he had replaced, bowl leg spin. It gave the attack a balanced spin combination. Even the Indians, fed on spin soon after birth, could not cope on a Sydney turner. Simpson took five for 59, Cowper four for 49. Australia won this time by 144 runs.

Lawry had a more than satisfactory start to his twenty-six Tests as captain.

Show pain, no gain

William Morris Lawry was still learning his trade as a plumber at Melbourne's Preston Technical College when he was picked for the Northcote club at sixteen and for Victoria's Second XI at seventeen. Two years later he was in the state team and known as 'Phanto' because of his liking for Phantom comics. There were similarities between Lawry and his comic book hero. The Phantom never flinched when punched on the jaw, although you read that he was unconscious on his feet for a split-second. When Lawry was hit by a bouncer, spectators would take bets on when he would rub the spot or flex the shoulder. On principle—he had a rule never to show weakness to a foe—Lawry would never react when struck. Usually a few overs after the hit, the 187-centimetre, lean opener with a prominent nose would roll his shoulder or give the bruise a quick rub.

It was the 1950s and 1960s when budding cricketers were taught by coaches never to show they had been hurt, even if a hand was too numb to hold the bat or if an elbow was aching. It was a time without helmets, armguards, painkillers, or the magic spray to anaesthetise welts. John Wayne, James Bond, Ron Barassi and Bill Lawry were macho heroes. It was a male sin to show pain and, heaven forbid, cry. If you did you were branded as a wimp, although wimp wasn't a word in vogue. But the same man who wrenched pipes, took bumpers on the body and hooked fast men had a soft side, more in keeping with a sensitive SNAG of the 1980s or 1990s. He was a bird lover. Pigeons were his fancy. He bred, named, nurtured and flew them with unabashed affection. The Phantom was also a jungle animal lover. Bill had more ornithological tendencies. Perhaps this explained his capacity for patience at the wicket. Those winged friends would sometimes race for days before returning.

That patience was important not just for his batting displays. He was forced to wait longer than most for a break into the big time of Test cricket. His name was not whispered loudly as a Test chance until the 1960–61 season, when Australia was doing battle with the West Indies and was well served by openers Colin McDonald and Bob Simpson (and before him, Jim Burke).

Lawry in that season scored a massive 266 in a 'defiant' innings (according to Victorian journalists—New South Wales journalists described it as 'painstaking') against New South Wales. It was enough to be chosen for the 1961 tour of England.

Everyone expected McDonald and Simpson to open in the Tests. They had shown courage above and beyond the call against Hall. They had earned their stripes and spots. But form in cricket is a season by season thing. The only way to break into the Test team was to make so many runs that you had to be considered. Lawry was twenty-four as the boat sailed and he knew that he had to make it on this trip or be relegated to state cricket for another five years, and oblivion.

Lawry batted first on tour in the second game against Yorkshire and scored just 29. It was back to the old firm of McDonald and Simpson for game three. Then it was on to the 'big' county game for the Australians, versus Surrey. This team had crushed Australia embarrassingly in the corresponding game of that awful tour of 1956. Lock and Laker had been the destroyers, with Alec Bedser not even needed. That game had set a pattern of decay from which the tourists never recovered. This time, there was a lot of pent-up feeling about facing Surrey at the Oval. Bedser and Lock were still in the side, but Laker had retired. Yet they were just names now, older and less potent.

Lawry took control from the first over of the game and wiped out fears for Benaud and his team about past disasters. He hooked, pulled and drove his way to a century in three hours. He crunched 101 between lunch and tea. Lawry was out half an hour after tea for 165. Benaud could declare at seven for 341 and then dismiss the county twice with ease. Australia won by ten wickets.

The lanky opener followed this up with a century against Cambridge University. The selectors could sniff something special in his form. They ran him for the third game in a row against Glamorgan. He hit 31 and 43 not out. His form was holding. Benaud was smiling. Instead of struggling to find a batsman on fire as in 1956 and 1953, he had everyone functioning on most cylinders. Benaud was like a billionaire with a furrowed brow over how to earn another few million. It was an embarrassment of batsmen. He left Lawry out of the next game but made sure he played at Lord's against the Marylebone Cricket Club on 27 May. This was an important game. The

Marylebone Cricket Club would field a near Test side. Australia did the same. Opening with McDonald (24), Lawry made his first appearance at the world's most famous ground and made 104. Just to show he wasn't dazzled by his own form, he settled in for a powerful 84 not out in the second innings, this time with Simpson (92 not out), as Australia cruised to a ten-wicket win.

Benaud's thinking was obvious. It wasn't now a question of Lawry opening in the first Test; it was a matter of with whom—McDonald or Simpson. In the final two games against Oxford University and Sussex before the Tests, Lawry hit 72, 12 and 30. McDonald was given the job of starting the innings with his fellow Victorian. Simpson's form had been very good too. He made the team batting at number six. Lawry made a creditable start with 57, about ten above what would be his career average. Australia amassed nine for 516 and the game was drawn.

It was on to Lord's. England won the toss, batted and was held to 206, thanks to Alan Davidson's sensational display of left-arm swing and bounce. He took five for 42. Lawry pushed his nose down over a lowered bat handle to keep the tricky bounce on the Lord's ridge under some sort of control. He was 32 not out at stumps, with Harvey on 6 not out. The next day, Lawry played the innings of his life. His temperament came to the fore on one of the most difficult wickets ever seen in a century of big cricket at Lord's. There would be no century in a session on this Friday of 23 June.

Australia moved from four for 111 at lunch to five for 183 when Burge (46) was dismissed. Lawry was on 99 not out. He clipped a single off Statham to reach his first Test century in his second innings. He went on to 130 and was the match winner. No one else scored more than 66. Australia won by five wickets.

Lawry made another century—102—again the only one in the vital Fourth Test at Old Trafford.

Bill Lawry's series aggregate was 420 at 52.5. On tour he hit nine centuries out of his 2117 runs. Lawry had left Australia a spare opener and had come back a Test hero. His decade-long career at the top was under way.

In 1962 he married Joy Barnes. They had two daughters.

Lawry's lightning

Much was expected of Bill Lawry after that mighty tour, and he seemed set to emulate it before the Tests in 1962–63 with his 133 for Victoria versus England. The state team had been sent in on a moist wicket. It was a slow grind that brought more jeers than cheers, but Lawry became the innings backbone.

He was just 'serviceable' in the 1962–63 Ashes in Australia, scoring 310 at 34.44, with a top score of 98 and two other fifties. In the final Test at Sydney, he was under orders from Benaud to just stay there as Australia fought out a draw. Lawry dropped a large anchor for four hours in which he garnered just 45.

At one point he belted two fours in succession. The restive crowd jeered more in hope that he would lash out than derision. 'Bloody hell!' one barracker on the Hill yelled. 'Lightning does strike twice!' This was followed by, 'Come on lightning, strike again!'

In the following home season Lawry lifted for the series against South Africa and collected 496 at 55.11 with a top score of 157 in the Second Test at Melbourne, his only century. He had a heavyweight struggle for supremacy with the Springboks' speedster, Peter Pollock, who tried to bounce him in every Test. Lawry took him on with the best hooking of his career and won the battle. Pollock only removed him three times in ten innings in the series. The speedster later nominated him as one of the best two openers he ever bowled to.

On his second trip to England in 1964, Lawry took a while to crank up in the Tests with 78 in the Third at Leeds, 106 in the Fourth at Old Trafford, and 94 in the Fifth Test at the Oval. His returns were 317 at 39.63. It wasn't quite the heroics of 1961, but still he was a mainstay at the top of the order with Simpson, as Australia retained the Ashes for the third successive time. Lawry also notched five centuries on tour.

Barnacle's pinnacle

Lawry's best season was 1965–66. He was twenty-eight and at his peak in terms of his ability to concentrate. He hit a record (by any Australian) of 979 runs in eleven innings (seven in the Tests) against Mike Smith's England tourists. They took him 2490 minutes, or a run every 2.5 minutes. He was a key in Australia's struggle to retain the

Ashes, but he was not entertaining. The contest against England brought out the best and worst in him. While he couldn't be removed, Australia couldn't be beaten, but the cricket was so tight that it was dull for the average punter. Lawry's efforts epitomised the grim struggles of 1958–59, 1961, 1962–63, 1964, 1965–66 and 1968. It wasn't pretty. You had to love Test cricket to enjoy it. Ashes were both the result and prize of wars of attrition from both batsmen and bowlers.

Lawry's scores in the 1965–66 Tests were 166, 88, 78, 0, 33, 119 and 108—592 runs in all at 84.57. When he made a duck at Sydney there was palpable relief and even joy from the stoic Poms. Each bowler and fielder imagined a day without facing him. Cowper, Burge and Booth were a pleasure to chase.

Only Victorians could forgive Lawry for his tardiness. Yet serious cricket fans everywhere saw the value in his opening-series knock of 166 at Brisbane. They were with him when he fought back with Simpson in an opening stand of 244 at Adelaide when Australia was one down in the series. In the Fifth Test at Melbourne, fans watched or hovered near the TV and radio for his 212-run stand with Cowper, who was en route to immortality with the first (and only) triple century in a Test in Australia.

Late in the season, Lawry continued in an indomitable mood of defiance for his beloved Northcote in the Melbourne district final. Before he went out to bat, he told his line-up he just wanted some of them to stay with him. There was no doubt in Bill's mind that he would bat for two or three weeks, as the game was only played on Saturdays. None of his fellow bats had any second thoughts either. Lawry performed as if in a Test, showing the opposition bowlers the same respect he would Trueman, Hall or Gibbs. He made 282 out of nine for 514, batting on three successive Saturdays. Northcote beat Essendon in the final. It capped off a tremendous season for him.

Bill Lawry came back to the pavilion more quickly in South Africa in the next season, 1966–67 with just 296 at 29.6, and a top score of 98. The Springbok attack of Eddie Barlow, Mike Procter, Pollock, and left-arm medium-pacer Trevor Goddard were tough competitors. Yet only

Goddard, the pick of them with twenty-six wickets at 16.23, snared him three times.

Lawry was back to his annoying best for the opposition in the four Tests of the 1967–68 season against India with an even run of scores— 42, 0, 100, 64, 45, 66 and 52.

Now captain, it was a sure bet that Lawry would be even more intent on defending his wicket. He felt the responsibility and was determined not to fail as a batsman while skipper, or let Australia be beaten. In the 1968 Ashes, he began with an astonishing burst of scoring after lunch on day one in the First Test at Old Trafford. He attacked off-spinner Pat Pocock with 2 sixes and 6 fours in his 81 that set his team on the way. Inspired, Doug Walters (81), Paul Sheahan (88) and Ian Chappell (73 run out) took Australia to four for 319 at stumps. Australia was all out for 357 on the morning of day two, but this enterprise took England by surprise. The tourists won by 159 runs and moved one up.

Rain cut the Lord's Test in half and guaranteed a draw. Lawry's finger was broken in the Third Test at Edgbaston, and on 6 he retired hurt but not humiliated. The game was drawn. Rain again reduced play by a day.

Lawry missed the Fourth Test at Leeds, when Barry Jarman led the Australians. But it was Lawry, in the dressing room, who took the flak for the decision to defend for a draw to retain the Ashes rather than go for a win.

Lawry's 135 at the Oval in the Fifth Test took him 450 minutes and earned him the sobriquet 'the corpse with pads' from English journalist Ian Woolridge. Yet it was the only century by an Australian in the series. He stood between England and victory. When corpulent Colin Milburn caught him off 'Big Dave' Brown for 4 in the second innings, John Woodcock noted: 'If the English side could have thrown Milburn aloft they would have.' He added, 'Lawry is a great battler and a wonderfully sound judge of length. All too often he has been the rock on which England foundered.'

The series that began so boisterously for Lawry and his team ended one all. But the skipper was not crestfallen. He had defended the Ashes. They were still retained by Australia.

Prolific peaks

Bill Lawry arrived back in Australia and geared himself for an expected onslaught by the West Indies during the 1968–69 series. But Griffith and Hall were slowing up and injury-prone. They collected only sixteen wickets at about 45 each in the ten innings in which they bowled. Sobers too was off the boil, taking eighteen wickets at 40.72. The second stringers weren't a problem and only off-spinner Lance Gibbs, with twenty-four wickets, was a worry, but even his scalps cost 38.46 each. Lawry had his most prolific series, scoring 667 at 83.38, including scores of 105, 205, and 151. He was only upstaged by Doug Walters (699 at 116.5).

Australia won three–one, thus avenging its one–two loss in the West Indies in 1964–65.

Lawry emerged as a relentless skipper. He berated his bowlers if they didn't perform and was uncompromising in his attitude to opposing batsmen, not even allowing a drink for a thirsty foe other than at the normal breaks. Yet his way was effective in producing wins for Australia.

Lawry had further success in India, winning three–one under the most testing conditions yet endured by Australians abroad. In Bombay during the First Test, the crowd rioted after a caught-behind decision riled them. Thick smoke engulfed the ground. Bottles were thrown. People began to push on a fence that looked likely to collapse. Ian Chappell urged his skipper to group the players at the end of play so that they could leave the field as a united squad. Lawry didn't seem to hear. 'Hell,' he said, 'we need a wicket badly.'

The captain got his wicket. India was all out in the second innings for 137, leaving Australia just 64 to win. It lost two wickets reaching them before another riot.

More than once the Australians were pelted with stones on the tour. Doug Walters, who had completed national service, was picketed for his part in the Vietnam War. Six people were killed while queuing for tickets to the Test in Calcutta.

It set a sad tone that deteriorated into abuse on the final day as Australia chased just 42 to win. Fans threw bottles and rubbish from the stands. The mess had to be cleaned up and there was a threat of worse action. But Lawry was not leaving the centre until he and Keith Stackpole picked off the runs.

During the break, Lawry used his bat to prod an Indian photographer, who had run onto the ground. Australia secured the runs and the opprobrium of the media. Lawry had offended Indian photographers by pushing one of them away with his bat. They wore black armbands in protest at the tourists' next match. It prompted the media in general to increase their criticism of the Australian skipper. The media had been biased; now it turned nasty. It incited crowd behaviour rather than attempting to placate it. Media reaction reached absurd proportions after Lawry pulled away from the wicket when a woman in a sari walked in front of the sightscreen at Bangalore. He was accused of insulting Indian womanhood.

Lawry had an ordinary series with 239 runs at 34.14 but had now led Australia in four successive undefeated series.

Wheels off

In South Africa in 1969–70, the wheels fell off the Australian winning train. It was thrashed in each of the four Tests. Bill Lawry had his worst series yet, scoring just 193 at 24.13. It was a form aberration, but it put his captaincy in jeopardy.

He lost it during the next Ashes series in Australia in 1970–71, when Australia went down nil–two in six Tests against the equally obdurate Ray Illingworth and his strong squad. The English team included hostile, effective speedster John Snow with the ball, and Geoff Boycott, England's answer to Lawry. Bill Lawry's form was steady, but his stodginess at the crease had turned off observers, including selectors. This was despite his gritty bat carrying for 60 not out of his team's pitiful 116 at Sydney. His steady aggregate of 324 at 40.5 was not enough to save him.

Lawry was sacked following a draw in Adelaide and Ian Chappell took over as skipper in the final game at the Sydney Cricket Ground. No one from the Board of Control bothered to inform Lawry and he received the news from team-mate Keith Stackpole, who heard an item on the radio en route to the airport. Lawry, just turned thirty-four, had been dumped from the last Test.

Lawry was also a shock omission from the tour of England in 1972. Critics felt he should have been on tour, especially as no one could fill his place. While Keith Stackpole had a good series, he had no partner who could stay with him. Opening stands were woeful. Just one was more than 24 runs. Perhaps there was a case for leaving Ian Chappell unfettered by not having his former leader looking over his shoulder. Yet both men seemed secure enough not to cause a problem. The 1972 Ashes was tight, with each side winning twice. Lawry's inclusion would have swung it Australia's way.

But it wasn't to be. Bill Lawry went out of Test cricket with an aggregate of 5234 runs at 47.15, with thirteen centuries—seven against England and four versus the West Indies. In first-class cricket he scored 18,734 at 50.9, with fifty centuries and 100 fifties, which, showed his importance at the top of the order.

Lawry later managed the Victorian team and became a popular TV commentator on Channel Nine. He wasn't able to emulate United States President Ronald Reagan by making clichés sound original, but his familiar, repetitive comments—'There's a good crowd in'—and shrill cries—'Got 'im! Yes!' and 'It's all happening!'—amused but didn't offend the vast TV audience. He was even the subject of mimicry by comedians, a sure sign that he was a national 'household name'.

Bill Lawry led Australia to the top of Test cricket in the late 1960s. He ranks, along with fellow left-hander Arthur Morris, as well as Bob Simpson and Bill Ponsford, as one of the top openers Australia produced in the twentieth century.

33

BARRY JARMAN

17 February 1936 –

Tests: 19; Captain: 1; Draws: 1

THE SHADOW

Barry Jarman walked out to toss the coin as Australian captain at Headingley during the 1968 series and told photographers not to miss it. The 'historic' moment was a toss between two vice-captains. England's Tom Graveney was deputising for injured Colin Cowdrey. Jarman was leading because Bill Lawry had broken a finger.

Jarman won the toss, but not the approval of critics. On day four Australia increased its lead to 250 by tea. Instead of going for quick runs in the last session, the batsmen were ordered to stay there until stumps. They scored at 1.5 runs an over. An appeal against the light wasted thirty minutes.

The innings dragged into the final day, changing the game's complexion. England was not set under 300 in more than a day, but more than 300 (325) in under a day—300 minutes. Yet still the game might not be lost as a spectacle and an exciting contest. If Jarman gave his spinners, particularly John Gleeson, most time at the crease, England might be tempted to strike out, and Australia could win the game. But at the crunch he used medium-pacers Garth McKenzie and

Alan Connolly to keep the runs down rather than use spinner Gleeson to attack and 'buy' wickets.

Most observers reckoned the approach was very unlike Jarman. The defensive hand of the Phantom, Bill Lawry, in the dressing room was behind the tactics. There were plenty of chats between them at the breaks. Jarman was playing Lawry's way, whether he was conscious of it or not. The Australians were leading one–nil with this Test to be decided and one to play. Lawry didn't wish to go down in history as a skipper who lost the Ashes. He felt there would be more to lose by taking risks.

Jarman's excuse for giving Alan Connolly twenty-four overs without a break was that he was keeping England below the 4 runs an over needed to win. But Gleeson's series figures—he was conceding just over 2 runs an over—were more economical than Connolly's. If he had bowled more, along with Bob Cowper, or Ian Chappell, who could deliver a fair leg-break, then England's bats might have been tempted, especially as it was down nil–one in the series. The game might have come alive. Had Australia lost, there was still one Test to play.

In the end the game fizzled to a draw. Australia lost the final Test and the series was drawn one all, with the tourists retaining the Ashes. Jarman's caution had thrown away the chance of a lifetime. But he and Lawry would never see it that way. The Ashes, which had been responsible for more dead Test cricket than any defensive, dour bat or even leg theory, had caused the cheerful and enterprising Barry Jarman, for one, to go against his nature and experience.

Barrington Noel Jarman, the son of a market-gardener, was in Woodville's A Grade side at fifteen, and four years later in 1955–56 made the South Australian side. He was a stocky 86 kilograms and 171 centimetres tall, and on first glance people would be sceptical that he could keep with agility. But his appearance was deceptive. His reflexes were quick. He was famous in club and state cricket for his dives to gather deflections either side of the wicket. Great strength in his legs gave him bounce from a pronounced squat. It also gave him durability. Jarman seemed to have just as much energy at the end of an innings as at the beginning.

In 1956, aged twenty, he married Gaynor Goldfinch and later had three children.

In the 1957–58 season, at twenty-one, he was chosen to tour South Africa in Ian Craig's squad. He was understudy to thirty-year-old Wally Grout from Queensland. Grout had waited a decade for Don Tallon and Gil Langley to vacate the keeper's seat in the Test side. The tour selectors—Craig, Neil Harvey and Peter Burge—couldn't make up their minds about who should keep. In the end, Grout's marginally greater capacity to keep to Richie Benaud's leg spin was the deciding factor. But it was line-ball. Grout began an eight-year, 51-Test career for Australia, with Jarman his standby.

An injury to Grout allowed Barry Jarman, at twenty-three, to be chosen for his first Test at Green Park, Kanpur, during the 1959–60 series against India. He took a catch in each innings.

Jarman toured England in 1961 and was selected for several county games without getting a Test. His capacity as a hard-hitting bat came to the fore in a festival match at Scarborough against Tom Pierce's XI. Jarman slammed 26—6, 6, 4, 4, 4, 2—in one over from burly off-spinner David Allen.

Jarman's next Test chance came against England in the 1962–63 season when Grout's jaw was broken. Jarman had three successive Tests and took seven catches. The best dismissal was a dive to grab a leg-side deflection from left-hander Geoff Pullar off McKenzie in the second innings of the Second Test at Melbourne. Jarman was in top form during the season, dismissing ten in one match against New South Wales. A year later, in 1963–64, he removed forty-five batsmen in eleven matches, which gained him selection for his second tour of England in 1964.

In 1964–65, Jarman stood in for the injured Grout against India at Bombay in the Second Test of the series and hit 78, which was second-top score to Peter Burge (80) in an innings of nine declared for 320. He kept well to the spinners (Bob Simpson, Tom Veivers and Johnny Martin) and took three catches in India's first innings. His first stumping came in India's only innings of the Third Test at Calcutta. The bowler was Brian Booth.

Against Pakistan in Melbourne during the one-off Test in December 1964, he took four dismissals in Pakistan's second innings.

When Grout retired at the end of the 1965–66 season, Brian Taber took over behind the stumps for the 1966–67 tour of South Africa (Jarman was unavailable for the tour, due to business reasons). But Jarman was restored as the nation's number-one keeper for the 1967–68 Indian tour of Australia. He took eleven catches and made one stumping in the four Tests. He had a top score of 65 in Melbourne for the Second Test.

In Jarman's third tour of England in 1968, he was Lawry's deputy. He broke a finger in the nets during the Lord's Test. He showed courage in batting, but a ball from David Brown struck him on the injured finger and did further damage. He stood down from the Third Test (which was kept by standby, Taber), but came back as skipper for the one and only time in the Fourth Test at Headingley.

In four Tests against the West Indies in 1968–69 Jarman took twelve catches and one stumping, but was dumped for the Fifth Test in favour of Brian Taber again.

Jarman retired at thirty-three. In nineteen tests he had fifty catches and four stumpings. He scored 400 runs at 14.81. In first-class cricket he made 560 dismissals—431 catches and 129 stumpings—in 191 matches. He scored 5615 at 22.73 with five centuries, which were figures more indicative of his batting prowess.

Barry Jarman ranked as one of Australia's better keepers, with an ability to take a spectacular catch. He was a capable state captain. He did not give free rein to his aggressive instincts during his one opportunity as a Test captain. More chances might have seen a different approach.

34

IAN CHAPPELL

....

26 September 1943 –

Tests: 75; Captain: 30; Wins: 15; Losses: 5; Draws: 10;
Win ratio: 50 per cent

LARRIKIN LEADER

Ian Chappell was the captain for the 1970s Australia had to have. The collapse of the national team during the 1970–71 Ashes meant the skipper, Bill Lawry, a dour leader of the 1960s, had to go. It was begrudgingly acceptable to be thrashed by South Africa away, as Australia was in 1969–70, but inexcusable to be beaten by England at home. A fresh, aggressive approach, more in keeping with Richie Benaud's winning way (1958–1963) was needed.

Ian Chappell was like Richie Benaud in some respects. They were both gutsy and attractive as cricketers; never-say-die and adventurous as captains. But that's where the similarities ended. Benaud, a journalist by profession, was a consummate media man, a natural public-relations spin doctor who knew how to avoid bad behaviour and publicity. Chappell didn't give a taxidermist's delight about protocol. He banned dinner suits on tours to England, which meant the cricketers cut back on formal functions. He wanted more focus on the cricket. Like Benaud, Chappell made an effort to work with the media. He cared what they said in print. But if he didn't appreciate what was written he would say so. He was the same off the field as on. Some observers like to suggest that sledging, that questionable art of put-down comments to unsettle an opponent, began with Ian Chappell in the 1970s. It did begin in the seventies—the 1870s, when Test cricket began. Players right through from that era have had words for and with the opposition. England's great W G Grace was big on games-manship. He chipped at umpires, opposition and his own players alike. In the 1880s, the volatile Australian George Giffen, who once refused vehemently to leave the crease when given out, wanted to have a punch-up on the pitch with his captain, Jack Blackham. They had to be separated by fellow Australian Hugh Trumble. A notable abuser of batsmen in the 1930s was Bill O'Reilly, whom Bradman regarded as the finest bowler he ever faced.

Chappell was Australia's most aggressive leader. Under him were probably more characters with offensive (as opposed to defensive) mental attitudes than ever before, although 'light banter', as he called it, wasn't confined to them. Barry Richards, the South African star opening bat, remembers even Paul Sheahan, who played in teams captained by Lawry and Ian Chappell, giving him a 'barrage of abuse' during the Tests in South Africa in 1969-70. (It must have been mild. Keith Stackpole could never recall Sheahan, now headmaster of Melbourne Grammar School, sledging anyone.)

According to players and umpires who performed with Chappell, he only went beyond the 'chippie' comments when he thought a player was not worthy of being at the level of the game, be it club, first-class or Test. According to a former Test umpire, Chappell would also respond abusively, for example, if after he had appealed from slip for a catch at the wicket, a batsman turned and gave him a 'you've got to be kidding' look.

Australian umpires' unwritten code, at least until now, has been to let sledging go if it is part of the cut and thrust of a match. Something like, 'let's see if this showpony can really bat under pressure', would be allowed. But the moment it got personal with:

'You're nothing but an *expletive*, *expletive* showpony,' would see an umpire step in. It might lead to a report. Today in a Test it would see a report, especially with certain international umpires standing games.

Chappell restricted himself to short of the organised or 'institu-tionalised' sledging and intimidation prevalent in the current game.

Nor were these measures necessary when he had two great fast bowlers—Lillee and Thomson—in his Test line-up. Thomson's speed and oft-quoted remark that he liked to see 'blood on the pitch' was intimidating enough without the need for anything further being said on the field. Chappell on odd occasions became heavier but it was unpremeditated. While on tour in New Zealand in 1974, he abused New Zealand opening bat Glenn Turner following a misunderstanding about whether Brian Hastings had hit a six or a four.

Chappell, reflecting on the incident in the March 2000 edition of the cricket magazine *Inside Edge*, said, 'The main reason I spoke to Turner the way I did was because it's me.' Apparently being Ian Chappell excused him from the normal niceties. 'I got extremely annoyed about the whole thing,' he added, 'and if I'm annoyed I'm liable to speak to people like that.'

Turner wanted an apology. Fat chance. Chappell's response to a request for an apology was, 'What happens on the field, stays on the field.' But did this mean no matter what occurred on the pitch—abuse, cheating, even a punch-up—there was never a need to admit a mistake or wrongdoing and say sorry? The more the media pressured Chappell on this, the more he dug in.

Legless legends

That notorious short fuse aside, Ian Chappell was the best leader for the key players at his disposal. A decade earlier, Benaud had champions like Alan Davidson, Neil Harvey, Norm O'Neill, Ken Mackay, Colin McDonald, Wally Grout, Brian Booth, Ian Meckiff, and Bill Lawry. Gentlemen all with courage to burn, and just right for Benaud's command. Several loved a drink but controlled it. But the late 1960s and 1970s spawned characters such as Dennis Lillee, Rod Marsh, Doug Walters, Jeff Thomson and Terry Jenner. Who else could run them but Ian Chappell?

The team was split between the drinkers and the more temperate. Getting legless was okay, a perverse kind of 'sporting' achievement in itself. Marsh became a 'legend' when he set the tinnie-guzzling record for a Qantas trip from Australia to Heathrow (later broken by David Boon). Lillee was accorded similar status when (according to Chappell in his biography *Chappelli*) after celebrating too much, he was able only to say 'G'day' when introduced to the Queen and Prince Philip

on the 1972 tour of England. This was at the same time that Bob
Hawke, who held another beer drinking record at Oxford University,
was running the Australian union movement in preparation for the
job of prime minister of Australia. Boorish behaviour of any kind was
acceptable. It even won votes. And as long as Chappell kept winning
on the field, he would stay the leader.

Chappell had been a Test player for nearly seven years when he
took over. The timing of his appointment, February 1971, was
exquisite. Neil Harvey likes to take most credit for twisting Don
Bradman's arm over the choice of Ian Chappell. Bradman, then
chairman of the Board of Control and also the selectors, wasn't mad
keen on Chappell, according to Harvey, but he came around
concerning his suitability at the helm, as Sir Donald would do if a
cogent argument was put to him. A majority of the Board then supported Chappell's elevation to the top job. How smart the Board of
Control was to sniff the mood of the nation and realise that a different
kind of leader was needed for the 1970s. Someone who could be anti-
authoritarian and a winner; larrikin and leader. Just when young
Australians were snubbing their noses at tradition and looking for
rugged, profane young heroes who would boisterously shed the clean-
cut look of the stuffy 1950s and 1960s, they gave us Chappell on our
TVs and in our papers. He was a born leader of men—direct and
forthright; the original in-your-face leader. Just right for the times. He
was more hirsute than hairy rockers—more Led Zeppelin than
Seekers. Chappell challenged the establishment. He was more Bob
Hawke than Bob Menzies. Just when advertising men were wondering
how to harness the pent-up mood for protest following the Vietnam
War, and Gough Whitlam was learning how to blow-dry his hair to
appear 1970s, not 1960s, there was Ian Chappell, leading the
national cricket team. If that sort of image was directing the way
genteel old cricket was played, it was time to cash in on it. Sydney ad
man John Singleton led the way in packaging jingoistic fervour and
created that creature of the 1970s, the 'ocker'. It was vacuous and
gauche, but it appealed to the youth and made lots money for those
selling products to the youth market.

When Kerry Packer decided to take over world cricket when he
didn't get the rights to broadcast the game on Channel Nine, Chappell
was just the man to sign twenty-seven top players around the world.

They were to perform in Packer's World Series Cricket 'circus'. It was a direct threat to the organisation of the game as it was.

World Series Cricket (WSC) rocked the establishment at Lord's and Melbourne. Ian Chappell was a prime mover. Once the players and crude facilities were in place, Packer pulled in the marketing and advertising gurus from his network and the agencies, knowing the exact poll-driven market to target: the under-thirties. They had admired Chappelli, Lillee, Marshie, Dougie and all the other 'ees', who played it hard, fast and entertainingly. Hardheaded Ian, the Australian Super Test captain, donned a helmet and invited the most brutal bowlers on earth to try and knock it off. At first the crowds stayed away. But when the promotion cranked up and Packer managed to turn the lights on at the Sydney Cricket Ground, it was a case of shut the gate, the house was full. Chappell's efforts for his good mate Kerry meant the media mogul didn't lose his shirt after gambling millions setting up WSC. The Australian Cricket Board (ACB) decided the fight was too costly and gave Packer the right to televise cricket. It meant he would make his money back a thousand-fold over the years. Packer was most grateful to Chappell and others like Tony Greig on the field, and Benaud and Bob Cowper, who were consultants, off it. Chappell, Greig and Benaud virtually had tenure as cricket commentators at Channel Nine from then on.

Pedigree potential

Cricket—or at least talent with ball games—was in Ian Michael Chappell's genes. His father, Martin, was an Adelaide club cricketer (Glenelg) and baseballer. Genes from his mother, Jeanne, were also useful. Her father was former Australian cricket captain Victor Richardson, who was one of the best all-round sportsmen ever from South Australia.

Ian Chappell faced up to a cricket ball when he was two and a half. That was all that was ever bowled in the back yard. From an early age, he loved the hook, the most courageous and difficult shot in cricket. If you miscued off an accurate fast bouncer, you might be caught out. If you missed it altogether you might be knocked out.

According to Ian, his father, who was not greatly loved in grade cricket for his aggressive approach to the game, was a hard taskmaster. Once, when twelve, Ian was allowed to play in his father's C-grade

team. Ian batted, made 9 in half an hour and faced down the opposition's fast bowler. Later at home his father accused him of once
backing away from a delivery, and he admonished him for it. Ian was
adamant he hadn't made any moves towards square leg. He was
satisfied he had not shown fear. Martin finished the argument by
telling him he wasn't ready to play at that level. 'Those words really
hurt,' Chappell wrote in his autobiography, *Chappelli*. He said he
lived to regret that game.

Ian Chappell's suppressed feelings would come out later in
different ways, and complement his exceptional and natural leadership
skills. He would fight to gain authority over other nations and make
Australia number one. He would battle authority figures anywhere,
especially those who tried to impose their will on him. As he matured
and gained self-confidence, his feelings sometimes manifested as
anger, usually against those who criticised him, such as journalists.
Those over whom he had authority and who accepted his style of
leadership saw a different figure. They admired him. They would go
through fire for him.

Like Joe Darling, Chappell had an upbringing influenced by a
tough-minded father. But that's where the similarity ended. Domi-
neering Darling Senior attempted to impose his will on his son in his
own interests, which Joe didn't agree with. He put financial pressure
on Joe, who had to fight to do what he wanted through much of his
adult life. Martin, by contrast, seemed, probably unconsciously, to live
his own unfulfilled dreams through Ian. Yet Martin's dreams became
Ian's and Martin went out of his way to guide his talented son. Unlike
Joe, Ian was appreciative of his father's interventions and drive. The
early imposed disciplines in batting, in both defence and attack, set
Ian up for advances beyond Martin's attainment. After that alleged
stepping-away incident, Ian redoubled his efforts never to show fear
against speed.

Ian's father had coached him until he was five. From six to sixteen
the main job fell to former country cricketer Lynn Fuller every Sunday
morning for a few hours. Ian loved the hook shot. But both his father
and Fuller tried to suppress this adventurism. As Ian matured, he made
decisions himself and gave free rein to the hook. It brought many runs.
Chappell weighed it against the number of times it led to his dismissal
and decided he would continue to use it.

A useful experience was playing for his school, Prince Alfred's College, which competed in the South Australian Cricket Association's second grade competition. That was a tough league for schoolboys. Once through it, youths were ready to go higher.

Chappell played for Glenelg in his teens and got his break in state cricket at eighteen at the end of the 1961–62 season, when Gary Sobers, who had been playing for the state, returned to the West Indies for a Test. Chappell was picked to play against Tasmania, which was not then in the Shield (now Pura Milk) competition. He only made a few runs. In the next game he made a fighting 59 against Victoria. South Australia's captain was the attacking Les Favell, who opened and inspired his team.

After leaving school, Chappell got a job in the clerical department of an Adelaide stockbroking firm in 1961 and spent two years there. It was the place he got to know Kay Ingerson, whom he later married at twenty-three.

In 1962–63, Ian Chappell found himself coming in after a strong state line-up of Favell, John Lill, Sobers, Ian McLachlan, Neil Dansie and Ken Cunningham. He learned much from all of them and particularly enjoyed the experience of performing with Sobers. He made 149 that season against New South Wales, partnered by Cunningham and the popular all-rounder Neil Hawke.

Chappell left his stockbroking job to spend an unproductive 1963 northern season in the Lancashire League. He was just nineteen and too young to appreciate, or take advantage of, the experience. All he did was add unwanted weight to his 180-centimetre, 78-kilogram frame by drinking beer and eating English food. (Nearly thirty years later, Shane Warne had the same experience at the same age. But he did better, and got bigger, topping 100 kilograms. The Lancashire League was a hunting ground for many a budding young cricketer. The price for the development was rotundity.)

Ian Chappell returned to Australia in October 1963 and joined W D & H O Wills, the cigarette manufacturer (where he was to stay, in 'promotions', for eight years until 1971).

Favell stepped Chappell up to number three in 1963–64 and from there he made his highest first-class score, 205 not out versus Queensland. It helped push him into the Test side during the next season. Chappell had already made the Australian baseball team in the winter of 1964. But before the year was out he had made the Australian cricket team, to play Pakistan in December at the Melbourne Cricket Ground.

Chappell was again thrown into the number three spot. As he scratched around for 11, the nation was aware for a brief time of a player with a multi-tic: in turn he paid feverish attention to gloves, box and pads before settling over his bat. Chappell had some influence in that Test by taking four slips catches. It was to become a speciality.

He had to wait thirteen months until the middle of the 1965–66 Ashes season to get another chance in Tests. The selectors wielded the axe after England won the Third Test and picked Ian Chappell and Keith Stackpole on debut. Chappell stayed for 17 in the Fourth Test and also took a 'blinder' at slip to send back the troublesome Geoff Boycott. In the Fifth, when Bob Cowper made his record 307, Chappell made just 19. He was disappointed but the selectors had faith in him.

In 1966, Ian Chappell married Kay and was selected to tour for the first time, to South Africa. In the same year he again played baseball for his country.

Ian Chappell had just earned his place in the team for the 1966–67 series against South Africa, making 196 at 21.78, taking six catches at slip and five wickets with leg spin for 296. There had to be an improvement in the next season of 1967–68 in Tests against India or Chappell would be dumped. He began poorly at Adelaide, scoring 2 and 13. He had now played nine Tests without a big score. Chappell felt the Second Test at Melbourne could be the last chance. Coming in at three for 246, he was dropped a couple of times early. It would have been a long way back after a fair run of chances. But luck was with him. He went on to a fine knock of 151—his first Test century—as Australia amassed 529. Chappell made 212 at 30.29 from seven knocks in the series. He was again effective at slip. But the Indians had no trouble with his leg spin on Australian pitches. He took one for 175.

The Chappells' daughter Amanda was born in early 1968 and he was chosen for the tour of England. It was this series that established him. He scored 348 in the Tests at 43.5, with a top score of 81 and 4 fifties in an even performance under tough English conditions.

A clear delineation in thinking between Bill Lawry and Ian Chappell was seen at the end of the Fourth Test at Headingley. The cautious tactics of Barry Jarman, acting for the injured Lawry, made sure of a draw on the last day when more aggressive tactics might have engineered an Australian win.

Ian Chappell walked off the field with the team and threw his cap in a corner. 'If that's Test cricket,' he said, 'you can stick it up your jumper.'

'What's wrong, Ian?' asked Lawry, who had been waiting for the team.

'We could have beaten England and taken a two–nil lead,' Chappell replied.

'We've done what we came over here to do,' Lawry replied without rancour, 'and that was to win the Ashes.'

Lawry's calm response made Chappell reflect later that it was the 'first real lesson in what England–Australia Tests' were all about. But it highlighted a difference in mentality. Chappell's natural instincts were to chase a win. Lawry's were to make sure Australia didn't lose.

Chappell topped the 1968 tour averages with 1261 at 48.5 and a highest score of 202 not out against Warwickshire. In three Test series, his average had lifted from the 20s, to the 30s, then the 40s.

There was more to come. He was again put at number three against the West Indies in Australia a few months later during the 1968–69 series, and made 117, 50, 165, 33, 76, 96, 1 and 10 for an aggregate of 548 at an average of 68.5. Added to this were ten catches at slip.

Chappell's batting form as the permanent number three continued on the 1969–70 tour of India, in which he scored 324 at 46.29 (top score 138 at Delhi). The team went straight on to South Africa for a four-Test series, with many of the squad suffering from fatigue, weight loss and lack of nutrition. It didn't help against a strong South African team that thrashed Australia four–nil. Chappell, after being billed by Lawry as the best bat in the world, failed, with 92 runs at 11.5. He had trouble with the pace of Peter Pollock and the swing of Eddie Barlow. The team came back to Australia in late March 1970 and received heavy criticism. It had the winter to regroup before facing a strong England team led by Ray Illingworth for the 1970–71 Ashes series in Australia.

Change of the guard

England was on top in a sometimes bitter encounter. Bill Lawry was dumped after the second-last Test and Ian Chappell, at twenty-seven, took over as captain for the final Test at Sydney. His attitude was to attack from the outset and that 'there was nothing to lose'. A win would square the series and see Australia retain the Ashes.

The game was marred by a series of events that led Illingworth to take his team from the field. John Snow felled Terry Jenner with a bouncer. The umpire, Lou Rowan, warned Snow about intimidatory bowling. Snow back-chatted the umpire and Illingworth stepped in to support his bowler. The crowd erupted. A spectator on the boundary then jostled Snow. The England skipper saw this as enough reason to leave the ground. He returned after a short break.

Australia lost the game by 62 runs and the series nil–two.

Chappell's consistency in scoring 452 at 37.67 from twelve innings was a fair return, but he had trouble with England's accurate speedster, John Snow. Snow was the star of the series, taking thirty-one wickets at 22.84. He removed Chappell five times in succession, causing trouble with the short ball. Chappell's natural instinct was to hook, but this had been thwarted when he was advised early in his Test career by Bob Simpson not to play the shot. It was too risky. Yet it left him without a counter to Snow, who bombarded him and all the Australian line-up.

During the 1970–71 season, Don Bradman, then in his final season as a national selector, came into the dressing room at Adelaide after a Shield game. 'You used to be a good hooker,' he said to Chappell. 'What happened to that shot?'

Bradman in his usual direct manner had said exactly the right thing in the right way. Instead of mulling over any negative he cut straight to the problem. Rather than saying, 'You should do this,' in an authoritative or dictatorial manner, Bradman at once praised him and seeded a positive solution that would release Chappell from a cricketing straitjacket, imposed first by his father and coach Lynn Fuller, and later on by Bob Simpson. Chappell responded. He said that this comment from Australia's 'greatest batsman ever' convinced him it was time to reintroduce his favourite stroke, which he had hidden in his locker for years. There was not the time to do it against Snow. He would have to retrain himself at the end of the season. He had his brother Greg bounce a baseball at him from close range on a concrete pitch until he conquered it. (It irritates Chappell now that players who struggle with the short ball, such as Michael Bevan, don't tackle it head on as he did.)

Now with the responsibility of the Australian captaincy, Ian Chappell left his job in cigarette promotion and began his own journalism, promotion and advertising set-up: Ian Chappell Enterprises.

South Africa was banned from touring Australia in 1971–72 and this caused the Board of Control to hurriedly scrape together a 'World XI' to tour and play a five-Test series against Australia. Chappell had a terrific run in the 'Tests', scoring 634 runs at 79.25, his best return in a top-class series. His scores were 145, 106 (both in the first match at Brisbane), 56, 21, 41 (run out), 17, 119, 18 and 111 not out. He also hit 95 against the World XI while playing for a Combined XI. Chappell's aggregate was the highest in the series by 114 runs and he was the only player to notch four centuries.

The World XI won the five-match series two–one, yet it was excellent preparation for the tour of England in 1972, which was drawn two all. Australia didn't win back the Ashes, but it showed real fight under Chappell to come back and win a thriller in the Fifth Test at the Oval. He and brother Greg combined for a 201 partnership in the first innings (Ian 118, Greg 113). Chappell ended the series with 334 at 33.4, and he took another eight slips catches.

Ian Chappell, Rod Marsh, Dennis Lillee and others in the team loved fraternising with the opposition after a day's play. They would whip the top off a few coldies and sit down with the on-field 'enemy'. But Chappell was shrewd. He learned much about his opponents this way. Geoff Boycott stunned him by letting him know the strengths and weaknesses of his fellow England players. Chappell encouraged the loquacious Yorkshireman and later put the knowledge gleaned to good use on the field.

In the 1972–73 summer, Chappell returned 341 at 68.2 in five innings of three Tests versus Pakistan. His top score was 196 in the First Test at Adelaide. Australia won the series three–nil and Chappell was confirmed as a successful, attacking leader. He was a tough skipper, who pushed his bowlers and dragged extra overs out of them, when they themselves thought they were spent. However, Chappell engendered spirit in the side. He believed in his players and they in him. It was half the battle for success, especially on overseas missions, such as the one to the West Indies in 1972–73, that quickly followed the victory against Pakistan.

The Caribbean tour was Ian Chappell's biggest challenge yet, especially as the team was without the injured Lillee. Australia drew the first two Tests and should have been without Chappell for the Third Test. He twisted his ankle two days before the game. Showing determination, he had to prop while batting in his scores of 8 (batting six) and a painful 97 (back at number three), which helped give Australia a chance. On the last day at lunch the West Indies was 66 runs short with five wickets in hand. Chappell, in a particularly inspired address, told his bowlers to concentrate on line and length and his players not to give up or whinge about things not going their way. Medium-pacer Max Walker and spinner Kerry O'Keeffe took the wickets for just 21. Australia scraped in by 44 runs.

In the Fourth Test Chappell hit 109 and Australia won by ten wickets. This gave Australia the series two–nil. Chappell scored 542 at 77.43.

In six Tests (three in each country) versus New Zealand from December 1973 to March 1974, Australia won three–one. Chappell hit 486 at 48.6, including 145 and 121 in the match at Wellington. It was the second time he had done it in international cricket.

When the New Zealand media was informed that Chappell had abused Glenn Turner in this series, journalists gleefully dubbed him and his team 'the Ugly Australians'. The British press picked up on the theme.

Caribbean and other clashes

Undeterred, Ian Chappell continued on his winning way. He had the great speed combination of Lillee and Thomson at his disposal for the next series versus England in Australia in 1974–75. The Australians destroyed England, taking 58 wickets between them. Chappell hit 387 from twelve innings at 35.16, with a top score of 90 in the first innings of the series at Brisbane.

Only a few months later, Chappell was leading his team to England

Benaud the bountiful. Richie Benaud, a top all-rounder, led with brilliance from 1958 to 1963, at a most competitive time in cricket history. He never lost a series as captain.

Australian cricket's all-rounder.
Bob Simpson maintained Australia
at the top of the world cricket table
in the 1960s and a decade later
made a comeback to stabilise a team
weakened by defections to World
Series Cricket. He was an
outstanding contributor to all facets
of the game over forty years.

Cool determination. Ian Chappell at
Arundel where he started his Ashes
campaign of 1972. Chappell was
Australia's most aggressive post-war
leader. Like Benaud and Bradman, he
never lost a series as captain.

Portrait of grace. Greg Chappell was handed a challenging chalice as captain by his brother Ian in 1975–76 just before the drama of cricket's 'World War Three', when World Series Cricket divided the game. Greg was one of cricket's elegant stylists—in the same vein as Victor Trumper, Charlie Macartney and Mark Waugh.

Kim of Lilliput. Kim Hughes is dwarfed by a celebratory champagne magnum. He had a giant task as skipper, post World Series Cricket, when morale in the national team was mixed and unity disrupted. He batted with fine style, which pulled the crowds.

Profiles of understudy, deputy and leader. Allan Border (right), with his deputy (Mark Taylor, centre) and Steve Waugh (who would follow them both as captain) at Durban during Border's last, of a record 93, Tests as captain. Border, the highest run-scorer in Test history, fumed, fought and forced Australian cricket back to pre-eminence in the early 1990s after the doldrums of the mid-1980s.

On the rise. Allan Border's victory ride after winning the World Cup in 1987 at Eden Gardens, Calcutta. It proved to be a premature dawn in Border's single-minded effort to lift Australia through the ranks of international cricket. But the win showed it could be done.

Earning the urn. Allan Border holds the miniature Ashes urn trophy. Stung by defeats in England in 1981 and 1985, he did not rest until he had righted the ledger for Australia with wins as captain in 1989, 1990–91 and 1993. His record in England ranked him with Bradman and Armstrong.

Taylor made. Mark Taylor shows his passion for the Ashes trophy. He continued the domination of England after Border by leading Australia to wins in 1994–95, 1997 and 1998–99.

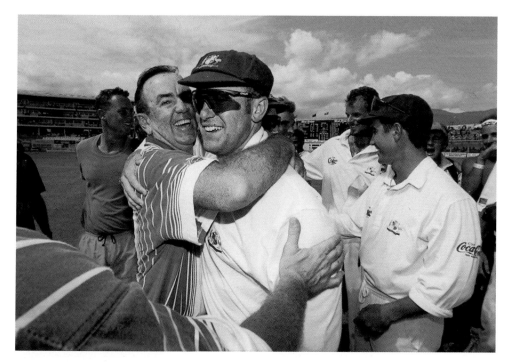

Shades of the ultimate victory. Coach Bob Simpson (left) hugs Mark Taylor after Australia's historic victory over the West Indies in the Fourth Test at Jamaica in April–May 1995. After this game Australia was back on top of world cricket for the first time in nearly two decades.

Waugh, what is he good for?—Winning! A beaming Steve Waugh with Bill Brown and beer during the Second Test at Hobart (against Pakistan) in the mighty millennium summer (1999–2000). Australia, under Waugh's leadership, won nine Tests out of nine during the extended season. Brown, as captain, kicked off Australia's post–World War II Test ascendancy with a win over New Zealand in March 1946.

Waugh's way. Steve Waugh shows power, balance and control here in one of his favourite shots—through point. In his first year as skipper, he set successive win records in both limited-over and Test cricket. In the 1990s he proved to be Australia's best bat, especially in the games that counted.

for the first ever one-day World Cup, to be followed by another Ashes contest.

Chappell was in a combative mood on and off the field by mid-June 1975. When he pulled up abruptly in a car at Swiss Cottage, North London and got out, he heard someone in another car shout in an Australian accent, 'Hope you can bat better than you can drive, Chappell!'

Chappell for a split second look confused. This wasn't a Pom having a go, but it was a form of criticism, even if it may have been said in fun. He took a step forward, employed his much-loved middle-finger gesticulation, and delivered his favourite gardening directive: 'Get rooted!'

The car from which the gratuitous, mild sledge emanated took off in haste.

Chappell was on the front foot all tour. He led his team astutely to the one-day final versus West Indies. The West Indies rattled up eight for 291. Australia, with Chappell, 62, leading the way, went down fighting at 274.

There was only time for four Tests. Australia won the series one–nil, with the Third Test at Leeds abandoned on the last day when vandals sabotaged the wicket. Chappell hit 429 at 71.5, including a top score of 192 in the final Test at the Oval.

Chappell surprised the cricket world by retiring from the captaincy after this series. He was at his peak. He had always maintained that he would go out on his terms and not those of the Australian Cricket Board (ACB). He had been shocked by the way the board had dumped Bill Lawry and had vowed it would not happen to him. Chappell felt satisfied. He had led his team from the depths to the top of Test cricket.

Apparently relaxed now he was free of the burdens of the national captaincy, Chappell dropped his trousers while adjusting a troublesome thigh pad during a state game late in 1975. Cameras at the Adelaide Oval picked up shots of this unintended 'mooning' of the South Australian Cricket Association (SACA) committee enclosure. It reinforced the public perception of Chappell as a 'bit of a larrikin'. Shedding the Test leadership had also allowed him to step up his militancy against officialdom. Richie Benaud remarked in the introduction to *Chappelli* that he sometimes did it sensibly, sometimes stupidly, and sometimes with an inbuilt knowledge of how far he could go.

'Sometimes it is difficult to believe he has any commonsense at all,' Benaud commented. He cited the example of Chappell being involved in a strike of South Australian players because the state selectors had wanted to take a thirteenth man on the eastern tour of Australia during the 1975–76 season. He and his men thought this excessive given that the SACA had been reluctant to pay laundry bills and other incidentals when there were just twelve on tour. Dirty jockstraps were just the trivial surface of a deeper issue for Chappell. He was having other troubles with boards at a time when he was mulling over his future. Should he go on or keep playing? He loved the game, but should he take up a new career? And if so, what? Chappell responded by lashing out against the superficial when bigger matters were on his mind.

Around this time he also encountered trouble over wearing striped Adidas boots, for which he was paid a sponsorship fee. It was part of the ongoing problem of older players—Chappell was thirty-two—with families attempting to stay in the game while being paid a pittance. The board banned the boots. Chappell contemplated dropping out of Test cricket. Adidas saved his career by paying out the sponsorship deal without him having to wear the striped product.

Brother Greg took over as skipper for the 1975–76 series versus the West Indies, in which Lillee and Thomson again took a huge bag—56 wickets—together in a series. Australia won five–one. Ian Chappell scored 449 at 44.9, with a top score of 156. He also had the satisfaction of leading his state to a Shield victory.

He made himself unavailable for Test cricket and then began secret negotiations with Packer to set up an alternative international cricket competition. Chappell had always fought for better conditions and pay for his players. Cricketers were still being paid poorly, despite the increased demands on their time. Now he was involved in events that would change cricket and payments forever. Packer's 'Super Tests', which included most of the best cricketers of the time, was successful enough after two years to see Packer given the rights to televise Test and one-day cricket. Chappell hit 389 at 43.22 with a top score of 141 in five of the WSC Tests (nine innings) of the 1977–78 season in

Australia. In the following season, 1978–79, his aggregate from seven innings in four WSC games was 181 at 25.85. In five more games in the West Indies from February to April 1979, he scored 323 at 35.66 from nine games. It was a first-rate record considering he took on the speedmen Roberts, Holding, Garner, Croft and Daniel.

During the Fourth Super Test at Bourda, Georgetown, the crowd rioted and the Australians were forced to barricade themselves in the pavilion. The next day, Chappell clashed with a Guyanese official whose incompetence had precipitated the riot. Chappell's stored anger had found another outlet. The local police chief saw the contretemps. Chappell was charged with assault. It was alleged that he had punched the official in the stomach. He was fined.

Tongue tensions

Later in 1979, Ian Chappell was thinking of making a return to the 'official' Test team once the ACB and Packer had reached an agreement over television rights. The team for 1979–80 against the West Indies and England would include WSC cricketers. Chappell was thirty-six. His form had held. If anything, he was a better cricketer and captain after the demanding two seasons with WSC. He would have been well placed to lead again. The other main candidates for the captaincy were Kim Hughes, who had not been in WSC, and Greg Chappell, who had. Rod Marsh was also mentioned as a possibility.

In November 1979 while playing for South Australia, Chappell abused an umpire, who reported him for swearing at David Boon on the second day—Sunday—of a game against Tasmania at Devonport Oval. Chappell was unsettled by the incident. He had transgressed his own code by verbally attacking an umpire. In the next twenty-four hours, he realised the incident would weigh against him in the choice of next captain.

On day three, Monday, he announced he would not be available for 'personal reasons'. He was in a fragile mood at a media conference at the end of play. When asked who he thought would be chosen captain, Chappell replied, 'Ask the bloody selectors.'

Journalist Bill Lane (brother of ABC radio broadcaster Tim) asked Chappell if he would be prepared to play under any player the ACB chose as captain.

'What do you blokes want me to do?' he said. 'Cut my own throat?'

Chappell knew that if he criticised another candidate, especially if the individual concerned became the leader, he would not be chosen as a player. He would not have fancied playing under Kim Hughes. His brother, however, would be acceptable. Ian Chappell then swore at two journalists for asking such 'smartarse questions'. Next, he rounded on Lane, saying, 'You can fuck off out of here!'

Lane was already on his way, microphone under his arm. 'Gladly!' he called.

The journalists had not been critical, but in this state, Ian Chappell was striking out against those who appeared to judge him, all at a time that he was—as he said—having problems of a private kind. But no one seemed to accept his explanation. Most observers thought it was just Chappell being Chappell.

Chappell lost his composure once again at an official luncheon on Tuesday, day four. He attacked a reporter who had covered his blow-up at the media conference in an article that appeared locally on Tuesday morning. 'You want to get your bloody facts right,' he said.

It was a popular refrain from Chappell. But the reporter had the correct facts. The integrity of the story was intact. The reporter stood his ground, telling Chappell that he mustn't have read the story correctly.

The running confrontation was the talk of media circles in Tasmania. Journalist Mike McCann witnessed it all. His editor at *The Examiner* asked him to write an article editorialising against Chappell. McCann was reluctant. 'It was daunting,' he said. 'Here I was just twenty being asked to comment on a famous Australian cricket captain.' McCann wrote the piece and concluded that Chappell was not handling the 'pressure [in big cricket] the way he once did'.

Also in 1979–80, Chappell abused another umpire in Adelaide, although observers on the pitch felt the situation that led to the abuse could have been handled better.

'There was a way of handling Ian,' one South Australian umpire from the era said, 'and it wasn't to be officious. If a jumper he had thrown short of you fell on the ground, you didn't tell him to pick it up. If you rolled with the flow of the game and the fierce competitiveness in that era, it was really enjoyable being out there.'

Despite these incidents, Chappell was selected to play three more

Tests under brother Greg's command during the 1979–80 season—one against the West Indies (for 2 and 4), and two against England (for 42, 9, 75 and 26 not out).

Chappell could still deliver with the blade, but he decided to hang up his Test boots for good. His entire official Test career saw him score 5347 runs in seventy-five Tests at 42.42, with fourteen centuries. He took 105 catches and twenty wickets at 65.8. Those figures exclude his 634 runs and four centuries against the World XI in 1971–72, at an average of 79.25 (eight completed innings), and his fourteen WSC Super Tests, for an 893 aggregate and one century (twenty-five completed innings) at a 35.82 average.

A more complete look at Ian Chappell's career shows he played in ninety-three 'Tests', including WSC matches and games against the World XI, and scored 6872 runs from 159 completed innings at 43.22, with nineteen centuries.

In first-class cricket he hit 19,680 runs at 48.35 with fifty-nine centuries.

Life after cricket was still cricket for him. And Chappell was still Chappell. He joined Channel Nine's commentary team but was suspended briefly for swearing on air. He now had to curb his tongue, at least on air. His livelihood was at stake.

After divorcing his wife, Kay, he married WSC employee Barbara-Ann Loois, in 1982.

Ian Chappell began a long career as a commentator. His humour was at times iron-booted, but his observations were acute, especially on the psychology of players and the moment. Like Richie Benaud, he had learned not to tell the viewers what they could see for themselves, but to augment the visual with telling comment. Chappell rarely sat on the fence, which made him, like Geoff Boycott, interesting to listen to. He criticised most captains. He even gave his brother a serve for the underarm affair. He was tough on Graham Yallop, Kim Hughes and Steve Waugh. He favoured Shane Warne for the captaincy after Mark Taylor and said so. He recognised a bit of himself in Warne, who he thought was a larrikin (although Warne didn't see himself this way).

While Ian Chappell supported aggressive Australian tactics, he was against intimidation going too far both verbally and physically. He didn't favour the institutionalising of sledging under Steve Waugh. He had not encouraged sledging himself while captain, despite his own lapses. There was a distinction between Chappell's occasional unpremeditated, foul-mouthed blow-up at an opposition player or an umpire on the field, and Waugh's match-by-match clinical planning of comments made to opposition players.

Ian Chappell's loyalty to those who played under him was demonstrated at Adelaide in the early 1990s with former Test and South Australian leg-spinner Terry Jenner. Jenner had been in gaol for three years for embezzlement. Chappell told his former charge that ABC broadcaster Neville Oliver wanted to talk to him on air about Shane Warne, whom Jenner had been coaching. Jenner wrote in his book *T.J. Over the Top*, that he wanted to go around the back of the stand to the media box. Chappell would have none of it. He told Jenner he would escort him round the front of the stand in full view of the members. He instructed Jenner to look up.

Chappell reminded him he had paid his price. He had every right to walk tall. Jenner did as directed and was forever grateful to his former skipper for giving him confidence and for sticking by his former teammate. It was a turning point in Jenner's rehabilitation.

In terms of the figures, Ian Chappell ranks as Australia's most prolific number-three batsman (Bradman excluded) since the Second World War. In that position in fifty-four Tests he scored 4469 runs at 53.2, and hit thirteen centuries. This again does not include his 634 runs at 79.25 with four centuries at number three for Australia versus the World XI in 1971–72. By comparison, Neil Harvey from fifty-one Tests, scored 3544 at 45.88, with twelve hundreds; Greg Chappell in twenty-four Tests hit 1677 at 44.13 with five centuries; David Boon had sixty-five games, scoring 4452 runs at 45.89; and Justin Langer twenty-nine Tests (up until the New Zealand series of March–April 2000), at 41.62 with six centuries.

Most knowledgeable observers judge Ian Chappell to be among Australia's greatest ever skippers. Bradman ranked him highly for his on-field performances. He said in 1975 after Chappell had stepped down from the captaincy, 'Choosing between them [Benaud and Chappell] was a photo finish: a slight edge in flair and initiative got Richie my vote.'

Performances in WSC matches and other efforts in Tests prompted Benaud to choose Chappell as the one to 'bat for his life', quite a compliment from a player with few peers for courage and application.

For some, particularly those who played under him, Ian Chappell was a cricketing hero. Others found his explosive, sometimes abusive personality unpalatable. When his long-held anger and aggression was directed into his cricket it brought winning results for his country. Its channelling into better conditions for players and WSC led twenty years later to full professionalism at the top of Australian cricket. Thanks to Chappell's early efforts and others such as Tim May in the 1990s, no current-day Test player struggles financially or is torn between playing on without security or finding another job. Outstanding players such as Adam Gilchrist, Justin Langer and Damien Martyn have had time to overcome waits and setbacks, rather than being forced into obscurity without the chances to have their skills come to fruition. Australian cricket has been the beneficiary.

35

GREG CHAPPELL

7 August 1948 –

Tests: 88; Captain: 48; Wins: 21; Losses: 13; Draws: 14;
Win ratio: 43.75 per cent

MR CLASS AND SUBSTANCE

No other captain ever had it as good as Greg Chappell on becoming the leader. He was a seasoned champion bat with an elegance rarely seen at the crease in Australia, where most successful batsmen tended to have a less-refined style than, say, their English or Indian counterparts. Greg Chappell was twenty-seven when he turned up at the Gabba to toss the coin with the West Indies' Clive Lloyd in the first of six Tests in 1975–76. Greg Chappell then had five year's Test cricket behind him. And in all but a handful of Tests, he had played under his illustrious elder brother, Ian, five years Greg's senior. Greg for some time had a feel for leadership. He had led Queensland for two seasons, and had been vice-captain to his brother. But his sense of what 'captain of Australia' meant went way back. Even as a four-year-old, a former Australian captain, Greg's grandfather, Victor Richardson, at fifty-eight, bowled to him. Greg would be dressed up in full batting regalia, complete with pads, gloves and protector.

Thoughts about captaincy were in his mind ever since he could retain anything, even if he were not conscious of it. By the time he was a mature top cricketer he had his own ideas, but he still learned much from his brother's approach to every aspect of the game. On top of this, Greg Chappell had a strong, seasoned team at his disposal. In batting, his two best assets were Ian and himself. His keeper was the talented, aggressive Rod Marsh. In the bowling department he had the left-handed fast-medium Gary Gilmour and the best off-spinner since Ian Johnson, Ashley Mallett. They were useful back-ups to Lillee and Thomson, the most lethal fast-bowling combination to pound a cricket field since Ray Lindwall and Keith Miller in the 1940s and 1950s, and the short-reigning combination of Ted McDonald and Jack Gregory in the 1920s.

Lillee and Thomson more often than not softened up the West Indies' strong batting line-up to such an extent that a certain fire went out of the Caribbean torch for the rest of the game. In six Tests they sent back fifty-six batsmen. Gilmour added another twenty. Greg paced his bowlers well and so maximised their benefit for the team. No one was overbowled under him. The only complaint was that six Tests was one too many. It put physical stress on the pacemen.

Even with his exceptional pedigree in cricket, athleticism and sport generally (he was a talented baseballer like his brother, father Martin, and grandfather Vic), Chappell had to deliver as both skipper and batsman. He was more a doer than an exhorter. In that First Test at the Gabba he performed in a way that no amount of pep-talks, speeches, pushing or cajoling could match. After the West Indies had been rolled for 214 the lean, long-limbed Chappell (188 centimetres tall and weighing 76 kilograms) strode in at two for 142 and made an unhurried yet attractive top score of 123. Australia reached 366. Then the West Indies, with grand answering hundreds from Kallicharran and Rowe, notched 370, and left Australia with a nagging, middle-range challenge of 219 for victory. It looked tough when Australia was two for 60, but Greg, in superb touch, with shots all round the wicket, hit another hundred—109 not out—and became the first Australian ever to score a century in both innings of a Test *twice*. Just for comfort he had his determined, strong-willed brother Ian (74 not out) at the other end for company. A 159-run partnership gave Australia an eight-wicket victory. Chappell the younger was under way in much the same way that Chappell the elder had left off as leader.

There was a hiccup in the Second Test at the WACA, when Greg only made 13 and 43 and the West Indies (585) won by an innings and 87 runs. Yet this seemed only to act as a spur, a wake-up call for Australia to fine-tune its performance and hone its determination to beat these highly competitive and talented opponents. Australia went on to win the next four Tests, which gave it a five–one series victory. Greg hit a graceful 182 not out at Sydney in the Fourth Test. His series aggregate was 702 from eleven knocks with five not outs. His average was 117, an amazing return against such a strong opposition, which boasted three great bowlers in its line-up—speedsters Andy Roberts and Michael Holding, and off-spinner Lance Gibbs.

It seemed that Greg, like his brother, thrived on the added responsibility of leadership.

Educated to rule

If Australia had a classic route to leadership, it was the one taken by Gregory Stephen Chappell. He arrived on a scholarship in 1963 at Prince Alfred College, where three Australian captains had studied before him: Joe Darling, Clem Hill and Ian Chappell, who was then playing for South Australia and on his way to the top job.

Young cricketers encountered such good wickets at Prince Alfred College that Test players liked to work out at the school's practice nets. The coaches were good, without imposing themselves on the boys' styles. They had their limitations. Bradman watched Greg Chappell play and suggested to his school coach, Chester Bennett, a former state player, that the sixteen-year-old play more off-side strokes. He had a habit of pulling the ball from well outside off stump to wide of mid-on. It ran contrary to Bradman's logic that you don't play such a shot unless field placings dictated you chase runs in on-side gaps. Bennett spoke to other coaches at the school and decided not to advise Greg. It was a general rule to let a good player develop in his own way. But this restriction in Greg's play would stand out as he progressed.

Another advantage for young players at the school was the B-grade competition that they played in on Saturday afternoons. It contained senior players, many of whom were up to the standard of A-grade, from whom state players were chosen. This was a wonderful, toughening, fast-track experience for those destined to go on.

In the last match for his school, against the hated foe, St Peter's

College, Greg made a patient 107. More than seventy per cent of his runs came from on-side shots. It wasn't a 'problem' as such, but it was limiting for such a brilliant natural stroke maker.

Greg Chappell left school with a poor academic record, but he had applied himself mainly to sport and particularly cricket with distinction. Cricket was to be his future and he knew it.

He came on quickly, perhaps too fast for his maturity. At the beginning of the 1966–67 season, aged eighteen, he scored two centuries for Glenelg and was rushed into the state side. Greg made 53 and 62 not out against Victoria on the Adelaide Oval in November 1966. In January 1967 he scored his first century, at the Gabba against Queensland.

In 1967–68, his penchant for on-side shots prompted his state captain Les Favell to say he hoped Greg didn't 'lose sight of the fact that there were two sides of the wicket'.

Bradman, then South Australia's chairman of selectors, had his say one morning before a state game. Greg, who had been signing bats in the dressing room, stood near the door, bat in hand. He saw the familiar figure walking past the door and said, 'Good morning Sir Donald.'

'I'd change that grip if I were you,' Bradman remarked in his usual direct way. Greg asked what grip he should use. Bradman took the bat and held it with the vee between the thumb and the forefinger of both hands pointing straight down the bat handle.

'That's the way I used to hold it,' Bradman remarked, 'and I think that's the best way to hold it to be an all-round-the-wicket player.' He handed the bat to Greg. 'The grip you've got now is very good for the on-side,' Bradman went on, 'but you'll never be a good off-side player with it.'

Greg, always polite, thanked him.

Bradman advised Chappell it wouldn't be easy to make a change. It needed practice. It would be uncomfortable to start with but he would get used to it. Bradman began to walk away, then turned and added, 'I've given this advice to one other player who used to play for South Australia. He didn't take the advice and he's no longer playing for the state.' The individual concerned was Alan Shiell, who went on to be a cricket writer.

Greg made a dash for the nets and had others bowl to him. He tried the new grip and felt comfortable enough with it to use it that day in the match. He hit cover drives that had eluded him in his short career. From that day, he became an all-round-the-wicket player, with the cover drive a specialty. Greg lost nothing in his on-side shots.

Some might have arrogantly ignored this vital information. Others might have been too lazy or dim to bother about it. But Greg was a listener and learner when it came to the game he loved.

Greg Chappell made 154 against Western Australia towards the end of the season. He had had 'lessons' in the field from early grade games when older players, with axes to grind from his father, Martin's, playing days, sledged him. He received more in state games, notably from Victoria's vociferous keeper, Ray 'Slug' Jordon, and in that Western Australian game, from ex-England spinner Tony Lock. The latter hissed that he was a cheat for not walking after edging a catch behind. The teenager came through it all wiser and tougher. He demonstrated a fine temperament. The more he was pressured or sledged, the more he dug in. It was one thing to be one of the best-looking cricketers in Australia's history, for height, stance and elegance of stroke play. It was another to have mental strength. No one who played with or against Chappell in that first season had any doubt about him. He was a Test player in waiting.

In the northern summer of 1968 and 1969 he played with Somerset in England, and so progressed his experience of conditions and bowlers another notch. Fred Trueman, near the end of his career, was more abusive with his tongue than the ball. John Snow, near the start of his career, let his short-pitched deliveries do the talking. Greg tried to hook him, was hit and ended up in hospital with stitches around the eye socket. Like Richie Benaud before him, he survived and went on hooking.

Chappell made enough runs in Shield cricket in 1968–69 and 1969–70 to be on the verge of Test selection. He toured New Zealand early in 1970 in an Australian Second XI. Greg averaged 60 in eleven innings. It looked impressive against the averages for the concurrent tour of South Africa by the senior side, where only Paul Sheahan (30.88) and Doug Walters (32.25) topped 30. Selectors went on the sight of players performing. Yet they always consulted the figures, just to verify an opinion either way.

Greg was selected for his first Test, against England in the 1970–71 series. The game was at the WACA. England made 397. Greg came to the wicket on day two with the score at five for 107. He felt like a spectator watching England, particularly Snow, pummel Ian Redpath with short-pitched bowling. Greg was inspired. He reckoned his brother Ian had guts. 'Redders' was on a par with Ian for sheer determination not to be intimidated or dominated.

Greg took sixty-seven minutes to notch up his first ten runs, but was 48 not out at tea. He reached his century an hour after tea with a blistering run of shots, mainly on the leg side and with slaps over mid-wicket of anything short. It was an inspirational knock, even for his brother, who thought he had better improve or he would soon become 'the other Chappell'.

Greg misinterpreted Richie Benaud's advice straight after his innings to always play his shots, whether in good or bad form. With that advice fresh in his mind, he tried to play strokes early in the next few innings that he was not quite ready to deliver. He had several low scores before the Sydney final Test of the eventful 1970–71 series, where he hit 65 and 30. His 248 aggregate in seven completed innings gave him an average of 34.71.

In the off-season of 1971, Greg, at twenty-three, married Judy Donaldson of Sydney. (They later had three children, Stephen, Linda and Jonathan.)

In 1971–72 Greg Chappell replaced Paul Sheahan in the last three of the five unofficial 'Tests' versus a World XI and notched 425 runs at 106.25 with a top score of 197 not out in Sydney. The week before he hit 115 in his first innings of the series at Melbourne.

He was a sure pick for the tour of England under Ian, and scored 437 at 48.56 with a chanceless top score of 131 at Lord's in the Second Test. It took him six hours and he faced 301 balls. Trevor Bailey judged it the best innings of the series. Bailey, a fine English all-rounder, who by contrast to Greg was less than an enterprising bat himself, recognised the sheer class being presented to England for the first time at Test level. In English eyes, Greg should have been one of them. His style had a similarity to Colin Cowdrey, Peter May and Tom Graveney, who starred in the 1950s and 1960s. Greg confirmed his status with 113 in the final Test at the Oval. His century took him 190 minutes and he hit 17 fours. It was chanceless again. Greg partnered Ian (118) in a 201-run stand—the first time brothers had made centuries in the same Test. Greg's figures were 437 at 48.56.

At the beginning of a long run of Tests during 1972–73, he scored 242 at 60.5 in three Tests against Pakistan, with a mandatory match-winning effort, this time at the Melbourne Cricket Ground, with 116 not out and 62 run out.

After that series ended in January 1973, the team was off to the West Indies for five more Tests. Greg was consistent, scoring 342 at 48.86. He managed a good score (40 or more) in every game, with a top knock of 106 at Bridgetown.

Greg moved to Brisbane at the beginning of the 1973–74 season in order to captain Queensland. It was a sensible career move. If he was ever to take over from his brother as Test captain, he would need to step out of Ian's shadow to test his own leadership skills.

In 1973–74, Chappell played six Tests against New Zealand. In the first three, which Australia won two–nil, his form was mediocre, with 110 runs at 36.67. But in New Zealand, where the result was one all, he lifted in tougher conditions and created a sensational double of 247 not out and 133 in the First Test at Wellington. His final figures were 449 runs at 89.8.

At home in 1974–75, he was at last in a winning Ashes team. He was the most important batsman of both teams, with 608 runs at 55.27, with another fine two-innings effort at the Sydney Cricket Ground in the Fourth Test—84 and 144. This demonstrated yet again that Greg Chappell had one of the strongest minds ever to pull on a baggy green cap. Rarely did players present themselves as well or better in a second innings after a brilliant first dig. Chappell had done it several times now at Shield and Test level.

His powers of concentration under stressful conditions, where he shut out all else as if in a plastic bubble of his own, were exceptional. This capacity has been rare in the game's history. Ponsford, Bradman, Morris, Ian Chappell, Harvey, Border and Steve Waugh were some of the others who had the capacity for the big innings, or a big score in both digs.

Greg's stamina was not evident from his build, but he had that too in his prime at twenty-six. He began the Tests with 58 and 71 at Brisbane and after eleven innings he hit 102 in the last at the MCG in the Sixth Test.

His on-field demeanour had been shaped. He began as a shy, polite type in contrast to his more brash, elder brother. But that shyness was knocked out of him after eight years in big cricket, where all the chest-beating fast men and opposing players had attacked him both physically with the ball and verbally. It was something they would have been less likely to do with Ian, who looked as determined as he was. Greg would never be a 'hard' man, but he developed iron in his soul. He had to survive and then conquer. Off-field, this manifested in a dry wit, especially in his speeches.

In Ray Robinson's book *On Top Down Under*, Greg Chappell told how he liked to relate an experience he had had when making a speech one night to a club. One man told Greg it was the worst such talk he had ever heard. Greg related this insult to the club president, who displayed a very dry wit himself, or none at all, when he commented, 'Don't worry, Greg, he's not worth worrying about. He just goes around saying what everyone else thinks.'

Greg's rule

Greg Chappell was off the boil in most of seven innings in England in 1975, making 106 runs at 21.2, with a top score of 73 not out at Lord's. But he was out of touch only in the Tests. In twenty innings for the season he made 762 at 44.82, with two centuries. One of them against Glamorgan came up in seventy-seven balls.

Then Ian stepped down from the captaincy and Greg was named his successor. The new leader had thirty-four Tests behind him and had scored 2507 runs, including nine centuries. Ian had broken him in on the tour of England, where, as vice-captain, Greg had taken over in five out of fourteen games.

Greg Chappell lifted for a magnificent Test series against the West Indies in Australia in 1975–76, and became the third Australian cricketer after Monty Noble (1903) and Lindsay Hassett (1949) to score a century in his first Test as captain. When he made a second in the same game, he was voted man of the match. Greg showed he was in a class of his own by playing the West Indies' spinners on a worn track with great acumen. He partnered Ian, who turned the strike over to Greg and played second fiddle in the interests of the team. Australia won easily. Greg's 182 not out in Sydney in January 1976 was one of the best ever big 'crisis' innings by a skipper. His team was in trouble at three for 103 chasing 355. He was still there at the end with the score at 405—50 ahead. The West Indies then collapsed under the swing of Gilmour and the pace of Thomson for 128. The runs were mopped up with relative ease, with Greg again not out (6) when the winning runs were scored.

Australia won the series five—one. Greg Chappell had begun his leadership from the front and in crushing style. Ian had pushed the team to the top. Greg was maintaining its elevated position. This was apparent in the next season of 1976–77 in a drawn series against Pakistan. Greg made 343 runs at 57.17, with another impressive double, 121 and 67, in the Second Test at the MCG. In New Zealand, he led the team to a one–nil series of two games, without doing anything startling himself. In March 1977 back at the MCG he had the lucky and extraordinary honour of leading his country in the Centenary Test against England. Australia won by forty-five runs, the same margin it had won by in the first game in 1877.

It was then on to England for the 1977 Ashes. Behind the scenes, Greg had secretly signed with Kerry Packer's World Series Cricket (WSC). The revelation of the breakaway competition broke in May 1977, just when the Australians were commencing their tour. The team was not strong. Ian Chappell had long retired. Lillee, a prime mover in the WSC creation with Ian Chappell, was 'unavailable' for the tour. Morale dropped to rock bottom, with Australian Cricket Board (ACB) members and team management angry with Greg Chappell. He was accused of 'betrayal' and 'deceit'. While he had not found the decision to be involved easy, the reaction from the establishment strengthened his resolve to be in the new movement.

It had begun with disgruntlement over poor player payments. Players had been belting their bodies for their country for years. Those without professions or trades had nothing to look forward to. They walked into that career void without any money after perhaps a decade of glory for Australia.

Despite the mental pressure caused by the WSC venture being made public, Greg still performed on the field, making 371 at 41.22 with a top score of 112 in the Second Test at Old Trafford. On tour he did better still, scoring 1182 runs at 59.1, with five centuries and a top score of 161 not out. Greg felt it was his last tour of England. He wanted to finish off in style. Yet his efforts were upstaged by Australia's nil–three thrashing in the Tests.

Then in 1977–78 he padded up for 'Australia' in WSC Super Tests, but not as skipper. He was happy to turn that arduous duty over to Ian. In six matches Greg scored 661 runs at 60.09, with a top score of 246 not out at VFL Park, Melbourne, a relatively unheralded performance because of the rebel status of the new comp. Yet the quality of the cricket was at least as high as conventional Tests and more demanding, given the high preponderance of bouncers directed at the Australians by some of the fastest quality bowlers in history, including Daniel, Holding, Roberts and Garner.

In 1978–79 in Australia Chappell hit 134 runs at 26.8 in three games. When the 'circus' moved to the West Indies at the end of that 'season' he amassed 620 runs at 68.88, with a top score of 150. In all he had batted sixteen innings with one not out for 1415 runs at 56.6. Considering the conditions and the opposition, Greg had put in a supreme effort to make WSC work. It did—to a point. The ACB came to an agreement with Packer that he could televise big cricket on his TV station, Channel Nine. WSC broke up. Players went back to playing conventional cricket again.

Australian cricket was in such disarray that the ACB gave Greg his old job back as captain of the Test side. It had to compromise if the country was to rebuild a quality team. A blend of the WSC players and the new men who had been coming on in their absence was the result. The hope that it would somehow create a brew strong enough to dominate a demanding nine Tests—six in Australia against the West Indies and England, quickly followed by three more in Pakistan—was soon dashed. It was wishful thinking. The sum of the parts was not as strong as expected.

The West Indians were very keen to crush Australia. Greg began in typical 'big occasion' fashion in the First Brisbane Test by scoring 74 and 124. He led a recovery that came within a session or two of winning. The game was a draw. After that, the home side was thrashed in the other two games. It was a reality blow. A true, sustained revival to make Australia number one in the world, as it had been in 1975–76, would take a lot longer than expected.

Greg returned 270 at 45. In three more Tests in the same season, Australia took out its frustration over their slaughter by the West Indies by beating Mike Brearley's England team three–nil. Greg returned 317 at 79.25. He finished off the summer with 114 and 40 not out, scores that were instrumental in an eight-wicket win.

There was more strife in Pakistan, when Australia was beaten first up by seven wickets at Karachi. Greg batted more than seven hours for 235 at Faisalabad, but a draw resulted. The same outcome at Lahore (Greg 56 and 57) gave the home team a victory of one–nil. Greg's statistics were 317 at 79.25. He and new man Allan Border held the batting together.

In nine Tests for the first reconstructed national team, Australia won three, lost three and drew three.

Greg led the team, now more settled, once more in 1980–81. First up were three games against New Zealand, which was crossing the Tasman as much as possible. The Kiwis fancied their chances against a weakened Australian team, but were well beaten two–nil. Greg made 180 at 36 from five innings with a top score of 78. This was followed by two Tests against India. Greg hit a magnificent 204 at Sydney and his performance led to an innings win. Australia just missed out on a second win at Adelaide. The game finished on 27 January.

The team had to immediately change into their coloured clothes for the WSC one-day competition, a legacy of the Packer intervention. There was a best-of-five final series between Australia and New Zealand, India having been eliminated earlier. And all games had to be staged inside a week before the final Test against India. It was ridiculous scheduling, and most players felt disdain for the one-day competition, especially as it was jammed in between Tests.

After two games, the series was tied one all. In the third final at the MCG, New Zealand had six runs to get off the last ball to make it a tie. Greg's younger brother, Trevor, was bowling. Greg was tired from a long run of games without a break. He wished to terminate this series as quickly as possible and so instructed Trevor to bowl underarm. He obeyed. The ball grubbed along the ground. The New Zealand tailender Brian McKechnie blocked it, then threw his bat in the air in disgust.

Hell's fury descended on Greg Chappell. New Zealand's prime minister, Robert 'Piggy' Muldoon, never known for his ambassadorial skills, wallowed in the folly, calling it cowardice. It was appropriate, he said, that the Australians wore yellow. Worse was condemnation from Richie Benaud on TV doing his game summary. Benaud said, 'I think it was a gutless performance from the Australian captain. It came about because he got his sums wrong.'

The reference to Greg's lack of courage was opinion. The remark about the 'sums' was incorrect. Chappell had meant to bowl Trevor and not Lillee at the death. But because Benaud had said it, Greg had the opprobrium of being branded as both lacking courage and being a little dumb, or at least innumerate.

It took Greg some time to appreciate the weight of the public opinion against him. He later appeared more contrite, and years later explained that he was not fit to be captain at the time. Greg said he was too mentally tired to think straight. All he wished for was the end of that series so he could have a break. Still, through the fog of fatigue, there was no excuse for such an arrogant act. Given that McKechnie was a hundred to one shot to hit a six, it was unnecessary too. It was a big mistake, one of the few Greg had made in an illustrious career. It would take some time to overcome. His reputation as one of the finest cricketers ever to play the game was besmirched by one act of thoughtlessness, which was out of character. Chappell had been more uncompromising than most as a leader, but this was a clear act of unsportsmanship, which appeared cynical in the extreme. He had contrived not to deliver a fair ball. Even a short ball (if within the rules) would have been lousy, but nothing like this. It was a classic example of an action being contrary to the 'spirit of the game'.

Greg Chappell returned to Test cricket a week later with the issue hanging over him and made 76 and a duck in a loss by 59 runs against India.

The underarm affair put added strain on his family in addition to the stress they suffered from Greg's long tours away from home. Chappell opted out of the tour of England in 1981. Instead, Kim Hughes led Australia.

It was a good series to miss. The tourists were beaten three–one. This strengthened Greg's case for being a skipper in place of Hughes, who had trouble with some of the players, including the headstrong Rod Marsh and Lillee. They thought that their experience meant they knew how to lead the team better than the new man. Lillee was tough enough to handle for someone whom he respected, such as Greg or Ian Chappell, let alone someone he had doubts about.

Watching Australia's losses on TV, Greg vowed to be part of winning back the Ashes. He returned to big cricket in 1981–82 against Pakistan and led Australia to a two–one victory. He notched his fourth double century in Tests—201—at Brisbane, which boosted his average to 50.2 from a 251 aggregate. This was followed by another three Tests against the West Indies. The series was drawn one all. Greg skippered well, but went through a period of the horrors with the bat. He scored seven ducks in fifteen innings (Tests and one-dayers), five of them in successive games.

Some players thought this experience enhanced him as a leader. After being humbled some claimed he became not compassionate but at least more understanding of the plight of other cricketers, especially lesser mortals.

In the 1981–82 three-Test series versus the West Indies, Chappell had his poorest aggregate yet—86 runs at 14.33 with a top score of 66 in the Third Test at Adelaide. Greg was a passenger for the first time. But he reckoned he was batting okay in the nets. He just couldn't get runs in the middle. It turned out to be a minor aberration in his mighty career. He scored 235 on tour in cold New Zealand in February and March at an average of 78.33, with a highest score of 176 at Christchurch in the Third Test.

Greg again withdrew from a tour, this time of Pakistan in September and October 1982. It didn't do his cricket career any harm. Hughes had to put up with a shocker of a tour. Australia was thrashed nil–three. Without lifting a finger, Greg enhanced his chances of again taking over as skipper against an English team led by Bob Willis. It was due to tour Australia for five Tests in 1982–83, straight after the Pakistan disaster.

Kim Hughes had a thin case for continuing, especially after leading Australia to two series defeats. Greg was elected captain and did as he intended, winning back the Ashes two–one. In a new look, he shaved off his beard. He notched 389 at 48.63 with two centuries— 117 in the First Test at the WACA, and 115 in the Third Test at Adelaide.

After the series there was a first-ever Test against Sri Lanka away in April 1983. Australia won easily. Greg hit 66, while David Hookes made 143. Later in the year, playing under Hughes' captaincy, he began his last campaign against Pakistan in five Tests in the 1983–84 series at home. He totalled 364 at 72.8, with a fine 182 at Sydney in his final Test. Greg couldn't have wished for a better ending. Australia won, to take the series. He passed Bradman's then best aggregate of

6996, and reached a final total of 7110 runs at 53.86 with twenty-four centuries.

In his first and last Test innings he scored a century. He played eighty-seven matches and had 151 innings—seventy-one more than Bradman to arrive at about the same total. Yet nothing could take away the fact that he had scored more runs than any other Australian in Tests. He also took forty-seven Test wickets with his medium-pacers at 40.7, with a best return against Pakistan of five for 61. Greg was also a fine slips fieldsman, snaffling 122 in all.

Then there were the fourteen WSC Super Tests for twenty-five completed innings and an aggregate of 1415 at 56.6, including five centuries; and three matches against the World XI of 1971–72, for four completed innings, and an aggregate of 425 at 106.25 with one century. Factored in, they gave Greg expanded figures of 104 'Tests', 183 innings, twenty-two not outs, and an aggregate of 8950 runs at 55.58, with thirty centuries.

In first class cricket, he played 322 matches, for 24,535 runs at 52.5 with 74 hundreds. His bowling at this level was more penetrative, with 291 wickets at 29.76. He also took 377 catches. Greg had a good record in 74 one-day internationals, scoring 2331 runs at 40.19, with a highest score of 138 not out. His accurate trundling was more appropriate for the short game. He took seventy-two wickets at 29.11.

Greg Chappell became an Australian selector after retiring and was one of three responsible for appointing Allan Border in 1984–85, a decision that would lead to the Test team being the best in the world again a decade later. After three years, Greg gave up being a selector and became a commentator. After various sports marketing and investment ventures, and a stint as coach of the Australia A one-day team of 1994–95, he took up the more demanding job of State Manager of Cricket, at the South Australian Cricket Association in 1998. He coached the state team with distinction and gained the respect and admiration of top players such as Darren Lehmann during the 1999–2000 year, when Lehmann was named Shield Player of the Year.

Greg Chappell was one of Australia's great batting stylists, in the line of Victor Trumper, Charlie Macartney, Lindsay Hassett, and Mark Waugh. He ranks eighth in terms of win ratio (43.7 per cent) of Australia's most successful captains who have led in fifteen or more Tests. Greg was more steely than his benign appearance suggested. He preferred leading from the front and was a big-occasion performer. His batting efforts won or saved many a Test for his country and his average of 53.86 placed him second only to Bradman in Australia's cricketing history. Greg Chappell was recognised for his feats by being named in the Australian team of the century.

36

GRAHAM YALLOP

....

7 October 1952 –

Tests: 39; Captain: 7; Wins: 1; Losses: 6;
Win ratio: 14.29 per cent

LEADER BY DEFAULT

Graham Yallop had one of the toughest jobs ever handed to an Australian captain, and the roughest first-Test experience in history. He was appointed skipper by default during the 1978–79 season, the second of Kerry Packer's World Series Cricket (WSC). In the first year, Bob Simpson, at forty-one, had his second coming in big cricket and filled in when Greg Chappell defected to Packer. But the selectors felt someone else had to be blooded as leader. Yallop, twenty-six, was given the job. If not for the advent of WSC, Chappell would have carried on as skipper until 1981, when Kim Hughes stood in for him. Yallop would never have been considered.

The lean (77 kilogram) Victorian had his first Test as leader against England in Australia in 1978–79. The home team could not be considered as other than a second XI. It faced a strong English team, led by Mike Brearley, that would not be sympathetic to the old enemy's plight. On the contrary, England would be trying to crush the tyros. It was the best chance to humiliate Australia since the 1932–33 bodyline series, which England had won four–one.

At Brisbane in the First Test Yallop won the toss and batted. The team returned a second XI effort of 116, the lowest score ever at the Gabba by the home side. Yallop managed 7, coming in at two for 5. When England batted, the skipper missed a tough catch at slip from Derek Randall, who went on to top score with 75. Sceptical eyes followed the new captain's moves, and lack of them, like spectators at a chess match. His worst error was not to give leg-spinner Jim Higgs a bowl early in England's innings. Yallop felt the wicket was not a turner. Higgs and off-spinner Bruce Yardley seemed an afterthought when they came on for six and seven overs late in the innings.

Keith Miller was critical. He would have used leg spin as a surprise, something to throw the English bats off balance. The sameness of Alan Hurst, Hogg and Trevor Laughlin irked the ex-champion all-rounder. To him and others, Yallop's efforts in the field were worse than bland or unimaginative. Yallop hadn't taken control. He didn't look like a leader. Ian Chappell, whose involvement in WSC had led to the situation where a Graham Yallop was required to lead the 'official' Test team, thought Yallop 'on the negative side'.

Thanks to Rodney Hogg (six for 74), the tourists were contained to 286. When Australia batted again, Yallop came in after another poor start at two for 2 and did what Ian Chappell and others had demanded by 'leading from the front'. Yallop and Kim Hughes (129) combined in a 180-run fourth-wicket stand. It was slow going but changed the game's complexion. Yallop reached 102 and joined that small band of players who had scored a century in their first effort as skipper. This verified that his nerve was okay. Behind that quiet, retiring exterior was fibre. The question raised by those passing judgment was whether he would learn on the job and bring out a hitherto hidden flair for it. Not all skippers were like Ian Chappell or Keith Miller, whose natural aggression caused them to take risks and try things. They were doers. Would Yallop surprise?

Australia reached 339 the second time around. No one else except for Hughes and Yallop reached 20. But for them it was still a second XI–type scoresheet. England had little trouble scoring the 170 needed, with seven wickets in hand. In the Second Test at the WACA, Australia once more looked inferior and lost by 166 runs. Yallop made 3 and 3.

At the Melbourne Cricket Ground in the Third Test over the New Year, Yallop won the toss and batted on a wicket with variable bounce.

Graeme Wood's 100 and Yallop's 41 were dogged as Australia compiled 258. Hogg did the damage to England, taking ten for 66 for the match. Australia won by 103. The series was alive. England got out of gaol and won the Fourth Test at Sydney thanks to Randall's 150. Yallop again came in for attacks over his lack of aggression, especially for not using Higgs in a more attacking way. He didn't pressure England enough.

Image was also important. Yallop had chats with players between overs. He didn't appear to know what he was doing, even if he did. When the media put that to him, he stopped the consultations and did more pre-planning. But after Simpson's knowledgeable leadership, Australia seemed rudderless. Field placings were criticised. Bowlers should not have been left to their own devices, unless the captain had no idea. At times, it seemed he had few clues, except to fall back on defence. One result of uncertainty was poor fielding. The skills seen under Simpson evaporated. Catches went down. So did heads. More fielding errors followed. In up to thirty-six days of cricket there was no way of hiding or covering up inadequacies in any of the game's departments. The worse indictment was a lack of fight from the underdog. Fans sensed this and stayed away. It was no surprise to see England run on to a five–one series thrashing. Yet Yallop salvaged a personal effort of merit, scoring another century—a brilliant 121—in the final Test at Sydney. He made the runs in 186 balls in the fastest hundred of the series. That innings made up 61.11 per cent of Australia's 198. Only a few batsmen in history ever had a higher proportion of an innings of eleven batsmen, with Charles Bannerman's 67.34 per cent in the first Test ever played being the best. (Bannerman made 165 retired hurt out of an innings score of 245.)

Yallop's 391 aggregate (at 32.58) was Australia's best. Only England's David Gower (420 at 42) did better.

The selectors realised low-key Yallop had the temperament at the crease. But they didn't feel comfortable with his captaincy. They decided to give him one more chance—against Pakistan at the MCG in March 1979, a month after the Ashes debacle. The game was marked by controversy. Hogg, the star bowler of the series, took four for 49 to help roll Pakistan for 196. Then in Australia's innings he was run out when he thought the ball was dead. The Pakistani skipper, Mushtaq Mohammad, sportingly asked the umpire, Clarence Harvey, to reverse the decision. Harvey refused. Hogg smashed his stumps down in disgust. According to *Wisden*, Yallop didn't help his cause as captain by commenting, 'I was surprised that he left one stump standing.'

Australia had the game in its grasp at three for 305 with just 77 needed to win. Yallop had been run out for 8, but Hughes (84) and Allan Border (105) had restored Australia to a strong position. Then Sarfraz Nawaz snared seven for 1 in thirty-five balls. Australia was beaten by 71 runs.

Yallop tore a calf muscle and missed the next Test against Pakistan. Kim Hughes took over at the WACA. Australia won by seven wickets. Graham Yallop was to play for his country again but he had led for the last time.

Graham Neil Yallop was the son of a castings foundry owner. He first came to notice at Melbourne's Carey Grammar, where England's former top paceman, Frank Tyson, was a teacher and cricket coach. Tyson knew talent when he saw it. Yallop was a fine left-handed stylist with all the strokes, with a good head for concentration and a lot more determination than his low-key mien indicated. Yallop made runs and Tyson spread the word about a Test player in the making.

Yallop was playing club cricket for Richmond at eighteen and was in the state side by twenty, but he couldn't hold a place, despite scoring 55 in his first innings for Victoria. Tyson advised him to obtain experience in England in the winter, which he did for three seasons. He played for Walsall in the Birmingham League in 1973 and Northamptonshire Seconds in 1975. In that year he met Welsh girl Helen Perkins and married her two years later.

At twenty-three in 1975–76, he consolidated a place in the Victorian side. Mid-season he was a surprise inclusion in the Test side for the fourth game of the series against the West Indies at Sydney. He replaced the popular Rick McCosker, who had made 42 runs in six innings to that point. Ian Chappell and some of his teammates were furious at McCosker's omission. They took it out on Yallop, who was made to feel most unwelcome. It was an ugly moment in Australian cricket. 'I was lucky to find my locker in the dressing room,' Yallop noted in his book, *Lambs to the Slaughter*. 'I was rudely awakened to the facts of life at Test level,' the quiet, unassuming Yallop said, 'thanks, or rather no thanks, to Ian Chappell and the rest of the team.'

Skipper Greg Chappell made Yallop bat in the hotseat at number three against the West Indies' Michael Holding and Andy Roberts ahead of the Chappells. Yallop made 16 and 16 not out, and was at the wicket when Australia won by seven wickets. He demonstrated resolve by making 47, 43 and 57 in the remaining games of the series to record an aggregate of 179 at 44.75.

Yallop was dropped for the 1976–77 season and missed the 1977 tour of England, although he was there, playing Second XI cricket for Glamorgan. WSC struck in 1977–78 and Yallop made the depleted side belatedly in the Fifth Test of the series against India after a superb double of 105 and 114 not out versus New South Wales at Sydney. He triumphed by making 121 in an Australian win in a close match. He went straight on to the tour of the West Indies and acquitted himself well against Caribbean pace, getting a score of 40 or more in the four Tests he played. His aggregate was 317 at 45.29 with a top score of 81. He had a strong tour, scoring 660 at 55, including a brilliant 118 against Guyana before having his jaw broken by Colin Croft.

Graham Yallop toured India from September to November 1979 and collected 423 at 38.49, with a top score of 167 in the Fifth Test at Calcutta. When WSC folded and the two squads amalgamated, Yallop lost his place and didn't appear during the six Tests of 1979–80 in Australia. Yet the selectors remembered his skills against spin on the Indian tour and picked him for the tour of Pakistan in early 1980. He made 172 at Faisalabad in a 217-run partnership with Greg Chappell (235). His aggregate in five innings was 237 at 47.4.

Yallop missed another couple of series and then toured England in 1981, where he was a disappointment (316 at 26.33 in twelve knocks), but for a defiant 114 at Old Trafford in the Fifth Test.

At thirty-one, Yallop reached a peak in Test cricket with a magnificent series against Pakistan in 1983–84, when he scored 554 at 92.33. His finest moment came in the Fourth Test at Melbourne, when he concentrated his way to 268 in 517 balls and 716 minutes with twenty-nine fours. It was the highest score of his first-class career, and the best score of either side for the series. At that point it was the sixth-longest innings (just under twelve hours) in all first-class cricket and the third-longest for Australia in Tests. That innings enabled him to eclipse the Australian record for runs in a calender year, which had been held by Don Bradman for fifty-four years.

A few days later he injured a knee sliding into the fence at the MCG and missed the tour of the Caribbean in early 1984. Realising that his Test days were probably over, he joined Kim Hughes's rebel tour of South Africa in 1985. Yallop's thirtieth and last first-class hundred was 182 not out against a South African Invitation XI at East London's Jan Smuts Oval early in 1987. He played club cricket in Melbourne until the 1990–91 season, when he was thirty-eight.

In Tests, Graham Yallop scored 2756 runs at 41.13 with eight centuries in thirty-nine matches. In 164 matches of first-class cricket he hit 11,615 runs at 45.9.

Yallop never excelled as a captain, but he took over the weakest side to represent Australia in the twentieth century, and at the toughest time. Bob Simpson, Greg Chappell, Kim Hughes and Allan Border didn't do much better in the upheaval of WSC and the weakened state of Australian cricket that followed in its wake for most of the decade from 1977–78. Yallop's 1983–84 series against Pakistan demonstrated that he was capable of scaling great heights with the bat. Given a 'normal' run he might have achieved more.

37

KIM HUGHES

....

26 January 1954 –

Tests: 70; Captain: 28; Wins: 4; Losses: 13; Draws: 11;
Win ratio: 14.29 per cent

THE DASHER FROM THE WEST

Kimberley John Hughes was all solicitous energy looking after his players as they arrived at various times at his hometown of Perth for what would be Kim's first game as skipper. The match was the Second Test of a two-game series against Pakistan, in March 1979. Hughes's enthusiasm was infectious as he met them at the airport, escorted them by taxi to their motel and confided in his players with such lines as 'This is what I want you to do, mate ...'

He chaired meetings with bowlers, batsmen and the team together. He made sure more experienced players dined with the new lads. Players who did not know each other were roomed together. Breakfast was a unified event, instead of players straggling into the dining area in dispirited groups.

Hughes stayed with the team instead of at his home. He took the team as a group to the WACA for the warm-up. His aim was to boost confidence in each individual and the unit. Confidence in the team was rock bottom, especially among the batsmen, who had been removed for under 200 in ten of their previous 14 innings against

England during the 1978–79 season and against Pakistan.

Good-looking, lean and fair-haired Hughes, at 182 centimetres, was a charmer, the first one Australia had had at the helm for decades. Yet he had a hard enough edge to be direct to his players and sometimes blunt, as he was to Dennis Lillee late in his career. It was a unique combination, and in that WACA Test the players responded to the new personality in charge. Perhaps they were pleasantly surprised after the strained time under his beleaguered predecessors, Bob Simpson and Graham Yallop, who had courageously taken the reins when Australia was at its weakest following the WSC defections. Maybe the change was as good as a holiday. Whatever the reason, the refreshment at the top led to a different Australia in the field and at the crease.

Hughes drilled the players on their roles and then fired them up after he won the toss and went into the field. His thinking was to use Hogg and Hurst on the bouncy wicket. Fielding first also allowed the team to settle as a unit. Pakistan succumbed early to Alan Hurst (four for 61), but Javed Miandad (129 not out) held his team together for a score of 277.

Australia made 327 (Allan Border 85, Rick Darling 75, Kim Hughes just 9). At practice after day two, Hughes stood on a speeding ball and twisted his ankle. Deputy Andrew Hilditch took over on day three. Pakistan made 285 in its second innings. Hogg, still 'aggro' after being unfairly run out at Melbourne, 'Mankaded' last man in, Sikander Bakht (that is, whipped off the bails when coming in to bowl, thus running out the cribbing non-striker).

The tension rose. When Australia batted a second time, Hilditch picked up a ball that had been fumbled by the bowler Sarfraz. The Pakistani appealed for 'handled the ball' after Hilditch handed it to him. The batsman was given out, the second man in Test history to be dismissed this way. (The first was Russell Endean early in 1957 against England, but in that case, the batsman had defended his wicket.) Hilditch's dismissal was an act of poor sportsmanship. The Pakistanis claimed they were responding to Hogg's action. In the end it made no difference to the result. Australia, with Border (66 not out) in the vanguard, cruised to three for 236 and a seven-wicket win.

Hughes had rekindled a winning approach in a team that had forgotten how to fight.

A career of living dangerously

The son of a headmaster, Kim Hughes followed his father into teaching, but in physical education. At fifteen in 1969–70 he was the youngest player in Perth ever to make a grade century. It was a pointer to an exceptional future. His training kept him trim at around 75 kilograms and he looked the part when he made his 1975–76 state debut against New South Wales. He scored 119 and 60 at twenty-one, another indicator of big things to come. Only four other Western Australians had scored a century on debut. Three games later he hit a classy century against the touring West Indians. In the following season, 1976–77, he hit a timely 117 versus the touring Pakistanis.

Hughes married schooldays sweetheart Jenny Davidson early in 1977 and then toured England under Greg Chappell. He had one Test innings and made 1 run. He played two Tests in 1977–78 at home against India under Simpson, scoring 64 runs in four knocks at 16. On the following tour of the West Indies Hughes was ill and didn't play any Tests.

In the next season, 1978–79, he entrenched himself in the Test side against Mike Brearley's tourists, making 345 at 28.75, including a chanceless 129 in the opening game at Brisbane. It took him six hours but the innings showed that he might be able to concentrate and curb a natural, flamboyant instinct to play adventurous shots.

At twenty-four Hughes found himself thrust into the captaincy versus Pakistan after barely gaining a firm spot in the Test side. Hughes's confidence was high after a 19 (run out) and 84 at the Melbourne Cricket Ground earlier in March 1979 in a Test Australia lost. After recharging the team for a win at the WACA, he took a team to England for the second World Cup. It floundered. Hughes made no excuses. There was no threat to his leadership from failures in the one-day game.

Hughes was given the reins in six Tests in India from September to November 1979. Although Australia lost nil–two, Hughes matured into a top-line Test player, with a series aggregate of 594 at 59.4, beginning with 100 at Madras. He and Border (162) put on 222 for the third wicket. Hughes went on to scores of 36, 86, 13 not out, 50, 1, 18, 40, 92, 64 not out, 14 and 80. It was a remarkable return of just three failures in twelve innings. He maintained this form all tour, notching 858 at 53.62.

Hughes's form avoided personal problems and helped his captaincy. Players were ill on tour and Hogg had no-ball difficulties, sending down forty-two in the two Tests. Hughes also found the South Australian speedster's volatility hard to manage.

World Series Cricket ended and Hughes lost the captaincy to Greg Chappell, who led the new-look amalgamated side during the six Tests of 1979–80 against the West Indies and England. Hughes scored 252 at 50.4, with a sparkling 130 not out in the First Test at Brisbane versus the West Indies. Against England he hit 186 at 36.6, with a top score of 99—another brilliant knock—in the first game at the WACA. He returned similar figures (182 at 36.4) on a tour of Pakistan for three more Tests from February to March 1980.

Centenary glory

Kim Hughes's glittering innings in the Australian summer were outdone by a magnificent double in the 1980 Centenary Test held at Lord's rather than the Oval, where the 1880 game had been played. In Australia's first innings he smashed 117, and in the second, 84. His 5 sixes brought brightness to a dull, wet affair, in which England failed to take up the challenge of going for a win when Greg Chappell offered it 370 runs to win in 360 minutes. The game was drawn. Hughes took the Man of the Match award. His reputation was enhanced.

He was appointed captain of Western Australia for the 1980–81 season, taking over from Rod Marsh. It caused some tension with Marsh and Dennis Lillee, who resented the transition. Hughes found these two difficult to deal with from then on.

He was vice-captain to Greg Chappell through the long summer of 1980–81, when six Tests were played. In the first three, against New Zealand, which Australia won two–nil, Hughes was subdued, hitting 109 at 27.25. He made 24 in the First Test against India at Sydney early in 1980. A few days later, his wife, Jenny, gave birth to twin sons, Sean and Simon. It lifted Hughes. In the next Test at Adelaide he hit a brilliant 213 in 301 balls, then the highest score by an Australian against India. (Twenty years later Justin Langer beat that score, making 223.) Hughes followed this up with 53 in the second innings.

Greg Chappell decided not to go to England in 1981 and Hughes resumed the leadership on what turned out to be an unhappy tour. It began well, with a two–one victory in the one-day Texaco Trophy, then a four-wicket win in the First Test at Trent Bridge (Hughes 7 and 22). A draw at Lord's left Australia with the initiative.

At Headingley in the Third Test, Hughes led the way with 89 in Australia's nine declared for 403 (John Dyson 102), then Lillee, Terry Alderman and Geoff Lawson routed England for 174. Hughes enforced the follow-on, and had the game won when England was seven for 135, still 92 short of Australia's score. Botham then played the innings of his life, making 149 not out, and was supported by bunnies Graeme Dilley (56) and Chris Old (29). England reached 356. Australia then collapsed to Bob Willis (eight for 43) to be all out for 111.

The 18-run loss was the cricket Houdini act of the twentieth century. The Australian side was demoralised. Learning that Lillee and Marsh had bet against Australia at long odds for a big windfall didn't help. When Australia failed again at Edgbaston to make a last innings target of just 150, the team was shattered. It lost the Fifth Test and drew the last, thus going down one–three. A little more application with the bat, tighter fielding and luck could have seen the result reversed. In the two games they lost, the Australians were on top throughout but went under at the death. England was only on top in the Fifth Test at Old Trafford and, even then, Australia fought hard, with Allan Border (123) and Graham Yallop (114) defiant.

Kim Hughes took the brunt of criticism at home and his own form (300 runs at 25) didn't help his cause. He lost the captaincy to Greg Chappell again, even though some commentators thought he should have been retained. He had at least toured. Chappell had shied away from the demands of an England summer on the road in favour of family life after years of unavoidable neglect.

In the 1981–82 home season, Hughes began well, with a century in the First Test at the WACA against Pakistan, but fell away for an aggregate of 193 at 38.6. Australia won two–nil and the side was at least settled after the debacle in England. It fought hard against the West Indies for a one-all drawn series in the final three games of a six-Test summer. Hughes had again started the series brilliantly. At Melbourne on Boxing Day, he came to the wicket at four for 26 against a great trio of speedmen: Joel Garner, Michael Holding and Andy Roberts. Hughes mixed solid defence with terrific driving and cutting, always employing his trademark flourish, which made it appear he was wielding a broadsword rather than a willow.

He was 71 with the score at 155 when last-man-in Terry Alderman arrived at the crease. To the joy of a big MCG crowd, Hughes made a dash for a century. The crowd warmed to his effort as he slid into the 80s, then rose to their feet as he crashed his way to 100 not out. The other ten Australian bats scored 83. The 15 extras brought the score to 198. Hughes's 260-minute stay, in what was his best innings ever, demonstrated that he had the ability to curb his adventuresome nature if he wished. Too often in his career, he tended to take his attacking play too far, a bit like the gambler who is compelled to put everything on one extra bet after winning plenty. Hughes would never have seen his batting as living outside his means. His vision of himself was as the dasher, which was accurate. The trick was deciding when to live up to it and when not. He got it right in this Melbourne knock.

The excitement generated by Hughes's heroic effort with the bat was matched by Lillee with the ball. He rocked the MCG with three wickets, including that of Viv Richards, in the final twenty minutes of the day. Lillee went on in the game to take the world record of Test wickets, surpassing Lance Gibbs's 309. Australia won by 58 runs, thus ending a sequence of fifteen Tests without defeat for the West Indians. Hughes's aggregate was 226 at 45.2.

The team went to New Zealand for three more Tests, making it a long season of nine games, one-day internationals and Shield games. Hughes struggled in his three knocks and scored just 29 runs at 9.67. The one-all result meant Australia had won a series and drawn two. In the structure of things, it had been restored to a middle power in world cricket a few years after the WSC split.

Greg Chappell again stepped aside to allow Kim Hughes to captain the team on a tough tour, this time to Pakistan. Lillee and Len Pascoe pulled out also. Australia struggled against poor umpiring, the heat, the spin of Abdul Qadir (22 wickets), bad food, substandard hotels, and a hostile mob at Karachi. Hughes had to lead the team off the field in three matches. The nil–three Test series loss and Hughes's own form (154 at 25.67) meant Chappell, who had remained comfortably at home, would be restored as leader in the coming Ashes series of 1982–83.

Kim Hughes took the decision in his stride and dominated the series, scoring 62, 0, 39 not out, 88 run out, 66, 48, 29 and 137 for a 469 aggregate at 67, the best figures of either side. Geoff Lawson (thirty-four wickets at 20.21) starred with the ball. Australia won the series two–one, which went a little way towards easing the pain of the 1981 Ashes loss. But players such as Hughes and Border, toughened by the experience, would never forget the humiliation of losing the unlosable.

Hughes led Australia in the 1983 World Cup in England. It was another disaster, with an unexpected loss to Zimbabwe and thrashings by India and the West Indies. David Hookes complained about Hughes's captaincy on returning home. Greg Chappell planned to make 1983–84 his last season, but not as skipper. He tried to persuade Hughes to step down in favour of Rod Marsh, who many felt was well equipped to lead the country. Hughes nearly resigned the job, but stayed on at the last minute, a decision that helped his final record.

In 1983–84 Australia won two–nil against Pakistan under Hughes. His batting remained strong. He hit 375 at 62.5 with scores of 16, 53, 30 and 106 (at Adelaide), 94 and 76. Greg Chappell retired. The pressures on Hughes were eased by the added retirement of Lillee and Marsh, who had never been close to their fellow sandgroper.

Hughes, with a prescience that would have surprised even him, fought the Australian Cricket Board (ACB) over player contracts that restricted them to 'authorised or approved matches'. This meant that if a player wished to play in South Africa he could not. Hughes and Geoff Lawson, using strong legal counsel, won the day.

But he was left with a depleted side for a five-Test assignment in the Caribbean. It was another poor series. Australia lost nil–three and Hughes managed just 215 runs at 21.5. Yet the selectors were most forgiving despite the fierce criticism from sections of the media, who wanted Hughes dumped as captain. There was no respite from press attacks or the brutal pace of the West Indians led by Joel Garner, Michael Holding, Malcolm Marshall and Courtney Walsh. The West Indies mowed Australia down in the first three Tests of the 1984–85 series, played in Australia.

Trial and tribulations by media

Ian Chappell, who liked to play kingmaker, used his Channel Nine platform to attack Kim Hughes. Chappell's comments made 'better TV' than Bill Lawry's defence of the skipper. Lawry felt 'the boot should not have been put in' when Australia was down. Hughes refused to answer Chappell's questions in the now regular quick, post-toss, TV interviews.

Hughes made just 34 and 4 in the Second Test at Brisbane at which the Australians were beaten by the West Indians for the second successive time. He resigned the captaincy in tears at a media conference. 'The constant speculation, criticism and innuendo by former players and sections of the media over the last four or five years have finally taken their toll,' he said.

Allan Border, who had tried to make Hughes stay on, became captain. In the Third Test at Adelaide he failed again with scores of 0 and 2 in a third loss. Hughes's confidence was shot. He made a pair in the drawn Fourth Test at Melbourne. There was no point in the selectors carrying him. He was dropped for the final 1984–85 Test at Sydney, which Australia won.

In seventy matches to that point Kim Hughes scored 4415 runs at 37.41 with nine centuries.

Kim Hughes was not chosen for the 1985 tour of England. He then led a rebel tour of South Africa. Australian politicians attacked him. Yet media and other polling found that he had public support. Up to seventy per cent of those surveyed ignored the apartheid issue and supported Hughes on the narrower argument that he should be allowed to carry on his 'trade'.

He did this for two seasons in South Africa. In seven rebel 'Tests' he scored 461 at 46.1, with a highest score of 97 not out. At thirty-three, Hughes was still capable of sensational and hard-hitting batting that attracted crowds.

He made a comeback to Shield cricket in 1987–88 but after 76 against New South Wales had a run of low scores that continued into 1988–89. Hughes then gave away first-class cricket in Australia in favour of skippering Natal. He played on until February 1991, aged thirty-seven. With a family of six it was time to move on.

Kim Hughes played 216 matches in all, amassing 12,711 runs at 36.52. He hit twenty-six centuries and sixty-nine fifties. As captain, Hughes did not achieve the heights he would have wished, with a record of just four wins from twenty-eight games. Yet conditions were often against him and he was dealt weak teams during the rebuilding after WSC. Kim Hughes was an attractive batsman, whose temperament didn't allow him always to calibrate the difference between straight-out adventure and creativity within the sustained batting effort.

38

ALLAN BORDER

27 July 1955 –

Tests: 156; Captain: 93; Wins: 32; Losses: 22; Draws: 38; Ties: 1;
Win ratio: 34.41 per cent

THE GREAT AUSSIE BATTLER

Allan Border never wanted the job of captain. He saw the pressure on
Greg Chappell and Kim Hughes, and never thought he could be as
diplomatic. Border felt he might be inclined to take on a critic rather
than turn the other cheek, which skippers mostly had to do. He would
have been much happier if Hughes had stayed on and Border could
concentrate on batting, fielding and even bowling a bit. But it wasn't
to be. In December 1984 Allan Border was made skipper when Kim
Hughes resigned the position. He now had the daunting task faced by
Bob Simpson, Graham Yallop and Hughes of leading a weak, inexperienced team. Not only that, there were still Tests in the series to play
against the world champions, the West Indies.

The enormity of that was driven home when Border won
the toss at the Melbourne Cricket Ground \ in the Fourth Test and sent
the opposition in. The West Indies rattled up 479 with Viv Richards
(208) dominating. Australia struggled to 296 in reply, Border making
35 and Kepler Wessels 90. Lloyd declared the West Indies second
innings at five for 186. Australia crumbled in its second knock, but

Andrew Hilditch (113) and Border (41) did just enough to allow the home team to avoid defeat at eight for 198.

Australia and Border sighed with relief. The West Indies had won the first three but now they couldn't make it a clean sweep. But Border was a realist. He knew the West Indies had dominated the Melbourne Test. Australia hadn't had a look in and was lucky to squeeze away without a defeat.

Nevertheless, he also knew that the Sydney wicket for the Fifth Test would be set up nicely for spinners. Bob Holland, a 38-year-old leg-spinner from Newcastle joined the left-arm finger spinner Murray Bennett. Border won the toss again and this time batted. Wessels made 173 and Border steadied the middle order—a habit of his—with 69, which pushed Australia up to nine for 471 declared. Then the spinners routed the might of the West Indies for 163 and 253, for an Australian win by an innings and 55 runs.

Allan Border was off to a fine start in his career as captain, which was to run for a decade and cover ninety-three Tests. But this early success could not mask the troubled, fragile façade of Australian cricket.

Knight moves

Allan Robert Border was the son of a wool classer. He played for his local Sydney club Mosman, at seventeen in 1972–73. Over the next two seasons, after leaving North Sydney High and taking a job as a clerk in the BP film library, he lost interest in cricket until the club's captain–coach, Barry Knight, cajoled him into taking the game more seriously. The veteran of twenty-nine Tests for England saw both the fight and ability in Border. He coached him during the winter of 1975. The stocky 175-centimetre, 80-kilogram left-hander, at twenty applied himself to becoming a top cricketer from the 1975–76 season onwards, and won a place in the New South Wales Colts.

He played village cricket in England in 1977 while Greg Chappell was leading Australia to defeat, and returned to play as a professional in the Lancashire League in 1978. World Series Cricket (WSC) hit and left openings in state teams. Border scored his first century at the WACA for New South Wales at the beginning of the 1978–79 season. It was enough for him to be rushed into the Test side a few weeks later against England. At twenty-three, Border had to pinch himself. Three years earlier he was half-inclined to give the game away. Now he was realising a childhood dream of playing for Australia.

He came to the wicket on 29 December 1978 at four for 189 and the 35,000 MCG crowd gave him a big welcome. England had won the first two Tests and the Melbourne crowd gave its full support, as ever, to the underdog. Border began with a drawn-faced determination not to surrender his wicket. It made him appear defiant rather than dashing; cautious rather than calypso. Yet his stillness of body between deliveries and head facing them signalled something special to the spectators in the vast amphitheatre. He could dance to spinners like Neil Harvey, and even though he seemed to play late at pace with a trademark push, sometimes like Ken Mackay, another durable left-hander of a previous generation, he was steady enough. He acquitted himself well, making 29. He was run out for a duck in the second innings. Australia won the game by 103 runs. Reluctance to change a winning combination saw him retained for the Fourth Test at Sydney. He hung on with the tail, scoring 60 not out and 45 not out while those around him disintegrated. It was a scenario that would be played out scores of times for the next fifteen years.

Australia was beaten. Border made 11 and 1 at Adelaide in another loss. His Sydney efforts were not fully recognised by the beleaguered selectors who had limited ranks from which to choose a Test side and he was dropped for the Sixth Test. Australia lost again, and England won the series five–one. A month later Allan Border was playing Pakistan at the MCG. He laboured over 20 in the first innings but made the fielders do the heavy work in the second, notching 105, his first Test century. He proved it wasn't a fluke by hitting 85 and 66 not out in the Second Test against the tourists at the WACA. Australia lost the first and won the second. But Border won himself a place wherever his nation's fortunes were swaying, by returning an aggregate of 276 at 92.

Six months later he was in India for a six-Test series. Australia lost nil–two, but Border advanced by scoring 521 at 43.42, with a highest score of 162 run out at Madras in the opening Test. He was brought down to earth hard in 1979–80 by the reigning world champs from the Caribbean, who beat Australia two–nil. Border could only muster 118 at 19.67 from six innings. Pacemen Joel Garner, Michael Holding, Andy Roberts and Colin Croft presented a different level of the game.

It was something that Border would have to come to terms with. He would be facing speed like this for the rest of his career.

He had a less demanding time against England in the follow-up three-Test series, still in 1979–80, scoring 199 runs at 49.75, with a top score of 115 at the WACA in the first game. Straight after that series, which Australia won three–nil, it was on to Pakistan for a nil–one loss. Border made 395 from five innings at 131.67, after hitting a brilliant double at Lahore of 150 not out and 153. The 303 runs took him ten hours. He hit 7 sixes and 32 fours.

This was followed in August 1980 by the damp Centenary Test, which was drawn. Border made 56 not out and 21 not out. He was content to be overshadowed by his friend Kim Hughes, who hit a dashing double of 117 and 84.

A few months later Allan Border was playing three Tests against New Zealand in Australia during the 1980–81 season. He returned just 100 at 25 in a two–nil series win for his team, before appearing soon afterwards in a further three Tests against India. This time he stepped up his rating and hit 228 at 45.6, with a top score of 124 at the MCG. The series was a one-all draw.

Border then toured England in 1981 and was the only batting success on tour, scoring 533 at 59.22 in a one–three series loss. He hit 123 not out in the Fifth Test at Old Trafford and 106 not out at the Oval in the Sixth. Border fought back when Australia was shell-shocked by Ian Botham with bat and ball, and Bob Willis with the ball. This series consolidated Allan Border as Australia's most reliable bat. He was twenty-six and in his prime.

After an ordinary 1981–82 series against Pakistan (won two–nil by Australia), he took on the West Indies for the second time. The three-Test series was drawn. Border hit 336 at 67.2, with a top knock of 126 at Adelaide. He had come to terms with the best speedsters in the world.

He had two more poor series against New Zealand (February to March 1982) and against Pakistan (September to October 1982), and then a steady run of performances against England in the 1982–83 series (317 runs at 45.29), with a top score of 89 in the Fifth Test at Sydney. It wasn't his best series, but he was more than satisfied to be in the team that regained the Ashes two–one after the 1981 debacle.

Border did better in the next series against Pakistan in Australia in

1983–84, scoring 429 at 85.8. He struck 118 at Brisbane and 117 not out at Adelaide in Australia's two–nil win.

His greatest series for performance and degree of difficulty followed soon afterwards in the Caribbean, when he collected 521 at 74.73. His finest Test (in his eyes) was at Port of Spain, where, against the full fury of Malcolm Marshall, Wayne Daniel and Garner, he came in at three for 16 and slammed 98 not out with hooks and cuts on tiptoe to counter the giants' missiles. In the second innings he was even more defiant—for just under six hours—in making his 100 not out in 281 balls. Border walked away unconquered and taller than his adversaries.

Australia lost nil–three but the West Indians couldn't defeat Border. His effort began another near-decade of struggle against them, beginning with a one–three loss in 1984–85, when he took over the leadership. Border had a rare ordinary series with 246 runs at 27.33. His record as skipper at the end of the series was one win, one loss and one draw. Had Australia turned the corner?

The cork pops

The answer came a few months later during the 1985 Ashes series. After four Tests Australia was well in the hunt, having won at Lord's in the Second, thanks to a mighty 196 by Border. Australia had lost the First at Headingley. But under the weight of scintillating batting from David Gower (215 and 157) primarily, Australia was crushed by innings victories in the last two Tests. Border himself had done well with the bat, collecting 597 at 66.33 (second only to Gower's 732 at 81.33), but he left England mightily displeased that Australia had not progressed from the one–three loss of 1981.

Cold analysis showed that Hughes's team had done better despite two pitiful collapses in close contests. In 1981 Australia was always in the contest. But in 1985 it showed little resistance at Edgbaston and the Oval in the final two Tests. Border took it personally. He thought in both series that the Australians had fraternised too much with the opposition. He liked Ian Botham and David Gower, but felt that the 'Poms' had it over his teammates in the psychological stakes. The chumminess seemed to carry on to the field. In 1981, when Botham belted 149 not out at Headingley, there didn't appear to be enough pressure put on him. Border felt the same when Gower dominated in

1985. England played as if they were superior, and whether they were or not, the Australian captain didn't like it. He would store away this dislike for future action when and if he ever returned to England.

He bottled his feelings in England but when Australia showed no great application in the Third Test of a home series against New Zealand, and lost, Border let his cork pop. In this game at the WACA, Australia made 203, then New Zealand 299. In Australia's second innings Border dug in for a stolid, defiant 83, but when he left at four for 195 the team fell in a heap to be all out for 259. New Zealand polished off the 164 and won by six wickets.

At the media conference after the game, Border was forthright. 'You start to wonder whether you are the right man for the job,' he said. 'If there was an obvious choice, who I believed could do a better job, I would be more than happy to stand down.'

Border was taking the foibles, weaknesses and lack of grit of others personally. They hadn't 'put in' for *him*. If there was someone else out there with a better capacity to inspire some grit and determination, he would let that person move into his job. It would sound like whingeing from anyone else. Border found it impossible to consider that perhaps England and New Zealand (with Hadlee at the height of his powers) were just too good for Australia. It didn't, *couldn't*, enter Border's head. He was an Aussie and Aussies never gave in, did they? They never admitted inferiority, did they? When his mortal companions didn't fight like he did he became irritated and angered, and this engendered his grumpy demeanour. Border couldn't relate to players who gave up. It was beyond his comprehension. If he could dig in, play hard, push an opponent, put pressure on, and 'win', then surely anyone else could.

But Border had something most others didn't. He had long been recognised as the foremost battler the country had produced. There was a solidity about him that gave you confidence in the man at the crease like no other, except for Bradman. Yet Border would play three times the number of Tests played by the Don over a similar number of years. Border figured in the national psyche as much as Bradman did, too. Television, the press, the frequency of Tests and now one-dayers as well made familiar the image of that unsmiling, unshaven, unforgiving face. The solid figure was often seen fighting out every inch of turf in conditions that were often the sporting equivalent of

Gallipoli, especially in campaigns against the formidable West Indian pacemen.

Through the years, Border began to realise that not everyone had his fire and refusal to be beaten. He disdained those who didn't and scoured the state and club players for individuals with his approach. That's why, for instance, he stuck with Steve Waugh and David Boon when others would have relegated them forever. That's why he was furious when Geoff Marsh, another fighter, was dropped in the early 1990s. They had a sense of invincibility about them. They were guys who were never beaten. He wanted bowlers around him like that too. He liked Craig McDermott, even if he had to give him a blast to fire up. He adored big, underrated Merv Hughes. Merv was a bullyboy bluffer on the pitch, and at times presented the image of a boofhead, but Border knew him close up. Underneath the menacing snarler–prankster was a character who put in when he had next to nothing in the tank. He carried injuries and made jokes about them. He came back to bowl at the end of the day when everyone else was desperate to get off the field. Merv also had that bit of mongrel in him.

Later Border would back the indefatigable spirit of a chubby blond spinner named Shane Warne, who bowled leg spin in the manner of an aggressive quick. Still later, at the end of his career, Border would 'verbal' a beanpole named Glenn McGrath in a state game just to see what he was made of. The response led to McGrath being recommended to selectors as someone with the right 'devil' in him. These were the sort of men Border wanted around him to help put Australia back on top.

Lashings at the low point

That embarrassing one–two series defeat by New Zealand in 1985–86 drove home to Border just how far down his country had gone. Yet despite the gloom his own form was strong. He hit 298 at 59.6 in the following three-Test series versus India, with a top score of 163 out of 308 at Melbourne in a rearguard performance that saved the match. His performances were similar in New Zealand for three further Tests and another series loss, nil–one. Border collected 290 at 72.5, with 140 and 114 not out at Christchurch in the Second Test. It was the second time he had managed the double. Yet not even that brought a sustained smile to his lugubrious features.

After the series and a loss in a one-day game, he blew up again. 'They [the team members] are really going to have to show me they really want me to play for Australia,' he said, 'and whether they really want to play under me.' Border said he would make a decision on his future after the next three one-day games. 'I don't think it's my captaincy,' he added, 'but if we continue to lose, you've got to start saying, "Right, someone else has to come in."'

His complaint in Perth had become an ultimatum in Auckland. *The players had to win to show they wanted him as leader.*

The team did perform a fraction better. Border stayed on. Deep down his feelings about opting out clashed with his natural instinct to fight. He would have no chance of putting Australia on top from his living room at home. His public remarks made the Australian Cricket Board (ACB) realise he needed help, not on a psychiatrist's couch but from a coach who could assist the players at every level. Bob Simpson was chosen. It eased the burden on Border. Simpson soon improved fielding, running between the wickets and fitness.

More of the sort of desperation Border was looking for came six months later in September 1986 at Madras (Chepauk). Border won the toss in the first of a three-Test series against India and batted in stifling heat. After David Boon had made a hundred and night-watchman Ray Bright 30, Border came to the wicket at three for 282 to join Dean Jones, who had been in for a day. During their partnership, Jones, dehydrated, vomited. He told Border he couldn't carry on.

'Okay,' Border replied, 'we'll send for someone with a big ticker . . . a Queenslander.' Greg Ritchie was next man in.

This was foolhardy given Jones's condition. His face had become a death mask. Yet Jones responded to the macho pushing, struggling on to 210, then to hospital on a drip and legendary status for his courage. Jonesy was just the sort of bloke Border wanted, and his performance the kind that would boost the image of the Australians. Border himself made 106 and the Test headed to a thrilling finish. The captain cajoled, reasoned and guided his bowlers on the last day as India crept closer to their target of 348. At five for 291, the home team had the game in its grasp. Border persisted with spinners Bright and Greg Matthews. The latter had to bowl the last over. Border talked him through it. India was nine for 347. It needed one run to win. Matthews trapped last man in, Maninder Singh, lbw for a duck and the game was a tie—the second in history. The other two games were drawn. Border had for the second time led Australia through a series without losing it. It was a beginning. He again contributed well—245 at 81.67.

There was no respite before running into a confident England again in Australia for the 1986–87 Ashes. Ian Botham (138) played his only good, rampant innings of the series in the First Test at Brisbane, but it helped England to a win, and a strong psychological advantage, given the previous Ashes series.

Allan Border found form with a century in each of the next two drawn Tests at the WACA (125 and 16) and Adelaide (70 and 100 not out). But at Melbourne for the Fourth, Australia (141) surrendered to the pace of Gladstone Small (five for 48) and the swing of Botham (five for 41) in the first innings. Border couldn't find the answer to opener Chris Broad, who hit his third century and did most to push England up to 349. Australia responded weakly with 194 in its second innings, with Marsh (60 run out), Border (34) and Steve Waugh (49) putting up resistance, but not nearly enough. Australia was beaten by an innings and 14 runs.

A dead-rubber win at Sydney by 55 runs saved some face. But Border was disappointed about the fact that he had now led Australia to two Ashes defeats. His own form—473 at 52.56—was an important consolation, considering that Border was now thirty-one. He had been in Test cricket for nearly a decade. If his form had slipped, his detestation of Australia's plight might well have seen him retire. But he was a professional cricketer. His performances kept coming. He looked as impregnable as ever.

With Simpson there to sort out certain areas, Border could focus on leading on the field. After the 1987 winter, he took his squad to India for the 1987 World Cup. Australia was written off without a hope by almost all observers, but came through to win the final against England.

It was a terrific boost for Australian cricket, even if it was a false dawn. At least the team had now experienced being 'the best in the world', even for a fleeting moment and in the form of the game still disdained by the purists. This winning mentality was sustained through the Australian summer, as Border's boys battled to win one–nil against New Zealand, drew a bicentenary Test early in 1988, and beat Sri Lanka by an innings at the WACA. Border was grimly determined not to lose ground, especially after Boon had hit 143 to do most for a win in the First Test against New Zealand at Brisbane.

In the Second Test at Adelaide, New Zealand ran up nine for 485. Border responded with 205, his highest Test score. The ten-hour effort was vintage Border: the sudden pushes with seemingly restricted backlift, the cuts, drives and stubborn defence. The game was drawn.

In the Third Test at Melbourne, New Zealand looked likely to mop up the Australian tail and square the series, but a little of the Border 'stickability' rubbed off on Craig McDermott and Mike Whitney. They managed to be there at stumps with Australia on nine for 230. They fell 17 short of the target, but didn't lose their wickets. Border's 288 at 72 was a typical return for him during these years of struggle.

Border stood up for the dreaded tour of Pakistan in September 1988. When Australia was hammered by an innings at Karachi in the First Test, Border expressed his hurt and anger at the pathetic umpiring, which seemed to the Australians to be more biased than normal. It was just another howl of protest against the Pakistanis at home, which had stretched back to the late 1950s, when the West Indian champion Gary Sobers was cut down by bad decisions. Border threatened to cut the tour short. 'Somebody has to make a stand,' he said. 'The situation is unacceptable and damaging to international cricket, yet nothing seems to be done.'

He felt it was tough enough trying to regenerate a national team without having to put up with unfair dismissals. Despite the gripe, Border himself did well, scoring 230 at 57.5, with a fine, defiant 113 not out at Faisalabad, but Australia went down nil–one. There were more genuine excuses for poor umpiring decisions, but these were as nothing compared to the long-term damage done by 'Sixty Minutes' and its front man, Mike Munro. They decided there was a story in Australia's complaints about umpires. Border and his men were portrayed as whingers and losers, a cruel indictment given the effort being put in to restore the national team's prestige.

It didn't help the team's morale to be facing the might of the West Indies a few weeks after returning from Pakistan. The Caribbean squad included a brutal line-up of fast bowlers—Marshall, Curtly Ambrose, Walsh and Patrick Patterson. Each man could bruise and would if he could. They all took wickets and rolled Australia in the first three Tests. The worst moment came in the Third Test at Melbourne. The West Indies set a target of 404 for the Australians. As one journalist observed, 'They fell apart like a Buck Rogers pocketknife', making 114. Every batsman was hit.

Border batted for nearly three hours for 20. After the game he remarked, 'I get absolutely no joy from Test cricket as it has been in this match.'

Again, anyone else would have been branded a 'loser' for this comment. But when it came from Border, everyone just shrugged and seemed resigned to Australia's inferiority to the West Indies. Their bats led by Viv Richards were better; their fielding sharper; their bowling far more penetrating.

However, yet again, Border's utterances belied the depth of his determination to continue to fight on. In the next Test, a dead rubber at Sydney, the captain himself provided the spin, with his orthodox left-arm tweakers, taking eleven for 96 (as well as making 75 and 16 not out) to win the match. The West Indies were reduced to clumsy lead-foots. The final game at Adelaide was drawn.

Border salvaged something from the one–three defeat. The West Indies bats were vulnerable to spin. They had all been brought up on a diet of pace.

Manufacturing Mr Mean

The big step forward for Allan Border came in the 1989 Ashes. He became 'mean' to the opposition and uncompromising with the media. Gower accused him of 'fierce sledging'. The words 'pretty boy Pom', 'front-runner', and richer remarks were heard. Border, in particular, had bitter memories of previous Ashes encounters. He had waited for this time for seven years and was not going to waste any advantage. His own batting was remarkably even. He returned scores of 66, 60 not out, 35, 1, 8, 80, 65 not out, 76 and 51 not out, for an aggregate of 442 at 73.67. He had Mark Taylor in his sensational first full series (839 at 83.9) and the maturing Steve Waugh (506 at 126.5) to back him up. Terry Alderman (forty-one wickets at 17.37) and Geoff Lawson (twenty-nine at 27.28) were the pick of the bowlers in Australia's four–nil victory.

After five years of struggle and few moments of joy, Border had broken through. Momentum was maintained through the 1989–90 summer. Australia won two and drew four of six Tests against New Zealand (1), Sri Lanka (2) and Pakistan (3). Border's team now hadn't been beaten in fourteen Tests since the disaster at Melbourne against the West Indies in December 1988. A final game for the long season at Wellington saw the end run. Border was not miffed. The loss had been a blip on the screen of wins and draws. He saddled up for the 1990–91 season against England in Australia, determined to keep the ascendancy over Gooch, Gower, Lamb and the rest. His bowlers, led by tall, thin Bruce Reid (twenty-seven wickets at 16) kept England down to just one score of 400 plus. Australia won three–nil. Border had another even series, scoring 281 at 46.83, with a top score of 83 not out. He was delighted to have squared the ledger as skipper with two wins and two losses in Ashes series.

Yet on his mind now was the challenge versus the West Indies away. He wanted to take away its crown as top cricket nation even more than beating England. It wasn't to be. The West Indies won two of the first four Tests, leaving Australia with a consolation prize of a 157-run win at St John's in the last game. But a one–two loss was closer than Australia had been to the world champs for some time. Border's own form (275 at 34.38) had slipped just a bit. He was not scoring hundreds so often. He was thirty-five. Time was running out if he was to beat those tough nuts from the Caribbean.

Old comrade and deputy Geoff Marsh was dumped during the next series against India in 1991–92. Allan Border objected and let the selectors know. Loyalty and courage were two characteristics that he loved and Marsh had been unwavering with both. But his time had come. It was a warning to Border that the fight could not go on forever.

Border scored 275 at 55 with a top score of 91 not out. Centuries still eluded him. Nevertheless, he had led a strong four–nil victory over a good Indian team. This was followed by a one–nil win over Sri Lanka in a three-Test series away. Border broke his run of scores under 100 with 106 in the Third Test. He kept up his steady output, this time 243 at 40.5.

Only the West Indians could claim to be a better unit. They came back to Australia for the 1992–93 series. Border had been pushing for the inclusion of leg-spinner Shane Warne. In four Tests he hadn't quite delivered but Border had faith in him. He thought the spinner had the gumption to stand up in a crisis as he had done at the death in the

First Test at Colombo against Sri Lanka in mid-1992, taking three for 11. The captain felt the West Indies would be vulnerable to spin anywhere, but the selectors dropped Warne for the First Test against the West Indies. The tourists hung on for a draw on the last afternoon. Border bemoaned the lack of a spinner 'such as Shane Warne'.

The selectors obliged for the Second Test at Melbourne. The West Indies were again exposed on the last day. Warne took seven for 52. Australia won the match and was one up with three to play.

Border tried to temper media and public expectations about beating the West Indies. They hadn't been tossed in a series for thirteen years. The Third Test at Sydney was drawn. If Australia could win at Adelaide it would take the series. In a dour affair, Australia was left 186 to win. It reached 184, due to a courageous last-wicket stand between McDermott and Tim May. The West Indies won by a single run. Border in the dressing room thumped a cricket ball onto the floor. After the years of struggle, planning, plotting and losing to this great side, he felt cheated by fate. The series was level one all. But a bouncy wicket at Perth played into the West Indians' hands. Ambrose took seven for 25 and two for 54. Bishop took two for 17 and six for 40. Australia was beaten by an innings and lost the series one–two.

Allan Border could look back on some sterling efforts against the West Indies from his 110 at Melbourne in the most recent series to his 98 not out and 100 not out at Port of Spain in 1983–84, when he scored 521 at 74.43. He was nearly thirty-eight years old and still hopeful of yet another tilt at the champions. In the meantime, he took his team back again to New Zealand for a one–all series, and then to England for the 1993 Ashes.

Border kept the screws tightened on the old enemy in the first three Tests, thanks to Shane Warne and Merv Hughes. In the Fourth at Headingley he hit 200 not out and made sure of several matters important to him. Australia won the game, Border was able to show his critics he still had the faculty for a big score, the memory of the 1981 Headingley loss faded and Australia took the series in time for Border's thirty-eighth birthday.

The four–one Ashes win meant he had now led Australia to three series wins against England, a result he would never have dreamt for during the dark days between 1985 and 1987. His own record of 433 at 54.13 demonstrated he could still deliver.

New Zealand bobbed up in Australia again for three Tests at the end of 1993, and Border was content that he had regained a sense of superiority over the combatants from across the Tasman. It had taken a long time. Australia won two–nil, with Border notching another century (105 at Brisbane) in an aggregate of 181 at 60.33.

The final challenge was against South Africa in 1993–94. The three games in Australia left the two sides with one win each. Border managed just 146 at 29.2. In the return series in South Africa, the result was the same. Border recorded 152 at 38.

Allan Border was now approaching thirty-nine and the selectors felt it was time for regeneration. He would have liked to travel on (as he did for Queensland) but could not. It was a hard time for him. Test cricket had been his life for sixteen years. He had played in a record 156 Tests (ninety-three as captain), scoring a record 11,174 runs at an average of 50.56 with twenty-seven centuries. No one in the history of cricket ever sustained an average over fifty for so long. He also took thirty-nine wickets at 39.1, and, if anything, was underbowled, especially by himself. Border took a record 156 catches, one for every Test he played.

Now he would have more time to rediscover family life with his wife of fourteen years, Jane, and their two sons. He played on for two seasons with Queensland, which included a Shield win that gave him much satisfaction.

In first-class cricket Allan Border played 385 matches, for an aggregate of 27,131 at 51.38, with seventy centuries. Border captured 106 wickets at 39.25, and took 379 catches. He played 273 one-day internationals, scoring 6524 runs at 30.63. He managed seventy-three wickets at 28.37 in this form of the game, where he was prepared to use himself more as the fifth option. He had always been a brilliant field. But in his position at short mid-wicket in one-day cricket he excelled like no one before him, especially with left-handed run-outs.

Life after cricket wasn't easy for Allan Border, and he took his time choosing his next 'career' path. He wasn't far from the action with TV commentary and coaching.

The Allan Border Medal was struck to honour the best Australian player annually. At the inaugural medal night early in 2000, Border was a happy man. He was being recognised for his invaluable contribution to Australian cricket. Each year in the future the medal would be the most coveted award in the game.

Many considered Border unlucky not to be included the 'Team of the Century' as chosen by a panel of twenty experts, including several former Australian captains. Border was named twelfth man.

Apart from being one of the best two or three fighters at the wicket that Australia ever produced, Border was the man most responsible for uniting the Test side and restoring it to a position where it could make a serious challenge for the title of 'world's best team'. His inner belief that there just had to be a core of like-minded players who could restore Australia to, in his eyes, its rightful position of superiority over all, found fruition a decade after he took over as skipper.

A year after he retired from Test cricket he was in the Caribbean happily witnessing Australia taking the world title. Allan Border's efforts to place his team where it could challenge were as important as any player's contribution in the actual 1995 series win.

39

MARK TAYLOR

....

27 October 1964 –

Tests: 104; Captain: 50; Wins: 26; Losses: 13; Draws: 11;
Win ratio: 52 per cent

A CAPTAIN FOR ALL REASONS

Mark Taylor marched out to bat with Michael Slater in the Second Test at Peshawar in Pakistan in October 1998 wearing a black armband. It was a mark of respect for former Test captain Ian Johnson, who had died in Melbourne at eighty. It put the Australians in a sombre mood. They were brightened a little by the news that speedster Wasim Akram had dropped out of the game with a throat infection. Taylor, who was not in touch, had been dismissed by Wasim for 3 in the First Test at Rawalpindi. Waqar Younis was still nursing an elbow injury and was also not playing. That left youngster Shoaib Akhtar and the open-chested seamer, Mohammad Zahid, to open the attack when Australia won the toss and batted on a lively strip. Taylor's relief turned to concern as he struggled against Shoaib's alarming speed and edged one close to the leg stump.

Shoaib dismissed Slater with the score at 16. The extreme heat meant that speed would be used in limited periods. Spin was soon tried and Taylor was dropped twice by Saeed Anwar off Mushtaq Ahmed.

Taylor was nearly run out at 55, but battled on, riding his luck.

When Shoaib came back with the new ball, Taylor pulled him to the mid-wicket boundary. Soon after he hoisted a six over the square-leg fence and was 112 not out (with Langer 97 not out) at stumps, drawn an hour early due to bad light. Australia's score was one for 224.

Day two saw Taylor's pre-tour fitness regime under Kevin Chevell pay off. The first session was three hours (Fridays finished early in Pakistan for religious reasons), and the Australian skipper picked up the pace in the trying conditions of the third hour, when all bowlers were flagging. He scored 50 in the last forty minutes and reached 100 for the session, something he would dine out on, tongue in cheek. He was 212 not out at lunch.

Taylor carried on and had soon passed 219, which had been his highest Test score to date, notched at Trent Bridge nearly a decade earlier in 1989. He had reached 260 at tea after a short middle session. During the short break, he thought of Allan Border's words when Taylor scored that double at Trent Bridge and got himself out stumped. Border suggested that he should have gone on to a triple century. Taylor now had a second 'chance of a lifetime'. He felt as fit as he had when he reached that other double century, even though he was now nearly thirty-four. He would knuckle down and attempt to go on to 300.

He donned a floppy hat to help beat the heat. He was a fraction careless running between the wickets and was nearly run out by Saleem Malik at 270. Yet the captain felt invincible. 'I knew exactly where they were going,' he said in his book, *Time to Declare*. 'Even with five men on the boundary I could still picture myself hitting a four—and would do it.'

Fatigue began to tell, but Taylor thought back to how he felt in the gym under Chevell, which he reckoned was worse. In the 290s, nerves rather than his fitness concerned him. He was close to that magic 300. It was daunting. At 298, he received a short one from Mushtaq and clipped it through the well-protected off side past cover for four. Taylor was now in the exclusive 300 club. He strode past Bob Cowper's 307 (scored at Melbourne against England in 1965–66) and Bob Simpson's 311 (at Manchester against England in 1964). He now set his sights on Don Bradman's 334 against England at Leeds in 1930. At 325 he was dropped by keeper Moin Khan off left-armer Aamer Sohail. Taylor reached 334 with two balls to go from Aamer. He tried to score that final extra run for the day, but both times hit it to Ijaz Ahmed, who was lurking at square leg.

Mark Taylor strode off three kilograms lighter and weary but a very happy man. The Australian team formed a guard of honour for him as he left the field. Then the questions began. What would the captain do: declare or go on in an attempt to reach 375, the record set by Brian Lara in 1994? Taylor didn't know. He chatted with vice-captain Steve Waugh, who pointed out he was in for glory whatever he decided. If he went on and took the world record, his name would be etched in the record books for a while before someone else took the record. Then he would be another name and statistic—however great—like those who were in front of him now: Walter Hammond (336 not out, England versus New Zealand, 1932–33); Hanif Mohammad (337, Pakistan versus West Indies, 1957–58); Sanath Jayasuriya (340, Sri Lanka versus India, 1997–98); Len Hutton (364, England versus Australia, 1938); Gary Sobers (365 not out, West Indies versus Pakistan 1957–58); and Brian Lara (375 not out, West Indies versus England 1994).

But if Taylor decided to declare, he would forever be bracketed with Don Bradman. This was never his intention. Fate had left him on the same score. Taylor first thought of batting on for twenty minutes to put pressure on Pakistan's openers, but soon dropped that idea. He then dismissed talk in the dressing room of going on to take Lara's record. Taylor knew that the Pakistanis would make him work for every run. He worried about getting bogged down on say 360, where the record, and not Australia's chance for victory, would be the paramount aim in being out in the middle.

Overnight Taylor decided to declare. Australia was on four for 599, more than enough to ensure it wasn't beaten. The decision disappointed some, but when the move sank in, Mark Taylor was hailed as a sportsman of the highest order. He had put the team's objectives over personal glory. And the fact that he had not gone on for an over or two and taken Bradman's record endeared him to all cricket followers. It was, for Taylor, a wonderful career move. He would only realise the importance of it as the years rolled on.

Rising star

Mark Anthony Taylor's answering to the nickname 'Tubby' said much about his character. He was solid, with tree-trunk legs, without being fat, yet he remained unconcerned by the implication that he was rotund. It was refreshing in an era when other players were sensitive about any suggestion of chubby cheeks, and when fitness gurus and coaches considered signs of body fat as sinful. Taylor never took himself too seriously and enjoyed his cricket, which he had done since he was a youngster growing up in Wagga Wagga in southern New South Wales.

The son of a roving country bank manager, the nuggetty lad put his bulk to work for him as an opening bat from an early age. The family settled in Sydney when Mark was fourteen. He attended Chatswood High School. At seventeen he made the Northern District Thirds and worked his way steadily to the senior team by the 1983–84 season at age nineteen. He came to prominence as a future state star in the Barclays Under-19 championship in January 1984 by compiling 334 (a number that would figure much in his life), which was second only to Steve Waugh (386). This led to him being selected to play for the Australian under-19 team against Sri Lanka a month later. Players so chosen in the early 1980s were given 'inside fast-track' opportunities to higher selection, just as those invited to join the Cricket Academy were later in the decade. Mark Taylor was already a player to watch.

A clue to Taylor's sporting and team mentality that would lead to his declaration on 334 not out at Peshawar was seen at age twenty-one while playing against Mosman in 1985–86. He had a chance to make his first double hundred in any form of cricket, but instead suggested to his skipper, Ross Turner, that it was time to declare. The team always came first. Tubby was that sort of bloke. Personal milestones and records were fine, but not at the expense of the team. To him cricket was a team game first and foremost.

That year he made the New South Wales state side when regular openers Steve Smith and John Dyson joined a rebel team in South Africa. Taylor made 12 and 56 not out against Tasmania and soon afterwards cracked centuries against South Australia. He was on his way to being a first-class bat and superb slips fieldsman with amazing reflexes. Taylor didn't allow much to get past him as a bat. But nothing, it seemed, got past him at slip.

Taylor progressed to become Northern District captain at just twenty-two during the 1986–87 year. It was clear to all that he was a natural leader. He communicated well, inspired his teammates and led literally from the front while still presenting an easy-going, friendly manner. In 1986–87 he compiled 765 runs for New South Wales at 40, enough during Australia's rebuilding years to bring him into consideration for Test cricket.

Taylor prematurely thought he had made the highest level when in January 1987 he was mixed up with Peter Taylor, the off-spinner. Mark was about to do a TV interview over his Test selection when the error was discovered. Off the field, he completed a degree in surveying at the University of New South Wales in 1987, which was to provide a back-up career should his rise through the cricket ranks fall short of Test level or a regular place at it.

Mark Taylor was uncertain about his chances for elevation after an unimpressive 1987–88 season for New South Wales. He had a summer as a professional in England's Bolton League with Green-mount. While he found the approach of fellow players slack compared to the fierceness of the Shield competition, he gained invaluable experience under English conditions. He returned for the 1988–89 home season a more rounded player with a greater range of strokes. His nickname in those early years had been 'Stodge', earned as a consequence of his scoring with nudges and deflections rather than cuts and hooks. His English season opened up a range of strokes, and he was for a time hailed as 'Slogger', before Ian Healy and others later settled on 'Tubby'.

Taylor's steady good form for New South Wales, and Australia's failure at the top of the order during the late 1980s, saw him selected for his first Test, against the West Indies at Sydney in January 1989. Taylor was in a Melbourne restaurant when journalists told him he was in the Test team. He asked if they were sure it was him. When assured Taylor, M, not P, had been chosen, Tubby called for champagne all round.

Curtly Ambrose dismissed Taylor twice for 25 and 3, although Australia won. In the Fifth Test at Adelaide Taylor was run out twice for 3 and 36 in a draw. It was the toughest introduction to Test cricket against a West Indian speed quartet that was always at the batsman with pace, bounce and bruising. Yet Taylor came through the baptism without the scars of some of his countrymen. Even though Australia lost the series one–three, he was yet to play in a losing side.

The making of Mark

Mark Taylor secured selection for his first Ashes tour in 1989 aged twenty-four, with twin centuries against Western Australia in the last match of the season. Soon afterwards he married Judi Matthews and then took off for England. He was at the crossroads of his career and needed to advance—at least gaining Test selection again and maintaining his spot as an opener. Coach Simpson was hopeful he could do it. He had been looking for a class left-hander to open with Geoff Marsh, with David Boon at three.

Taylor began out of touch in England and only produced two innings—97 and 58 against Somerset—before the First Test. But Border, Marsh and Simpson gave him his chance. He grabbed it and lifted his rating to be 96 not out on day one and out for 136 the next morning. Taylor had scored a century in his first Ashes Test and it boosted his confidence. He now believed that he was a player who could cope at the top level. His effort set Australia up for a massive seven for 601, with Steve Waugh (177 not out) building on the fine start. Taylor backed this up with 60 in the second innings, then a run of good opening scores—62, 27, 43, 51, 85 and 37 not out. After a jolly run-making time for Greenmount a year earlier in the backblocks of English professional cricket, he was now capitalising on that humble experience and scoring just as freely in Test cricket. He consolidated his place and helped Australia regain the Ashes by the end of the Fourth Test at Old Trafford with a three–nil lead.

In the Fifth Test at Trent Bridge, Taylor (141 not out) and Marsh (125 not out) put on 301 unconquered on day one, which was an Australian record for an opening stand in an Ashes Test, surpassing the 201 by Lawry and Simpson at Old Trafford in 1964. Marsh was dismissed next day for 138 at 329, and Taylor went on to 219 before being stumped.

Taylor added scores of 71 and 48 in the Sixth and final Test at the Oval in Australia's four–nil series win. His aggregate of 839 runs from eleven innings (at an average of 83.9) surpassed Arthur Morris's 696 (from nine innings at 87) in 1948 and placed him second only to Don Bradman's 1930 record of 974 runs (from just seven innings at 139.14). This mighty season saw Taylor named as one of *Wisden*'s Five Cricketers of the Year in 1989.

Taylor enjoyed that tour of England more than any other in his long career. Spread over four and a half months, it was the last of its kind for an Australian touring side since the first visit more than a century earlier. In the future the English campaigns would become increasingly truncated affairs, with fewer county games and more pressure.

Taylor had leapt in the Deloittes World Batting ratings from ninety-seventh to seventh. He continued on with his dazzling form with centuries in all but one of the five Tests against Sri Lanka and Pakistan (featuring Wasim, Waqar and Mushtaq) during the 1989–90 season in Australia. Taylor's scores read 9, 164, 23, 108, 52, 101, 77, 59, 101 not out, giving him 694 runs at 86.75—thus maintaining his 80-plus Test average for twelve Tests against three countries over eight months. To cap off a magnificent period, he took over from an injured Geoff Lawson as skipper of New South Wales in the Sheffield Shield final of 1989–90 and led the way to victory with centuries in both innings.

Return to reality

Mark Taylor came down to earth in the next series at home in 1990–91 against England, scoring 213 at 23.67 with a top score of 67 not out. It relieved him of the inevitable 'new Bradman' tag, which had dogged every champion since the Don retired in 1948. Australian critics stopped using it around the time Doug Walters emerged. But somehow, English journalists, in particular, thought it original for half a century to make the comparison whenever a new Australian Test batsman did something exceptional.

Despite the accolades, Taylor remained well earthed and realistic. He was disappointed not to be included in the one-day team. A broken finger at the start of the 1990–91 season set him back and his self-confidence dipped. Yet he lifted a few weeks later for a five-Test series on the toughest tour of his career, around the Caribbean in March and April 1991, scoring 442 at 49, with a top score of 144. It marked Taylor as a future Test captain. He was chosen to lead an Australian B side or Second XI in Zimbabwe during September 1991. His vice-captain was Steve Waugh, and the squad included leg-spinning prospects Shane Warne and Peter McIntyre, speedster Paul Reiffel and batsman Stuart Law. Team manager and selector John Benaud brought back an encouraging report of Mark Taylor's leadership skills.

Concerns about his weight developed when team coach Bob

Simpson and media critics were looking for slim athletes. Taylor began heavy gym work under physiotherapist Kevin Chevell and took off ten kilos, which seemed to satisfy everyone. But Taylor's figure, no matter how well he passed the pinch tests, would always appear burly because of his substantial hips, derrière and thighs. He thought many observers were 'fatist' and prejudiced. Myths abounded about his slowness and unsuitability for one-day cricket. He was selected in just two limited-overs games in 1991–92.

Yet Taylor sustained his touch at the top of the Test order in Australia during the season against India, with an aggregate of 422 at 46.89, and a top score of 100 in the second innings of the Adelaide Fourth Test. His average in Test cricket was levelling out to a realistic mid-40s, which placed him high in the list of Australian openers. When Geoff Marsh was dropped for the Fifth Test against India in 1991–92, Taylor, Marsh's opening partner, took over as Border's deputy. Something extraordinary now would have to happen for Taylor not to succeed Border as national leader of the Test team.

The one-day leadership was more problematic. The 1992 World Cup was played in Australia and New Zealand, and Taylor was still rankled by not being a main player in one-day internationals. He and Merv Hughes were effectively thirteenth and fourteenth men for the tournament.

Taylor had an ordinary series in Sri Lanka in August and September 1992, scoring just 148 at 24.67, which was not the best preparation for the 1992–93 series against the West Indies. Border and his men regarded this as the biggest challenge they had ever had. There was a raw determination to beat the Caribbean champions, who had been on top of the world for more than a decade. Yet Taylor felt there was not yet a self-belief that Australia could be victorious against them.

He was fit, after continued training under Chevell as a substitute for not playing Aussie Rules for a Sydney club in the winter any more. But after a promising century against the West Indies for New South Wales, he lost the plot against the barrage of speed from Ambrose, Walsh, Bishop, Benjamin and the other West Indian bowlers. Taylor managed an aggregate of 170 runs at 24.29 in the first four Tests. He was dropped to twelfth man for the Fifth Test at Perth.

The 1993 Ashes tour of England was looming. Taylor made the most of his chances in three Tests in New Zealand in February and

March, scoring 148 at 37, with 82 and 50 run out in his only two innings in the first two games. He was nowhere near the player of the last Ashes tour but his record was enough to ensure him a spot in the squad. Taylor regained touch in the first two Ashes Tests with scores of 124, 9 and 111, and performed as he had four years earlier. His Test series figures were indicative of Taylor's true level as he notched 428 at 42.8. He failed only three times in ten knocks to send Australia off to a fair start of an opening partnership of fifty or more.

With his confidence restored, Taylor went about demolishing New Zealand's thin attack at home later in 1993, scoring 296 at 95.33, hitting 64 and 142 not out in the First Test at the WACA. He was dominant early against South Africa in the first three Tests between the countries in more than twenty years. Taylor was fortunate to survive an lbw decision early in the first innings of the First Test at the Melbourne Cricket Ground, but went on to a commanding 170 in the wet, drawn game. His series figures ended at 304 at 60.8. The return games in South Africa early in 1994 saw him reduced through injury to four innings, in which he scored 97 at 24.25, with a top score of 70 in the Second Test at Cape Town.

Cap'n Taylor

Allan Border retired after the South African tour, and Taylor, at twenty-nine, became Australia's thirty-ninth Test captain. He also took over control of the limited-overs side. Taylor was a seasoned campaigner, well-drilled in leadership in club and Shield, and experienced in Test cricket. His preparation had been better than that of any previous leader, except for Greg Chappell.

He was off to a nervous start in Pakistan, scoring a pair courtesy of Wasim and Waqar at Karachi in a tight game that the home team was lucky to win by one wicket. It was marred by Salim Malik's failed attempt to bribe Shane Warne and Tim May to throw the match.

The tourists didn't quite recover from the First Test setback, and Taylor (106 runs at 26.5, top score 69 at Rawalpindi) returned home chastened but determined to do better. He compiled a first-rate, 'normal' quota for him in the 1994–95 Ashes series against England, scoring 471 at 47.1, with a highest knock of 113 in the drawn Test at Sydney. Australia won three–one and Taylor was away as a successful skipper. A few weeks later he led Australia into battle against the West

Indies in the Caribbean. The visitors took the series two–one and so knocked the Calypso Kings from their perch for the first time in twenty-nine series over seventeen years, the longest reign in big cricket. Taylor's contribution with the bat seemed ordinary on paper—153 runs at 25.5 with a top score of 55. But his effort in the field as a slipper (ten catches) and as a leader in and out of the arena was a major factor in Australia's success. He kept the lid on cockiness early and showed grit opening throughout the series. The series win put Australia on top of the Test cricket world.

Now Taylor's job was to maintain the team's drive and attempt to improve its record. First up at home in 1995–96 was a challenge from the confident Pakistanis, whom Taylor handled with verve as a leader by defusing the bribery scandal and then blunting its talented bowling line-up with the bat. He was consistent, with scores of 69, 40, 123, 47 and 59. Australia won two–one, dropping the last dead rubber. The Australians went one better immediately afterwards in the same season, beating Sri Lanka three–nil. Taylor (159 at 39.75) began well with a 96 at the WACA, while his partner, Michael Slater, went on to 219.

Mark Taylor led the one-day team into the 1996 World Cup final against Sri Lanka at Lahore and top-scored with 74. Sri Lanka won easily and rumblings began again about Taylor's perceived unsuitability to play in the limited-overs competition. It seemed unfair given that, the final aside, Australia had only been beaten by the West Indies, which it turned around and defeated in the semi-final. Another nail was hammered into the coffin of Taylor's one-day leadership during the 1996–97 season in Australia, when the home team lost five games in a row and missed the finals, which were contested by Pakistan and the West Indies. Pakistan won two–nil.

A test of character

This came amidst a miserable Test batting run for Taylor against the West Indies. Australia won the series three–two but Taylor, hampered by a back injury that restricted his footwork, collected just 153 at 17. If he had not been captain, he would have been dropped, as he was in the final game of the preceding home series against the West Indies in 1992–93. But while Australia kept winning, the selectors were reluctant to dump him. His woeful touch continued in South Africa, when he garnered 80 at 16. But Australia had a thrilling two–one victory and saved Taylor's leadership. His torment was continued in the one-day tournament that followed. He dropped himself after failing in the first two games of seven, which Australia won four–three.

There was no time for recuperation. Within a month after the South African tour, Taylor was packing his 'coffin' for another Ashes tour. It was clear that he and others in the Australian squad had been on the road at home and abroad too long without a substantial break.

He and his one-day team were soon reeling from a three–nil defeat to England. Taylor again missed out and the team was in crisis. It was not helped by a fearsome British media that was willing Australia's collapse. Taylor was still out of touch in the lead-up to the First Test. Only a dropped catch by Dean Jones, skipper of Derbyshire, which allowed Taylor to make 63, averted a catastrophe. Taylor would have been forced to step aside to make way for Steve Waugh as captain, thus plunging the squad and tour into turmoil. As it was, the leader's self-confidence was at rock-bottom and it was affecting team morale. Everyone was willing the popular leader to get a century, but he couldn't put a substantial knock, even a bright cameo, together. The selectors had stuck with Taylor until now, but the one-day series defeat and the prospect of further calamity in the 1997 Ashes series put everyone under pressure.

Taylor failed in the first innings of the First Test at Edgbaston with just 7. He strode out to bat in his second dig on day three knowing that if he failed his Test career was over, and in embarrassing circum-stances. No player of his calibre had ever been under more pressure in the history of the game. He decided on a cavalier approach. Taylor went for his shots and reached 50 in just sixty-nine minutes. By close of play he had scored a fine 108 not out. He went on to 129 on day four. This performance of exceptional character turned around the morale and mentality of the team, even though they lost the Test. Australia went on to a three–two series win, with Taylor hitting a modest yet useful 317 at 31.7.

The first blow to his position as Australia's cricket leader came during the 1997–98 home season, when he was dumped as captain of the one-day team in favour of Steve Waugh. Taylor was disap-pointed and expressed it publicly. He felt that two skippers would be divisive. The positive to come out of it was less cricket for him, which may have preserved his career.

Taylor returned to good form in 1997–98, first against New Zealand, where he scored 214 at 53.5 with a top score of 112, then against South Africa, with 265 at 66.25. Taylor carried his bat for a highest knock of 169 not out at Adelaide in the first innings of the Third Test. His innings kept South Africa out and helped Australia to a draw, which meant he had won another series, this time one–nil.

After another long summer, Taylor led Australia to India from March to April 1998, where the tourists lost one–two, ending a nine Test series winning streak under Taylor, the best by an Australian team. His aggregate of 189 and average of 37.8 were flattered by a dead rubber last Test score of 102 not out. He continued to complain that there should be only one leader for the two national teams. His words fell on deaf ears as Steve Waugh motored on as captain of the one-day side towards the 1999 World Cup.

Zenith in Peshawar

Mark Taylor led the Test team back to Pakistan in October 1998 with a score to settle over his first time as skipper four years earlier in 1994. Australia then lost one–nil and he began with a pair. He failed again at Rawalpindi in the First Test but the tourists won. At Peshawar in the Second Test, Taylor made history with his 334 not out and 92— a game aggregate of 426, which placed him second only to England's Graham Gooch, who scored 333 and 123 for 456 against India at Lord's in 1990.

Taylor's series tally was 513 runs for an average of 128.25. He returned to Australia a hero and was surprised by the attention he received. He now understood more of what Shane Warne had been through. Everyone wanted to shake his hand, get an autograph, stop for a chat. It galled Taylor at times, when he just wanted privacy with family and friends. Yet he rarely rejected a request to scribble on a miniature bat or piece of paper.

He began to comprehend the value to his reputation of his decision to declare with his score on 334 not out. It helped him consider life after cricket. Offers for TV, Olympic promotion, advertisements and endorsements swamped him. Taylor skippered on through the 1998–99 Ashes series against England in Australia. While his team won three–one, his form degenerated again to an average of 22.8

from 228 runs with a top score of 61. It gave the captain pause. The media began to speculate about his retirement. If he had averaged even 30 or 35 with another good hundred, he would have been able to answer his critics and say he was playing well enough to carry on.

Taylor was named Australian of the Year early in 1999 and procrastinated about stepping down. Pressures mounted. Those tempting offers for life after cricket were dangled in front of him. He wondered if they would be there in a year if he were not travelling so well with the bat and was forced out. There was also the thought that he could spend more time with his wife and two small sons, William and Jack, who had missed him.

In the end he retired after 104 Tests, in which he scored 7525 at 43.49. He hit nineteen centuries and forty fifties and took 157 catches as one of the country's best ever slippers. He played in 253 first-class matches, scoring 17,415 runs at 41.96, hitting forty-one centuries and ninety-seven fifties. Although maligned as a one-day player, Taylor's international figures were good. He played in 113 matches for 110 innings, scoring 3514 runs at an average of 32.23 with 28 fifties. Yet he hit just one century, against India in India in 1996, which underlined a weakness. An opener had to do more and at a faster rate than Taylor managed.

Mark Taylor built a formidable batting record over a decade of Test cricket. He ranks with the best Australian captains of all time, leading the team to the top of world cricket in 1995 where it remained until his retirement.

He was a flexible, cheerful skipper, who could be tough and would discipline players when required. Taylor had the gift of intuition, something possessed by only a handful of captains in cricket's history. It stemmed from his innate ability to 'read' a game, sense its rhythms and act on them to his team's advantage. His incessant gum-chewing was not nerves but concentration. He discovered the balance between treating the game as fun and a fierce international contest. Taylor never appeared grim or as if he carried the weight of the team's performance on his shoulders. Yet he was as determined as anyone before him to see Australia on top.

Taylor was an astute media performer, incapable of losing his cool even if goaded. He appeared the same in defeat as in victory. He was never begrudging towards the opposition, although he was annoyed by the Sri Lankans' failure to shake hands after the series in 1995–96. Taylor was always generous to the opposition, win, lose or draw, without ever conceding that his squad was inferior or superior. He condoned a certain level of sledging without indulging in it himself, or encouraging it. This kind of intimidation was beneath him and, he thought, a waste of emotional energy. He disliked how it tore at the game's fabric, which was designed on good sportsmanship. Verballing opponents would never have been institutionalised under the affable, yet tough Tubby.

Taylor was diplomatic with the Australian Cricket Board, but not a board puppet. He stuck with the players during pay disputes.

No finer man of character has led Australia. The way he handled his run of outs was an even greater measure of his exceptional mentality than his declaration at Peshawar. Though his gut was wrenched when his form slipped he kept an outward demeanour of dignity and command, of both the team and himself. By good luck and selectorial faith, some would say favouritism, he remained captain through the horror stretch. He never missed a beat in the field or in slips, behaving like a modest player who had just come off a hundred. The relief for his legion of admirers when he eventually struck form at Edgbaston said much for the public's appreciation of him, from the prime minister to the man in the outer.

Mark Taylor will be honoured for the rest of his days above all for his one unselfish, sporting act in Peshawar. This only highlighted his permanent way of performing and thinking.

40

STEVE WAUGH
....

2 June 1965 –

Tests: 128; Captain: 17; Wins: 12; Losses: 3; Draws: 2;
Win ratio: 70.59 per cent

CRICKET'S WINNING MIDAS

The Mark Taylor show, like that of Joe Darling, Don Bradman, Richie Benaud and Ian Chappell, was a tough act to follow. When Stephen Rodger Waugh took over to become Australia's fortieth Test captain in February 1999, doubters emerged from every quarter. He was branded as selfish, negative and unimaginative.

While Waugh's new responsibilities heightened rather than diminished his batting, he had his problems as leader during his first series against the West Indies in the Caribbean. Australia ran into hurricane Lara. Waugh seemed uncertain how to contain him, if in fact anyone could. The tourists scraped in for a two–all series. Steve Waugh was relieved that he had not presided over the dropping of a series to the West Indies after two decisive series wins in 1995 and 1996–97. Australia held on to the Sir Frank Worrell Trophy and Waugh the captaincy. There were more troubles in the Caribbean one-day series that followed, with unrestrained supporters and near-riots ruining two encounters. Australia again sneaked through with a drawn series.

It was then on to the 1999 World Cup in England. Australia was

343

sluggish and looked like being out of the tournament early. But somehow, Waugh, dour and defensive at media conferences, held everything together. He had to contend with a difficult media, injuries, grumbling in the ranks about alcohol curfews, a vice-captain who wanted to throw in the towel and selectors telling him he would lose the leadership if Australia failed. Waugh kept his iron will intact. At no point when asked did he suggest Australia couldn't make it. Even when it had to win seven games on end to take the cup, Waugh claimed his team could do it. No one but his squad believed him. It took a stupendous performance by Waugh himself against South Africa in the fifth of those seven games when he smashed 120 not out to give Australia a real chance. He knew that if he failed Australia would lose and he would be dumped as one-day captain. Instead of buckling under the strain or performing near his top, he went beyond anything he had ever achieved before. Waugh had never been a great one-day performer. In 265 previous games he had scored just one century. Australia won, then tied against South Africa, got through to the final and thrashed Pakistan to take the cup.

That success was a turning point for Steve Waugh as a leader. He was pumped with the feeling that he had teams under him that could achieve anything they desired, if they applied themselves with a will to win. There were hiccups in Sri Lanka in August and September 1999, when Waugh had his nose smashed in a collision with Jason Gillespie and wet conditions reduced the series. Sri Lanka won one–nil. In Zimbabwe a few weeks later Australia won again. Waugh's record as Test captain read three wins, three losses and two draws. He knew he had to lift that rating. The long millennium summer from November 1999 to April 2000 in three Test series versus Pakistan, India and New Zealand promised to be make or break for him as a leader. If Australia and he struggled the knives would be out again.

Before the First Test Waugh suggested to his team that it could win all six Tests in Australia. It would have sounded audacious from anyone but Waugh. His optimism seemed set to founder in Hobart in the Second Test against Pakistan, but mighty centuries by Gilchrist and Langer in chasing 369 won the game by four wickets. It was the third-biggest chase for a win in the last innings of a Test and the most accomplished ever, given the Pakistani bowling line-up of Wasim, Waqar, Shoaib and Saqlain.

That win was the turning point. The Australians now didn't believe they could win six straight, they *knew* it. Any side that could come back from that position could achieve what it wished. All the time, Waugh was building strategic plans, goals and tactics with new coach John Buchanan, who was never without his dynamic computer analysis of all players in the team and the opposition. Waugh also boosted the confidence of players in an unprecedented way both privately and publicly. He said Ricky Ponting was the way of the future. The tough Taswegian performed brilliantly through the summer. The captain put his faith in Justin Langer, who maintained such a high rate of runs, accelerating towards the finish in the series against New Zealand, that Waugh didn't sound silly when he said in April 2000 that the Western Australian left-hander was the 'best bat in the world at the moment'. Langer said often that Waugh's support did the trick for him. New keeper Adam Gilchrist, under pressure for taking over Ian Healy's Test spot, also responded to his chance and the skipper's encouragement. He not only batted with breathtaking power and aggression, he broke records for dismissals in both forms of the game. Waugh had also taken Shane Warne for a 'walk in the park' in London during the 1999 World Cup, when the spinner was about to retire because of shellackings on the field and from the media, and private problems. Warne was restored and eager to strike his way out of the doldrums, which he did with match-winning bowling efforts in the last three games of the World Cup. Then there was Damien Martyn, who had been made a scapegoat for a last innings collapse against South Africa in 1994 and discarded from Test cricket. Waugh backed him too, and Martyn came through a steady star with a cool head in both Test and one-day cricket, making a mockery of the reason for his original rejection. A clean sweep versus Pakistan removed the dead rubber blues that had struck Australian sides through the 1990s, when they dropped games that didn't impact on the series' outcome.

Before any of his many critics could draw breath, Steve Waugh was telling media conferences that he wanted a three–nil sweep against India too. Yearnings for Mark Taylor, heard in the West Indies, were now non-existent. Commentators who had maligned Waugh's leadership looked foolish. Many didn't understand the new regime with its emphasis on planning session by session, day by day, game by game, series by series. They were dumbfounded by Waugh's in-your-face brashness and psychological warfare.

India was expected to provide better opposition, but it folded. Australia's cohesion and planning, plus a superiority in all departments of the game, saw another three–nil series win. Waugh, who often spoke his own mind before clearing statements with the Australian Cricket Board (ACB), began a subtle public push for new fast bowler Brett Lee. Selectors picked him. Lee proved more than a counterpoint to the hype behind Pakistan's Shoaib earlier in the summer. The young New South Welshman bowled quicker and better. He was a destroyer from his first big game, and kept on mowing down the opposition, taking thirty-one wickets at 16.06 in his first five Tests. His success was in no small measure due to Waugh's solid support and a smooth, welcomed entry into the Test XI.

The fulfilment of Waugh's six–nil prophecy catapulted him into an unassailable position as skipper. In his first twelve months as leader he maintained his average of 50 with big hundreds every now and again. Barbed questions at media conferences all but dried up. Waugh seemed beyond serious criticism, but for issues such as sledging, which had become institutionalised under him, when verbal attacks were planned against certain opposition players to unsettle them. He even dismissed this as inconsequential, although some journalists regarded it as too important to let go.

Steve Waugh's demeanour changed with his success. Instead of being on the defensive, he was relaxed, with a ready answer to every query. His natural humour emerged and he smiled more. He could afford to be himself, rather than a stony-faced defender of the indefensible.

The amazing Test momentum spilled into the 1999–2000 one-day series. Australia lost the first game then won the next nine to take the contest with ease. Without a meaningful break, Waugh was on his way with his teams to New Zealand for a season too far. In other years, New Zealand would have picked off the tourists in at least one Test. But this squad was so full of its own commitment and buoyed by success that it even mowed down the confident Black Caps. The one-day winning sequence was extended to fourteen—a world record. The team lost only the last of a six-match series.

Observers wondered whether this might spell the end of Waugh's wonder run. There was bound to be a flop in one of the three Tests. But there wasn't. Australia even made two important chases for 174 and 210 in the Second and Third matches to win both times. Thus the last glaring team weakness—the failure to always secure small totals in a last innings chase—in Australian Test cricket over the last two decades had been eliminated.

Steve Waugh and his fatigued but very happy team flew home from New Zealand with nine successive Test wins over the millennium summer. The September 1999 win in Zimbabwe had made it, in all, ten wins in a row. This wiped out Warwick Armstrong's record of eight successive wins in 1920 and 1921. Waugh was now just one Test away from equalling the record of eleven wins straight, set by the West Indies under Clive Lloyd in 1984–85.

During the long season, Waugh developed a Midas touch. Unorthodox changes, especially in the field with bowlers, often paid off with a wicket. Waugh showed that, like his predecessor Mark Taylor, he could read a game. He wasn't squeamish or too rigid about bringing on a non-regular bowler like Greg Blewett or Ricky Ponting. Waugh handled Warne to perfection, especially during the 1999 Boxing Day Second Test at Melbourne against India. Sensing that the leg-spinner was the only bowler likely to dismiss Sachin Tendulkar in India's second innings, he kept Warne on for two long spells that allowed him to weave his famous spell around the great batsman and finally trap him lbw. Waugh also brought on brother Mark for two surprise wickets, and preferred new man Brett Lee to Glenn McGrath, simply because Lee was 'hot' at that moment. Waugh also demonstrated that he was far from negative or unimaginative and was willing to take calculated risks with the batting order and declarations.

His leadership during a gruelling six months over the 1999–2000 season saw him with twelve wins, three losses and two draws from seventeen games, a 70.59 per cent win ratio. This placed him ahead of a distinguished field of captains who had led in fifteen games or more, including Don Bradman 62.50 per cent, Douglas Jardine and Frank Worrell 60 per cent, and Lindsay Hassett 58.33 per cent. No one in the history of the game emerged with as much glory after one year as a Test captain.

Twinned ambitions

The young Steve Waugh came from a near perfect crucible for an extraordinary career in cricket. His parents, Rodger and Beverley, were accomplished sportspeople, who married young to raise a family. The emphasis of the Waugh household of four boys—Steve, his twin, Mark, and their younger brothers, Dean and Danny, was on competitive sport. In that environment, Steve would have developed into something in games, but he just happened to have an equally talented twin. Every time they played anything, they competed hard against each other. The obsession in every game from marbles to tennis was to win. Such rivalry between two budding talents with encouraging parents had to lead to the top.

The boys took the same path and their ability was recognised in many sports—tennis, cricket and soccer—when they were nine. At eleven in early 1977, Mark was captain and Steve vice-captain of the New South Wales Primary Schools team that won the national cricket carnival undefeated. They put on 150 in one partnership. It marked them early as boys with serious potential. At that point you could say with certainty they would both make grade cricket at least. Between thirteen and sixteen they dominated Moore, Watson and Green Shield representative teams. Now officials of the state underage competitions were branding them future New South Wales players.

Their characteristics were emerging. Mark had an attractive, orthodox style, all flow and technique. Steve liked to belt the ball and cared less for his appearance at the crease. Steve's leadership skills began to show out more than Mark's, although the latter's abilities here were underestimated. Steve was an aggressive young leader, who even then could read the game well.

Steve was shocked to be left out of a New South Wales Under-15 state squad, which included Mark. The reason given to an inquiring father was that Steve was 'too aggressive'. This could only have implied he was a 'slogger', without a defensive technique. Steve took the omission to heart but used it as a motivator. There was no way that he was going to let Mark streak ahead. He carried on scoring and taking wickets as a medium-pacer in lower grades for Bankstown and in the Poidevin-Gray Shield. His figures were good without being devastating. Yet no one could create statistics for his determination and strength of mind. If measurable they would have pointed to great achievement.

Despite the Under-15 setback, Steve worked on his defensive technique and was selected for the Under-16 state side. At seventeen, both twins made the Australian Under-19 team, a big leap forward. Several of this team in the early 1980s could look forward to Test selection. The twins smashed centuries in junior 'Tests' against Sri Lanka at the end of the 1982–83 season. Steve also took eight wickets and eight catches. In the following season, aged eighteen, Steve scored several big innings: 200 in the Schoolboys Carnival; 170 for New South Wales Combined High Schools against Great Public Schools; and 161 in a sixty-over match in the Australian Carnival. More important for Steve's advance were performances in 1983–84 in first-grade cricket. Centuries for Bankstown versus Sydney University and Waverley and three hauls of five wickets made state selectors take notice.

About this time, Steve gave up the possibility of a soccer career. Cricket was now the main focus of his life. He had no academic ambitions, and gave up teaching studies after a couple of lectures. His main aim, he would tell anyone who asked, was to 'play cricket for Australia'. There were no ifs, buts or qualifications. Even as a raw eighteen-year-old Waugh knew much about the power of positive thinking.

Yet he still had to earn a living. He tried several menial jobs but stuck at nothing. Then at nineteen Steve made the state side in 1984–85. It didn't solve his employment problems but did give him serious hope that his dreams would be fulfilled. He scored 31 and took none for 34 against Queensland. In March 1985 he clipped a fluent 94 versus Victoria at the Melbourne Cricket Ground and later 71 in the Shield final against Queensland, which New South Wales won.

Waugh played for Essex Second XI in the 1985 English summer and was surprised to have his employment and income problems temporarily solved by Kerry Packer. The Australian media mogul signed Waugh up on a three-year contract *not* to play rebel cricket in South Africa. Packer didn't want the ranks of cricketers depleted. He needed talent feeding through in Australia to make his televising of the game attractive to viewers.

Back in Australia Waugh attended a motivational course that helped him focus on developing the right attitude for his cricket career.

A Test break too early

Steve Waugh was selected for his first Test, to play India at the Melbourne Cricket Ground in the Boxing Day Test of 1985. He was twenty and not prepared for the sudden advance after scoring just two Shield centuries. He scratched together 13 but took a commendable two for 36 from eleven overs. Waugh hit 5 in the second innings but was inspired by his skipper, Allan Border, an authentic Aussie hero, who scored 163 from the team's 308. Waugh failed again in the next Test, but it was clear he would be carried. Border liked his aggressive demeanour with bat and ball and in the field. Waugh was seen as the type of cricketer who would succeed at the highest level. Ideally the selectors and Border would have preferred the tyro to have a better preparation at Shield level. But with a lack of talent in the mid-1980s, when Australia was at its lowest ebb in one hundred years of cricket, there was no choice but to bring on the best prospects.

Waugh made the team to tour New Zealand under Border but flopped for the fifth time in a row with the bat, making 11 in the First Test at Wellington. Just before he was given the chop, he made 74 in the next Test at Christchurch. His confidence up, he took four for 56. But in the Third Test at Auckland he scored 1 and 0, as the team collapsed to off-spinner John Bracewell. Waugh was humiliated. He stored away the experience for future accounting against the rivals across the Tasman.

Allan Border didn't appreciate it either and threatened to resign. Waugh would never forget the black mood in the Australian camp. He refused even then to accept inferiority to any nation.

Lack of competition allowed Steve Waugh to hold his place for a tour of India in September 1986. His batting average of 12.5 from nine innings was not enough to justify a Test spot. A series of not outs allowed him to fly away from India with a flattering average of 59. He took ten wickets at 36.7. This tour was followed by the Ashes battle of 1986–87 in Australia. Australia was well beaten two–one but Waugh made real progress as a Test player, scoring 310 at 44.28 and taking ten wickets at 33.6.

He and the team had a terrific boost in 1987 when Australia won the World Cup in India against all odds. Waugh performed well with the ball and earned the sobriquet 'the iceman' for his cool bowling at the death. It was an advance for Australian cricket if only in morale.

Waugh spent another year playing county cricket, this time for Somerset. He hit his first county century versus Surrey, which had the super-quick West Indian Sylvester Clarke in its line-up, and then another versus Gloucestershire, which included Courtney Walsh. These successes gave Waugh a confidence lift. He felt he could take on the Caribbean speedsters with some hope of success. His figures of 340 runs at 113.33 gained him kudos in England, where at that point he was more appreciated than at home.

In 1987–88 Australia won its first series for three years, beating New Zealand one–nil. Waugh had a modest series, making 147 runs at 36.75. A draw against England and a win against Sri Lanka in the first such Test in Australia between the two nations (in which Waugh took four for 33), made it appear as if Australia was emerging from its horror stretch.

Waugh continued his personal advance in the 1988 county season, notching a fine 1314 runs for Somerset at 73 in twenty-four championship innings. In all he hit eight centuries in the season, two of them in one-dayers. It was enough for *Wisden* to name him in April 1989 as one of the Five Cricketers of the Year (for 1988).

Downs and ups

Steve Waugh and the Australian team took a step backwards in September and October 1988 on an acrimonious Pakistan tour that was lost one–nil with two draws. Then they ran into a speed-packed West Indies outfit in Australia for five Tests in the 1988–89 series. The home team lost three–one. While Waugh was sobered by the smashing defeat inflicted by Malcolm Marshall, Curtly Ambrose, Courtney Walsh and Patrick Patterson, he was satisfied with his own performances. He hit 331 at 41.73 with two 90s, which was more than respectable. He also took ten wickets at 47.8, which did not reflect his ability to break partnerships.

Later in 1989 Waugh came of age as a top Test batsman during the Ashes series in England, scoring 506 runs at 126.5, with two big hundreds of 177 not out and 152 not out at Leeds and Lord's. His years in English cricket and his own steady application had seen him develop. He would from now on be known as a batsman first and a spare-parts bowler second.

Steve Waugh continued to bat at number six during the 1989–90 season in the Antipodes, notching 361 at 40.11 in seven Tests against Sri Lanka (2), New Zealand (2) and Pakistan (3). He had trouble with the ball moving away outside off-stump as presented by Wasim Akram, Waqar Younis, Imran Khan and Richard Hadlee. In England he could play his slashing cut with impunity. It was tougher on bouncier, faster Australian wickets.

Despite a retreat from his brilliant English summer, Waugh still managed his highest first-class score—196 versus Tasmania at Hobart. It demonstrated his growing capacity and desire for the big hundred. His concentration had improved over his five years in big cricket.

In the next season, 1990–91, Steve (216 not out) and brother Mark (229 not out), who had served a long apprenticeship in first-class cricket, put on a world record of 464 for the fifth wicket in a game against Western Australia, which had a strong bowling attack.

It marked the rise of Mark, the tortoise of the two in terms of elevation to Tests, and the fall of Steve the hare, who was dropped after three Tests of an Ashes series against Graham Gooch's tourists. Steve had scored just 80 runs at 20.5, and was forced to make way for his twin. He was selected in the 1991 squad for the Caribbean but still struggled in the few opportunities presented, making just 32 runs in three innings. Mark, with 367 runs at 61.17, stole a march on his brother.

Steve married his teenage sweetheart Lynette in August 1991 at a time when his future was uncertain. He was not selected for any Tests in the 1991–92 series versus India at home, and his first-class figures—472 from eleven innings at 42.9—did little to push his claim for reselection. He had to sit out another year, missing a tour in Sri Lanka and another three Tests, before he was returned to the Australian team.

When he was selected again, there was a catch—or two. He had to face the West Indies and bat in the number three spot that nobody else wanted, the toughest against the pacemen. He failed in the first two Tests at Brisbane and Melbourne with scores of 10, 20, 38 and 1. But he was kept in the combination after a sensational victory at the MCG, when Shane Warne spun Australia home on the final day. Waugh was once more down to his 'last chance', this time at Sydney. He hit a dashing even 100 in a drawn game dominated by Brian Lara (277). In the Adelaide Fourth Test, Steve hit a solid 42 against tough opposition as ever from the West Indian pace quartet, but only made 4 in the second innings when Australia fell 2 short of victory. Again, Waugh experienced the grimness of a loss, which was nearly as painful to skipper Border—because his team came so close—as the dark years of the mid-1980s.

Waugh (13 and 0) was part of the collapse to Ambrose that followed in Perth, which gave the West Indies the series two–one. He averaged 25.33 from nine innings and an aggregate of 228. Despite the disappointment, Border and the team had to pick up the pieces and move their caravan on to New Zealand for three Tests. Waugh lifted his rating and kept his place with 62, 75, 41 and 0 in a drawn series. It was then on to England for the 1993 Ashes.

Waugh revelled in the conditions again, gathering 416 at 83.2 and a top score of 157 not out at Leeds in the Fourth Test. A small problem in batting at number six behind a strong combination of Taylor, Slater, Boon, Mark Waugh and Border meant he missed out on some of the batting action. Still, a few not outs helped his average as Australia won four–one.

Waugh kept up this rating in the series against New Zealand in 1993–94 with scores of 44, 25 not out and 147 not out, giving him an unreal average of 216 as Australia took the series two–nil. Waugh had emerged since his reinstatement in the national side as a more determined batsman, restricting his cuts and eliminating hooks and pulls in order to avoid self-inflicted dismissals. His average began to creep up. He would now never give his wicket away with a rash shot, or at least that was his intention. He had reinvented himself as a dogged fighter like Border.

A leg injury caused Waugh to miss the first two Tests against South Africa—the first contest between the two teams since 1969–70—but he came back to make 164 and 1 in Adelaide. Australia won the game and levelled the series. In the return three-Test bout soon after in South Africa, Waugh hit 45 not out, 0, 86 and 64 in another drawn series. It was the last for Allan Border, who was replaced by Mark Taylor as captain.

Still in 1994, Steve Waugh collected 171 at 57 with a top score of 98 at Rawalpindi in a three-Test series against Pakistan away. Two things recurred: his wobbles in the 90s and hamstring problems that kept him out of the Third Test. Pakistan won the series one–nil.

Waugh again missed a century in the next series, making 94 in Melbourne in the Second Test and 99 not out at the WACA versus England in the 1994–95 Ashes series. In this second stage of his career he had decided not to take control of the game near the end of the innings when in the 90s, but to let the 100 come naturally. This meant he had to rely on tailenders to help him through to three figures. His series aggregate was 345 at 49.29. Australia won three–one. The series proved the perfect preparation for Steve Waugh and Australia to take on the West Indies in the Caribbean a few weeks later.

Waugh was determined to stand up to the Windies pacemen and show the way to beat this mighty XI after twenty-eight series and fifteen years during which it had not lost to any team in the world. His belief that Australia could win set a pattern in the first three Tests, when he scored three defiant sixties, two of them unconquered. The speedsters peppered him but he rode the bouncers and stayed at the wicket. His confrontation with Curtly Ambrose at Port of Spain, when he impolitely asked the tall bowler what he was looking at mid-pitch, was pivotal to the series' outcome. The West Indian had never experienced such in-your-face aggression. It sent a message all round the Caribbean that this side would not lie down as so many teams had before over the years. The West Indians thrived on physical intimidation. They feared they might have met their match. In the Fourth Test at Kingston, Waugh played the innings of his life, scoring 200 after a 231 partnership with Mark (126) that led to an Australian series win of two–nil. Steve collected an aggregate of 429 at 107.25 and was the player of the series.

This series completed his transition from a battler to a true champion of the game. He continued on through 1995–96 versus Pakistan (200 at 50 with a highest score of 112 not out) and against

Sri Lanka (362 at an average of 362, from 131 not out, 170 and 61 not out).

Australia made the final of the 1996 World Cup on the subcontinent but was beaten by Sri Lanka. This loss saw official thinking change about how a one-day side should be composed. No longer were Test players automatic selections for the short version of the game. This put the position of the skipper, Mark Taylor, in danger. He had never been perceived as an ideal one-day player.

Steve Waugh was part of another good series win (three–two) against the West Indies in Australia in 1996–97. He missed one Test and managed ordinary figures on paper—188 at 31.33. But he scored two good fifties when it counted in the series. He lifted for a three-Test series in South Africa, which rating agencies and *Wisden* were dubbing the battle for the world crown. Waugh hit 313 at 78.25, with a top innings of 160 in a match-winning partnership of 384 with Greg Blewett (214).

Australia won two–one, settling the world crown issue. It then went on and won the one-day series amidst turmoil, when Taylor's poor form saw him drop himself from the contest. Australian vice-captain Ian Healy lost his position for dissenting an umpire's decision by throwing his bat up the dressing rooms steps after his dismissal. Waugh took over as vice-captain.

There was very little time for the Australians to recover after this long season before they flew to England for the 1997 Ashes. The tourists flopped in the one-day series, losing all three contests. Taylor failed again and threw the squad into near-chaos as the English media swarmed around the tourists like sharks in a feeding frenzy. Taylor continued to get out cheaply. Waugh had to prepare to take over as leader in a most inappropriate way. But Taylor turned around his game with a fine hundred in the First Test of the Ashes at Edgbaston. Still Australia lost. It drew a wet Second Test at Lord's. The tourists went into the Third Test at Old Trafford desperate for a win. Waugh had failed so far with scores of 12, 33 and a duck at Lord's. Just when required, he turned on a magnificent performance, scoring a fighting 108 in the first innings and 116 in the second. This double, along with Warne's six for 48 and three for 63, did most to win the game. Australia went on to take the series three–two, with Steve Waugh managing 390 runs at 39.

Short-game leader

The selectors dumped Mark Taylor as one-day skipper and appointed Steve Waugh to take over for the 1997–98 season against New Zealand and South Africa. At the same time as he was advancing, the Australian Cricketers Association, of which he was secretary, pushed hard for a greater percentage of cricket revenue. It won significant gains for first-class cricketers, where 25 per cent of revenue would be paid to the players if the total revenue was $60 million or more.

On the field, Waugh hit 96 in the Second Test against New Zealand at the WACA, his seventh stoppage in the 90s. It was a mediocre series for him—130 at 32.5—that Australia won two–nil. He stepped up a gear against the South Africans, but was again stopped short of a century in his ninety-ninth Test, when he hit 96 at Melbourne, and then 85 at Sydney in his one hundredth Test. Both times Allan Donald removed him. Brother Mark upstaged him with 100 at Sydney. Yet Steve Waugh's form was consistent in Australia's one–nil series win. He hit 238 at 47.6.

Australia under Waugh couldn't win a preliminary game versus the Proteas in the CUB one-dayers. In the middle of the finals he inferred that the South Africans were 'chokers', players who succumbed to big pressure during the final series. Australia went on to beat South Africa two–one, the skipper improving his rating with scores of 53 and 71.

Waugh struggled with form and fitness in India a few weeks later in March and April 1998, making 152 at 38, including 80 at Calcutta while carrying another groin injury. India won two–one thanks mainly to Sachin Tendulkar, but Australia took the following one-day series against India and Zimbabwe. Waugh gained confidence from this series and the next in Sharjah versus India and New Zealand. Tendulkar was in touch and impossible to contain. Australia lost the Sharjah tournament final when he slammed 134 from 131 balls. Waugh realised he would have to work out a way to hold this champion if Australia were to have any chance in the 1999 World Cup, and in future Tests against India. Waugh worried about how to dismiss Tendulkar from then until their next encounter.

More Ashes

Steve Waugh led Australia in a one-day tournament at the Common-wealth Games at Kuala Lumpur. In an event not recognised by the

International Cricket Council, he starred with a century against India and a top score of 90 in the final, which Australia lost to South Africa. He was content to take away a silver medal and the great pride in having represented Australia at the Games.

Waugh resumed his place as deputy to Taylor on a tour of Pakistan, which Australia won one–nil. He notched 157 in the First Test at Rawalpindi, which allowed him to average 58.75 from 235 runs, second only to Mark Taylor, who notched 513 at 128.25 (including his 334 not out and 92 at Peshawar). Waugh then led the one-day side to a three–nil win. It was the first significant sign that Australia might have improved in this version of the game.

In the 1998–99 Ashes, Waugh opened the series with 112 in a drawn First Test at Brisbane, and then scored 59 at Adelaide in the Third Test won by Australia. He should have been a match winner at Melbourne in the Fourth Test when he hit 122 not out and 30 not out. But Australia 'choked' in a modest run chase of 175 for victory. Waugh refused to take control of the tail and it collapsed around him. He was consistent in his career policy of letting the tailenders share the strike in a 'normal' procedure. Yet the critics called him selfish for not taking the initiative. It was more likely a strategic error. He had overdone self-preservation at the expense of a team win.

Waugh carried on, scoring another 96 at Sydney (while his brother made a brilliant 121). Australia won this game and the Ashes series three–one. Steve Waugh's figures of 498 at 83 suggested he was at the peak of his form at age thirty-three. An injured groin kept him out of most of the one-day series.

Test leader

Mark Taylor retired and Steve Waugh was made captain in February 1999. His first Test assignment was the West Indies in the Caribbean, which was not an easy one. Australia won the First Test at Port of Spain. In the Second at Kingston, Waugh hit a fine 100 in Australia's first innings and was last man out, chasing runs. But West Indian captain Brian Lara stole the show with 212 and the West Indies won. In the Third Test at Barbados, Waugh went one better and hit a magnificent 199, demonstrating his greatness as a big-time batsman. Yet Lara again upstaged his counterpart with a flawed but fighting 153 not out. The home side won the game by one wicket. Waugh made the right noises in defeat, saying the match should be remembered as a great game of cricket, full stop. But at one–two down with one to play, he knew that he was not going to get away with such a comment. Critics said he was too negative and under pressure he had not handled his bowlers with flair, a code for 'bring back Taylor, all is forgiven'.

Steve Waugh dropped his vice-captain Warne for the last Test at Antigua. This was a tough decision but the leg-spinner had not delivered in the first three Tests. He was a luxury given that leg-spinner Stuart MacGill was in the team and performing better. Waugh won the toss, batted and was 72 not out in Australia's 303. Lara, like a whirlwind, slammed an even 100, but his team managed just 222. Langer (127) held Australia's second innings of 306 together. The West Indies failed to reach the target and it was beaten by 176. This squared the series two all.

Drained from combat, Waugh was relieved to have scraped out of the series without surrendering the Frank Worrell Trophy. Waugh may have faltered as leader first up (I'm learning on the job, he said), but he had an exceptional series, scoring 409 at 58.42. Only Lara with 546 at 91 did better.

The seven one-dayers ended a three-all 'draw', with one game tied in Guyana. Two games (at Guyana and Barbados) were ruined by crowd behaviour, but in all of them Waugh responded to criticism and experimented with the field, batting line-ups and bowling combinations. The series proved to be a kind of laboratory for Waugh's leadership. Yet Australia had not performed well enough to give supporters or observers confidence it would win the World Cup, beginning in England soon after the Caribbean tour. Still, there were good signs. Warne had returned to form. McGrath was fit.

Australia was sluggish to begin with but Waugh was the glue that held the shaky team together. It cranked up slowly and reached peak form in time for the semi-finals. Waugh won the super-six game against South Africa with 120 not out, then hit 56 in the dramatic, tied semi-final versus the Proteas. He finally led his team to a big win against Pakistan at Lord's. Waugh hit 398 at 79.66 in ten innings, a grand effort given his leadership responsibilities and the fact that if he had failed he would have lost the one-day captaincy. He had not just waved away his critics with the bat. He had hit them about the ears. For the moment, his position was unassailable.

In Sri Lanka his team was beaten one–nil in the Tests. Waugh struggled, partly because of a sickening collision with Jason Gillespie in the field in which his nose was smashed. The fast bowler, who broke his leg, was put out of Test cricket for at least a year.

A few weeks later in Zimbabwe Waugh made 151 not out in a one-off Test at Harare. He led his team home without a series win but a Test record of three wins, three losses and two draws.

Australia then steamrollered Pakistan and India at home and New Zealand away in a clean sweep of the 1999–2000 millennium summer, winning nine successive Tests. Waugh struggled against Pakistan but began the series versus India at Adelaide with 150 and ended with 334 runs at 37.11 after the six Tests in Australia. More realistic were his figures for 1999—993 runs at 49.65. This indicated that his form overall had not fallen away with the added responsibility of leadership. Australia won the one-day international series against Pakistan and India, losing just one game for the entire tournament—the first. It won the finals two–nil against Pakistan. Overall, Waugh's leadership skills had developed rapidly and he had certainly learned much in his first year. Gone now were nostalgic cries for Taylor. Waugh had added a degree of toughness to a team that had also developed flexibility under him. He could lay claim to a Midas touch. Whenever he made a change in the bowling, it seemed to come off. Waugh was helped by John Buchanan, who proved to be a most innovative coach. He added a dimension to Australia's strategies and tactics that helped Steve Waugh make the right decisions.

Austin empowers Waugh

Lynette had the Waughs' second child, Austin, late in 1999 (their first child Rosalie, was born in 1996), but Steve had limited time for his family, much to his disappointment. Soon after the home season, Waugh pushed himself and his side on to another tour of New Zealand, winning the one-day series four–one, and creating a world record fourteen wins in succession. Waugh hit 151 not out in the Second Test at Wellington. He had now scored 150 or more in an innings against every Test playing nation—a record. Waugh slipped into fifth position in the all-time run-making list behind Border, Gavaskar, Gooch and Miandad. His average in the New Zealand Test series was 53.5 from 214 runs.

At the end of the long millennium summer, Waugh had played 128 matches (204 innings) for 8373 runs at 50.43. He had scored twenty-two centuries (one double, 200 versus the West Indies) and forty-two fifties. His bowling statistics—eighty-nine wickets at 35.74—emphasised his importance as a top-class batsman who could bowl. In one-day international cricket he had scored 6874 runs at 32.27, while taking 191 wickets at 34.62. In first-class cricket at the end of the 1999–2000 season, he had scored 19,220 runs at 52.37 with a highest score of 216 not out. Waugh had scored fifty-eight centuries and eighty-six fifties. He had also taken 243 wickets at 31.98.

At thirty-five, Steve Waugh ranked as one of the five most successful batsmen—at least in statistical terms—in Australian Test cricket. Yet his value as a cricketer to his country over fifteen years goes far beyond this. He was the only player who had survived from the horror years in the mid-1980s. His revival and development as an inde-fatigable run-scoring machine allowed Australia to prosper by the mid-1990s when it became, by any measure, the top nation. By the end of the 1990s, Waugh as captain had taken Australia to the top in one-day cricket as well.

On top of maintaining Australia's ranking as the best Test team by every rating agency from 1995 to 2000, and taking the 1999 World Cup, Steve Waugh had led record-winning streaks in both forms of the game. And all this with teams that were not ranked higher by most expert observers than Bradman's 1948 Invincibles, or the teams of Benaud in the 1960s or Ian Chappell in the 1970s. By any measure Stephen Rodger Waugh must rank as one of the most successful captains in the history of cricket.

Index

PHOTO CREDITS

Cover photography
Don Bradman: The Fairfax Photo Library
Bobby Simpson: The Fairfax Photo Library
Ian Chappell: The Fairfax Photo Library
Allan Border: Allsport/Ben Radford
Mark Taylor: The Age/Bryan Charlton
Steve Waugh: Allsport

Author photograph: © Dean Golja and Associates

Inside pages:
The author and the publishers would like to gratefully acknowledge Ken Kelly
for permission to use the pictures of Dave Gregory, Billy Murdoch, the 1893
Australian team, Tom Horan, Hugh Massie, Jack Blackham, Henry Scott,
Percy McDonnell, George Giffen, Harry Trott, Joe Darling, Hugh Trumble,
Monty Noble, Clem Hill, Syd Gregory, Warwick Armstrong and team, and the
Australian team 1920–21. These pictures were previously published in *The
Ashes Captains* by Gerry Cotter (photographs and picture research by Ken
Kelly), first published by The Crowood Press, Great Britain, 1989.

The author and publishers would also like to acknowledge Philip Derriman
for the use of the photograph of Charles Lawrence and group from *True to
the Blue: A History of the New South Wales Cricket Association* by Philip
Derriman, published by Richard Smart Publishing, 1985; and also Alan
Young for supplying the 1957–58 photograph of the Australian team.

Acknowledgments are due to: *The Age* for the photographs of Woodfull and
Jardine (together); Harvey; Booth; Simpson and Bradman (together);
Richardson; Jarman; Hassett; Ian Chappell, Lawry, Simpson and Benaud
(together); Brown; Ryder; and Yallop; *The Herald and Weekly Times Photo-
graphic Collection* for the photograph of Hassett and Johnson (together) and
AAP for the photographs of Morris and Lindwall.

Acknowledgment is also due to Allsport and the individual photographers
of the following images: Don Bradman; Richie Benaud bowling; Bobby
Simpson (photographed by Don Morley); Ian Chappell (photographed by
Don Morley); Greg Chappell (photographed by Adrian Murrell); Kim Hughes
(photographed by Adrian Murrell); Border, Taylor and Waugh together
(photographed by Thomas Turck); Border with World Cup; Border with
miniature Ashes urn (photographed by Ben Radford); Taylor with Ashes
crystal trophy (photographed by Stu Forster); Simpson and Taylor together
(photographed by Shaun Botterill); Brown and Waugh (photographed by Jack
Atley); and the Steve Waugh batting shot (photographed by John Daniels).

Every effort has been made to identify copyright holders and photographers
of pictures in this book. The publishers would be pleased to hear from any
copyright holders who have not been specifically acknowledged.